Praise for Jeremiah Tower and

"I'm glad to have [Tower's] riveting, frontline persp⸺⸺ ⸺⸺⸺ is at once fascinating, illuminating, and poignant. Those of us who have built American hospitality careers over the past couple of decades owe a major debt to this bushwhacking pioneer of product, pleasure, and promotion."

—Danny Meyer

"Jeremiah Tower dishes better than almost anybody."

—Robert Mondavi

"This book is a celebrity-studded literary 'tasting menu,' combining the raw, tell-all energy of Anthony Bourdain with the worldliness of Jeffrey Steingarten."

—Rick Smilow, President, The Institute of Culinary Education

"Tower's place in culinary history is assured, and his message still needs to be heard by striving young chefs today."

—*San Antonio Express News*

"Jeremiah Tower is a beloved legend of America's food business. He was at the forefront of the new era when America got serious about its own cuisine. He ranks up there with Wolfgang Puck and Emeril Lagasse and all the other pioneers of today's great food styles in putting the new American cuisine really on the world map. This book is an absolute must-have for both the serious cookbook collector and the casual reader."

—Robin Leach

"His memoir is fascinating, offering tantalizing glimpses of restaurant operations and insights into many culinary personalities."

—*Library Journal*

"The food memoir is a dicey proposition for a writer: It takes real courage to sit down and decide that your individual eating experience is interesting enough for other people to care about. . . . Grub Street decided it was time to look back and assemble a list of the all-time best food memoirs. . . . 10. *California Dish* by Jeremiah Tower."

—"Great Books: The Top 25 Must-Read Food Memoirs of All Time,"
Grub Street, October 2013

Start the Fire

Start the Fire

HOW I BEGAN A FOOD REVOLUTION IN AMERICA

Jeremiah Tower

AN ANTHONY BOURDAIN BOOK

ecco

AN IMPRINT OF HARPERCOLLINS PUBLISHERS

HarperCollins books may be purchased for educational, business, or sales promotional use. For information please e-mail the Special Markets Department at SPsales@harpercollins.com.

FIRST EDITION

Designed by Ashley Tucker

Library of Congress Cataloging-in-Publication Data has been applied for.

ISBN 978-0-06-249843-4

17 18 19 20 21 LSC 10 9 8 7 6 5 4 3 2 1

To Elizabeth David, Richard Olney, James Beard, and the staff of my restaurants, and to all the players who made this history. For Daniel Isengart and Filip Noterdaeme, and to Ken Hom because we both made it through.

CONTENTS

One day in 1976, Jeremiah Tower was leafing through some old cookbooks, seeking inspiration for the next in a series of French regional menus at Chez Panisse, a modest restaurant in Berkeley, California, where he was the chef. In a turn-of-the-century collection of recipes by Charles Ranhoffer, the French chef of Delmonico's in New York, Tower encountered something unexpected. . . .

"I saw the title of a soup, Crème de Mais Verte à la Mendocino—Cream of Green Corn à la Mendocino," he writes in *Jeremiah Tower's New American Classics,* published in 1986. Why, Tower wondered, did a recipe from a French chef in New York refer to a Northern California town? "Like a bolt out of the heavens, it came to me: Why am I scratching around in Corsica when I have it bountifully all around me here in California?" The recipe, Tower discovered, was nothing but American ingredients prepared according to French cooking principles. "I could not contain my exhilaration," he wrote, "over what I beheld as the enormous doors of habit swung open onto a whole new vista. And I began to compose an American regional dinner—California, not Corsica." Chez Panisse had been open for five years. No one had yet uttered the term *California cuisine.* Proprietor Alice Waters and her friends were just cooking the way Americans do at home, using American ingredients to make recipes from classic cookbooks. They took a lot from France, the occasional dish from Italy or elsewhere in the Mediterranean, and a little from mom. But the elements were there, and inspiration met opportunity. Chez Panisse's previous menus had been written in French, but this one Tower couched in English. Significantly, the wines offered were from California as well. The menu crystallized Waters's vision of the sort of food Chez Panisse should serve—great local ingredients prepared classically.

—*Wine Spectator,* 2001

THANKS

To all the people whose backs I climbed over, and all the players who made this history.

Especially Lucius Beebe, my hero since college days. "If anything is worth doing," he once said, "it is worth doing in style and on your own terms—and nobody goddamned else's." I wanted to be as James Villas described him in a *Gourmet* magazine article called "Lucius Beebe: The Last Magnifico": the randy and dandy boulevardier, the "eminently polite, generous, witty, and kind gentleman, who was not out to impress anybody and simply relished a civilized evening on the town over 'a hot bird and a cold bottle.'"

SPECIAL THANKS

To Kit Wohl of Wohl & Company in New Orleans, who urged me to rewrite it and showed me the way. To Linda Ellerbee, who pushed her to ask me. To Dan Halpern at Ecco for saying yes as well as Kimberly Witherspoon at Ink-Well Management for urging them to. Especially to Anthony Bourdain, who made this rerun possible, and who, with *Kitchen Confidential,* let me know I wasn't the only one.

INTRODUCTION

"What the fuck is California cuisine?" asked East Coast chef Dan Barber in late 2014. I feel I should now answer his question. And what's the point? Culinary background and history may be fascinating and useful for some, but bore the crap out of others.

During a 2015 summer Blood Moon eclipse dinner at Dan Barber's Blue Hill at Stone Barns with six very smart, ambitious, and dedicated young men in their twenties who wanted to re-create Stars, I knew the point. After an hour of hearing them talk about American restaurants, food, and wine, I could think only of kids learning to swim the hard way. Thrown into the lake and told to kick. Move their arms. A lot of determined effort, a lot of flailing, little progress.

It had been a shock to me when we opened Stars on July 4, 1984, that my twenty-something kitchen crew knew nothing of America's culinary past. My eager young hosts at Stone Barns had heard of culinary America, had watched all the TV shows, but they also knew nothing about where it came from. Asking them the key to their futures, or what they could discard of the past to get on with an intelligent future, was pointless. I made do with "Does America, the world's biggest melting pot of cultures, have its own distinct culinary identity?" Or is it just about making a thousand errors, then connecting the errors? Is the American food revolution the realm of legend, of myth? After all, what this young group of cooks, waiters, and sommeliers know of the origins of the changes in culinary America is pure media. None were there at the beginning of the revolution or grounded in what inspired it. The new generation has adopted the terminology of "fresh," "organic," "local," and

"California," but how many of them had ever gardened or been on a farm? If the essential meanings of these concepts for them live only in the press, cooking magazines, and the floodlights of fame, one can hardly blame them. Some of their mentors were press-manipulating mythmakers.

Do we have that problem again?

The question gripped a group of chefs during the World's 50 Best Restaurants' first #50BestTalks event in New York in October 2014, put together as a forum to debate the future of American dining. The chefs group included Eleven Madison Park co-owners Will Guidara and Daniel Humm, Eataly's Mario Batali, British chef April Bloomfield of the Spotted Pig, Italian chef Massimo Bottura of legendary Osteria Francescana, Wylie Dufresne, Sabato Sagaria of the Union Square Hospitality Group, Nick Kokonas of Chicago's Alinea and Next, and Andrew Carmellini.

A veritable melting pot of Euro-American talent.

Dan Barber caught all their attention with his California cuisine remark, prefaced by "America doesn't have a cuisine. I was in California and someone stood up and talked about California cuisine." That's when he wondered aloud what it is. Massimo had a different answer. "I go to America to recharge my batteries. In Europe, we're not dreaming anymore: we have a sense of sadness filled with nostalgia." At least they know what they are missing. My young hosts would have been incredulous had I told them that in 1974, France's three-star Michelin chef Jean Troisgros told me in my kitchens in Berkeley's Chez Panisse restaurant that he envied my freedom.

The questions are relevant not just to the current and next generation of culinary professionals. As a restaurant goer, when you have finished the twenty or so courses at Blue Hill, have you wasted your three hundred dollars of eating-out money? How much can you believe of the "slips and stumbles" alleged in the *New York Times* January 2016 review by Pete Wells of New York's Per Se, with the conclusion that "in and of itself" (in other words, "per se") the restaurant is no longer worth the time and money? Unless you have something to refer it to, how could you know if a new restaurant's revival of nouvelle cuisine stacks up unless you knew something about the origin, successes, and failures of that kind of cooking? Or whether they are just blowing hot kitchen smoke up your nose?

Dishing the history is a palatable way to find out.

CHAPTER 1

FROM GONADS TO FOAM

Revolution: the cyclical movement of celestial bodies. From Delmonico's epoch-making restaurant in 1900 New York and its foragers on Long Island farms, to its re-creation in the Four Seasons in 1959, to 1970's Chez Panisse in Berkeley, California, to 1980's Stars in San Francisco, to Spain's El Bulli, with its famous foam, to El Bulli disciple René Redzepi at the world-famous Noma restaurant in Copenhagen. And now back again.

Or from what first inspired me professionally to what is influencing chefs today. The gonads from sea urchins I cooked in their spiny shells as soufflés for James Beard in the early 1970s, after which he exclaimed to the national food press the beginning of a new American cuisine—a highly exaggerated claim, but Jim always had a nose for something about to happen, even if he didn't live to see the world-conquering foam from El Bulli that changed restaurant cooking overnight.

Chefs were still debating which fork in the cooking road to take as late as 2013, as in an article by Hillary Dixler on Eater.com that quotes a well-known British chef complaining to blogger Fuchsia Dunlop, "This isn't food. It's got nothing to do with food, with the earth, with Spain, with what his grandmothers cooked. Ferran Adrià has fucked it all up." The chef goes on to explain that Adria has friends in Barcelona who complain that all the young chefs want to become "gastro-magician[s], . . . celebrit[ies], . . . superstar[s]." They want to invent and play but don't see the value of the basic skills. El

Bulli's creator, chef Ferran Adrià, himself started with those basic skills, beginning his culinary career first as a dishwasher and then a cook at the Hotel Playafels in Castelldefels, on the Barcelona coast, where the chef de cuisine "taught him traditional Spanish cuisine." Only later did he turn traditional Europe on its head and make a new haute cuisine in Spain.

ROOTS OF NEW AMERICAN CUISINE

"The Orson Welles of the food world," I was called by journalist Bruce Palling in his interview for the *Wall Street Journal Europe* in November 2010. Were I to make a film of this book I would subtitle it "The Roots of New American Cuisine." Perhaps the script would start with a 2001 *Wine Spectator* article: "One day in 1976, Jeremiah Tower was leafing through some old cookbooks," looking for the future in the past and inspiration for the next in a series of French regional menus at Berkeley's as yet unknown Chez Panisse— specifically from *The Epicurean,* the 1894 cookbook of Charles Ranhofer, the French chef of Delmonico's in New York,the American equivalent of France's culinary bible, Auguste Escoffier's *Le Guide Culinaire.*

The *Wine Spectator* goes on to say that although "Chez Panisse had been open for five years, no one had yet uttered the term 'California cuisine.'" Before I arrived, co-owner "Alice Waters and her friends were just cooking the way Americans do at home, using American ingredients to make recipes from classic cookbooks. They took a lot from France, the occasional dish from Italy or elsewhere in the Mediterranean, and a little from mom. But the elements were there, and inspiration met opportunity. Chez Panisse's previous menus had been written in French, but this one Tower couched in English. Significantly, the wines offered were from California as well." The menu, as the *Spectator* says, crystallized the way America should cook: great local ingredients simply prepared.

The 1976 "California Regional Dinner" menu at Chez Panisse created a new outlook on how to find a new cooking style in America. It was the match that lit the revolution, changing American food and the way we eat, and ingredients were what led it. But it had no name until we took a team from the Santa Fe Bar & Grill in Berkeley to a lunch at Beechwood, the Astor mansion in Newport, Rhode Island, in 1983 for one hundred food journalists. Days later their hundred or so national newspaper food sections proclaimed "California Cuisine Is Here," and "Grilling Is It." A few months later "California" became "American" when chefs from all over America came to San Francisco to cook at the Stanford Court hotel "An American Celebration" of chefs and their cuisine. When Stars restaurant opened in San Francisco on the Fourth of July in 1984, it continued the celebration, creating a new democratic and popular American brasserie style of eating out, as journalist R. W. "Johnny" Apple Jr. from the *New York Times* claimed, calling Stars "the only truly democratic restaurant in the United States."

Just as César Ritz at the beginning of the twentieth century had made it socially acceptable for women to be seen in a public dining room, San Francisco's Stars and Los Angeles's Spago, Michael's, and West Beach Café set the stage for the rich, the famous, and indeed the superstars to mingle in restaurants with those who were none of the above. At Stars one would find celebrities mixing with government clerks from the courts across the street, the owner of the hot dog stand next door, and groupies from all over town. Stars also created the superstar chef, raising the profession of cook out of the social gutter.

It was also the setting for the new casual. Uber-chef Mario Batali, who tasted a bit of his career at Stars, nailed the reasons for eating out ready-to-wear instead of couture. Speaking at the World's 50 Best Restaurants' 50 Best Talks event in New York October 2014, he said, "Fine dining came to be defined as a three-to-four-hour thing and that has faded in a life where you're busy. You still want delicious and nutritious food, but maybe you don't want to put on a jacket and long pants."

California did that.

CHEF OR TECHNO ENGINEER

Whatever the style of the restaurant now, ingredients still tell the story. American food writer John Mariani wrote in November 2013 in *Esquire*: "A great chef needs to do so little to make so much of what he finds perfect to begin with." If that's true, then why, before the 1970s food revolution in California and again now when that revolution has matured, are chefs trying to make perfect ingredients jump through hoops? Why isn't simplicity still just that simple? Can we still believe, like Robert Capon in his 1967 book, *The Supper of the Lamb*, that "[t]he purpose of mushrooms is to be mushrooms"? Or should the Massachusetts Institute of Technology have a culinary program, its textbook Hervé This's 2005 book, *Gastronomy: Exploring the Science of Flavor*, one of molecular gastronomy's bibles? Looking beyond gels, sous vide, and any other approaches to cooking, Hervé sees our future belonging to NbN, or "Note by Note" cooking. Olive oil becomes cis-3-hexen-1-ol. Or is this, as Dan Barber warns, a product of excitement about food that is now fetishized and privileged?

I thought about that question on my way to the 2014 MAD symposium in Copenhagen, hosted by chef René Redzepi of the world-famous and "best in the world" Noma restaurant. In a 2014 *Wall Street Journal* article, Jay Cheshes called the annual event the "Food World's G-20," where "international tastemakers convene to eat, drink, and be mindful." Evelyn J. Kim, writing in the *Huffington Post* of the 2013 MAD, called it "a mashup of TED and Burning Man." The 2014 theme was "What is cooking?" Subtitle: "The past decade has given rise to a great many things that we know cooking is *not*. Our goal is to remind ourselves what cooking *is*." NbN, or a simple mushroom soup?

The jet lag from Mexico to Copenhagen disappeared in a flash of pain as I ate the first course at Noma the night before the symposium. René Redzepi brought me a bowl of crushed ice with a langoustine on top, its tail shell removed. "It's very fresh, Jeremiah." The Yale culinary history professor next to me got it immediately and stuck his animal down into the ice. I didn't. As I picked it up in one hand to bite its tail, it bit me. Very fresh indeed. Definitely all about ingredients, spurring me to go back to my hotel for a rewrite of my speech to focus it even more on the ingredient revolution that had started in Berkeley.

Speaker Massimo Bottura, chef of Modena, Italy's, famous Osteria Francescana, stated that after revolution there's evolution. The question of where that leaves us all was addressed by Alain Senderens, famous for Paris's restaurants L'Archistrate and Lucas Carton. René asked Alain what keeps him going. What had inspired him as one of the creators of nouvelle cuisine? What made him give back his three Michelin stars when he changed the name of Lucas Carton to Restaurant Senderens? Alain talked passionately about going to the market and of the beauty and inspiration of ingredients that fueled his long and world-famous career. He made it clear that it was always about ingredients and still is, even more so now, when, carbon footprints aside, the whole world is our marketplace—hard to match that when I gave my speech following Alain's. I talked of the new world of cooking, with everything from Noma to food trucks, and the change from cooks as social pariahs to sought-after, tattooed superstar chefs. I discussed the ingredient marketplace, how the nineteenth century's ubiquitous American organic products gave way to industrial ingredients, to the cornucopia of the world market, and back to the local and the hundred miles around it. I also talked of the new hypocrisy of "pure" and "authentic" versus innately flavorful.

That is why we see René Redzepi traveling to the Yucatán, in love with its indigenous tacos, proving that a taco is now worth a journey. A market stand or food truck taco can be as satisfying a moment as a twenty-two-course meal at San Francisco's Saison, New York's Stone Barns, or Chicago's Next. It's different, no doubt, but in its own way equal in the weight of satisfaction, like the first course of perfect, just-picked tiny vegetables at Stone Barns and the radishes picked that morning to make the salsa for cochanita tacos in Mérida, Yucatán's Santiago market.

As for what keeps me going? As Elizabeth Taylor told me at my restaurant Stars after the 1989 earthquake, "When the going gets rough, put on your lipstick, pour a cocktail, and get on with it."

CHAPTER 2

EARLY PLAYPENS

Grilling was my first cooking lesson, fitting, therefore, that my national fame as a chef started twenty-five years later, standing over an outdoor grill at a press lunch in Newport. It started with a lesson when I was five. My teacher was an old Aborigine named Nick, whom I met peeling potatoes out behind the kitchen of an island resort in Australia's Great Barrier Reef.

PERFECT LOVE: GRILLS, GALAHS, AND BUDGERIGARS

Nick had taken me on as a cause. First he taught me how to spike coconuts on a log, whack them with a machete to clean the husks away, open them up, drink the water, eat the flesh. Sucking down the young coconuts, the meat still jellylike and mixed with fresh molasses from sugarcane, seemed to me so sinful, indulgent, and anti-parental that it is to this day one of my favorite things on a hot, steamy beach. Nick also tried to teach me about the birds and the bees, without the benefit of bees, making do with my little lizard (as he called it) instead. I preferred the cooking lessons.

From Nick's dugout canoe I caught a barracuda, which he showed me how to roast over a coconut-shell fire on the beach. It tasted awful, like a meat loaf with fish in it, but I put on a good face. I posed for a photograph eating it, and then fed it to the ravenous cats lurking in the banana trees outside the restaurant. As did my portion of the wild parrots, or galahs, which he cooked on spits on the beach. Eating those was to me like cooking the Australian family budgie. All I could see was the bright raspberry pink plumage of the birds in the palms above the beach, and even though there were thousands of them, I couldn't imagine killing one, let alone eating one. Seeing my disappointment in both these treats, my mentor took me off to the tide pools on the reef, some Olympic-size, some small enough to reach into for oysters, mussels, little crabs for frying, big black shiny sea urchins, and the short spiny purple ones we ate on the spot.

After that I was allowed to watch a fishing expedition carried out by the adults at dusk. It was in the failing light that the big and best eating fish like barramundi came in to shore to get away from the tiger and hammerhead sharks prowling close to the beach for their evening meal. My father, fueled with several pink gins, went chin-deep into the water to provide a strategic "anchor" for one end of the net while the other end was towed around in deeper waters by a little rowboat. The rest of us watched, breathless, from the shore, knowing that a scream from my father meant no dinner, at least not for us.

The ever-darkening waters were screamless. The catch was brought in, gutted, cleaned, and slathered in coconut oil, salt, and chili pepper. The coals of a big bonfire, started to provide light for the cocktail hour, were raked down into a three-inch bed, over which the grill grates were laid. When Nick declared them sizzling hot enough by spitting on them, the fish were set on the grill, big ones first, and then, in stages, all the rest. We ate our fish, crayfish, and grilled oysters while the fire-engine red and Macedonian-gold parrots, pink and gray galahs, and thousands of multicolored budgerigars swirled overhead, their deafening shrieks descending into murmurs in the inky equatorial darkness. Nick squeezed fresh limes on the oysters, sprinkled chili powder mixed with salt on the crayfish, and poured a sauce made from coconut milk, oil, fresh chilies, and lime juice over the cooked fish.

This, I realized, was how life must be.

Cooking these exotic animals from the sea in this tropical setting fixed a love for grilling in my mind forever. I didn't yet know the word *paradise*, but I knew the concept, and sensed that tropical islands meant abundance, color, and the perfumed life I would always crave. My instincts told me to savor every moment of it and, in the future, never to let those feelings get very far away.

ADVENTURIST

Deprived at an early age of being an orphan, I was forced to live with my parents. A childhood hardly suitable for children, at least to onlookers; to me it was an adventure.

In early 1947, when I was four, my parents moved us from Connecticut to Australia. My father was sent as a managing director of Westrex, part of the original AT&T's Western Electric manufacturing arm, to make sure their movie houses had the right equipment to take their soon-to-be-developed stereophonic sound.

I had never been on a plane, and the trip from San Francisco to Honolulu was airsick-horrendous enough for me to never want to get on a plane again. Fortunately there was a layover in Honolulu, during which we stayed in Waikiki at the very grand Royal Hawaiian Hotel, and in the first hour there I wanted to stay in Hawaii forever. All it took was a few minutes on the balcony; the bodies on the beach and the balmy tropical climate bonded me with Hawaii forever. Then with increasing misery I watched the hours go by before we had to once again get in that little DC-3 airplane for Sydney.

The three-day plane trip across the Pacific was so traumatizing that my memory of anything leading up to the coral landing strip in Fiji is almost entirely erased. But I do recall a few things from those eighty hours in the twin-engine DC-3 prop plane: the smell of the DDT bomb set off in the cabin before we left Honolulu, the dry air, the turbulent plunges, and the French convicts seated behind us on their way to a penal colony (only the French would send their convicts first-class), who kept propositioning my thirteen-year-old sister. I screamed, threw up repeatedly, and pleaded ceaselessly for the plane to be stopped. By the time we skidded to a halt on Fiji's bleached pink coral atoll, I was frantic to get out. As we arrived at the little corrugated-iron terminal building, I slung my arms around the nearest pole and shrieked at the top of what was left of my lungs that I would never leave.

I was approached by a huge man in a tapa cloth skirt, black hair teased straight up about a foot and tied with a red ribbon, his torso filling firmly a white military jacket with brass buttons. The fact that he had no shoes on his size-fourteen feet fascinated me so much I forgot that I was going to live and die on that pole. I loosened my grip with a failing of spirit brought on by the enormous, condensation-covered glass of golden yellow liquid he was holding, and by his voice, which was like a vibrating cello, as he told me to come and sit in his tapa cloth lap and have some pineapple juice. I am pretty sure that I had never heard of a pineapple, but as he waved the glass under my nose I knew I wanted to.

The smell and sight of that juice is my first and still one of my most vivid culinary memories. The pineapple had undoubtedly been picked only a few hours before in the cool morning and not refrigerated, just a few chunks of ice in it so the juice was kind to my teeth as it went down. The cool, sweet, refreshing liquid shut me up for the first time in two days, so when I asked for a whole pineapple that I saw in the terminal, my mother nodded wearily. The pineapple itself is my second culinary memory: a whole fruit seemingly half the size of me, its top cut off, and so ripe that I could dig into it with my whole hand and eat the entire inside with my fingers. The crew's irritation that greeted me when I returned covered in pineapple didn't matter. I had found paradise.

Promises of more juice for the twenty-four-hour trip to Sydney lured me back onto the plane. Their mistake. I drove the stewards mad with demands for more and more, until I was yet again violently ill, this time from all the acid of the canned variety. But I was hooked on tropical fruit, and within hours of arrival, now on firm ground at Sydney's Hotel Australia, I lunged for the ripe fruit that was sent up by the manager: a huge basket of passion fruit, ripe finger bananas, and, of course, more ripe pineapples from tropical Queensland.

From a culinary standpoint, we were lucky that wartime shortages were still in effect and electricity was sporadic. An infrequent refrigerator meant relying on an old stand-up Coca-Cola reach-in cooler on the banana-tree-covered porch. It was powered by ice blocks, which meant that we ate fruit—which now included papayas, mangoes, guava, rambutans, mangosteens, and custard apples—only ice chilled. By the time the thirties power stations were updated with American machinery, even with our refrigerator working, we knew that refrigerated fruit loses the scent of its ripening in the sun, of the heady vapors of tropical jungle plantations of papaya and pineapple. The ice chest remained. As did my later insistence, when I had my restaurants, on never refrigerating tomatoes and other fruits.

I loved all the tropical fruit, including the different seasons for the various varieties of mangoes, and the excitement when the garnet red, peppery-aromatic huge papaw arrived. But my favorites were the passion fruits, still warm from the summer sun, growing along our backyard fence. Listening to the kookaburras overhead in the gum trees, I would bite the top of a hot, ripe fruit and suck out the juices while inhaling the perfume. The taste memory came to play a constant part in my menus and recipes twenty-five years later in my Berkeley, San Francisco, and Asian restaurants. Perfectly ripe tropical fruit—the only thing I had in abundance in my early childhood—was a measure of happiness and success.

I was a stranger to my father until he came back from World War II when I was three. Our status had not changed much, deteriorating from the start when I bit him in the groin at our first meeting. Not much improved on moving to Australia, but he did provide a grand lifestyle funded by the inheritance from his family's and America's first oil company. Although we lived in the wealthy Vaucluse suburb of Sydney, the large size of our house was a distinct disadvantage during routine power outages, with their resulting lack of heat and hot water.

In cold weather we ended up living in one room with an illegal heater monopolized by the dog; the smell of singeing hair reminds me to this day of deprivation. Home was far preferable to school, however, with its bare stone chapel, rank confessionals, enforced silence, and promises of life perfect only after death. As a Yank, I was mercilessly brutalized by my peers when I wasn't subjected to the wandering hands of priests.

My oasis was our vegetable garden, which my mother opted for after enduring six months of Australian postwar rationed vegetables: cabbage and its entire family, huge potatoes and carrots, the potatoes revoltingly full of deep-set black rotting spots, the carrots more wood core than sweet flesh. The garden was laid out in an old tennis court at the back of the property. It was set ten feet below the level of the garden, the top of the retaining wall was planted with nasturtiums, and the whole face of the hundred-foot wall was covered in a blanket of multicolored flowers; so began my love for them. The nasturtiums attracted snails, and since I was paid for my small bucket full of snails, I took on the job of planting and carefully tending these flowers—my first gardening project. As a five-year-old I made sandwiches of nasturtium flowers (an Australian treat) and later, in 1974, put the blossoms in salads at Chez Panisse. Ten years later when I started a cooking demo on ABC's *Good*

Morning America, host Joan Lunden announced, "I hate flowers [in food]," and went to a commercial.

After my success with the nasturtiums, I chose what I wanted from a seed catalog airmailed from Burpee in the United States and took responsibility for five rows of beans: "runner," broad (fava), and lima. With great love and prodigious labor—Australia is the land of extreme climate, droughts alternating with monthlong deluges—we produced sweet corn that made the conservative Australians, unaccustomed to eating with their fingers, uncomfortable, but delighted our homesick American guests.

The rest of the Australian diet was lamb chops for breakfast, lamb sandwiches for lunch, and roast lamb for dinner, interspersed with a bit of flathead, a fish that was all we could come by when the fishermen were too nervous to venture out through the harbor for ocean fish. Fledgling communist terrorist groups had taken to blowing up Pan American flying boats anchored in the middle of the route out of the harbor. From our house we had the best view in Sydney of those explosions, but the thrill was significantly lessened by the thought of having to go back to eating lamb or flathead.

After a couple of years, things like fresh shrimp showed up in abundance, and my mother added a jambalaya to her party repertoire. Some of my fondest memories of that huge house are the sideboard groaning with the little there was to cook with, the jambalaya in the center of the display, and the arrival in Sydney of meat other than lamb, even if it was only silverside beef (top round), corned and as tough as nails. My treat on my way out of the butcher shop was to pinch some of the wet corning salt surrounding the beef as it sat in a ten-inch-deep marble table by the door, and suck on it until it dissolved.

CHEZ PRUNIER

The city's hotels and restaurants featured twee interpretations of English food in a Dame Edna Everage atmosphere. Whenever it was time for my annual visit to the one renowned French restaurant, Chez Prunier, because it was my mother's birthday, I would be beside myself with excitement. When the tolerant maître d' handed me a huge menu with a silk tassel longer than I was and all the words in French, my mind began to race. From my many visits over the next three years, I memorized the menu and would insist on ordering for myself—a source of pride to my parents and eye rolling from nearby diners appalled by my high-soprano French pronunciation. I loved Chez Prunier so much that I was an angel of restraint and good manners, but since arrival was an hour before my usual bedtime, the deep gloom then fashionable in deluxe dining rooms made me sleepy. The deal was that I could put my head down on the table and sleep between the main course and dessert, the course that woke me up.

As obnoxious as my mangled French must have seemed, the owner-chef was charming to me and always brought me special things to taste. I was enchanted by his glamour, this man in starched white who had such authority in his domain. And he was a long way from my grizzled, half-naked, Aborigine cooking teacher.

Forty years later, after a lunch promoting California cuisine at the Regent Hotel in Sydney, an old man summoned me to his table. "I'd have recognized you instantly: you're your father's son," he said. Then the owner of Prunier told his guests, "This is the little boy who used to order by himself in horrible French and after the main course put his head on the table to sleep it all off." Twenty-seven years later Prunier was still open, and this wonderful old man was still cooking.

On these foundations of my life at six years old, I fixed my attentions on our world of food, wine, and gardening. They were at once a balm and an escape into a private universe of glorious sensation, and my only potential realms of mastery. I knew food plucked from trees, pulled from the sea, and thrown on hot coals. Now in the glamorous grand dining rooms of the poshest restaurants and in the kitchens of luxury ocean liners or hotels, these passions—a love of things cooked with bravura in their elemental state, where they came from, how they were grown, and a fascination with "fine dining"— became the foundation and structure of my life.

CHAPTER 3

THE WORLD IS A DINING ROOM

In 1949 my father decided to get rid of the family for a while and announced the rest of us were going around the world. "The world" was still a vague concept in my mind, but missing two months of school was splendidly unambiguous. With a delicious sense of living well as the best revenge, I announced to the school's head priest that I was leaving for Ceylon, India, Yemen, the Red Sea, Egypt, Italy, New York, and San Francisco, before returning to Sydney.

The Italian ship was brand-new but would have made a fine steamer on Lake Como. Through the Great Australian Bight we hit a hurricane that nearly upended the ship. Many people were badly injured, the captain was seasick, and I begged for someone to kill me after smelling the banana oil used to clean up someone's smashed bottle of nail polish in the corridor outside my cabin. (To this day I cannot go near banana flavoring or the smell of heating bananas, Mr. Foster's delicious dessert notwithstanding.) Taking pity on me for the pounds I'd lost after three days of not eating, our stewardess, Maria (the one seen in the film *The Last Magnificent*), wheeled in a dish of eggs shirred in garlic and green Neapolitan olive oil. Green is what I turned. She took it personally when I threw up on the spot.

After these upheavals of every kind, all I could think of was cereal and cold milk. The only milk on board was canned unsweetened condensed milk, and after one taste of that on corn flakes, I gave up in disgust. It was a disappointment all the more felt because I loved sweetened canned milk, which at that point was the only thing I could cook by myself. Australian food lore, born out of deprivation, had designated sweetened condensed milk, cooked in boiling water while still in the can, a national delicacy. And it was, though one could hardly call the fabulous ensuing goo delicate. Now known as *dulce de leche,* then it was simply pudding and just what every kid begged for. Probably because it is as sweet as anything can be.

Pudding

14-ounce can sweetened condensed milk

Do not open the can, but take off the label and put the can in a saucepan 4 inches deeper than the can is high.

Pour water in the saucepan to cover the can by 1 inch. Bring the water to a boil, and continue simmering for 2 hours, adding water when necessary to keep the can covered with boiling water.

Take the can out and let cool completely before opening it.

Eat with a spoon right out of the can if you are a kid, and if an adult, think of something else to do with it, like make ice cream, or pour it over vanilla ice cream, or, if you are a real adult genius, like the late George Lang, use it to dip pretzels into.

If my mother thought I had been a pest about fresh pineapple juice on our first plane to Australia, on board the ship she could have killed me over an all-day nag for fresh milk. In those days I didn't know there *is* no point complaining about what you cannot change, so I begged and plotted. My mother and sister became alarmed when I insisted I'd find some in Bombay, our first port after two weeks out of Australia.

"Eat *nothing* from the vendors," I was told.

When we docked and I peered over the rail at the forty or so vendor boats pressed against the ship's hull, I saw a little canoe far beneath us selling fresh milk. Down went my money in a can on a string, up came the milk, and down my throat it went. It was tropically warm but, to me, ambrosial. Then it came up and kept on coming up, until the doctor, seeing that he could have put a pencil between my ribs and it wouldn't have rolled away, gave me up for dead. My mother courageously washed me with cool, jasmine-scented towels and tried to fill me up with chilled Schweppes India tonic water, the only thing that had a prayer of staying down. Within a day or so I rallied, and to this day I am not sure which acts more as a tonic in difficult times, Schweppes and gin, or jasmine anything. Although my first brush with the "East" had nearly killed me, having been for the first time the center of so much attention I was now forever hooked on its flavors, smells, and unending exotica.

After Egypt and Port Said, we were soon headed up the Mediterranean and into Rome and my first truly grand hotel. While my mother went shopping I was left in the care of the hotel staff. They had been warned to make sure I touched no dairy. If I stole anything to drink, they were instructed, it had better be wine.

It was at this wonderful old hotel that I discovered room service, the kind that only great luxury hotels can give. The Quirinale was like the nearby presidential palace of the same name. And it had milk, which, despite my sister's best efforts, I managed to order from room service and scarf down. Only minutes later was it on its way up again, and this time my family said, "Why not just let the little bugger die?" Quite rightly. But my second near-death experience left me surprisingly sanguine, as I could now luxuriate in heavy linen sheets and silk bedcovers and listen to the soothing clatter of horse carriages and the presidential guard outside the huge windows. From that week on, hotels like the Quirinale became an obsession and room service my favorite hobby.

The pampering would continue on the vast American ship the SS *Independence,* which left Genoa for New York. Because she was completely modern, with identical stainless steel and pale enamel walls throughout the public areas, I was always hopelessly lost. I did remember the way from my cabin to the dining room, however, and decided to spend all my time in the latter. In those days the menus of luxury liners were enormous, with more than sixty items for breakfast alone. It was my first real encounter with American food, and the only impression I took away was of quantity. My brother ate pancakes, waffles, and French toast with maple syrup until he could no longer stand. I ate rafts of smoked salmon.

We landed in New York, settled into the Waldorf-Astoria, and hit the city's restaurants: Cavanaugh's, Lindy's, Lüchow's, and Schrafft's, all of which had the same huge menus I'd seen on the ships. Certainly Lüchow's dining room, "The Gourmets' Rendezvous," was the size of an ocean liner's. Here I found fried Long Island scallops (a princely $2.35) and lobster Newburg, a favorite because it was served tableside by a maître d', and everyone in the restaurant would turn and look. At Lindy's I discovered Maryland lump crabmeat, and jumbo shrimp "cocktails," and Welch's Concord Grape Wine, a very grown-up moment since I couldn't get the real thing. I loved Lindy's menu because it was a voyage in itself, like the painting on the wall of American travel spots. There was Boston sole, Maine lobster, Nova Scotia salmon (my new favorite), Great Lakes sturgeon, Canadian bacon, Jersey pork chops, and California strawberries. I ate as much of it as I could. The only dud was the Cold California Fruit Salad, with Cottage Cheese and Raisin Bread, which put me off "California" food for years. As did the "Halekulani Salad" I had at the St. Francis Hotel in San Francisco on the way back to Sydney. It was a Fresh Half Pineapple, Papaya, Prunes, Banana, and Cottage Cheese. Suddenly full of nostalgia for Fiji and the Queensland pineapple fields, I ordered it, despite some misgivings now about bananas, let alone prunes. At its arrival I knew my experience at Lindy's was true, and for the next several years whenever anyone in Australia or England asked me about food in California (the land of Hollywood to them), I told them it was all about canned fruit and cottage cheese, and to be avoided at all costs.

DELIGHTS AND PREJUDICES: AMERICA'S FOOD

In 1950 the news came that we were moving again, this time to England by way of the United States. My father felt we knew nothing of the heartland of our native country, so he decided to show it to us. His plan was to fly to California, purchase a car, drive leisurely across the country with stops at major landmarks, sell the car in New York, and board the HMS *Queen Elizabeth* for Southampton, England. My memories are of the restaurants on each coast, with something of a blank in between.

The highlight of our West Coast leg was a pair of trips with my grandfather in and around Carmel, California, where he had retired. The first was to a California Spanish hacienda restaurant on the Holman Ranch, an oasis at the center of hundreds of acres of sunburnt, golden brown hills. We sat on a raised terrace beside a courtyard where white-robed and red-sashed Mexican staff gathered around huge grills and spits. It was a series of firsts for me: Caesar salad tossed at the table, garlic bread in huge rustic slabs, wild boar sausages grilled over mesquite charcoal, avocado "pears," and two-inch-thick T-bone steaks. The memory of a perfect evening lingered: the brown summer hills of California suffused in pink early evening light, an ambush of bougainvillea, the dense dark green of live oaks, the perfume of the fully flowering jasmine hedge mingling with the smells of charcoal-cooked wild boar, and my first taste of California wine. Later, as a professional chef in California, the place remained a benchmark of pleasure for me: simply grand food and perfect service in an unpretentious but beautiful setting. Let alone grilling.

The second excursion was to the Garrapata Trout Farm, located in one of those magical canyons off Big Sur. Catching fish in the pond was guaranteed, and we soon had enough to grill on open fires under huge overhanging California bay trees. Again the smells and aromas invaded and captured my brain: the summer-baked grass, the spice of the bay leaves, the charcoal smoke, the fish wrapped in sizzling bacon. The family was happy as a group, something rare enough in itself to incise this day into my memory. When I started working at Berkeley's Chez Panisse, live Garrapata trout were among the first resources to which I turned.

Heading east in California we stopped in Needles, home of motels, pickup trucks, dust, and an enormous sign with thousands of lightbulbs flashing in sequence that read "The Cocky Cactus." Bedazzled, I begged my parents to stop there for dinner. The decor was an original of the "family restaurant," a prototype for copies that soon lined U.S. interstates before the industrial food complex took over. The menu was Pacific seafood, steaks, salads, and flaming desserts like hot plums ladled over a gigantic pile of coconut ice cream. I adored it. But what kept it in my mind was the birthday card the restaurant sent every year for at least the next decade. Years later, when I opened my restaurant Stars in San Francisco, I put two lessons from the Cocky Cactus at the top of my list of principles: a restaurant can be fairly humble and still feel world-class, and nothing will build loyalty like "loving" relationships with customers.

The dinner in that dusty town was the last thing I remember of the trip until our stop in Washington, D.C., except for an endless succession of stainless steel diners serving fresh pies and wonderful regional American food. In Washington we visited my aunt and Russian uncle. Both would come to play an enormous role in my culinary upbringing. My Auntie Mame was my mother's sister, the eldest in a wealthy Irish Catholic family of thirteen kids. But she had been raised apart. Bedridden from a childhood illness, she was passed to my grandfather's even wealthier brother and his wife, who brought her up as a debutante in opulent Philadelphia Main Line settings. Her first marriage, to a polo-playing prince of Philadelphia society, had ended after her husband's alcoholism became more pronounced than his homosexuality.

The uncle I knew was her second husband and was my hero, a celebrated space travel scientist who, as an eighteen-year-old Russian naval cadet, had captured an imperial frigate in communist hands, and then as captain of the ship had sailed it to India to escape the revolution.

I loved my aunt's meticulous sense of order, her beige, white, and navy blue wardrobe, her passion for galleries, Russian emeralds, a perfectly made-up face before lunch, old textiles, restaurants, and perfect, simple, cooking.

When I had told her that in New York we'd be dining at Lüchow's and Lindy's, she gave a shudder and handed me a small pad of English blue notepaper. "Write these down," she commanded. "Delmonico's, the Colony, and Le Pavillon."

"Are those your favorites?" I asked.

"No," she replied. "Those would be Le Voisin, L'Escargot, and Maud 'Chez Elle,' but don't write them down."

I did. And when I showed the entire list to my mother, she swore to keep me away from my aunt forever. My father was impressed, but asked me who was paying.

I never made it to any of them, but they've been anchored in my mind ever since. Especially Delmonico's, whose cookbook, *The Epicurean,* triggered the Chez Panisse California Regional Dinner in 1976. In 1985, after opening Stars, I tried to buy L'Escargot to have a Stars in New York. When that fell through I posted a 1953 menu of Le Pavillon in a place of honor above the Stars kitchen entrance and incorporated quotations from its imperious owner, Henri Soulé, into our training manuals.

Michael and Ariane Batterberry's *On the Town in New York* says Soulé was "to French cuisine what de Gaulle was to the Third Republic," but that his personality was closer to Napoleon's. He was a martinet and a snob, but above all a perfectionist who lived for his art. Nothing compared to his mentor Fernand Point. According to George Lang, the first great promoter and manager of the Four Seasons in New York and later owner of Café des Artistes, Point once threw out a party of four at his restaurant La Pyramide because one of the men was holding his glass of champagne by the bowl instead of the stem, ruining the otherwise perfectly achieved temperature of the wine.

What would I have eaten if my parents had taken me to Le Pavillon? What would I eat now? There were eleven ways to start the meal, from smoked salmon to cherrystones to crabmeat (all in French of course). Following those were eggs (ten dishes), fish (eleven), plats du jour (fourteen), grillades (seven), cold plates (six), vegetables (nine), and desserts (eight). Traveling on ships and trains had made me fall in love with cold plates like York Ham and Tongue, but I would have mercy on my guests and not confuse the order of the meal by ordering them (since no one knew any longer where to put them in the order of dishes served).

I'd begin with the Bayonne ham with a glass of champagne for sure, most likely followed by the Goujonettes de Sole, Sauce Tartare. Then, though tempted by the kidneys from the grillades section, or the Rognons Maître d'Hôtel (with a simple unmelted butter mixed with parsley, salt, freshly ground pepper, and lemon juice), and wondering about the daring of featuring "Irish Stew," I would have the Poached Chicken Bordelaise with fresh little peas steamed in lettuce. For dessert my eye would light upon the Désir du Roi as I looked on the Duke of Windsor or the Aga Khan across the dining room. Knowing that one of my companions would have a wild strawberry soufflé, I would order the Coupe aux Marrons, as I always did as a child. The cost for my meal would have been ten dollars.

Would anyone not want to join me?

CHAPTER 4

THE CUPBOARD IS BARE

In 1951, boarding the Cunard liner *Queen Elizabeth* in New York, I found that the enormous cabin reserved for my brother and me was filled with huge trays of canapés, more than the two of us could eat, and our first caviar and goose liver. We were in heaven. But this very grand ship was to teach me more than how to fill my belly with wonderful food. The first morning I found the promenade deck and a deck chair with a card that read "Master J. Tower" in its holder. After tucking me into my blanket, the white-coated steward served me hot beef bouillon in a bone china cup. Too small to see over the rail, I stared at the sky and listened to the hum and vibrations of the ship, allowing myself to be voluptuously enveloped in the perfection of the moment. I remember thinking that whatever my future held, the freedom of this morning without adults, the only supervision from a perfect waiter folding blankets around my feet and providing delicious food, would be what I'd live for. Whatever happened (and it usually did, I thought), I would always have this.

The next area to conquer was the dining room. My brother and I were scheduled for the first dinner seating, my parents the second. Since my brother was embarrassed to sit with me (he wanted Cindy, the beautiful daughter of the Firestone tire heir), I was left alone with the waiter and the immense menu mostly in French. I found the things I knew I liked. Sydney's Prunier had trained me to know Saumon Fume écossais, Caviare, Jambon de Paris, Homard à la Newburg, and Pommes Chips. The Mock Turtle Soup and

Baked Alaska in English were easy, so I had those too. Then I had the Assiette de Petits Fours all to myself. Within days I was bedridden, sick as a dog from greedy and enthusiastic overeating.

Most any calm-sea afternoon before my downfall, I could be found in the dining room waiting for dinner, or waiting to be asked into the kitchens, where I had become something of a mascot. So one evening when I did not appear, my parents were compelled to explain that I was in bed, incapable of looking at more food. That night, there was a knock at my cabin door. In came a dining room waiter—not a cabin steward but my real dining room waiter. I was honored, but then my stomach tightened at the sight of the trolley piled high with domed dishes, among them an enormous silver cloche that obviously held a huge roast beef or goose. My heart sank. I knew if I said, "Please go away and let me die," I'd insult the kitchen and lose my standing. If I ate any of it, I doubted I'd survive the night.

I should have noticed the sympathetic smile on the waiter's face and the grin on the steward behind him. I recoiled in horror as the waiter, with a dramatic flourish, removed the dome. My queasy stomach perversely expected fatty meat, but I saw only a small green earthenware pot. My pal from the dining room laughed as he removed the lid to reveal a dish of simply water, lamb, potatoes, a hint of sage, and nothing more. The clean aromas of a Lancashire hot pot wafted across to my bed, and my appetite was immediately restored. The next morning I felt good enough to consume a quantity of smoked salmon, but I never dove blindly into a menu again. The chef had taught me balance, if not moderation.

We left the ship in Southampton in November as I was about to turn eight. England was in the midst of postwar rationing, just like Australia. There were no signs of it, however, as we headed up to London by the Golden Arrow Boat Train, with a wonderfully magical dining car and its afternoon tea of Toasted Teacake, Buttered Toast, Crumpets and Scones, Hovis Bread and Butter, Teatime Biscuits and "Quality Cake." I was in heaven, although how much so I was only later to learn, when we got to London and found ourselves in the desert of nationally rationed and very scarce food.

It was cold, damp, and thick with fog as we made our way to the Hyde Park Hotel, our rooms looking out on trees, Royal Horse Guards in red and blue, and nannies whose big black strollers could be seen vaguely through the gloom. The Roman hotel had been vast, but these hotel rooms were the biggest I had ever seen. My brother's and my suite was so large that I don't remember him there after this. Maybe he was in school. Alone and bored, the city too fog-swathed to venture into by myself, I turned to the only entertainment I knew: room service and the dining room.

During the day I'd run the carts around the corridors with my favorite waiters, Bill and Ben, who would let me accompany them into the rooms of the less uptight guests. They showed me how to carve game birds, open wine bottles, and hold the tops of huge tureens as they ladled out turtle soup or consommé Célestine.

Meanwhile, my first lesson in shopping for perfect ingredients was just a few Knightsbridge blocks away at Harrods' magnificent Food Hall. I went every day to see the twenty-foot-high, ten-foot-wide display of fish and shellfish, the fish laid out on a sloping, light gray marble slab, so fresh they needed to be cooled only by a mist of water. It must have been all the fish in London. But as food became more readily available in the next two years, sometimes the white belly of a forty-pound turbot would be decorated in a Prince of Wales fleur-de-lis of tiny shrimp, their pink in contrast to the orange coral of sea scallops still in their shells; sometimes it would be covered in an arabesque of fresh herring and lobsters. If the fishing weather had been bad, the display would be all smoked fish, with miles of kippers and mounds of smoked salmon and four-foot-long smoked eels biting down on the tails of whole smoked sturgeon.

Even with rationing, the poultry section had the usual domesticated Aylesbury ducks, if only two. Anything wild and shot was there in abundance. Mallard ducks, pheasants, plovers, teals, wood pigeon, and more I didn't recognize hanging in rows along the marble hall. I was astonished not so much by the numbers of hares and rabbits as by the fact they were there at all: in Australia, rabbit was known as "bush chicken" and so common a pest that no one ate it. In England in those days, before U.S. battery systems were introduced, chickens were more expensive than beef. They were hardly any of those. The meat section boasted a couple of whole Welsh lambs, a half Scottish beef carcass, and every kind of offal, including calves' heads scrubbed and white and ready for Tête de Veau, Sauce Gribiche, my favorite lunch at the hotel. My routine was to order something new on the hotel menu and then run to Harrods to see what it looked like raw.

My career as a food tourist was cut short one night when my parents unexpectedly stayed in the hotel for dinner and I, seizing my chance to have some wine, sat down at their table. Bill, Ben, the headwaiter, and the maître d' all came to greet me. This caught my father's attention, and he looked at me with new focus. "What are you doing here?" he asked. "I thought you were in school."

"I am," I said. "They're teaching me to slice smoked salmon."

Admiration and disgust were in a close race on my father's face, but he knew I had him for the moment.

It says something about the size of our adjoining suites that I had been in residence for two months without my father noticing. It says something about my father, too. He turned to my mother, and I could read the looks on their faces. Each wanted to say to the other, "I thought you put him in school!" The waiters and I were devastated: my reign as Eloise of the Hyde Park Hotel was over.

That evening was about the extent of my parents' attention span with me, because we remained at the Hyde Park for another month before eventually landing in a very *Separate Tables* hotel in the Surrey countryside nearer schools. It was another month before they found one. In the meantime, I attempted to reproduce my old routine by befriending the chef and the room service waiters. I failed. The entire staff thought I was a pest. So I turned my attention to the guests, particularly to an ancient English lesbian dressed in impeccable tweed suits. Mrs. Charlesworth let me take her two Russell terriers around the grounds while she played canasta with the beautifully mannered unmarried colonels, reverends, and female gym teachers who lived in the hotel. Then she'd let me finish off her gin and have a puff on her ivory cigarette holder.

Finally, I was sent off to school. I was miserable. For the first time in my life I had to eat bad food. At the hotel the menu had been very English, with very good ingredients, and I learned to love most of them. But unlike life at the Hyde Park Hotel, at school we were on English food rationing coupons. I had two eggs a week, no sugar or desserts, bread fried in bacon fat, and steamed puddings. Never did I see the actual bacon. It was a long way from shipboard lobster Newburg and grand hotel roasted teal duck.

The school food was cooked for hours and covered with sauces reconstituted from powders labeled "brown," "fish," or "custard." It was a diet made for scurvy; in my six years at English private schools, I never saw a piece of fresh fruit.

For that I would have to wait for the weekends. After the country hotel we moved to a manor house near Guildford, forty miles from London. It had a three-acre garden, which included an enormous "kitchen" garden. At last my mother had a kitchen and an orchard soon to be full of fruit.

MY MOTHER'S ENGLISH KITCHEN

My mother was a beautiful, passionate, intelligent, and multitalented alcoholic woman, a great natural cook in several cuisines, her favorites being American and Mexican. My memory of her is of the two forces holding sway in her—elegant in Jean Patou suits, pearls, and Cartier diamond brooches pinned to her lapels on her way to those endless parties; or plunked down in old mannish clothes in the garden dirt all day with no gloves, the rings taken off and put in a nearby flowerpot. Food and entertaining were the way my mother communicated. She had never cooked before her marriage, but she was a natural and quickly learned her way around the kitchen. My father's making light of all her talents save cooking and gardening meant they became her only artistic outlets. Hopeless in most maternal respects, she took food and hospitality very seriously. Parties meant mountains of food, rivers of drinks, and the carpet rolled up at midnight for dancing to tangoes and Pedro Vargas's Mexican music until dawn.

Rural England in the throes of rationing meant that the only meats and poultry in plentiful supply were locally caught wild things. I would walk down the streets of Guildford ogling all the wild hare and rabbits hanging outside the shops, with little buckets under their noses to catch the blood for "jugged hare," or *lièvre à la royale*. In 1953 sugar became available and in 1954 meat and everything else. Now wild game was the luxury because no one could afford gamekeepers anymore. When I was at home, my mother and I would often shop together. She took me to the greengrocer, the butcher, the poulterer, the fishmonger, and, twice a week, the farmers' market, where one could find fresh herbs and salad greens, honeys, more game, and potatoes dug that morning. Everything was local or regional because it had to be. There were no large industrial farms and no refrigerated transportation, very little gas for anything but local transportation.

At the fishmonger's they would try to frighten me with tasting a raw oyster, a game I kept up for as long as I could, and in the greengrocer my mother taught me to pick out the best Channel Islands new potatoes and green beans. They had to be small and of the same size so they would cook evenly. The watercress had to shine, the Brussels sprouts had to be tiny and firm, and the lettuces had to have no brown spots. The vegetables and fruits we bought were to supplement our orchard of pears, apples, and quinces, and our vegetable garden of herbs, edible flowers, green "runner" beans, and American crops like squashes, corn, and lima beans, which the gardeners thought were devil's work and most of the time the weather agreed. There were also strawberries and raspberries (both of which were my project and responsibility), and blackberries, mulberries, and hazelnuts from the wild "common" land where I'd go horseback riding.

On several occasions, when I managed to get myself suspended or expelled from school, my exile to the garden was a haven, not an exile. Even if Mullins, one of the gardeners, did insist on pinching my bottom, I got used to it after a while. This was England, after all.

I cannot think of a more important education from my mother than gardening, and certainly no education I enjoyed as much. There were no big concepts like "organic" or "pesticide-free"—I'm not even sure there were chemicals. It was all manure and plowing under, and double digging, and the dung from our horse stables, and my pet twin goats kept the strawberries and asparagus very happy. "They need to be fed a lot," my mother would explain, firing my imagination about plants that had to eat before we ate them.

When my mother's ambition didn't outlast her martini consumption, and the housekeeper-cook had no idea about the food, I often ended up cooking. There were memorable disasters, like the time we received a shipment from the U.S. embassy of what appeared to be vegetable shortening, which I promptly used to cook eggs. It was only after the house was made uninhabitable by the smell that we all realized I had just fried with pure lanolin meant to keep naval leather in good condition at sea. Her most memorable was a Saturday night when I came home from school, sniffed the air, and said, with dripping contempt, "What are we having, fried cheese?" Her face fell. One whiff from her of the kitchen and she knew the wild pheasant had been hung according to true English tastes, to their desired level of putrefaction. Into the garbage it went and off to the martinis went my mother. I looked in the "larder," which, since as ever money talked, was full of the usual. On any given day there would be a whole poached wild Scottish salmon, a fresh ham (meaning leg of pork brined and poached), leftover game birds and beef, as well as cakes and pudding made by the housekeeper. I put it all out on the dining room buffet and everyone was happy once the smell of heated freshly rotten game bird had cleared.

My mother was not an alcoholic in the usual sense. She didn't drink during the day. What she had, I realize in retrospect, was a problem metabolizing alcohol. She'd consume two martinis and it was as if you'd hit her with a sledgehammer. So I was used to taking over the kitchen. But the large summer garden parties were the most dramatic and heart pounding for me. At age fourteen I would find myself with the housekeeper and waiters doing the second half of a meal for a hundred people, carefully removing huge wild Scottish salmon from their poaching liquid, peeling them and decorating them and giving them to waiters to take out to the garden tent. The boiled leg of mutton served cold with *sauce gribiche* or the grilled steak would have been done in advance, and I had been taught how to carve and slice a few years before, so they were no problem to finish. Nor were the green bean salad vinaigrette, the twenty-odd pounds of strawberries served in a bowl my mother had had made in Venice for that purpose, or the ice cream, usually wild blackberry, that we had taken turns all day churning. The quantities were heart-stopping for me, but our waiters Bill and Ben from the Hyde Park Hotel knew how much to put out and when to replace it.

If alcohol drove a wedge between my mother and the family, it was my one point of connection with my father. I lived for the wine ritual that anchored my one-day weekend, when I'd return from school, determine what was being served at Saturday's dinner, and discuss with him the appropriate bottles. I would push for my favorite wines, of course, even when they were too expensive for the occasion. He didn't always appreciate my maneuvers, but on the whole he was pleased by my performance as his private sommelier, and proud that I would accompany my mother to Berry Brothers in

St. James's (London) to taste and pick out the English bottlings of "Claret" or "Pomerol" house wines for the year.

Retrieving the bottles was nonetheless fraught. The four-hundred-year-old cellar was cavernous, with five or six rooms, and I had to descend a long, gray stone staircase in darkness before I got to the ten-watt gloom. I had seen all the Hammer company's horror films, so I had nightmares about those rooms throughout my teens. Yet I made the white-knuckled descent, because of what was ahead of me: choosing, decanting, tasting, and finally drinking them with dinner. When there was no company, we served only red wine, since my father considered white "effeminate" and champagne "frivolous." Perhaps that's why I adore both.

HOME ALONE

In the summer of 1958 my mother left for the United States to put my brother in Brown University. My father decided to stay in London and he and I were alone in our Knightsbridge mews flat. By that time I was sixteen, so my parents felt I could hold down a kitchen of my own. It was my job to cook. I had Harrods to shop in, and food was plentiful, even though I blew the week's budget the first day. The first dinner in the flat, one for my father and his Australian mistress, was a success despite melting the plastic colander over boiling water while keeping the rice warm to go with my Veal Marengo.

My aunt in Washington wrote constantly with cooking advice: "I have an easy recipe: Take a cut-up bird—chicken, grouse, or what have you (even rabbit)—wipe it dry and clean, and brown it in butter (salt and pepper) in a pan on top of stove. When brown pour heavy cream over it, put a tight lid on pan and turn heat low, and let cook half an hour. Serve with wide noodles in butter and a green salad." When she told me about whole Mediterranean sea bass baked in the oven and I cooked it, my father was aghast at the expense, which only mounted as more recipes arrived: "the first and second ribs of beef," "wild mushrooms with potatoes," "an honest to goodness Indian lobster curry," "coquilles" in their shells, and "last but not least, chicken livers in 100-year-old Madeira."

Before the summer was out my aunt and uncle decided to send me Paris to eat, learn, and buy them truffles. They told me which restaurant, and my thank-you note to them says I had "six escargots, a *croustade de crabe, salade verte, gateau des pêches (de la maison),* and *café.*" The crab was in a white wine sauce (very light) and served on a vol-au-vent. "I don't usually like them, but this one was exceptional. The food was good and down-to-earth! So many restaurants have very fancy food that tastes of nothing but money."

Money was a problem if you were a young glutton, even a subsidized one. I wrote of passing Fauchon's, "which makes Fortnum & Mason look ill. Fresh truffles, mangoes, mountains of chocolate truffles, cakes enough to make you smash the windows to get at them. The only trouble was it reeked of money, so I was forced to stay out—just as well, I suppose." But my father was just as indulgent when it involved teaching by traveling. In 1956 he sent my brother and me alone to California and back, traveling on the French ship *Liberté* from Southampton to New York, the 20th Century Limited crack train from New York to Chicago, and from there the California Zephyr to San Francisco, stopping in the Rockies to pick up wild trout for the dining car.

Such indulgences could not last, and I was soon back in boarding school, where I finally complained to the headmaster about the food. For breakfast there was white bread, margarine, and cheap marmalade; for lunch, typically shepherd's pie and bread pudding with powdered custard sauce; and for the evening meal a repetition of breakfast. I was surprised when he offered a challenge instead of the usual caning for speaking out. "Cook a meal that could be reproduced, on a given budget, for the students." I enlisted a boyfriend and cooked veal and beef meat loaf with fresh peas and little white onions, watercress salad, and an upside-down apple tart served with cheddar. I was applauded—and the boardinghouse food stayed the same.

But nothing of English food and ingredients had prepared me for the weird swill dished out at the Connecticut prep school Loomis, to which I moved for two years starting in 1959: chipped beef in flour sauce on a rusk that would choke a giant, and lime Jell-O with marshmallow and bacon. I thought of a hunger strike but decided instead on illegal trips to town for the newly discovered luxury of hamburgers and malted milk shakes. Threats to expel me didn't work (been there, done that), even after I tried to run away to Cuba anyway and join Che and the revolution. I was made head of the student committee on food, a position that meant nothing in the face of a phalanx of dietitians drumming up Jell-O. For the headmaster, it was an admirable act of revenge.

CHAPTER 5

THE CHAMPAGNE PALACE

Two years later, in 1961, at Harvard College, the Freshman Union eating hall was worse. Worse even than the food I had at army camp in England with the Royal Fusiliers when I was a fifteen-year-old cadet. Once again I spoke up, this time to the deaf ears of a home economist and the huge women cooks who had been serving that slop for thirty years with firmly muttered Boston Irish oaths. So I backed off, and plotted to get out of Harvard's "houses" and into a house of my own. Or anyone's, for that matter. "Anyone" appeared in the form of a teaching fellow from Paris, and soon I was ensconced in a Directoire-decorated apartment on Beacon Hill's Chestnut Street I called the "Champagne Palace."

STEAK AND JACK DANIEL'S

The teaching fellow turned out to have lived in Paris, so we loved the same things. The champagne flowed, the candles stayed lighted, and the Piaf songs played on. There wasn't much of a kitchen, but I did manage a mean *steak au poivre*. Since my aunt continued sending recipes, I had to improvise and we enjoyed a chicken in cream, spaghetti in clam sauce, lobsters, and all sorts of risottos and omelets. The apartment was above the English consul general's house, the site of constant English theater cast parties, so many a bored actor found his way up the stairs at the advice of the consul's (and our) risqué maid.

Here I could practice my own full-blown candlelight Alexandria Quartet hospitality and impromptu cooking for the first time. The guests were whatever actors, hustlers, pill pushers, and Etonian consular sons and cousins appeared in the wee hours of the morning. A college diary entry in 1961:

Freddy and the Champagne Palace
Steak au poivre
Jack Daniel's
Chambolle-Musigny
Courvoisier
Pills
Substitute Chicken Club, Omelet

After two years of this masked ball, my Champagne Palace friend became unhinged, and the creditors showed up and commandeered my Directoire gilt-bronze swan-neck and dolphin chandelier. So after a few more parties, the palace was disbanded and bare, and I went back to my allotted rooms at Adams House. Deprived of a kitchen, my time was now filled with Baudelaire, Mallarmé, William Burroughs, studies of Egyptian funerary temples, and wishing I didn't understand why Oscar Wilde would take a cab to cross the street. My great friend and roommate, Michael Palmer, already on his way to becoming a first-rate poet, developed friendships with Louis Zukofsky, Allen Ginsberg, Gary Snyder, and the Robert Creeleys, who were among those who visited our room. After smoking marijuana for the first time, I said I preferred a good champagne, Lafite-Rothschild, or Otard cognac, and offered some to that evening's guests. But I still needed to cook for whoever had the munchies.

I set up a kitchen in the closet with the hot plate and blue Le Creuset frying pan sent by my aunt, who was worried that years of bad school food would stunt my mind. Recipes and advice on how to entertain my friends kept coming: one for romaine lettuce dressed with sour cream, mayonnaise, and imported Parmesan cheese; others for her incredible coleslaw; iced coffee with ice cream and vanilla bean; and the names of importers on the East Coast that sold Ratsherrn bock beer and a particular 1957, Rosé d'Anjou (with advice never to spend money on any older ones).

At the end of that letter in 1962 she wrote, "Your uncle's prediction for the past five years came to pass yesterday—two Soviets in space and he expects them to try for a rendezvous and to train for a rescue in space." Back on earth, she knew it was time to check out my mental health, so she invited me with several of my friends, including Michael, still uninitiated in the lessons of aristocratic Russia, to come to Washington.

THE OLD WORLD FIRST

My friends had indulged in my aunt's chicken liver with hundred-year-old Madeira recipe, which I'd cooked in our college room's closet. Before we disbanded from Harvard, I wanted them to experience the source and lifestyle of the only perfect harmony I had ever known—a grand world whose real players were about to disappear. I wanted my friends to hear the conversations at the table with my uncle's circle of aristocratic Russians, their talk ranging from underwater missiles and galactic travel to space stations and the real story of Rasputin's death. The storyteller was Count Cheremetev, childhood friend of Prince Yusupov, Rasputin's assassin. My favorite of the group was a discreet crown prince of Poland. When my aunt had offered an aspirin to a guest complaining of a headache, the prince said: "Take the *France* instead; it sails at eleven."

So in our junior year we made the trip to Washington, D.C. My friends paled when they saw the silk and malachite apartment, but it was nothing compared with the pallor they'd acquired after three vodka toasts: "To our meeting!" "To the promise of your young minds!" and "May you leave the world a better place than you found it!" Only a Russian could greet you and speak to your death within five minutes. It was normal for me.

As were the famous chicken livers as hors d'oeuvre, vodka, and caviar blini for a first course. The first Russian culinary lesson was that blini should be drenched in enough melted butter for it to run down into one's lace cuffs, if one had them. The second was in the social nerve and dexterity to pick up a vodka in one hand, a beluga-laden, butter-soaked, sour-cream-covered blini in the other, and pop the whole blini in one's mouth seconds after the burn of the vodka hit one's throat.

After several more courses and lots of wines, dessert was a quart of ice cream per person. Then my uncle repeated the before-the-war/after-the-war tutorial, giving each of us a taste of his favorite liqueur partnered with its far more magnificent prewar incarnation. The pousse-café to settle our stomachs was what legends are made of: a sixteen-ounce Scotch and soda. Our lessons had begun, and we returned to Cambridge, Massachusetts.

BALENCIAGA FOOD

Stories of this Russian meal survived better than we did, and it became a challenge to repeat as much of it as possible back in Cambridge, though now it was at least easier with a kitchen of my own. When we couldn't stand Adams House any longer (or they us), Michael and I took a little two-story house with a garden on Green Street in Cambridge. I pulled out my Elizabeth David *Gourmet* articles on the London restaurateur of the thirties X. Marcel Boulestin; put aside Radiguet and Ho Chi Minh, and opened Prosper Montagné's *Larousse Gastronomique*.

We never did get around to planting the planned little lettuces and mesclun in the garden, but the kitchen was well enough equipped for serious cooking. Michael loved food as much as I did. He came from an Italian family in Scarsdale, New York, with several maiden aunts who specialized in organizing Old World feasts. His Wellesley College girlfriend, Cathy Simon, loved cooking as well. Her Danish mother in Manhattan was a friend of the legendary cooking teacher Michael Field, and Cathy had learned from the best. Not that she needed much education: she was one of the best natural cooks I had ever seen. And our Texan friend John Sanger, another passionate cook and Michael Field fan, had the allowance to cook all the things like whole Smithfield hams that we others couldn't afford.

For my junior year birthday, Michael had given me a can of truffles and a book of H.D.'s poems, setting the tone for the coming year, one spent in the college library listening to tapes of Noël Coward and Gertrude Lawrence read Coward's play *Private Lives,* and cooking. Nothing else seemed to make much sense.

Once we had our kitchen, I couldn't wait to use the truffles and the other gift from Michael, an 1884 Madeira.

First Dinner in Our Own Kitchen
Cambridge 1964

Pâté
Frozen Vodka
Consommé Madrilène
Saumon en Gelée aux Truffes
Pouilly-Fumé 1962
Filet de Boeuf Périgourdine
Chateau-Neuf-du-Pape 1957
Strawberries and French Cream
Asti Spumante
Coffee
"Napoleon" Armagnac
Sercial Madeira 1884

Guests at that dinner included Cathy, John Sanger, and my boyfriend Colin Streeter, the most beautiful young man at Harvard and, it was said, just out of the arms of Leonard Bernstein.

Fired up by this success, I filled my notebook with recipes for salt beef, how to make hams, turbot with Meyer lemon salad, sturgeon with cream and caviar, green bean and nasturtium flower salad, and Soufrières lime punch. I wrote that my goal was to cook the way Balenciaga cut clothes—simple in form, without ornamentation, always in harmony with the lines of the body. For "body" read ingredients.

BEEF AND CHATEAU D'YQUEM

Everyone who had been on the Washington trip wanted to test what Cheremetev had told us was Prince Yusupov's definition of decadence: drinking Chateau d'Yquem with roast beef. The Russians considered the point of it to be the richness of the fat (it had to be prime and aged beef) and the age of the wine, which could not be too young or too old. Too young, the wine would lack the complexity to match the richness of the meat, and too old, it would pale under that same richness. A twenty- to thirty-year-old d'Yquem was thought to be just about right.

We served the beef with a 1955 d'Yquem because that was all we could find and afford. But the ten-year-old wine did its job: I remember the moment of silence that fell around the hot, early summer kitchen as I cut salty fat off the roast ribs and everyone (as instructed) sucked on a chunk while washing it down with the cool wine. One felt a stagger in the knees, the body sending a silent but eloquent message to the brain to stop! We had reached the benchmark. Or so we thought.

Our final dinner, a year later, just before we graduated in June 1965, was in a kitchen that had reached one hundred degrees by the time I had roasted the goose. I served it at room temperature with more d'Yquem. The fatty goose and its Peking duck–like skin, paired with the old sweet wine, pushed us momentarily out into a world where eating and tasting were as powerful forces as any we knew.

But enough of all that, I thought. We were leaving the college nest, and so time to find a job. An offer from *The New Yorker* seemed from the other side of the moon, so I thought of architecture. And Italy and Greece. Would they move me enough to go back to school for more?

I sailed for Europe.

CHAPTER 6

OLD WORLD AGAIN

My mother's treat for surviving Harvard and for never having successfully made it all the way to Cuba to meet Che, or to Venezuela for the Peace Corps, was to take me to her ancestral Ireland before we went on to England. I chose the liner *Maasdam* because of my parents' stories of Trimalchian feasts on Dutch freighters before the war. I had great expectations of eel and rijsttafel, of two-hour midmorning breakfasts of cold fish and fowl followed by more of the same throughout the day. But the food was so bad that I spent my time writing an outline for a cookbook called *Quick & Cheap*. It included a fifteen-minute tomato soup, green bean salad, citrus chicken, and a lamb-potato casserole modeled on the hot pot that had saved my life aboard the *Queen Elizabeth*. Then I wrote a regimen for a carbohydrate-free diet (fish, eggs, smoked salmon, melon, prawns, clear soups, watercress salads, trout, vegetable ragouts) before drawing up a list of all the famous restaurants in the world and a travel plan to visit them.

We landed in Galway, on the west coast of Ireland—a country that in those days had no famous restaurants, so we were a bit adrift after a few days in Ashford Castle, with its ease and splendor and fine old Amontillado. On the way to Dublin we ended up at the Welcome Home guesthouse, where it was a shock to learn that if you didn't eat a high tea of eggs, fried bread, and grilled tomatoes at 6 P.M., you didn't eat at night at all. Gone were the famous teas of Lady Portarlington, who replaced tea with Sidecars, and gone as well the fashion of cold grouse washed down with ancient Malmsey. Now it was store-bought cold sausage rolls.

All this my mother forgave when she discovered that every tiny village grocery store had a bar, and that a little tot of enlightenment was always just around the corner. Never one for whiskey during the day, I distracted myself by keeping records of every meal, in macabre fascination at the contrast between the richness of the countryside (lily-covered peat bogs and endless undulating hills covered in rhododendrons and fuchsia hedgerows) and the ubiquitous watery tomatoes, powdered oxtail soup, and canned peas.

In England I retraced my childhood culinary past. At Brown's Hotel, beloved of my aunt and Russian uncle and a mecca for country eccentrics, gone also were its breakfasts of cold meats and ptarmigan, haddock, eggs and kidneys, ham and nectarines, and small mountains of scones and buttered toast. Gone were Brown's vodka iced to perfection, and the hundreds of different kinds of pies that Leonard Woolf said had limbs peeking through the crusts. Gone the grand dinners with ten courses and the suppers that followed of deviled chicken and potted shrimp and a huge brandy or Scotch and soda. Gone also was this last attempt at something timeless in everyday life, like the party in Sir Alfred Munnings's painting *Tagg's Island*. These thoughts cascaded through my mind in the bar at Brown's while I listened to the Texas, not my old-school Wiltshire, accents. I shed a tear into my champagne for everything wonderful that had passed, and we headed for the village of our old house, an hour southwest of London in the county of Surrey.

TWO PIMMS BEFORE LUNCH

We stayed in Surrey with my English guardians. They had been my parents in 1958 when I was left at school in England as my parents returned to the States. They shared my mother's passion for gardens and gardening, and their grounds were an ocean of enormous careless poppies, ceanothus scented like honey, columbines in various shades of night, fritillaries and delphinium, and a whole garden of roses, both tea and peace. Filled with nostalgia, we rushed to see our old house, with its acre kitchen garden lined with box hedges and framed with rose-covered arbors and trellises, its lawn tennis courts, vast orchard, goat paddock, stables, barn, and croquet lawn that held the huge tents of my mother's garden parties. Eight houses now sat in its place.

Two Pimms before lunch, enjoyed back among my guardians' flowers, assuaged the growing sadness that you can never go back. I learned that even this huge garden of my wealthy guardians was probably doomed by the vast cost of keeping it up. I realized that gardening, which so far was the only thing life had prepared me for, was not a way out. My mother went back to New York, a piece of her heart forever left in the eighteenth-century perfect Georgian property we had seen in the Wicklow Mountains outside Dublin, my father having decided they would live in Connecticut. I would have stayed in Ireland happily, but not Connecticut, so looked around in England for a job.

I had no leads for any, so perhaps the wine business could be the answer? My first visit to a wine company led only to the director's bed and the advice that I was too ambitious to settle for never being able to own this, his boss's family's company.

Cooking was my last hope. But for whom? Back in Surrey I ran into my old girlfriend, the daughter of the publican at the Horse & Groom, next to where our old house had been. It turned out she was fed up with cooking the simple pub menu and offered me the job. The prospect of requisitioning ingredients and facing a row of orders at the rush while using such strange equipment as infrared steak griddles and deep-fat fryers was terrifying, but not as much as being penniless. The food, I figured, would be easy. All I had to do was cook everything a little less than this English kitchen had, put some butter and cream in the mashed potatoes, banish packaged sauces, and salt the previously tasteless soup. After a few disasters—among them not shutting the valve in the fryer when filling it back up with oil—I got the hang of it. Or so I thought. The customers hated my Frenchified food, thinking the mashed potatoes with butter and cream too rich and strangely flavored. Perhaps Napoleon had returned. Their thumbs-down gesture meant that after two months I was out pounding the pavement again.

I had just finished reading James Baldwin's *Another Country*, with its line about security as a vast, gray sleep, so I fell on my grandfather's offer to pay for graduate school in architecture, as long as it was back at Harvard, and left England for good. As the Belgian freighter docked in New York in hundred-degree heat I had my great-uncle's fur coat over my arm and a handkerchief wet with the tears of an admiring chief steward in my breast pocket. My family took the wetness in my own eyes as a sign of my happiness to be back in America.

CHAPTER 7

AMERICA AGAIN

I set out for Cambridge. Cathy and Michael were back in the same Green Street house, but this time they had planted the backyard garden with rows of baby lettuces from seeds brought from Italy and France. That street held too many memories for me, so I found a place in Boston's Italian North End to be near the food markets, in the romantic notion that it would be like living in Europe. But the only European thing about the neighborhood was that it was more violent than Naples. The Italian mama across the hall turned out to be the mother of the local boss, so I was declared off-limits to stranger bashing, but my friends were not. Brushing aside the pasta hanging in the corridor, I made my peace with Mama and crossed the Charles River again. This time it was for a blue-collar Irish block near Inman Square in Somerville, where the rents for large houses with kitchens and dining rooms were cheap. There was also a decent fish market called Legal Sea Foods, where after a few months I convinced the owner to use the space next door as an experimental restaurant. Use up all the leftover fish in fish and chips so that what's in the case each day is fresh, was what I told him. Later I was his first customer.

CHAMPAGNE WHILE THE WORLD CRUMBLES

Protests against the Vietnam War were breaking out across the nation, and Harvard Square was no exception. My disdain for a revolution without the proper Jacobite fashions had brought down polite but dedicated calumny on my head, so I decided to cook for revolutionaries instead of marching with them. Two street-kid dancers, poets, my brother—just in from Vietnam for R&R, radical architecture students, and the son of a senior counsel at the FBI were the guests at dinner to discuss my artistic and revolutionary stance.

After a few Polish frozen vodkas, the veins of their currently politically correct thinking ran not as deep as when they had first walked in the door and seen the enemy, my brother, who at my request was in full-dress Green Beret–Special Forces uniform. By the time we were deep into the red wine, they all saw him as having the same dignity as the rare and expensive Chateau Beychevelle 1962. Then I asked my brother's advice for making Molotov cocktails.

"Use strong bottles."

We filled the now empty bottles of Dom Pérignon with gasoline siphoned from my car, ripped up an old Hermès scarf to use for fuses, and hauled them in a Tiffany shopping bag to the campus. My champagne Molotovs bounced off the architecture school building, rolled down the street into a storm drain, and exploded.

So much for my militant radical phase.

I had about the same success at the Harvard Graduate School of Design. My passion for designing in-sea or underwater architecture habitats and resorts were too radical for Harvard. My other obsession, a bridge-and-tunnel design for linking England and France, went over equally badly. The professors insisted instead I involve myself with the real world of public housing. My reality response was a multimedia effort: cooking, film, music, and drugs. "Champagne While the World Crumbles." A film loop of the atom bomb going off amid footage of the worst public housing projects and urban sprawl I could find. The music was Lou Reed, the food a huge platter of hashish fudge from *The Alice B. Toklas Cookbook*, the drink champagne.

Despite a sign saying eating more than two was at the eater's risk, all the fudge was consumed. Most didn't know what they were. At least five were gobbled up by a juror professor. Found three days later in some louche sink in Boston, he later told me that I was lucky not to be kicked out of school, and that I would have been had there not been a student revolution going on. In my senior year, he said, I would have to work on socially responsible projects. Over the summer I would have to think long and hard about myself.

I did.

And I realized that food was a more powerful weapon than architecture.

––––––

Mary Jane Butter

The quality of the grass you use to make this butter is up to you and your budget. We used to use whatever leftover sticks and seeds there were after harvesting the leaves. Obviously fresh is better. As for quantity, anything from two to six handfuls.

The butter is very good under the skin of a turkey to be roasted for Thanksgiving.

Handfuls cannabis   2 pounds butter

Put the cannabis in a 4-quart saucepan and fill ²/₃ with water. Add the butter and bring to a boil. Simmer over very low heat for 1 hour, adding more water if necessary.

Drain through a fine sieve, discarding the plant material. Put the water with the butter floating on top in the refrigerator until the butter is hard. Discard the water, unless you have a penchant for it, and use the butter for cooking.

––––––

Mary's Cookies
Makes about 20

2 cups all-purpose flour, sifted

½ cup powdered sugar, sifted

¼ teaspoon salt

1 cup Mary Jane butter (see above), cut in 1-inch cubes

Preheat the oven to 325 degrees.

Mix the flour, sugar, and salt in a bowl, and then mix in the butter. Form the mixture into a ball, and then roll out on a very lightly floured surface until ½ inch thick.

Cut out into your favorite shape with a cutter, place the pieces on a cookie-baking sheet, and bake for 30 minutes.

Cool on a rack and eat while still just warm.

––––––

EATING THE REVOLUTION

My only plans that summer of 1969 were to give political revolution one more chance—at the Black Panther conference in Northern California—and to sweet-talk my grandmother in Carmel. My grandfather had just died. The question of my generous allowance was very much up in the air. A week after the academic year ended, I packed my copy of Carlos Castañeda, started a new journal with a quote from John Cage about circumstances being in charge, and began a cross-country trip in my little green MGB GT. I had no set itinerary since I dreamed of a Norman Douglas *South Wind* kind of life (of giving in to one's "fool") and followed my stomach. What was to have been a tour of American architecture turned into a tour of its food, especially Louisiana and Southwest culinary festivals, New Mexico chili cookouts, and Texas barbecues. After a stop at my aunt Mary and Russian uncle's for a dinner of those livers in eighteenth-century Madeira and my requested chicken Kiev, I set off for Louisiana, out of Washington and southbound down the Blue Ridge Parkway.

In Lafayette, Louisiana, I headed straight and ravenously for the crayfish festivals and a gumbo and crayfish dinner ($3.65) at the famous Normandie. Then to Morgan City and Don's with its dozen freshwater oysters for $1.50, and on to New Orleans's Hotel Pontchartrain, where I thought to myself if there was better Creole food in the United States it must be in heaven itself. After a breakfast at Brennan's and "buster" crabs at Casamento's, I headed west for Texas.

It was too late at night for any restaurants to be open, so I ate peyote instead, driving along the interstate listening to B. B. King and watching the oil burn-off lighting up the wide-open Texas night sky. In the ninety-eight-degree heat my iced ripe white peaches, dipped in freezing Coca-Cola from my backseat cooler, were heaven. Then after a wrong turn, I ended up in Houston's ghetto and found an all-night and all-black soul food cafe where I had perfectly delicious barbecued meat loaf, even if eaten in a silence from the locals as thick as the glutinous mashed potatoes.

I stopped in San Antonio to visit some friends of my mother's whom she adored for their huge warehouses of chilies and every conceivable Tex-Mex seasoning as much as their love of dancing tangos till dawn. After a five-hour lesson in southwestern spices, I headed to the Four Corners and the chili at

Kelly's Bar in Chama, New Mexico. After the superb green chili, which I noted was hotter even than the rocks of the Sangre de Cristo Mountains at high noon, I tore myself away, drove my four cylinders up into the Rockies, drove west, and drank from the cool upland glacier springs in Yosemite. Then it was down to the coast and into Carmel to negotiate my allowance and stock up for the Black Panther conference with a 1959 Lafite and 1963 Romanée-Conti from a local market.

Annoyed by the crude fascism of Students for a Democratic Society (SDS), I headed back to nearby Big Sur to see the trout farm again, and to meet a forbidden couple.

Now that my grandfather was gone, I was finally emboldened to look up the Big Sur legends Emile Norman and Brooks Clement. My step-grandmother couldn't have dealt with two male artists living together with scandalous frankness and enormous success, so her ancient Cadillac and I were off alone down the coast to the top of a mountain and their house set in the center of four hundred acres. After I knocked on the door, it slid open to reveal Emile Norman clad only in a towel. I was dressed in a jacket and tie as I would have been for lunch on my grandmother's terrace.

"You can stay just the way you are, or get naked for lunch. It's up to you."

The Naked Lunch did it. Until this trip, I had never been seen in public without a jacket unless it was at a pool or on the rugby field. So this was a turning point in my life, and why I had come to California.

With pounding heart I took off my clothes and joined the two of them at a table set by an indoor pool surrounded by a vegetable garden in planters. The sun shone through an overhead vine of New Zealand climbing spinach, from which Emile was cutting leaves for a salad, while Brooks played Bach on an organ that was a replica of the composer's own. Standing with my glass of champagne, looking out over the brown hills to the Pacific Ocean, I realized then that one could love and cook in a world entirely of one's own choosing.

After a couple of magnums of red Burgundian Pommard and a screening of films they had taken of the young Masai holding hands and elephants and giraffes doing things no nature program had ever shown, it was time for the next course.

"May I help with dessert?" I offered.

"Yes, you may. You are the dessert."

In no time I was telling Emile I would be moving to California as soon as possible.

DRINKING THE REVOLUTION: LAFITE IN THE STREETS

Back on the East Coast there was more revolution in the streets, Moratorium Day, and the March on Washington. Two dancers I'd met the previous spring took up residence with me in Somerville, and when Rudolf Nureyev came to town, my new friend the Harvard undergraduate and painter Philip Core called him. We went to see him at the Ritz. Philip had with him his script for a ballet on Nijinsky with Rudi in mind. While my favorite dancer spent an athletic night with Rudi, he with a bottle of Stoli in one hand, a boy in the other, Philip and I drank champagne, smoked Sobranie cigarettes nonstop, and read the script aloud. In the morning Rudolf told us that Margot Fonteyn was coming to town, and that we should look after her.

"Most often it's lonely being famous," he told me, "and she's both."

A few weeks later we summoned the nerve to call her and invite her to dinner at my house in Somerville, an invitation which, to our huge surprise, she accepted.

We had three hours to shop and cook. One of the streetwise dancers called me from the store. "I have some wine called L-A-F-I-T-E. Is it okay?"

It was, but who had the money?

"Don't worry about that," he said. "Is a ten-pound rib roast big enough?"

Half an hour later he returned, triumphantly. With no time for questions, I started to cook. Two hours later, when we answered a knock at the door, there was a breathtakingly beautiful Margot in floor-length white mink covering a basic black Yves St. Laurent dress and ropes of pearls, with a huge, disarming smile. And a slightly Cockney accent: "May we come in?" Her partner in dance—Richard Cragun from the Stuttgart, also in black but full leather, his crotch delicately festooned with chains—stood behind her.

Dinner for Margot Fonteyn, Richard Cragun, Philip Core, and the Street Dancers
February 16, 1970

Salmon Canapé
Roast Beef Ribs

Château Lafite, 1962
Creamed Spinach
Château Lafite, 1964
Green Salad Vinaigrette
Raspberry and Lemon Sherbets
Pirouettes
Café
Cointreau

After Margot's second slab of beef and heavily into the Lafite, she commented on my generosity. I said she'd have to thank the two dancers as well. With great pride at having ripped off the Establishment, the dancers related that to support the revolution, they'd stolen the Lafite, beef, and Cointreau. I blushed, the boys beamed, Richard helped himself to more Lafite, and Margot let out peals of laughter. "Well," she said, "if it has to be Lafite in the streets, so be it."

A blizzard had set in during dinner, so I drove them back to the Ritz in an old silver Porsche, the boys squashed into the tiny back, Richard in the passenger seat with Margot on his lap. As we skidded around the deserted streets, all I could think of was how many millions of dollars of legs I had in that car, and how to drive passing a bottle of pink Veuve Clicquot champagne around so as not to spill it over her white mink.

The next morning the dancers and I awoke to riots in the streets again. We headed to Harvard Square. As we sat on the roof of the news kiosk in the center of the square, we were suddenly surrounded by police. One of the dancers pushed me off the roof into the arms of the other, did a grand jeté onto the roof of a squad car, and rebounded down into the subway with the two of us in hot pursuit. I went home to work on underwater space stations again, and after that close call the boys were in the mood for revolution eighteenth-century French style: more for dining while America burned than for burning it.

THOUGHT IS MADE IN THE MOUTH

Soon after, while having an all-aquavit dinner with my new girlfriend, Annie Meyer, a wonderful cook and granddaughter of the *Washington Post* and

Newsweek founder Agnes Meyer, the windows of her apartment were blown out by some firebombing "students" in the street. We decided it was time to get out of town. I thought that it was time to grow up, or at least that that time was fast approaching. So I decided to leave the dancers behind and to move in with Annie. We rented a farm in Prides Crossing, north of Boston in the town of Beverly, where we started a vegetable garden and raised birds. But first we packed up the cats and put them into her Aston Martin DB5 and headed north to her family's island in Maine.

The first day I read Euell Gibbons's *Stalking the Wild Asparagus,* and as I contemplated the difference between stealing great ingredients and walking outside and gathering them, cooking took on a whole new life for me. I switched from reading Escoffier's *Ma Cuisine* to a culinary mix of Rachel Carson, a nineteenth-century American housewives' companion, and James Beard.

Dinner in Maine Having Read Euell Gibbons
May 22, 1970

Four nests of Eider ducks, each with four eggs.
In one, the eggs still wet. Took one.
Found samphire, sour sorrel, and lovage—or seacoast angelica.
As well as young dandelion.
Mussels, a bushel or so, some for salad.
Steamed Mussels with Samphire
Niersteiner Meisterkroner 1967
Spinach-sorrel noodles
Wild Asparagus, Vinaigrette

For lunch the next day we had a mussel salad with a mayonnaise made with more wild sorrel, shallots, wild horseradish, and mustard, thinned with a reduced white wine mussel broth. In the evening I dressed cooked lobster meat with a "lobster cream"—a paste of the coral, the fat lining the shell, and the liver mixed with mayonnaise and garnished with sea sorrel. We drank a perfect ten-year old Bollinger champagne from my favorite year of 1961.

Back in Prides Crossing I noted that my life now was books and food, when my Harvard college friend Philip Core sent me a note: "Food and Wine are the sex of art, and pasta is the bridge between the two." I wrote back with

Tristan Tzara's "Thought is made in the mouth." Cooking for friends was now more eloquent a revolution than politics. The directness of the menus said it all:

Lunch at Prides Crossing
Cold Salmon, Fresh Herb Mayonnaise
Château d'Yquem 1947
Strawberries
Château d'Yquem 1966

The next night, after a pound of caviar and 1962 Dom Pérignon, Annie made the accusation that the only way I could communicate was by writing menus and then cooking them. True. We decided to take some time off from each other. While she was in Washington visiting her aunt Katharine "Kay" Graham, I read my dandy hero Robert de Montesquiou, wrote the outline for a book from one of his best phrases, "A Carnage of Geraniums," planted fifty, and cooked.

YOUTH ON THE PROW AND PLEASURE AT THE HELM

I finished my "politically acceptable" public housing project—but my notebooks were now filled with the glories of old American picnics, systems of ocean farming and aquaculture (using dolphins as the staff), designs for the World's Fair in Hawaii, which I heard was to be on the water, and California wines I should try. The allure of California and Hawaii became real, but not before one last-gasp attempt to create the European world that was as comfortable to me as old clothes—and as increasingly tattered.

I tried to make a living in Prides Crossing designing gardens for the rich. But they were not as rich as the people who had built the gardens, and thus knew and cared little about them. So I ended up just a gardener. It was a year in which our band of aesthetes graduated and dispersed—a year, as Philip Core said, that was "crowded with the wreckage of exhumed conversations."

Meanwhile, I followed the advice of Carl Van Vechten, "Write as you feel and you will discover that your feeling is greater than your knowledge of it," because I wanted to know what I did feel. I wrote "An Outline of Pleasures" after Colette, subtitled "The Sauce for Being Served Up." I loved her "Pride in giving pleasure relieved them of the need for any other pleasure," and "To receive from someone happiness—is it not to choose the sauce in which we want to be served up?"

I found myself truly beginning to travel into the silent and self-absorbed world of cooking in 1970 when I read Richard Olney's just-published *French Menu Cookbook*. It bowled me over. I adored his claim that cooking the first time for his mentor, Georges Garin, he dared only "simple preparations." I had a sneaking suspicion that I must be one of the few readers who felt calm at his calling Artichoke Bottoms with Two Mousses followed by ortolans, then cheeses and a "Tepid Apple Charlotte," simple.

When I read, "The rock on which my church was built was the provincial kitchen of my home in Iowa," I wondered what he would think of my rock: eccentric lives and the life of travel around the world with its great hotels, ships, and trains. I had been, like Olney, "cooking with a passion that could be gleaned from books—Escoffier, in particular." Olney's rock was Iowa. I looked around for mine. I wrote Richard, opened a bottle of 1888 Boal Madeira, and jotted down a rash of titles for proposed cookbooks: "Casting Pearls Before Wine," "Culinary Suicides," "Mental Cuisine," "Octopus Bouquet," and "Fraises Musclées."

Something had to give.

Just as I was rethinking that old offer to work at *The New Yorker*, a call came from an old pal, Clay Shaw (the New Orleans architect who was accused of masterminding the Kennedy assassination), to work on the revival of New Orleans's French Market. It was tempting, but I knew if I lived there I would fall even further back into my longing for the past: I would never leave lunch at Galatoire's. So I left Annie and the farm, and headed on down to my sister's beachfront apartment on the Jersey Shore to put aside my "Carnage of Geraniums" and rewrite it as my memoirs, "Camphor Ice." A cure for what itches.

Perhaps then I could put the past behind me.

In June 1971 I finished *Camphor Ice*. Writing it did not cure my itch for the past, so I decided I could find the cure in Big Sur—the land of Emile Norman's naked lunch. I cooked a last dinner on the East Coast for my sister's fortieth birthday, finding parts of the menu from my new bible, Lucien Tendret's *La Table au Pays de Brillat-Savarin*. I served Tendret's famous "Le gateau de foies blonds de poulardes de Bresse, baigné de la sauce aux queues d'écrevisses." Or baked loaf of blond liver mousse of Bresse chicken, bathed in crayfish sauce. I poured my last two bottles of wine, a 1962 La Tâche and an unlabeled 1927 vintage port. So now, with no wine and no money, I set out for California.

CALIFORNIA: AN IMMEDIATE OPENING

Heading west in a huge old Lincoln rental car with a childhood friend from England, we landed in San Francisco with seventy-five dollars, not enough to fund the final leg of my journey to Honolulu with my designs for the World's Fair half under and half above the water. I showed the project around architectural offices, with no success. So once again I worked as a gardener.

The rest of the year was one of agony and attacks of nerves that left my nights full of demons, my days full of looking for a job, my skin scrofulous, and me writing a letter at 4 A.M. to Philip Core, the only pal who would understand. "As I lie here recovering from yet another evening of unsuccessful job-seeking charm and brilliance, wondering how could I again, in a room full of Indians from ancient Mexican jungles, Chinese, Japanese Burroughs, Swiss and Argentinian *L'Uomo Vogue* bathing-suit extravaganzas, end up tangoing 'til dawn in the arms of a Garcia Lorca lesbian from Cuba? Feeling like a venomous orchid, and am teetering on an edge beyond bankruptcy which has led better men than me to prison and to say 'the only vice is shallowness.' These last weeks have been a tornado of vortices, leading nowhere."

On my thirtieth birthday, in 1972, I was down to twenty-five dollars.

I wrote in my journal: "Good thing to do at 1:15 A.M.: sit on toilet, drink beer, and read Dumas' *Grand Dictionnaire de Cuisine*." The bookmark that fell out of that book was a menu from the RMS *Mauretania* dated forty-three years before, to the day. An omen, if the food was not. My father, at President Herbert Hoover's table, ate grapefruit Maraschino before a *petite marmite*, fillet of sole, roast pheasant, *pomme chips*, salad of the season, and *pouding glace Nesselrode*. After reading the menu, I fell into a troubled sleep. From my notebooks of the time:

5 A.M.: In a Dream—In a Restaurant:
Steak with marrow bone filled with marrow soufflé

Baba (au rhum)
Puree of celery root
Sauce Périgord on steak
All on plate together.

My last hope, I felt, was the cure of Big Sur and Emile, who had given me the courage to embrace the freedoms of California in the first place. At a lunch he gave for Elizabeth Gordon (later editor of *House Beautiful)*, the menu was cannelloni stuffed with wild boar, followed by persimmons with a mayonnaise flavored with fenugreek (to this day I love this dish). Over a superb, velvety Chapelle-Chambertin 1961 Elizabeth talked for hours of Alice B. Toklas, with whom she had traveled. Even on a trip to Venice when Alice was very old, Elizabeth said, she showed great courage and knowledge of where to find the best food in the markets along the canals. At the end of the lunch Elizabeth said, "Alice would have loved cooking with you." I took that as an omen as well.

The next day at 1 A.M. I was werewolf awake at the sound of Big Sur coyotes outside my door, my sleep plagued with Mozartian black-sheeted figures trying to strangle me. After writing a suicide note—"The last of my silk shirts just died"—I read Wilde's essay "De Profundis" again and the next day, back in San Francisco, cooked a last meal: goose soup and a Chambertin 1934, Cuvée Héritiers Latour.

I recovered and decided to live.

In San Francisco for a New Year's apartment sitting for Michael and Cathy, I made a feast for one, and recorded the menu.

Dinner for One
San Francisco, 1972

"Simple pleasures are the last refuge of the complex." Oscar.
The virtues of boiled garlic.
Spread on new bread and French butter.
I put it with marrow, a paste for toast.
Château d'Yquem 1967

When Michael returned, he told me that the little French cafe in Berkeley we had visited a couple of months before was looking for a chef. He showed me the ad in the newspaper.

"So what?" I said.

All I remembered from my one visit there two months before was the most perfect slice of fresh raspberry tart I had ever tasted. But by now any job was looking good. It seemed he could be right when he replied: "There's more to it than a simple raspberry tart."

Or could be.

THE LANGUAGE OF MENUS

To me, menus are a language unto themselves.

I have been collecting and reading them since I was seven, composing and acting them out since I was a teenager. They spoke to me as clearly as any childhood fantasy novel. Reading an old menu slowly forms in my mind's eye its era, the sensibility of the restaurateur or the chef, even the physical details of the dining room. I can picture the guests even when I don't know who they were. Sometimes I can conjure up an entire evening, a three-act play orchestrated around the food. And from my own past, it's the menus and the food that are the fixatives for the memories. When I think again about one of my mother's summer garden party menus, the whole day is conjured up—my mouth waters as I see, taste, and smell the lovage-mayonnaise covered poached whole salmons laid out in the tents. I can see everyone who was there.

I have used the language of menus as the basis for dialogues with mentors, colleagues, and friends. And I had always assumed that this language was universal. When I began to write this book, I outlined it with menus—some that had aroused my appetites, others that I'd designed and cooked myself—and eagerly passed them on to a few editors and publishers as a way of revealing my mission.

The silence was deafening; broken later by only a single comment posed in a question: What do they mean? After a long pause, that question was followed by two more: What were the stories behind the menus, and were any famous people present at the meals? I couldn't have been more stunned. I thought the menus told their own stories. And eloquently.

Menus are liberally sprinkled through this book, and so that you do not find them silent, let me tell you how they speak to me.

I transcribed what I had read in the December 1961 *Gourmet* magazine article on "The Art of Table Decoration" into one of my mid-1960s culinary notebooks: "A treat need not be a luxury; a banquet need not include caviar. Imagination is the most important ingredient." Then I wrote a menu knowing at that time only that a dinner was given by Cecil Beaton in a private dining room in Paris's Lapérouse restaurant, for two dozen male friends, and probably in the early 1930s.

Beatonmania

Fat of a Turtle

Château d'Yquem l860

Cold Foie Gras

Truffles Poached in Champagne

Canard Rôti Lucullus

Burgundy (a priceless one)

Doyenne de Comice Pear, Juste à Point

Coffee

Crusted Port

Cognac Napoleon

Romeo and Juliettas

At first glance it seems way over-the-top. But it has a discipline. The kind created by Beaton in the horse-racing scene in *My Fair Lady,* with its miles and miles of extravagant ruffles and hats, but all in black and white, and the singing in a controlled chant about the perfection of the Ascot afternoon . . . until, of course, Liza screams, "Move your bleedin' arse," to her horse lagging in third place. In this menu, that scream is the duck.

The mixed language suggests an Englishman wrote it, since a Frenchman would never use English with food, and with the same taste and delight in the language as in the food. *Gras* has a onomatopoeic ring to it, but only when pronounced by a lower gratin butcher from Marseilles. Using the English word for it, *fat,* tells you that in relishing the word, probably pronounced with the very upper-gratin Oxford accent so that it sounded like *fiat,* the dinner guests were undoubtedly rail-thin young things in perfect Boldini-portrait tailored frock coats and Charvet floppy bow ties, giggling at the irony of slipping so much of that fat between their tightly compressed lips, otherwise opened only for the latest quip, gossip, or fingernails-on-metal analysis of the most recent *Brideshead Revisited*–type scandal. And I would automatically, without thinking, have used *rôti* once *canard* had been used, and slipped into French once the word *doyenne* had been put on paper. It would just be natural, without affectation, in bilingual company.

Following the turtle fat with *foie gras* tells me also that whoever ordered the menu was very securely a gourmand with a deep appreciation for the art of dining: knowing how to push one's guests' sensibilities to the limit without embarrassing them with a troubling surfeit later in the meal. Obviously they all were aesthetes, and saw themselves that way. They were not unfamiliar with this kind of expensive living, and whoever was paying was wealthy. Maybe a younger Tennant or Devonshire son, if his millionaire father had him on a liberal leash.

I have never been in a private dining room at Lapérouse, but one can count on it having a rectangular table seating two at each end, leaving no room for dropped conversation. And just as the meal was far more than a token, so the table decor would not have been one shrimp-pink geranium in a vase—a degree of sophistication with which Beaton would have been out of sympathy. Rather there would have been an impression of enthusiastic spontaneity. Probably there was a *tulipière* filled with enough camellias so that after each guest was served one for the buttonhole, enough were left to make an impression on the room of expense but not extravagance.

Very likely there was a small sofa in the corner. Somewhere off the room fur coats, top hats, and silver-tipped Malacca canes were stored, since it was obviously winter. It was the kind of scene Ken Russell portrayed in *The Music Lovers,* but with more restraint, at least until the port showed up, at which point the sofa was the scene of more intimate conversations, the waiters long since having ceased entering before knocking, after the "my dears" among the young men had become a bit thick.

And the food?

Our minds now might reel at a slab of turtle fat apiece. Even at this dinner the cold-blooded English, who would easily rip out the throat of a partridge with their teeth, might have thought twice to plunder further an endangered species so baldly. So the slab of fat in the Limoges soup plate in front of each of the two dozen guests must have given them a slight frisson. I had fat of a turtle in my youth, but only small cubes in turtle soup. Here it is obviously served hot, perhaps moistened with a little sherry-perfumed consommé (but only a little), since it is followed by a cold foie gras. Well, not exactly cold, more like the temperature of the pantry off the dining room, which in those days clocked in at a bone-chilling (were it not for the cashmere-lined silk waistcoats) sixty degrees. Obviously Beaton knew that to stimulate the senses and keep them going is to sample something hot, then something cold, then something hot again.

To follow turtle fat with foie gras—100 percent more fat—is a heady statement in an already heady room. I remember the turtle fat texture as more foie gras than even meltingly fatty hot foie gras itself, and I love the knowledge here that, as the turtle should be hot, the foie gras should not. Heated until the fats are released, foie gras seems to me too slippery; the flavor is deeper and more satisfying when the fat melts slowly in one's mouth. A reluctant companion in excess, rather than a dancer in your lap.

Next, a whole truffle per person poached in champagne, served in a starched napkin, says again, "This is a person who knows the best of the best," and needs no ostentatious show of it. The roasted duck Lucullus, however, gives one pause. What duck dish could be worthy of the name of ancient Rome's most sumptuous banqueteer? I don't know what the preparation consists of but need to believe it had no truffles, and ideally no coxcombs, testicles, or sweetbreads either. "Doyenne de Comice pear"—housewife's pear, a frivolous and funny label that could easily rev up the fragile conversation. The simplicity is pleasantly startling. And then the "crusted" port: nonvintage, but to those in the know, a much more satisfying value for your money, all the while accompanied by Havana's best and most expensive cigars. The waiter appears again for the last time, to crack open the windows for the fresh air of the Quai des Grands-Augustins to end the evening.

WIMSEY

In college I devoured all the Lord Peter Wimsey books. In my diaries at the time I noted a menu that to me is still perfection in language, balance, and progression of food. In 2014, Chris Kimball of the TV show *America's Test Kitchen* told me, "You are the Lord Peter Whimsey of your food generation—flamboyant, sharp-tongued, talented, and in love with the style of the thing as much as the thing itself." I replied that I loved the comparison and that it was true in "the way in which something is presented, even if hardly presented at all. Keep the beluga in its blue tin. Remember it sitting in the hollowed-out belly of the ice Buddha in the film *Auntie Mame*. Nothing more is needed."

Oysters

Chablis Moutonne 1915

Chevalier Montrachet 1911

Consommé Marmite

Sole

"Echter" Schloss Johannisberger

Poulet

Lafite 1875

Pré-salé

Clos Vougeot 1911

Dessert

Genuine Imperial Tokay

True "Napoleon" with Seal

I wrote "Short and lovely" in my college culinary notebooks when I first read it.

Auguste Escoffier, the father of modern French cooking (and chef to César Ritz of the famous hotels), considered oysters such a natural way to raise one's juices and expectations for the food following that he hardly deemed them part of the "opus" or the main part of the written menu, and often left them off. Or merely listed them as "Natives," deliciously the same word in French and English. Here they are part of the menu, and probably Colchesters or flat oysters like Bélons. A great Colchester is rich enough to need a palate cleanser, but as importantly, a dozen of them would need a mental one so that they didn't dominate the beginning of the rest of the food. That is up to the sole.

The consommé of a simmered beef broth from a marmite works better here than a lighter chicken, since white poultry broth wouldn't send the oysters into memory quite completely enough.

A bachelor like Peter is used to simple food. So I guess the sole is simply *meunière* or *grillée,* since his mouth will be hungering for a bit of richness after the consommé broth, with or without a splash of sherry, though not enough so Peter would recoil at the fish being covered with lobster sauce. The chicken, however, is obviously *à la crème* after the austere fullness of the sole, as simply served by Henri Soulé years later in Manhattan's Le Pavillon. Obviously the *pré-salé* is that perfect lamb from the salt marshes of Brittany around St.-Michel, or from the coast lands of Suffolk or Cornwall. Simply roasted.

And the dessert? Well, no need to call that out, since it's chosen from a trolley of them. Peter would have either a little *baba au rhum* or just a big plate of raspberries covered with Devon or Jersey/Guernsey cream—if the chicken was not.

After reading this I wrote myself a note: "Taste an old Lafite and Tokay."

Years later in Berkeley I would taste the Tokay, and then in my San Francisco restaurant Stars, at a West Coast tasting of the old Lafites, finally taste the 1875.

COUNTERREVOLUTION

Cecil Beaton was definitely in the air my spring of 1969, when I wrote a self-consciously "decadent" menu for a dinner in my Somerville, Massachusetts, house. This was at the height of the counterculture, when revolution was in the air.

Pirozhki
Vodka Wyborowa
Prosciutto and Figs
Niersteiner Spiegleberg Spätlese Kabinet 1966
Consommé Marijuana
Roast Beef, Sauce Nature/Madère
Château Beychevelle 1962
Spinach Cream Puree

Pommes de Terre Chateau
Watercress Salad Vinaigrette
Fraises, Crème Carême
Korbel, brut, California
Coffee
Meringues
Madeira (Cossart)
Cigars Royal Jamaica, Churchill

It was hot outside and inside, and since nothing gets a party going or the juices flowing faster than a slug of vodka right out of the freezer followed by anything warm and rich, that's what we did. The vodka was bison-grass-flavored Żubrówka. We immediately popped a little pastry, *pirozhki* or "little bites," into our mouths, the bison-grass perfumes playing off against coriander-flavored buttered cabbage-filled pastry, the burn of the alcohol in our throats smoothed over just in time by the butter. Heaven.

Then prosciutto and figs, salty and sweet, dry against moist fig flesh (not dry against wet, like melon), the complex flavors brought together even further by the fruity young Spätlese.

The consommé cleansed the palate, and this one, from marijuana plants, the stems soaked in a rich chicken stock, provided another level of stimulation. But not before its time. The brew takes forty-five minutes to reach the brain, by which time, as planned, we were on to dessert, tasting strawberries and cream as we'd never tasted them before. Meanwhile, the bitterness of the creamed spinach was a perfect foil against the fat of the roast beef, its juices bolstered with sweet Madeira. The second-growth Bordeaux accompanying the meat was from an especially hard year that I adored and defended for its non-easy virtue. The wine did not yield easily, but when its personality finally and stubbornly emerged, it proved a glorious match.

Why serve roast beef in ninety-five-degree weather? In love with memories of my own and in the spirit of Beaton at Lapérouse, it was the way I knew best to push culinary senses to the limit. The fat of beef I had dry-aged for thirty-four days had all the complexity of the long-cellared wine with which it was paired, with a kind of power that met the intensity of the hot weather. The beef, the heat, the wine said all about what it meant to be at table that night: our manners meeting the challenge of the menu, ingesting forbidden drugs, and talk of my heroes Ho Chi Minh, Che, and Nureyev, whose pictures were on the kitchen wall.

Watercress with vinaigrette was a different kind of bow to the heat, and cleared the palate. The commercial strawberries were tossed in fresh red currant syrup, a trick that always intensifies their strawberryness. Served with a custard containing white Maraschino, this simple cream has so many layers of flavor that you can't put your finger on what makes it so mysteriously and magically delicious. And of course the drugs would have just been kicking in . . .

———

Consommé Marijuana

6 cups rich chicken stock

1 packed cup marijuana stems and seeds

½ cup fresh basil leaves

1 loose cup freshly picked nasturtium flowers (mixed bright colors)

sea salt

pepper mill

Preheat the oven to 275 degrees.

Bring the chicken stock to a boil in a 4-quart saucepan.

Meanwhile, spread the marijuana out on a metal cookie sheet or tray and put in the oven for 10 minutes. After the stems and seeds are "toasted," put all of them in the chicken stock and turn off the heat. Steep for 1 hour.

Put the stock through a very fine strainer, and return to the cleaned-out saucepan.

Chop the basil leaves coarsely (⅛ inch), and shred the nasturtium flowers. Heat the consommé to boiling. Put the basil and nasturtium in warmed soup plates, and pour the consommé over. Pass the sea salt and pepper mill separately.

———

RICHARD OLNEY

My early outlaw efforts notwithstanding, it was reading Richard Olney's *French Menu Cookbook* in 1970 that firmed up my ideas of what a seriously enjoyable but also controlled menu should be. I wrote to him that in the progression of his dishes I could see the workings of his mind and heart, his discipline, and his sense of play. In his first chapter, he lays out principles of menu creation that I live by to this day, even while tweaking them:

> Each course must provide a happy contrast to the one preceding it; at the same time the movement through the various courses should be an ascending one from light, delicate, and more complex flavors through progressively richer, more full-bodied, and simple flavors. Essentially the only thing to remember is that the palate should be kept fresh, teased, surprised, excited throughout a meal. The moment there is danger of fatigue, it must be astonished or soothed into greater anticipation until the moment of release and postprandial pleasures.

Inspired by his philosophy, I created the following menu in 1971 for a late-winter dinner with Annie Meyer and friends at our Prides Crossing farm. We ate to the sounds of our barking dogs, partridge and quail chirping, geese chattering, and guinea fowl screaming.

Winter Dinner with Annie Meyer and Friends

Pâté de Foie (perdrix) Moelle

Frozen Vodka Wyborowa

Garlic Soup

Perdrix à la Souvaroff

Château Léoville 1959

Château Ausone 1937

Soufflé of Hominy

Chateau Cheval-Blanc 1959

Salade Doria

Stilton (aged)

Martinez Port 1927

I made a pâté of beef marrow and the livers of the farm partridge(*perdrix*), spread it on wonderful country bread, and served it warm with freezing bison-grass vodka. I wanted that satisfying jolt at the beginning of the menu: the rich game flavors, the scent of its juniper berries, the perfumed bites of black pepper and cold vodka. The garlic soup brought us back to earth. Long-simmered and very mild, it was like a consommé with a vegetable pure, rich and austere at the same time. The partridge was stuffed with a truffled foie gras, while the hominy (white cornmeal) soufflé that accompanied it was simple and clean, the perfect foil for the luxurious meat and liver. The Léoville had a slightly truffled aroma and was particularly good with the partridge stuffing. Of course, in those days there was no fresh foie gras and I had to use canned.

No dessert—the rest of the menu was so rich—but a flashy salad instead. Potatoes with asparagus tips in white truffle mayonnaise with red and gold chopped baked beets sprinkled on top. Aged Stilton and the 1927 port stopped time. The best part, actually, was the breakfast the next morning, when I made a mousse of all the leftover foie gras stuffing and partridge meat, spread it in a gratin dish, buried coddled eggs in it, and covered it with fresh cream before baking it just until it started to bubble. Served with Black Velvets (half champagne, half Guinness), it blew what was left of our minds.

NEW OLD FOOD

A menu doesn't always need to be a grand wallow.

In summer, in particular, it is best to be calculatingly offhand as well as to indulge in the occasional roast beef gesture. Begin, for example, with bruschetta because it's colorful when made with yellow and red tomatoes, light, immediate, and delicious. The acid and sweetness of the fruit and the olive oil, the spice from pepper, the aromas of garlic and fresh herbs make for a perfect palate teaser.

A great summer menu can be as simple as this one, cooked by Cathy Simon to cheer me up following the harrowing experience in June 1969 of my year-end presentation at Harvard's Graduate School of Design:

Cathy's Dinner to Cheer
Cambridge, June 1969

Asparagus, sauce alsacienne
Niersteiner Domtal
Tuna, Fresh, over Charcoal
Salad, Lettuce of the Garden
Mushrooms

Pie: Strawberry and Rhubarb
Scotch & Soda

The asparagus was poached and served at room temperature with a thin demi-glace and olive oil; the fresh grilled tuna was showered in basil from the garden, which also supplied the lettuce salad served alongside mushrooms mixed with cream, mustard, and olive oil. Strawberry and rhubarb pie and Scotch and soda were accompanied by the sound of chanting students bent on overthrowing the established social order, but I, for one, was happy to keep the best of the old one (its food and cellars) while investigating, by cooking, a new one.

FOUR MENUS

For these four menus I had no thought in my mind other than the power of simplicity and the ease of cooking it, for creating the most effect for my guests. Foraging on the beaches of islands in Maine, and tasting lobsters and mussels right out of the water, had reminded me of the power also of perfect, and perfectly fresh, ingredients.

Dinner for Two Street-Kid Dancers
My House, Somerville, 1970

Avocado-Lobster Mayonnaise
Chateau d'Yquem 1959
Chicken (cold) in Tarragon Butter
White Asparagus
Cheesecake with Garden Strawberries

Lunch in the Heat, Using Up the Somerville Cellar
June 11, 1970

Poached Red Snapper, cold
Dom Pérignon 1959, 2 bottles

If I had had some caviar, I would have thinned a little cream and mixed them for a light sauce, like that perfect lunch dish from *The Alice B. Toklas*

Cookbook, Filet de Sole à la Ritz, or cold sole with a sauce of whipped cream and fresh horseradish, but the cupboard was bare so I left it just as it was, no mayonnaise since it would have killed the champagne. My last two bottles, one each, and that was the point of the lunch as well as finding that perfect snapper at Legal Sea Foods around the corner from my house.

Lunch by Myself at the Farm Eating the Produce Before Moving to California

May 3, 1971

Hot Pheasant Liver Toasts
Iced Lemon Vodka
Cold Roast Pheasant
Vosne-Romanée 1961 (superb!)

In this case the produce was the last of the birds. I couldn't catch the guinea fowl, but the pheasant were willing.

Lunch with Annie, for Michael Palmer, in from California

Prides Crossing, Massachusetts. July 1971

Cold Poached Salmon, Garden Mayonnaise
Château d'Yquem 1947
Caesar Salad
Wild Strawberries
Château d'Yquem 1966

The Caesar was a flop since it was impossible to find good lettuce. I wrote in my notes that we must grow our own lettuces again, including mesclun and eight-inch-long romaine. These were not to be seen for another twenty years, though we did raise some as soon as I took on the job of head chef at Berkeley's Chez Panisse a year later. Michael raved about the wines he was trying out there in California, and we drove down to the local store to look for some. All we found was bulk California "Burgundy."

CHAPTER 8

TRUTH OR MYTH

The great enemy of truth is very often not the lie—deliberate,
contrived, and dishonest—but the myth—persistent, persuasive,
and unrealistic.
—John F. Kennedy

My first meeting with Alice Waters was scheduled for 6 P.M., an unusual time to interview a prospective chef when the kitchen was taking the first customer orders. But Chez Panisse was less than a year and a half old. Did anyone know any better?

I had arrived early on the bus from San Francisco, with plenty of time to survey the building in which I hoped to work for the next few months to get enough money to continue my journey to Hawaii. The remodeled old Victorian house looked like a cross between Frank Lloyd Wright and Charles Rennie Mackintosh, with a little bow to Berkeley's Julia Morgan. There were a couple of brick steps dodging under an enormous monkey puzzle tree, then a few more leading up to the front door, which said, "Pull."

At one minute to six I did.

The ice in my stomach did nothing to stop the hot fear bubbling into my throat. When I'd applied for jobs in the past, it had always been through an introduction by family or friends, but this time there was no one influential to set up this appointment. My terror of entering was quickly overcome, however, by how little money was left in my pocket after the bus. And I still needed to get back to San Francisco.

The ad in the newspaper read:

IMMEDIATE OPENING in a small, successful, innovative restaurant, provincial French cuisine, for inspired energetic CHEF to plan and cook single entrée 5-course dinners weekly, Fernand Point and Elizabeth David style. Send resume menus. Chez Panisse, 1517 Shattuck, Berkeley, California. U.S.A. (415) 548-5525.

As I soon found out, it had appeared in desperation. When the first chef, Victoria Kroyer (later of Pig by the Tail charcuterie, across the street), left in 1972, a year after Panisse opened, the kitchen had been staffed by any friends of Alice's and her partners who could cook.

The clue of their situation was their pairing of Point and David in one style. No plural *s*. How could anyone put these two icons, England's greatest twentieth-century culinary writer and France's greatest chef, in one style? I had read both of their books a couple of times, David's *Provincial Cooking* and Point's *Ma Gastronomie*. Point had simplified the grand cuisine of the nineteenth century and started the modern cooking movement in France, but there was no clue that Point had breathed life into any of the old Panisse menus I was given to guide me. Perhaps in the turkey sandwiches and Cristal dinner that Gene Opton, the woman running the restaurant at the time, and one of the partners had wooed me with, but nothing else.

Point was in the provinces but his unadorned versions of the great classics were not "provincial" by any stretch of the imagination. He had famously commanded the kitchen staff (including the young Paul Bocuse) to make a *gratin de queues d'écrevisses,* or gratin of crayfish tails, every day for two years before he thought it fit for the public—and this for a dish with only five ingredients! Where in the San Francisco Bay area would I find the makings of my favorite dishes from his great book? The *omble chevalier,* or arctic char, woodcock, goose foie gras, fresh black truffles for the famous salad, partridge, wild boar, and doves for the Aga Khan's favorite *palombes en béatitude?* All are available now, but no one had ever seen any of this in California then, except for the wild boar, which I later found high above Carmel valley at the ranch owned by the heirs of Stuyvesant Fish.

I stuck to what I thought was "provincial" French cooking, and saved Point for later. My eighteen sample menus were without desserts, which were the bailiwick of the raspberry tart maker and Chez Panisse pastry chef, Lindsey Shere:

Tuesday

Gougère à la Bourguignonne
Haricots Verts Natures
Matelote à la Normande

Wednesday

Oeufs Rémoulade
Consommé Madrilène of Beet and Onion
"Haricot" of Oxtail, Alice B. Toklas

I could make the cheese puff *gougères* in my sleep since I had used them a lot at my dinner parties in Cambridge; the green beans had been drilled into me by my growing them as a child and by my mother and D.C. aunt's fierce teaching; I had already made a lot of fish stews; the eggs rémoulade were a personal favorite from all those hungover days with Philip Core in New Orleans for Mardi Gras at Maylie's restaurant; the consommé was another dish made in advance and just heated to order; and the oxtail, once made, was easy to serve out to a hundred people without compromising any of the quality, as if it had been made for six.

The night of the interview with Alice, menus in hand, I walked into an unheated dining room that had fresh flowers in marmalade jars, unmatched old silver, and checkered oilcloths. The room was small, the floors bare; it was anything but formidable. Through a door to the tiny kitchen I glimpsed a confusion of bodies under the direction of a diminutive, bandannaed young woman who seemed oddly in and out of charge.

"That's Alice. I'm Tom Guernsey," said a friendly tall, blond, and whiskered waiter. "Just go in."

At the door I was stopped by a man with a black beard, severe eyebrows, and wire-rim glasses (Willy Bishop). "Alice can't see you now," he said, frowning. "She says come back tomorrow."

I left, down the first set of steps, through the bare courtyard, dodging the lethal leaves of the huge monkey puzzle tree, to Shattuck Avenue. Then I did the math. My round-trip fare had used up a third of all my money. I'd have barely enough to return, let alone come back again. Biting my lip, rubbing sweat from my palms onto the backs of my thighs (where it wouldn't be visible when I reentered the restaurant), I strode back along the irregular brick sidewalk. I turned into the unruly honeysuckle-covered gate and went up the steps, sliding my right hand along the railing to wipe off the last of the perspiration, hard to remember that this panic had nothing to do with fame or famous people. There was and were none in Panisse in those days. The cold sweat dripping down my back in that foggy Berkeley winter air came from fear of this new position of supplication. I was not used to being on my knees. For a moment I envisioned a safer route out of poverty: perhaps I should ask for the job of gardener. By the looks of the garden, they needed one as much as they did a chef.

At the kitchen entrance once more, I declared that an interview had been scheduled and an interview there would be. To my amazement, Alice received me with a beaming smile, then swiftly returned to finishing the dinner that was already overdue in the dining room. "Do something to that soup," she said.

I turned to the biggest aluminum pot I had ever seen, twenty gallons, full of a liquid puree of some kind. I stuck a finger in and tasted it. All it needed was salt, but I added a bit of white wine and cream, to show off.

Alice took a spoonful and smiled. "You're hired!" she yelled across the counter.

I stood there awkwardly, the taste of uncooked white wine in my mouth, imagining her next words would be "On the other hand . . ." But there was no other hand.

The man with the beard and the severe eyebrows shot a furious glance at Alice, then turned to me. "Call Gene. And come back tomorrow," he said curtly. It wasn't a promising start for our relationship, but this man— my soon to be sous chef, Willy Bishop—would turn out to be my greatest ally.

The menus had gotten me in the door; salting the soup got me the job.

The next day, Gene Opton, who had kept Panisse financially afloat in those haphazard first years, gave me a cash advance to pay for the next two weeks' buses. Two days later a letter appeared:

Dear Jerry,

We would like to offer you the position of chef, with the responsibility for developing and executing the cuisine of the restaurant—assuming a common interest in integrity and high quality without pretentiousness.

HEAD AND ONLY CHEF

I knew I was imprinted with cooking integrity and high quality; lack of pretentiousness I wasn't so sure about. It was sobering to read the rest of the letter, which said that in addition to menu planning and food preparation my responsibilities would include "directing kitchen operation and personnel, ordering of supplies, budgeting food costs, ordering and storing food, maintaining inventory control, routine cleaning, and all other considerations that are relevant to making the restaurant a smoothly operating, profitable enterprise." Thirty years later I received another letter from a friend of that time: "All I can think of is that rainy night when I went with you on the bus to Berkeley and you interviewed at Panisse. I remember that on the bus back home you said you weren't sure if you could do this, and I said, if you don't try, you'll never find out."

I accepted the job. The salary was four hundred dollars a month.

My official entrance early one morning a week later coincided with the arrival of the produce, which was stacked at the dining room entrance to the kitchen. As I was fresh from my farm in Massachusetts and my foraging hunter-gatherer menus from summers in Maine, the stack of commercial-grade crated fruits and vegetables was not promising. I separated out the more pathetic specimens and told the delivery boy to take them back. "But," he protested, "they usually just sign the invoice." I told him that a chef has to approve all the ingredients (how would I know?) and that the green beans were especially a joke, so large and tough that even one of my goats would pass them up. I told him I'd come across the road to look for replacements.

Seconds more than the time it took for the goods to make their way from the restaurant back to Ron's Produce Center, the kitchen phone rang. It was Alice. "You can't send produce back to Ron," she said. "He's a friend."

"That very well may be," I told her, "but this is junk. The green beans are ridiculous. I'm going over to find whatever looks good." Precious time was being wasted. I still had no idea how to cook for a hundred people. But I knew mediocre ingredients when I saw them and was prepared to hold my ground.

A few minutes later, Alice appeared with two members of the restaurant's board, one of them a rock-star attorney. Her eyes told the story, and her mouth agreed. The lines around it defiant. At a nudge from Alice, the lawyer explained that I was out of order and would not be allowed to refuse product from suppliers who were part of our community. I was confused by the quick intervention of a stranger, not yet used to Alice's technique of using front men to carry out unpleasant tasks.

I took off my apron and laid it on the butcher block table, watching it all in slow motion, throwing away a paycheck more sorely needed than anything in my life. My money was gone. I was living with a friend and a dog in a San Francisco ghetto dump across the hall from porn stars. I felt especially bad for the dog, who deserved to go hungry even less than we did.

"If that's the way it's going to be," I heard myself quietly say, "you cook."

That was probably the moment my reputation for being "difficult" was born. The tag has been glued to me ever since. My knowing exactly what I wanted and East Coast manners were oil in the Berkeley waters, and not extra-virgin.

Alice backed down. As Willy Bishop arrived, she was squirming and cooing to get that apron back around my then thirty-two-inch waist. He laughed, if a bit grimly, having seen her act before.

The altercation had used up a couple of hours on my first day of work, and panic was beginning to set in. As the apron strings tightened, so did the feeling of a noose around my neck. It would all be up to me now. Me, that is, and the bearded beatnik menthol-cigarette-chain-smoking, English-atomic-mint-sucking painter, drummer, and sous-chef Willy Bishop. And the dishwasher, who came out from hiding, after the altercation, to peel potatoes.

THE MENUS BEFORE ME

On that first day in the first week of February 1973, Alice gave me the menus for the week her team would have cooked if I had not taken the job. The first menu for six dollars a person was also a confusion of languages, and I wondered where her loyalties lay.

Quiche d'Aubergine
Velouté Volaille [sic]
Gigot d'Agneau, Sauce Soubise
Salade or Fromage
Fruit and Coffee

An eggplant quiche seemed no problem, especially since I had a pastry chef to make the shells. I had no idea what Alice intended for the white *velouté de volaille* since, unadorned, it's the roux-thickened French version of chicken soup. The leg of lamb was easy, but for eighty people a daunting task. The white soubise of onions cooked lovingly down and mixed with some long-cooked flour-based Bechamel was definitely easy, something I had cooked many times before, although I wondered if anyone wanted it after the flour-based rich soup, or if anyone in Berkeley knew that Count Soubise had been executed for politically incorrect sexual crimes. My other menu challenges that week, beyond the variable produce, included game hens that arrived frozen solid and a menu that included a "saupiquet de jambon." I'd cooked that before, too, but for only five people and with a week to cure the ham. Smithfields were the only decent hams around and we couldn't afford those even if appropriate.

To get a better angle on the Panisse style, I read what had come out of the kitchen in the previous year and a half and how it had been received. Gene Opton gave me press clippings, all local, and the gist was reassuring. Reviewers felt warmly toward the restaurant: "What faults there are seem somehow more tolerable than they might be elsewhere," wrote one. "Funny how much easier it is to appreciate a slightly flawed culinary work of art than a mass-produced, perfect appearing but tasteless meal."

The reviewer's biggest complaint was that a black-truffled-under-the-skin chicken in half mourning or "Chicken Demi-Deuil" (not entirely black) had no truffles. Since there were no fresh truffles to be had in those days in California, I wasn't surprised. But she loved the "remarkable raspberry tart," viewed as doubly remarkable in December, with raspberries out of season. There were more winter out-of-season amazements, among them "hors d'oeuvres varies" [*sic*]: marinated broiled green pepper and early summer fennel. There was disappointment in "a tasty substance on a buttered crouton that seemed like lamb marrow but no one could identify for sure since that particular cook had gone."

The most important Bay Area restaurant reviewer was Jack Shelton, and in May 1972 he introduced his review by saying that the food in the "unassuming circa 1900 wood-frame house" had shaken him with "imbalances" in some menus, and "slipups" in presentation. But, he added, "I have never, ever been bored."

He said also that the soup "called for a soupçon more salt"—which brought a smile to my face.

I took note of his final warning: "Watch your marketing"—an astonishing comment given the reputation later of Chez Panisse for fresh ingredients, but prior to my arrival they were not thinking of foraging, growing their own, or using anyone but the usual commercial suppliers.

Gene had also given me a sheaf of menus. The format was a different menu each night with no choices, printed a week in advance for regulars to pick up and decide which meal they wanted to eat. Sunday through Thursday menus started with "hors d'oeuvres varies" and included one dessert, with more available à la carte. For Monday, November 1, 1971, at $4.50 per person:

Hors d'oeuvres Varies
Calamari Farci

Salade

Zabaglione

For Friday, November 12, the menu cost $6.00:

Celery Mimosa
Fresh Tomato Soup
Lamb en Croute
Salade
Cheeses
Mousse aux Poires

Other menus of the period featured Consommé Bellevue, Crab Quiche, Manicotti and Meat Balls, Orange and Carrot Soup, "Gigot de Provence," and lots of "Poulet Basquaise."

I was confused.

Seasonal it wasn't, with tomato soup in November. Nor was it Elizabeth David, who stood for "[e]xcellence of ingredients, simplicity of preparation, seasonality, and respect for tradition, and for region." She would have hated the lamb *en croute*: In her books, lamb is braised or grilled. Nothing is served in pastry unless charcuterie, a tart, or pie. It wasn't the cooking of Fernand Point, either, but it was all food that I wouldn't mind eating. Except for the *croute*.

Looking at more menus from 1972, when Alice was in the kitchen with anyone who would help, the menu on Saturday, October 21, was again "Celery Mimosa," followed by:

Onion Soup
Chateaubriand
Salade or Cheese
Apple Tart

The cost was now up to $7.50 per person, and the dishes did not as a whole thrill me. I took heart when I saw the 1972 New Year's menu, just months before I'd been hired. For $12.00:

Pâté de Poisson à la Guillaume Tirei [sic]
Consommé Royal a l'Oseille
Pigeoneaux Farcis
Choux Rouges Braisés
Fromages Varies
Gateau Moka, Paris Brest ou Tartes aux Oranges
Bonbons Assortis Chez Panisse

Of course the "tirei" meant Guillaume Tirel, or the famous Taillevent, the master chef to the fourteenth-century Valois court of France. And having been to the Paris restaurant of that name, this was more along the lines of where I wanted to go, and where I had gone in the menus I submitted. From eating Russian I thought of my version of their ravioli: chicken breast *pelmeni* sauced with a little raw onion juice, parsley, and butter or "pellmenes de blancs de volaille au beurre"; a hard-boiled egg gratin from my favorite English chef and restaurateur of the 1930's, X. Marcel Boulestin; *Queches de Nancy* from Alice B. Toklas; and then "potage Untel froid; cervelles de veau froides â la crème," and the "poulet farci a l'ariégoise." Cold green turnip soup, poached veal brains in cream as a cold first course, and a chicken dish now lost to memory.

Shelton had written that Panisse was a "rule-breaker" if not a "revolutionary." Reading that I thought of my revolutionary hero, the Doors' Jim Morrison, and his manifesto that was always on a wall where I lived. "The most important kind of freedom is to be what you really are. You trade in your reality for a role. You trade in your sense for an act. You give up your ability to feel, and in exchange, put on a mask. There can't be any large-scale revolution until there's a personal revolution, on an individual scale. It's got to happen inside first." In this case, my mask was the lie that told the truth and, as my Dom Pérignon–bottle Molotov cocktails would suggest, I had revolutionary aspirations, even if somewhat elitist ones. But I knew that I had to learn the rules of running a restaurant before I could break them.

THE PANISSE CREW

With a lot of support from Alice and Gene, and devoted teamwork from Willy, it took six months for me to hit my stride. They patiently guided me through the mysteries of quantity. Willy and I would look at the numbers from the previous week for each day and make a guess about how many would turn up that night. Then he would draw a chalk mark on the soup pot and say, "Make soup to here."

You could tell that Willy had been a drummer by the way he'd turn twenty pounds of button mushrooms into a mound of finely chopped duxelles in about ten minutes. He'd lay the mushrooms out in a long row along the six-foot butcher-block table, then attack them with two Chinese cleavers while moving around and around it. Unlike those of the young male cooking school graduates I would later see, convinced that the louder their chopping the more virile they'd look, Willy's blades barely touched the wooden top. It was a light and soothing staccato, the sound of an unassuming master at work.

Willy's real love was painting. His works were in the style of early Francis Bacon, complete with toilets, sexual emissions, and text (Mallarmé, Genet, *Fear and Loathing in Las Vegas)*. Cooking gave him money for cigarettes, rent, and a weekly blowout of oysters and drinks at one of the local fish restaurants. Later it would keep him in cocaine. Barely.

Willy was the only one who consistently saw through Alice's wiles. He called her Tiny, in part because of her stature and in part because whenever she'd be caught in some brazen act of manipulation, she'd try to become small; she'd raise one hand to her mouth to hide the lower part of her face and emit little squeaks of contrition. Later, at the end of service, with a glass of wine, she would sit in his lap and coo sweet nothings to calm him down, and it generally worked. Alice was good.

I am often asked about Alice's role in the kitchen in those early days, and the truth is that we worked together, but in different realms, she in the dining room and I in the kitchen. Our relationship was like an alternating current: little shocks backward and forward between us, a current of creativity. I was Apollinaire to her Breton. But most of the time it was Willy and me against the world.

We all believed in the Panisse no-choice, five-course, single-menu system. It focused all my attention on three courses, some burden lifted by the waiters, who made the green salads and cut the cheese, and by Lindsey Shere, whose stunning desserts were by far the consistently best food in the restaurant when I got there. It was like a dinner party, albeit for an average of eighty people, and I loved the novelty of cooking something different every night: a repertory theater with a new play each day.

Less clear to us was how to make this particular theater great. I knew the grand things I had grown up with and had cooked for my friends, but "grand" was not a part of the Chez Panisse persona. And it was all too clear that we were a long way from Harrods' Food Hall, my favorite street markets in Paris, my farm in Massachusetts, and the wild beaches of Maine. But I was determined to bring a bit of my hero Euell Gibbons's philosophy to Chez Panisse, as laid out in his 1962 book, *Stalking the Wild Asparagus*. In contrast to industrial and processed food, he says, "[w]ild food grows in the clean, uncultivated fields and woods, and has never been touched by human hands until you come along to claim it. No artificial manures, with their possible sources of pollution, have ever been placed around it. Nature's own methods have maintained the fertility that produced it and no poisonous sprays have ever come near it. Wild food is clean because it has never been dirty." That was how I wanted to provision the kitchen.

I started immediately to write my own menus.

CHAPTER 9

FROM ELIZABETH DAVID
TO FERNAND POINT

I didn't yet know Alice well, but I could tell she was a kindred spirit. She loved the way I encouraged the fishing boat boys to come to the back door with stuff that no one else would accept—wolf eels and other unappreciated "trash" fish. It didn't take long to find Sacramento River Delta crayfish; whole wild boar I'd pick up at the Stuyvesant Fish ranch in Carmel; trout from my teenage stomping grounds in Big Sur's Garrapata; and fresh spot prawns from Monterey's Fisherman's Wharf, where my grandfather had indulged my childhood insistence that we survey the fish stores before hitting the restaurants there.

MY MENUS

By the summer of 1973, my menu format had an English version on the back page. Panisse, the "experiment in dining," was becoming a real restaurant. A menu in July shows the food was now heading more into the Fernand Point *Ma Gastronomie* style, but the price was still six dollars per person:

Salade de Champignons
(Salad of fresh mushrooms)
Potage à la Florentine
(Cream of spinach soup)

Truite Jurascienne
Trout Jura Style Cooked in Rose Wine, served with a Hollandaise Sauce
and Buttered Croutons

In another few months the price had gone up fifty cents, the food another more luxurious notch.

Escargots en Cocotte Languedocienne
(Snails with garlic, fennel, ham, and wine)
Crème de Champignons
(Cream of mushroom soup)
Thon Poché, Sauce Beurre Blanc
(Fresh poached tuna with shallots, butter, and white wine)

I had always loved my parents' books of the compiled *Gourmet* magazine articles of Samuel Chamberlain and his wife on their tours of the gastronomic regions of France, so I came up with the idea of doing special dinners of the regions of France to teach the restaurant staff and increase the range of customers beyond Berkeley. And catch the attention of the national press as well. Among the inspirations were my books by Curnonsky (1920–30), Austin de Croze (1931), Urbain Dubois (1856), John Evelyn (1699), Robert Courtine (1970s), Ali-Bab (1928), Lucien Tendret, my handy 1931 *Larousse Gastronomique*, and the incomparable *Almenach des Gourmands* (1803) by Grimod de la Reynière.

In September 1973 I wrote the menu for the region "Brittany" and decided to charge $8.50 per person, pushing the prices for a Wednesday night. Attendance had been forty-five to seventy on weeknights and seventy to ninety on weekends; weekly gross sales were averaging $3,600. If I was ever going to earn enough to move out of my flophouse—not to mention make it to Hawaii—I needed to raise the revenue, then my salary.

Local or "Native" Oysters on the Half Shell
Mussel Crepes
Roast Duckling with Baby Peas
Watercress Salad
Pont-l'Evêque Cheese
Almond Cake with Almond Paste and Chantilly

The attendance was 104 and the sales $1,200 for one night. I knew then what we had to do.

A month later I wrote the "Provence Region" menu, our first local foraging and sourcing. The menu started with our take on the famous *aioli de province* of fish, vegetables, and snails, followed by sea scallops, then spit-roasted pork loin with wild sage (from a Sonoma ranch), a whole small artichoke, not stuffed with saffron milk cap mushrooms (*barigoules*) but the more contemporary version, *artichauts à la barigoule,* stuffed with onions, garlic, and chopped carrots and braised with white wine. Then a course of California goat cheese. The finale was fresh figs we'd picked in the Sierra foothills and poached in red wine, served with crème fraîche we made ourselves since there was no other way of getting it. That was another weekday night, and another 104 people came, boosting the weekly revenue to five thousand dollars.

I was convinced we were on a roll, so I decided to tempt the gods on November 29 by serving a Champagne dinner featuring a real *truite au bleu,* or live trout cooked in vegetable broth.

Champagne Regional Dinner
November 29, 1973

Boudin de Lapin à la Sainte-Ménehould
(White sausage of rabbit breaded and grilled)
Truites au Bleu au Champagne
(Fresh trout poached in champagne)
La Brioche de Ris de Veau au Champagne
(Sweetbreads in a brioche pastry with a champagne sauce)
Salade Verte
(Field greens salad)
Plat du Fromages de Champagne
(Special cheeses of Champagne)
Sorbets de Poire et de Cassis

We charged a then astonishing ten dollars per person on a Thursday night. We offered various champagnes from the middle sixties. Roederer Cristal was sixteen dollars and Dom Pérignon a dollar more. Best of all, we debuted the new and superb California Schramsberg Blancs de Noir for eleven dollars.

The first time I ever saw *truite au bleu* was at Stonehenge, the Ridgefield,

Connecticut, restaurant of Albert Stockli, the first chef of the Four Seasons. In 1968 I asked Albert if he would cook live trout au bleu for me. Not just for the spectacle of watching the live fish caught from the pond outside the dining room window just after it was ordered, but because I wanted to see it from a master I admired. Albert served it perfectly "blue," meaning none of its color-giving protective slime had been rubbed off as he gilled, gutted, and immersed it in a bath of simmering vegetable broth. Minutes after it was netted, the trout would appear on a huge silver platter, this time swimming in an inch of melted butter. Then, in one magnificent gesture, Albert would slide the skin off and serve the fish with whipped cream–lightened hollandaise sauce spooned over.

The day of our Champagne dinner, the trout arrived from Big Sur in a huge tank on a flatbed truck that Jerry, the headwaiter, had driven there and back. We filled every available sink with the Big Sur mountain stream water in which they'd been raised, and kept the water bubbling and aerated with a compressor from the garage across the street.

The printed menu notwithstanding, the trout weren't poached in champagne. Some pink champagne was poured over them before they left the kitchen and the rest I drank so that I could face killing more than a hundred trout myself.

Then it was killing time.

The first trout slipped out of my hands and went flapping into the dining room, spraying slime over some dowager's ankles. The entire neighborhood heard her ensuing shrieks. My last trout, at around fifty, was worse: it looked up at me as I prepared to bash it over the head, and croaked a complaint. I couldn't go on—the dishwasher had to finish off the rest.

Blue Trout in Pink Champagne

4 eight-ounce live trout

1 gallon vegetable broth

1 cup clarified butter

½ bottle pink champagne, at room temperature

1 cup savory (shellfish) sabayon

Prepare the trout: Being very careful to handle the trout as little as possible so that the protective slime is not rubbed off, hit it over the head, put your fingers into the gill opening, wrap a finger around the esophagus, and pull out the entire intestinal tract along with the gills. You will get really good at this after the fiftieth trout, so just do your best with the first four.

Bring the broth to a gentle simmer. The moment you have cleaned the trout, put them in the hot broth and cook for 8 minutes.

Have ready a heated rimmed 2-inch-deep platter that will just hold the trout and melted butter. Stand the fish up on their bellies on the platter in a swimming position and pour the butter over each trout. Take the platters to the table, open the champagne, and pour the pink wine over the trout.

Serve the trout with the champagne butter from the platter spooned over them. Each person draws back the skin, then spoons some sabayon on each bite of trout.

———

Success we could bask in seemed just around the corner. A letter from the head of KQED, one of the country's flagship National Public Radio stations, had waxed lyrical about the Champagne dinner, saying it was "extraordinary for the originality of the courses and concept . . . the best of Panisse." Our work, he added, was as important to the Bay Area as that of San Francisco Symphony conductors Kurt Herbert Adler and Seiji Ozawa. We'd become a cultural institution.

THE YEAR OF EXPERIMENT ENDS

Nineteen seventy-three was a year of experiments culminating in a menu that I hoped would set the stage for the new Chez Panisse. We charged fifteen dollars per person.

New Year's Eve Dinner, 1973
Crabe au Macôn, Sauce Moutarde
(Fresh Dungeness crab poached in Macôn wine, mustard sauce)
Tarte de Bresse Nantua de Lucien Tendret
(Tart of chicken livers and fish quenelles with a crayfish butter sauce)
Civet de Lapin Lyonnais
(Civet of rabbit cooked in red wine)
Fromage Saint-Marcellin
(Saint-Marcellin cheese marinated in olive oil, juniper berries, and garlic)

Sorbet de Cassis aux Poires

(Pears poached in red wine served with a black-currant sorbet)

In June 1974 Panisse received a local review from the newsletter *À La Votre.* "The few flaws we found [earlier have] virtually disappeared, and there is a feeling of life and creativity." It used terms like "poetic" and "a wonder." The reviewer also applauded our effort to promote California wines on our list, among them the Santa Cruz and Ridge Geyserville Zinfandels. She gave us three and a half stars out of four, saying she needed to keep a half star back to give us something to strive for.

And strive we did. As one of the equal five general partners in Chez Panisse I was still hoping one day to collect my winnings and finally head off to Hawaii. If we were starting to become famous, we were a long way from rich. The restaurant's finances were in a shambles, and the lone partner with financial smarts, Gene Opton, had also been alone in regularly standing up to Alice. The upshot was that Alice had successfully lobbied the rest of us and the bank to buy her out.

Alice pretended she didn't care about profits, until she needed them to travel or buy a new car, or to subsidize the business of one of her close friends, a crazed but wonderful woman who looked like Marlene Dietrich in *Touch of Evil,* lived with ocelots, and ran a vintage clothing shop. Disarmingly casual about expenses, Alice would take a bunch of checks and never bring back the dupes, so operating as we did on a day-to-day cash flow, it was common for me, as the principal food buyer, to be in constant fear of the bouncing checks—a waste of energy. And energy, in the days before cocaine fueled a chef's eighty-to ninety-hour week, was what it was all about.

I commandeered the checkbook and took over the books, keeping track of the food costs and attendance each day. After twenty-eight years of the world's most expensive schooling, I still had no experience handling money. In college when I had problems balancing my checkbook, I would just give in to my grandfather's constant offers to send me more money. But I was determined, some said ruthlessly, to make money and get out, and I quickly learned my way around accounting. If my Irish side promptly spent whatever I made for myself, with my inherited Yankee Puritan grandfather's instincts I fiercely guarded the restaurant's takings.

Our first financial statements of the new partnership were an exciting "grown-up" moment, even if no one knew how to read them. For the first six months of 1975, we had assets of $24,000 and a long-term debt of $60,000. Sales averaged $25,000 a month, and the profit was 12 percent, a huge improvement over the previous year. We still owed Gene ten grand on her investment, but with $5,000 in the bank, things were looking up!

CHAPTER 10

A WEEK IN THE LIFE OF CHEZ PANISSE

My week would begin on the day it ended, the one day we were closed, Monday. First I would look to see if we had any money. Then I would look at the menus for the coming week, which I had written the previous week or day off for posting to the public on the preceding Friday. The Panisse regulars knew I would change much of the menus depending on what I found in the market or what foragers brought in, but also that I would try to stick at least with the main courses. Then I'd make up purchasing lists and call purveyors to alert them to what we would be needing. With luck there would be a few hours left in which to do personal things before the stores closed and the bars opened. Then I'd be off to Oakland's Trader Vic's to collapse into a martini.

A '66 LITTLE RED DART

The real inspiration for the menus came from wandering around the markets. At six on reopening day morning I would head off in Alice's little red car to buy the food for the day and snoop around for the week. The trip to San Francisco was a logistical nightmare because the ancient, battered, powerless, ugly but faithful Dodge Dart couldn't go up hills. At its age and level of decrepitude the car should never have run, but it never broke down.

First stop was Chinatown, for ducks, fish, shellfish, and the occasional vegetable far fresher than I could get from other suppliers. I would watch the little old Chinese women blow air up a chicken's anus to see if it was fresh. I'd see the vendors sneaking ice into the boxes of fish before weighing, then taking it out with much gesturing and laughing in Chinese insults when I called them on it. With ducks and fish loaded in I would ritually confront the parking meter "dykes on bikes," then head over the Bay Bridge to Oakland.

By the time I got there the pressure was on, since I had still to get back to Berkeley and cook lunch for sixty by myself. In Oakland there was one beef and veal "jobber," where whole animals, hanging by their feet, would whiz past me down steel runners from huge trucks into the warehouse. As they swept by I would stand at the end of the ramp with my bucket and grab the sweetbreads and kidneys. The Sicilian workers, covered in dried blood and specks of animal fat, wondered aloud why I didn't just go into the freezer and pick up boxes of already butchered meat. And they were really fascinated, in a Hammer Films sort of way, when I rolled up my sleeves and got shoulder deep into the big drums filled with the blood and livers of calves. I wanted only the blond ones with the mildest flavor and texture that reminded me of foie gras. No one, not even the old geezers, knew what I was doing, and I didn't have the energy to explain. It was too long a story if you didn't know the short one: buy fresh, buy the best.

I did get a lot of their respect for my beef project. I had reserved space in one of their dry walk-ins, bought New York sirloin strips on the bone, and left them there for another twenty-one days. The stress on the cash flow was worth it. Those Sicilians hadn't seen anyone do that since the old days and soon learned plastic shrink-wrapping in Cryovac were dirty words to me. The blood from that packaged beef smelled dead. My dry-aged beef smelled like mown grass (with a lot of mold thrown in), and that, I knew from my childhood visits to English butcher shops, meant perfect steaks.

From the butcher's I would have to hit the dangerous section of Oakland, and here that old red jalopy came in handy. The door locks had long since failed, and the poultry and fish blood leaking into the spare tire well in the back of the car had congealed, but not before raising green-miasma aromas in summer that kept thieves away. But it also drove off valet parkers, who'd retch and refuse to park the car.

I had to make my peace with that car, since it was our lifeline. I didn't want commercial-grade, usually frozen stuff, but that was all we could get from companies big enough to have vans and Bay Area–wide deliveries. Spices, extra-virgin olive oil, and decent cheeses were unavailable anywhere except Italian specialty stores, which didn't deliver. It fell to us all to find what we needed, and to me to devise menus around what we could find.

If I hadn't come up with enough fish in Chinatown, my last hope for live crab, fresh shrimp, and still-kicking Baja spiny lobsters was Oakland's commercial fish market or the vast walk-ins at Spenger's Fresh Fish Grotto, located on the bay in Berkeley. The Bay Area's biggest restaurant had its own boats and wholesale fish business. But detours to both meant cutting into lunch-preparing time.

With luck I'd make it back to Chez Panisse with two hours to cook—although I still hadn't figured out what Berkeley people wanted for lunch.

My spirit had been badly shaken the first Christmas season, when we proudly imported California's first fresh black French Périgord truffles and I stuffed them in omelets. I knew that charging ten dollars was asking for trouble, but not the kind that showed up. The first customer ate the eggs but carefully piled the truffles around the edge of the plate. I felt trapped in a barbarian land. The second order was completely eaten, but the plate came back with a butter-drenched fly on it. "Flies in December?" I shrieked to the waiter. "Give me a fucking break!" I needed every penny from that omelet to cover the exorbitant cost of the truffles. Next Christmas the fly came back again, and I swore I recognized it as well as the customer. Did he keep flies in his freezer to get free lunches? I made him pay me for his omelet personally.

Lunch was usually a bit of a blur, since my mind would be already on overdrive for dinner. There was a huge amount of work and only two of us to do it—although the dishwasher and a busser would help out in a pinch, a collaboration that turned out happily over the years. Several (like Steve Sullivan, who went on to open the famous Acme Bread Company) became cooks and entrepreneurs themselves. Another reason for anxiety was that, despite the published menus, I was unsure what we were cooking until the amateur foragers showed up with the promised wild mushrooms, octopus, or hand-harvested mussels.

At 2 P.M. Willy would come in, and while I was finishing off the last lunches I would go over the evening's menu, telling him what the planned vegetables were and how he was to cook his dish. I had two dishes and he one, usually something that he'd never done before. It was by necessity of time a rushed and inexact conversation, and then Willy would wing it. I prayed every day for an easier, less harrowing way. A few hours on the "day off" over oysters and clams at Spenger's was a start, but then the martinis and fatigue would erase the talk.

Finally, at six, the guests would arrive, and sometimes we'd be ready for them, if with tempers frayed and nerve endings as raw as the bloody livers I was still cutting up.

One of my more talked-about intemperate moments came when a busser started to carry plates out of the kitchen with his fingers in the food. I banged my spoon on the table in fury. "What is it about 'keep your fingers out of the food' that your little cockroach mind can't grasp?" I yelled over the Puccini blaring through the kitchen music system. He blanched but held his ground:

"I am a person, too, you know."

That was too Berkeley for me.

"What's your point?"

That was only the beginning. An hour later Tom Guernsey, the very sweet upstairs manager and a partner in the restaurant, came in with two plates that guests had returned. "Bugs again," he said with a sigh. Sure enough, two or three little red centipedes were swimming around in the cream sauce on fresh morels gathered that afternoon in the hills above the restaurant. "Jesus Christ!" I yelled, picking out the insects and replating the food. "Don't they know this proves they're eating the only fresh morels in America?"

A fresh and even louder scream was heard above the Maria Callas tape, freezing staff to the spot and curdling the food that had just hit diners' stomachs. A dishwasher staggered out of his corner, blood spurting through his fingers. Some idiot had put a knife in the pot sink.

In a restaurant as small and understaffed as Chez Panisse, everyone is critical, and we'd just lost both the dishwasher and the employee who had to rush him to the hospital. I was frantically putting lobster claws in four different bouillabaisse pots and plating six others when the kitchen phone rang and a voice on the other end demanded, "Where is the finger?"

Two anxious waiters, shifting from foot to foot like racehorses eager to get out of the chute, were drafted to finish plating the bouillabaisse while I tiptoed over to a sink full of water as gray as my face, pots, and, evidently, one knife and one finger. I wasn't certain which I wanted to find first. "Do fingers float?" I asked Alice, now looking over my shoulder. I rolled up my sleeve and gingerly reached through the congealing inch-thick layer of grease, coming first upon the knife, then upon the severed member, which I slipped into a Ziploc bag and handed to our last remaining busser, who dashed out the door and into a waiting taxi.

By then there was a serious backlog in the kitchen, but the guests would have to wait. It was a champagne moment. I opened a bottle of Clicquot, drained a glass in one long and sensual draft, and went back to cooking.

The scream had softened up the customers, who by now must have figured that any more food coming out of the kitchen would be a miracle. So after catching up with the orders, I knew it was time to visit the dining room. First I reassured the guests that the injured man was well cared for. Then I showed Californians how to get Maine lobster meat out of the claws. A waiter had spilled the beans that the bouillabaisse contained a wolf eel, and the news had traveled around the dining room as fast as that scream; I explained that wolf eel was not poisonous and that it really did give the broth a wonderful punch of authenticity. I informed one group that the salad oil was not "weird" but only "extra-virgin," and that the fresh California goat cheese did not smell or taste like the rear end of a billy goat because the milk came from a dam with clean udders. That sent a neighboring table into paroxysms of giggles.

More champagne.

"THAT PRICK"

Just as we were getting back to a kind of normalcy in the kitchen, a waiter announced with great self-righteousness, "I am not serving that prick!" I recoiled in shock. It would take something very rare indeed for a waiter to talk like that to a chef. But with opera blaring in the kitchen to obliterate staff chatter, I hadn't heard the waitstaff's powwows about the politically undesirable "shithead" in the dining room. It was H. R. Haldeman.

"He's paying, isn't he?" I told the waiter. "Take the food out *now*."

The mutinous staff stood firm. H.R.'s food was getting cold. Then Jerry Budrick, the headwaiter and another partner, stepped up to the plates and said, "I'll take them. But for this you owe me big-time."

Haldeman was dining with his daughter, who was graduating from the University of California, Berkeley, a schooling choice I thought a bit off the wall, if not downright dangerous. Alice was with the staff on this one, but I was adamant that the man would be served and served well. As somewhat of an outcast myself, I sympathized. Throw Molotov cocktails as a political gesture I did, but intentionally serving bad food was not in my repertoire.

I noticed all the phone lines on my wall phone blinking. Most of the customers and half the staff were trying to call out—to reporters or for reinforcements, I was not sure. I went back to cooking, hoping Jerry would handle whatever came through the front door. Then I heard anarchist Willy say "motherfuckme"—or words to that effect. I looked up to see him staring, false teeth at snarling half-mast, over my shoulder. I turned around to see Haldeman advancing on me with a smile and an outstretched hand.

The best part about English public school training is that, when all else fails, your manners take over. Mine did. So I watched my hand as it rose slowly to clasp Haldeman's.

"Thank you," he said. And for not shaming him in front of his my daughter, "Thank you for that."

He was nice.

Somewhat blessedly, Alice and the staff did not speak to me for a week.

On a normal night we would be finished and cleaned up by about eleven—as long as Alice had not overbooked the room. If she had, Willy and I would do the loaves-and-fishes act, albeit not always as successfully as the original. Then Willy would once again pull off his apron and threaten to quit unless Alice promised never to do it again, a vow that came off her lips as easily as Willy accepted her cooings and proffered glasses of old Chambolle-Musigny. The time I spent holding both sets of hands (no one wanted Willy gone) was time I needed for planning the next morning's sorties.

But I was not entirely out of sync with Alice on the subject of late walk-ins. They were almost all profit (who had heard of overtime), and the sales were always needed.

The rule, though, was that she had to check with the kitchen around ten to make sure there was food for those late diners. When she didn't it would be cause for panic, since she would always seat her friends, whether the famous or any filmmaker like Nicholas Ray, Fassbinder, Pasolini, or Coppola.

They were brought in late by Alice's ex-boyfriend Tom Luddy of the Pacific Film Archive, and there would always be a table for them somehow. But the most disastrous night for Panisse was when she seated, without checking, her current lover, Robert Finigan, who was also the Bay Area's most powerful restaurant critic.

As we were getting ready to clean up the kitchen, the order came in for a first course, triggering what I knew would be a crisis with the now-finished main course, leg of lamb. I looked down with dismay at the plastic buckets with lamb leg bones bare of servable meat. All that remained were the "souris" (little mouse) part of the shanks; that and some crisp bits that tasted delicious but were totally unpresentable to paying customers. The waiter was dispatched to ask if steaks would be acceptable instead. The answer was a firm no. He wanted lamb and Alice had told him he could have it. In those days I thought it improper for a chef to go out and talk to a local restaurant critic, so Finigan and company got what they asked for. ("Inordinately gristly," he would write.) The plates came bouncing right back, the waiter (a friend of the restaurant volunteering for the night) announcing they'd demanded better lamb.

"Tough shit," I said. "Where's Alice?"

"At the table."

In an instant Willy flung his apron down, his brows and beard twitching. "Get Tiny now," he growled.

TINY

I searched the buckets again for lamb I knew wasn't there and looked up to find Alice, red-faced and shedding not her usual crocodile "please forgive me" tears but genuine ones, of rage. "How could you?" she said.

It turned out that the volunteer waiter had repeated—in violation of a cardinal rule of the kitchen—my offhand comment. He'd told Finigan, "The chef says tough shit."

All of this led to an hour or so of recriminations over many drinks, and we left around midnight, so that I could try to be asleep by 1, up by 6, and into San Francisco's Chinatown by 7 A.M.

It never occurred to Alice to consider the role she had played in bringing about this embarrassing episode. In a 1978 article on the history of Chez Panisse, she typically shifted the blame to someone else. "I almost died," she said. "Jeremiah just got fed up. It was not amusing at the time."

She never bothered to tell the reporter why I'd been fed up and how even less amused we were in the kitchen to serve unpresentable food.

Finigan explained it nicely: "Had I not been visiting Chez Panisse in a professional capacity [with his lover the owner sitting with him], I might well have decorated the waiter with the *gigot rôti* and then set out for the kitchen, but instead I cooled my outrage with sips of the remarkable 1972 Mt. Eden Pinot Noir." Years later I became a great friend of Bob and he finally, for the first time, heard my account of the incident, and could laugh over another glass of Mount Eden.

Alice may have nearly died, but a few days later I was more worried about customers in convulsions after having eaten American white truffles. Linda Guenzel, Panisse's most devoted customer and later author of the first Chez Panisse cookbook, had brought some from Texas. She found squirrels digging them up in her mother's front lawn. After calling UC Berkeley we found out they were *Tuber texense,* and that there was no record of anyone eating them. They had certainly not been served in a restaurant. I had called England's culinary encyclopedia, Alan Davidson, and for the first and only time, he was stumped. He knew about Terfezia, the North African dessert truffles so beloved by the imperial Romans, but Texas? White Oregon truffles had not been heard of yet, so he cautioned me to try one first and wait a day. But there wasn't time; we were to serve them that night. Alice thought I was mad—if not criminal.

END OF THE DAY

After sixteen hours of shopping and cooking, I couldn't look at food for at least two hours. That meant if we ate dinner at all, it would start at one in the morning, and that I'd have only four hours' sleep before heading back to Chinatown to sniff the bloody gills of fish and hold down my rising gorge.

The dilemma in my few hours off was how to recharge my batteries instead of depleting them further. The mental onslaught was never-ending. Even in sleep. restaurant operation nightmares are famous in the industry.

And drugs were easier to organize than sex, unless it was casual, which usually meant with one another. Who else would put up with us? So on a day off, temporary oblivion was what we sought. On that day, after I had written all the menus for the next week, done the accounts, and planned the next PR coup, and before a four o'clock lunch with some of the staff, I would head off to the Japanese baths for a long soak. In later years, when I was a bit more flush and certainly more famous, I would be invited out, sometimes by San Francisco's elite restaurateurs. But in those early and not so well-funded days, it was either Trader Vic's in Oakland for its tandoor oven-cooked food and expert bartenders, or Vanessi's in San Francisco for tomato and anchovy salad, tortellini in butter, a great filet mignon cooked on charcoal, and zabaglione for dessert. We ate like pythons coming out of a long sleep. As cooks we had not really eaten during the week, just tasted and picked.

It was no surprise that, after six months of these ninety-plus-hour weeks, one night I wandered into the dining room, empty except for Alice and some staff sitting around a bottle of old Le Corton from Doudet-Naudin, and burst into tears. All my strength and discipline were gone. The months of a relentless attempt to make it all work with so few hands had done me in. "I am out of here," I told the astonished group. "See you in a week." I added, "And, Alice, you will just have to do the menus if you don't like the ones I have done."

She did, and took over the kitchen for a week. A photo of her and Willy from when I was away tells much: Alice is dipping her finger in a container of sauce, hesitancy and doubt pervading her face, and Willy is looking on with the scolding frown he reserved for her alone.

The most creatively lonely places in the world are beaches, and it's on warm ones that I do my best thinking. Thirty hours after leaving the staff openmouthed in the Panisse dining room, I was sitting on the white sands of Yelapa, Mexico, down the coast from Puerto Vallarta.

I was the only guest in the hut "hotel" on a beach visited every day at lunch by a boatload of tourists from Puerto Vallarta. When the boat arrived I would retire to a hammock in the trees, to which my soon-trained waiter would bring perfect fresh ripe-lime-juice margaritas every thirty minutes. I managed a lot of thinking while sipping those drinks, some of it brilliant (between the first and third margaritas) and a lot of it junk (thereafter), but I returned to Panisse ready for battle, snippets from my just-read Sun Tzu's

Art of War still buzzing in my brain, my tactics outlined and ready to put into action.

On the beach while listening to my tape of Sidney Bechet's soprano sax, I remembered that he was as famous for never sticking to the score as he was for his excuse for being always three days late for work: "The taxi driver got lost." I figured I'd never be famous by sticking to the score, so I might as well do big, outlandish, nontraditional things based on traditional principles. If and when I got into trouble, if the revolution failed, I could always continue to Hawaii.

CHAPTER 11

BACK TO THE FUTURE

A chance for a new score came when my ex-roommate and now San Francisco poet Michael Palmer reminded me that it would soon be the one hundredth anniversary of the birth of Gertrude Stein. For the Stein–Alice B. Toklas dinner, I selected dishes from the *Alice B. Toklas Cookbook,* Michael wrote the menu text, and Willy Bishop designed the menu card with a drawing of an old-fashioned stove that was Gertrude, with Alice in her oven.

> *Dining. Dining is west.* **Mushroom sandwiches.**
> *Upstairs.*
> *Eating. Eat ing.*
> *Single fish. Single fish single fish single fish,*
> **Sole mousse with Virgin Sauce**. *I wrote it for*
> *America.*
> *Everyone thought that the syringe was a whimsy. Mousse and mountain*
>   *and a quiver, a quaint statue and a pain in an exterior and silence.*
>   **Gigot de la Clinique** *a cake, a real salve made of mutton and liquor,*
>   *a specially retained rinsing and an established cork and bracing*
> **Wild rice salad**. *She said it would suit her.*
> *Cake cast in went to be and needles wine needles*
> *are such. Needles are.* **A Tender Tart**. *That*
> *doves have each a heart.*

Nobody ever followed Ida. What was the use of following Ida.
Cream Perfect Love.

February 3, 1974

On the strength of Michael having invited his good friend, the poet Robert Duncan, to read from *The Making of Americans* for after-dinner entertainment, the audience was even more eclectically diverse than our usual patrons: high-minded Berkeley street poets, the Birkenstock brigade of both sexes, hunched-over academics from the university, anyone haunted by Gertrude, and the usual troublemakers. Like my sister. When Robert seemed out of his element reading from Stein, my sister took his place. As she sat down, she unconsciously took the posture of Gertrude in the portrait by Picasso, and a hush fell over the room. Years later my sister described to me those hours: "I have never felt so free, so comfortable and secure, so lovely, and surrounded by acceptance. It was a wonderful evening—a magic dinner."

The year before I had contacted James Beard in New York. Since he was the most powerful food journalist in America, and the high priest of American food, I invited him to the restaurant. Afterward, in his annual widely syndicated reminiscences column, he called Chez Panisse "fascinating." But even with Beard on board, no national press had responded to my notice of the Stein-Toklas dinner.

We did better locally: For the first time since it opened, Panisse appeared in the top San Francisco press. I invited Herb Caen, the Walter Winchellian gossip columnist for the *San Francisco Chronicle*. He telegrammed his regrets. "Jeremiah: Would that we could be there for the signal event but alas, it is impossible. Much luck, merci mille fois-gras, and vive le Gertrud-inus one. T'jours, Herb Caen." But he mentioned the dinner twice in his powerful daily column, starting an alliance that would boost my career as much as anything else. Later, Caen would put Stars in San Francisco at the top of the list of Bay Area places to be.

I didn't have the nerve to put hashish in the after-dinner cookies, although not for lack of supply. I had learned to steer clear of it. The problem with smoking marijuana is that all food tastes just wonderful and cooking to a schedule becomes meaningless. We learned that lesson during the Moroccan

Regional Dinner, when for atmosphere we burned some marijuana stems in braziers under kitchen tables and got so stoned that instead of the smoke our burned best efforts went up the flue.

A DRUG-FUELED KITCHEN

I didn't like it much since the really good marijuana from Hawaii and Jamaica was a far cry from the low-grade stuff that in college I could smoke all night. One night a Panisse friend handed me a cigar-size joint as I was cleaning up. I smelled the powerful resin from the new "Maui Wowie" or sinsemilla and said, "No thanks." But the waiters kept pestering me as I was trying to finish up and join Alice and a group of eight food journalists, so I had one puff, pushed open the swinging doors to the dining room, took three steps toward the writers' table, and passed out. When I came to I heard Alice screaming I was dead and Willy telling everyone to calm down, cancel the ambulance, and get me a glass of champagne.

A few months later we were all at a late-night party celebrating the opening of a local bakery when someone handed me a cigarette with black resin on the end. It was opium. I had tried it once in a village in the hills outside of Tangier with a blind Moroccan boyfriend and was curious to try it again. I quickly knew the most perfect moment of my life: I was fused emotionally, physically, and mentally in one perfect state—and I knew within seconds I must never use opium again or there would be no coming back.

Later there would be nitrous oxide canisters in the kitchen and a case of them at home. One night I was gazing fondly at a poster of the SS *France*, which I'd hung across from my bed so it would be the first thing I saw in the morning and the last thing at night. It stood for my planned escape. After taking several little canisters of gas, I completed an entire crossing without leaving the room.

But these substances were diversions. The only drug friendly to the restaurant business is cocaine. It was cocaine that became the fuel for the energy that changed the way America dines, and for the high-profile and all-consuming peripatetic schedules that launched the superstar chefs.

At Chez Panisse it started on the restaurant's third birthday, in 1974. We planned an open house at five dollars per person, wine included, so we needed something cheap to serve. I had to come up with it fast since the poster for the party by David Lance Goines, one of Alice's lovers, was almost in production. I grabbed a favorite cookbook, Jacques Médecin's *La Cuisine du Comte de Nice,* and saw a recipe for something called, aptly enough, "Les Panisses," a flat pancake type of thing with something boring on top I knew I could improve upon. Excitement caused haste. I didn't read the recipe carefully, but I did write the menu.

Chez Panisse Menu for Third Birthday
August 28, 1974

6 P.M.—midnight

Hors d'oeuvre Variés
Panisses
Salade Verte
Glace de Fruits
Demi Carafe du Vin
$5.00 tout compris

—and sent it over to David at his St. Hieronymus Press for printing.

Soon the day arrived for me to tell everyone what a "panisse" was and to order the ingredients. The recipe called for chickpea flour to be mixed with water and fried in olive oil. I drove down to my Italian delicatessen in Oakland, bought all the flour they had, and made a "panisse." It was disgusting. So I decided to lie. When anyone asked what a panisse was, I said, "Basically just a little pizza." Alice and everyone else were happy with that. So pizza was what it had to be. We had no ovens that would cook regular-size pizzas. Individual ones were the way to go. What went on top had to be cheap and easy. I decided on a fresh California goat cheese (still new to the world in those days) and Sonoma beefsteak tomatoes, a fine idea until a hundred or so people more than we expected showed up and the cheese and tomatoes were all gone. In our walk-in refrigerators there were still fresh ingredients from the previous night's bouillabaisse (clams, prawns, squid, crab, lobster, onions, saffron, garlic, and fennel), so I decided to scatter everything on top. What came out of the oven changed every hour depending on what was left, but little bouillabaisse pizzas they were.

Searches for ingredients caused delays, and soon a line formed to get into the kitchen. I was flagging a bit, and everyone was buying me champagne, which slowed me down even more. Word went out that the chef needed a boost. In sauntered a friend of one of our waiters with a black-leather-coated accomplice. Flashing a gold-toothy smile as he glided by me, he pulled a plastic bag out of his coat, then dumped half a pound of white powder on top of the chest freezer at the back of the kitchen. He cut it into several long lines and handed me a straw fashioned from a rolled-up twenty-dollar bill. In an instant, I was back at the stoves. Then a conga line formed (this time not for the pizza), snaking out through the kitchen, into the dining room, and up the stairs into the bar.

The demand for pizza evaporated with anything left to cook, so that was good. And there was more cocaine and more champagne. The night was a huge success, premiering three new trends: individual pizzas, the freedom to use any topping one wanted, and the drug that made all the long hours possible, then impossible, in the kitchen.

Meanwhile, as our cocaine intake got out of hand, I would think someone on the staff was in love with me; Willy would be stone broke and more interested in scoring than cooking; my partner waiter Tommy would spend the whole night at the Stud and, after hours, the gay baths in San Francisco; and headwaiter Jerry would shoot up the telephone with a friend's .38. Alice disapproved of using cocaine, partly the result of her New Jersey suburban background and partly because she knew it interfered with the proper running of the restaurant. Still, inasmuch as she knew it was a release from the mad pressures of maintaining and improving upon an increasingly famous restaurant, she turned a mostly blind eye. Lindsey and Charles Shere never partook: they regarded us as naughty children, with Charles stentorianly pronouncing doom for all.

I don't know the source of the dispute that got our original dealer killed, but he was replaced by another waiter's friend, along with a few new runners. All was peaceful, in the drug world that is, for a few years, until Willy stabbed someone in a San Francisco bar for hogging the coke lines in the bathroom and was carted off to the state penitentiary—but not before we had cooked hundreds of marvelous meals together. Panisse somehow survived our love affair with champagne and cocaine. And I had long given up using it in the kitchen. Willy sent me a drawing from prison, missing our days off watering inspiration with champagne.

JOSHUA

We had hired a lunch cook. Now that I no longer had the killing responsibility for being alone behind the stoves at lunch, I looked forward to more elaborate menus. But that ship hit a reef and her name was Lydia "Lili" Lecocq. She was, in her words, "just a peasant from the Savoie," but with that said in the kind of way where if you agreed with her you'd never be forgiven. She reminded me of her peasant heritage every morning, when I returned from market with all the things she said she'd love to cook but couldn't. I had a very trying time with her until I figured out that I was the problem. Lobster Bordelaise she couldn't do, but with a potato gratin Savoyard she was a genius. I forgave her mustache, her nasal whine sounding like a slowly opening warped cupboard door, and her flirtatious looks intended to make me like her. All I knew was how helpful it was to have her at those stoves when I was shopping and gearing up to cook the eighty that had now turned to 120 dinners. And her food when I left her alone was delicious.

In crises I could draw assistance from Alice or the staff. One night, when Willy bowed out early and the waiters were lined up, their desperate sighs audible over the blaring *Rigoletto*, I asked a fifteen-year-old dishwasher named Joshua to come over and watch me make a sauce. "Now taste that and remember the taste," I said. "Then duplicate it." He did. Very well. So I said, "Do it again, and quickly." As the waiters looked on hopefully, Joshua Kohn made the sauce even faster and better. He was a natural. I kissed him, work resumed, and we had a fifteen-year-old cook, and I had a new obsession stronger than the allure of Willy's white powder.

"REVOLUTIONARY BUT MAGNIFICENT"

By now we had located, grown, or imported a lot of ingredients that had not existed a year before in California, and the kitchen had a new assurance. So in midyear I decided to push the envelope again. A menu from June 1975 included Fernand Point's classic, expensive, very time-consuming dish of shelled crayfish tails sautéed in cognac, covered with a cream and crayfish sauce and gratinéed; duck consommé with pureed red cabbage and sliced red cabbage cooked in walnut oil; marinated loin of pork roasted over a charcoal fire with fresh herbs, fresh herb butter sauce; and salad of spinach wilted in olive oil and sherry vinegar.

Other dishes included an egg dish from Alice Toklas and her love for "corse" or forthright food: Oeufs Knapik, or coddled eggs with a fresh basil, lemon, caper, mustard, and garlic sauce. And one too grand for her: Filet de Boeuf Nantua, grilled filet of beef served on a crouton spread with mushroom duxelles and sauced cream, crayfish butter, and vermouth.

Another successful menu was the "Sauternes Dinner," inspired by my favorite childhood Russian, Count Cheremetev, and his stories of Rasputin's assassin, Prince Yusupov. I was also intrigued to drink Sauternes throughout the meal. *The Chez Panisse Menu Cookbook* (1982) prints the menu in English, but the original was in French:

Sauternes Dinner
Jambon de Virginie aux Pruneaux
Colombines de Saumon Nantua
Entrecôte de Boeuf
Pommes Chez Nous
Salade Alice
Tarte Chaude de Fruits
Blanc Manger
Noix Caramélisées

After this dinner Alice thought I walked on Sauternes.

She said the meal was "revolutionary, but magnificent in effect." She also said that the menu and evening was a "turning point for the restaurant." I could not have done it without Lili cooking lunch, without the five co-owners' willingness to provide service for a meal with four added courses, without Alice's gift for explaining our mission to the guests in the dining room, and without a new confidence in the kitchen that we could cook the food correctly and on time. It did feel revolutionary: a menu in which sweet wine could be drunk from beginning to end was surely a first, and this one followed Olney's principle of keeping the palate fresh, teased, surprised, and excited.

The "but" in Alice's "revolutionary, but magnificent" implies the concepts for her were mutually exclusive, whereas I believed there was no oxymoron. Although the food at Panisse was no longer what would restore the soul after a romp with the police in People's Park without compromising one's principles, it did make a political statement. The revolution from radical to radicchio that started with the college dropout Alice Brock in the Back Room in Stockbridge, Massachusetts, was, as Arlo Guthrie sang and told us about in "Alice's Restaurant" and when he dined at Panisse, all about fresh, healthful food. But while half my gaze was still on France, the intent was to use American ingredients for themselves rather than as substitutes for unobtainable French ones.

OUT OF THE BOX

Drugs had not dulled our ability to create a wonderful restaurant or my instinct for public relations, so in 1974, well into the French regional dinners using old texts, it was time to liven up the menus with some contemporary culinary giants. Though fairly unknown to the United States, Richard Olney was my first choice. We had finally met a year before at Williams-Sonoma. "Yes he is what I hoped and expected," I wrote in my journal. "Could easily spend some time with him, and cook. He knows I will see him again. That eye understanding was established." I put in the back of my mind that, before the year was out, I would go to France and cook with him.

But we had still the already-planned French culinary regions festival to finish, and the last one had ventured beyond the penultimate Morocco-Tunisia to Corsica. The Corsican menu pushed me over the edge. I didn't know what the Corsican version of "priest-strangler" *strozzapreti* were, so I called the walking food dictionary, Darrell Corti (of the still-famous Corti Brothers specialty food stores in Sacramento), and asked what they tasted like. "Think of them as "quenelles of summer greens," he said. That was easy. Even without the authenticity of *brocciu* cheese. The next course was Stocaficado à la Corse. Caught up in a frenzy for authenticity, I found the "real" stockfish—dried-out cod as hard as an air-dried plank, and just as palatable. But since salt cod was second nature to me, I was not worried—until I cooked this version. The dish was authentically inedible. My low point. I could feel I was nearing the end of slavishly French cooking but could not give up overnight. I needed a break. A surreal holiday in Mustique, where Lord Colin Tennant tried to persuade me to stay as Princess Margaret's chef, gave me an idea.

On my return I wrote a festival of menus from the cookbook of "The Divine Salvador Domenech Philippe Hyacinthe Dalí for Gala," warning the public they were about to see their favorite restaurant, now thought predictable, take a surrealistic leap. The first week was "Dinners for Gala," the second, "Galas for Dalí." Among the dishes were "Un Délice Petit Martyr Sans Tête," a toast of avocado, brains, almonds, Mexican liqueur, and cayenne, and "L'Entre-plat Drogué et Sodomisé," a leg of lamb injected or "sodomized" with Madeira and brandy. One diner wrote to me, "My god, that dinner last night was more memorable than a Dalí crucifixion and a lot less painful to contemplate." But others were not so happy, like "the pillow-breasted shrike" who demanded a green salad and soup in the old style of Panisse. If the unhappy ones had seen me sodomizing legs of lamb every day with huge syringes full of tangerine juice, Madeira, and brandy, they might have been even less confident.

All these challenging menus called for more ingredients than we could find. Our attempts in the last two years (1974–75) to have Francis Ford Coppola buy the Niebaum-Inglenook estate for a Panisse country inn and farm had not worked out, but the idea seemed still our only way to find the ingredients we needed. The list of what we couldn't get seemed endless. When I hauled out my college notebooks filled with garden and country inn projects, I came up with some new ideas. I reread my notes on Robert May's seventeenth-century *Accomplisht Cook* and saw recipes for salads calling for Alexander buds, or black lovage. I put a salad of watercress, sliced oranges, lemons, currants, and pears on the menu—without the buds. Then I read my notes on a 1950s *Farmers' Weekly* section on "Farmhouse Fare" to grow mountain ash (for rowan or "rodden" berries), to flavor vodka as my Russian uncle had shown me, and whortleberries for stuffing game birds. We had bought some goslings and taken them up to Sonoma so they would be ready for the fourth Panisse birthday, on August 28, 1975. For that night we cooked a lineup of cassoulets with real confit of goose made weeks earlier. The result of such public acclaim was that I was now under pressure to make more cassoulet nights, and I nearly fell back into the comfortable lap of French bourgeois cooking.

The plans to make our own culinary region was not so much then a conscious movement as a race to have quality fresh ingredients available in enough quantity to keep up with more and more ambitious menus.

REALITY CHECK: RICHARD OLNEY'S FRANCE

To see if I was on the right track, I needed a reality check. In mid-October, after serving our first in-house smoked California salmon, I put a side of it in my luggage and headed for Paris to join Richard Olney at a special dinner at Lucas Carton given by the Club des Cents for the legendary Madeleine Decure, the head of the magazine *Cuisine et Vins de France.* From there we journeyed south to Solliès-Toucas near Toulon, to his little house on the hill above the town. The place was still fairly primitive. Unfortunately for bathing, but fortunately for cooking. We did a lot of it in the fireplace, over coals that burned twenty-four hours a day to keep the house above freezing.

After we got the sex part of our affair out of the way, we got down to other business. The long winter nights were filled with single-malt whiskey, old French music hall records, and talks about food. I had never been to Chez L'Ami Louis (I couldn't afford it), so I listened in awe to Richard's stories of the ortolans cooked in butter, the perfume of premortem Armagnac anesthesia still lingering in their bodies; of the huge slabs of duck foie gras served with raw country ham; of the woodcock in the fall and the tiny legs of lamb for two at Easter. We shared stories of Alexandre Dumaine, who, with Point, were the greatest twentieth-century French restaurant chefs. And of Dumaine's work at his L'Hôtel de la Côte d'Or, particularly his adaptation of Lucien Tendret's "L'Oreiller de la Belle Aurore." In Olney's words this greatest of dishes was a large pâté intricately cross-sectioned in a mosaic of "pistachio-speckled dark and light forcemeats, alternating with striped layers of dark game and white meats, punctuated with fingers of red tongue, white back fat, and black truffle." Richard promised to make it for me, but an exploration into the glories of the Bresse chicken cooked in the fireplace took over. He talked endlessly about his first days in Paris and later in Grasse cooking for a bunch of opium smokers, including the head of a well-respected travel guide. Dinner had to be ready by ten o'clock, but sometimes the group didn't sit down to table until two in the morning.

Richard was forbidden to get caught up in the opium, but he didn't mind since he was too busy fending off the most famous chef in France at the time, Georges Garin, who was in love with him, a hopeless notion since Richard was in love with a male black Folies-Bergère dancer introduced to him by James Baldwin. I knew in a bizarrely comforting way that Richard had been as mad as I when I heard the story of the look on the dancer's face upon seeing the broken-down shepherd's hovel on the Solliès-Toucas mountainside that he was supposed to exchange for the makeup mirrors at the Folies-Bergère.

In 1975 Richard was trim and still youthful. He was not beautiful, but the sight of him walking fully tanned around the vegetable garden in a turquoise cotton bikini, a bottle of Krug chilling in an ice bucket under the grape arbor behind him, could be thrilling. I minded not at all his under-the-surface melancholy for past grandeurs and true loves, as he didn't mind my simultaneous reverence for the past and obsession with the future. After a couple of glasses of champagne, we were in perfect sync. From all this talk of eating and love we decided to do a festival at Chez Panisse in celebration of his new book, *Simple French Food*. But first a lesson in ingredients.

I waited patiently in line at the neighboring town fish store, admiring all the varieties of fresh sardines and anchovies that I couldn't get in California. One particularly intrigued me for its freshness. I asked the woman behind the counter what it was. She ignored me. I asked again, only to be ignored again. Finally I turned to Richard, who asked her. "Ils sont étrangers" was her disdainful reply. Foreigners? I asked Richard if I had heard correctly. He laughed and explained that the fish were caught more than twelve kilometers from the shop, so they were "foreign" and not fit for selling to him. "Wow," I said to Richard, since the fish looked better than any I could get in California. "If that's the standard, California is sunk."

To complete the lesson he took me to lunch at Domaine Tempier, in Bandol. The wine was unavailable in the United States at that time, and Richard thought that since we were going to cook his food in California, I should have his favorite local wine to go with it. We tasted all the wines from barrels, then sat down to sea bass cooked on a fire of dried vine cuttings, served with a sauce of its roe made in a huge marble mortar; spit-roasted leg of lamb; and a deeply ripe and perfect apricot tart.

SIMPLE FRENCH FOOD

I asked Richard if we could finish the preliminary menus I had sent him for a two-week Olney festival in the spring of 1976 featuring simple French food and his 1974 book of the same name. I also wanted feedback on the menus for an upcoming "California Zinfandel" festival I had written. We decided to combine the two, and wrote the menus listening to the forty-year-old recordings of Mistinguett, Freyel, and Piaf while drinking Niagaras of Krug, other great wines, and the ever-present Glenmorangie. The original paper-work (now available with my other culinary papers in the Janice Bluestein Longone Culinary Archive at the University of Michigan) shows we changed our minds at least four times, and constantly reworked the order of dishes and the sequence of evenings so that Saturday night, at my insistence, would be the crescendo. The final versions weren't ready until after I returned to Berkeley.

Back in Berkeley, I tasted the Tempier wines with my friend George Linton, the brilliant eccentric vet who had started Connoisseur Wine Imports, and by April the first cases of Domaine Tempier arrived. I was eager to proselytize on behalf of the Mourvèdre grape that made Tempier's wines so good, but started by commissioning and helping blend a Beaujolais-nouveau style with Joseph Phelps Vineyards in Napa to go with Richard's menus. The menu read: "Richard Olney Autumn Menus to Celebrate Gold Rush Zinfandel from Amador 1975 County Grapes of Frank Dal Porto Vineyards Produced at Joseph Phelps Vineyards" and included dishes like "Rich pork stew garnished with vegetables, pigs' ears and tails" as well as "French moussaka with watercress" and "Fresh white goat cheese in vine leaves."

But first the year 1975 ended with a menu of French food influenced by rereading the great Lucien Tendret's La Table au Pays de Brillat-Savarin. I'd found a hundred-year-old salad very similar to the one I had seen in Escoffier's 1908 magazine Le Camet d'Epicure and which Richard and I had seen together at the great Jacques Manière's restaurant, Au Pactole, in Paris. It was the "Salade Gourmande" or "Salade Folle." The green bean puree was an homage to Georges Garin, the turnip puree was Richard's Puree Blanche, and the rest was elegantly easy. But no one except Alice understood or appreciated it, and over a few glasses of yeasty champagne, I suddenly had the feeling that I'd gone about as far as I could go at Panisse.

New Year's Eve Dinner: Chez Panisse
December 31, 1975

*Salad of lobster, chicken breasts, black truffles, squab breasts,
mushrooms, and shrimp with a mustard vinaigrette*

*Prime sirloin of beef with truffles, roasted and served with a
truffled Madeira sauce*

*Puree of green beans and puree of turnips, leeks, and potatoes
with garlic*

Champagne sherbet

Fruit tartlets

Bonbons Chez Panisse

Many thought I'd gone mad charging twenty-five dollars per person—
and I almost did when the truck carrying the fresh truffles and foie gras hadn't
arrived from the airport until six fifteen, fifteen minutes after the first guests
had been seated. That one had me sweating. We couldn't charge so much
without the truffles, although even at that menu price we were hardly making
any money. It was truly time to reassess once again what we were doing.

CHAPTER 12

CALIFORNIA KICK-STARTS THE FUTURE

The instrument of change arrived in the form of the 350-pound James Beard, who came to Panisse for dinner the day after Christmas in 1975. The menu started with a trio of oysters: one an oyster soufflé with shellfish sauce, the others Escoffier's "Favorites" with cream and black truffles, and cold "Natives" on ice. This was followed by filet of beef with beef marrow, and then California goat cheeses.

I showed him the press we had been getting that year. The pieces were a paean to the accomplishments of our little band of amateur owners. They are worth repeating to see how much difference a few years had made with the food press and what they now felt a "serious" restaurant could be.

James Beard had said that Panisse had become "a superbly authoritative restaurant." A Bay Area critic reported "unrelentingly superb quality in food preparation, innovativeness in menu planning, purchasing only the finest ingredients, and resolute attention to even the smallest culinary details." In the October 1975 issue of *Gourmet*, Caroline Bates summed up what we had achieved: "Jeremiah honed his palate at an early age and now, like many creative young chefs in France today who have turned away from the pretentiousness of *La Grande Cuisine*, he strives for the simplicity and directness that characterize French regional food with its emphasis on fresh ingredients and the integrity of each taste." So why did I tell Jim that I was still not satisfied?

I moaned to him that size of the profit line was still a vital question for me; that places like Ireland and England, not to mention Italy and France, still had better ingredients, and that they had the courage to put them on the plate without much interference from the chef. I told him that I had not turned my back on *la grande cuisine* in its purest and most perfect form (as in Tendret's book), but that I was beginning to doubt a three-star French restaurant could ever be achieved at Panisse prices.

"DARLING"

Jim gave me the smile he reserved for young men he held in favor.

"Darling," he said, "keep your mouth shut about all that. You have a good thing going here; you're on the right track. Just stick with America." I promised to reread his wonderful 1972 book, *American Cookery.*

The next morning at the Stanford Court Hotel, where Jim's own court of cooking classes was held each day, I bandaged his feet (devastated by lack of circulation), giving his devoted servant Marion Cunningham a rest from her daily chore. His robe had been left open where it "fell," exposing a belly as vast as Yosemite's El Capitan, which swept down to reveal what he could have been proud to reveal were Jim not the exception to the rule that large fingers are also a measure of the family jewels. Jim did have very big hands. This was a morning ritual, exposure to which I had long since become familiar and with which I'd grown comfortable over the years I'd known him. After a little hug or two, we talked about Alice, about Marion, about *Gourmet* magazine's "simplicity and directness" as the path to continue following, about my career, and saying it was fine not to make money. We talked about Delmonico's and the time, a hundred years earlier in New York, when the great restaurants listed the provenance of their ingredients on their menus. We talked of the great William Niblo in his Old Bank Coffee House in 1814 serving ingredients with their origins called out on the menu: "Bald Eagle shot on the Grouse Plains of Long Island." And the Four Seasons restaurant in New York, where Jim had consulted starting in 1959, and which did the same thing.

Jim had rethought his earlier position about sticking where I was, but going American. He asked me if I wouldn't be happier in New York, since the Bay Area press had begun to see me as "pretentious," "autocratic," "royalist," and so on. "Perhaps you should start wearing Birkenstocks to work," he quipped. "Whatever you might think, there is no love lost for you here." I showed him a letter in the *Berkeley Independent-Gazette* that complained of paying ten dollars for "pork and beans"—meaning the cassoulet I'd made from our confit of our own geese! He also read a *San Francisco Bay Guardian* article from November, in which Alice said the restaurant had reached a "plateau." She complained that the telephone lines were always clogged and that 60 percent of the customers were now from out of town instead of the East Bay regulars. "It's extremely frustrating," she concluded.

I wasn't frustrated so much as impatient to go to the next level. Jim knew that Alice's ideas of success were going to conflict with mine, and sooner rather than later. "Jeremiah, they're jealous," he said. "And if they aren't now, they will be. Get out."

"But, Jim," I protested. "I have to work. No one wants an under-ocean architect!"

We pondered this for a while.

Then I was out the door to go to work when he boomed out and waved me back with a huge, effete hand clustered with loose gold wire bracelets.

"How about a restaurant of your own?"

I went back in and sat down.

"But what kind?"

I reminded him of his recent comment that if he had to go back to four restaurants in the United States they would be Tony's in Houston, the Coach House and the Four Seasons in New York, and Chez Panisse. I hadn't been to Tony's, but I knew it was "Continental" and red plush. The top famous restaurants in San Francisco at that time—L'Étoile, Ernie's, and La Bourgogne—were similar: they had severe dress codes and even more severe headwaiters, who would flick open menus half the size of the table and call you "Madame" even if you weren't.

AMERICA'S FOOD

We went on talking about food in San Francisco and the rest of America in 1975. Locally there was Dungeness crab, Petrale sole, and abalone at Sam's

and Tadich Grill, and a great mutton chop at Jack's. Trader Vic's had surprisingly forward-looking ingredients (mahimahi, fresh mangoes, and tiger
prawns). In Los Angeles you could eat simple and direct food like sand dabs,
more Dungeness crab, and prawn cocktails (Chasen's), and even crabmeat
baked in papaya with cream (Il Padrino), which always sounded better than it
was, and it didn't sound too good. You could get Mexican lobster tail (frozen)
with California avocado in La Jolla's Top of the Cove. In Baltimore there was
Danny's with its Chesapeake Bay blue crabs, crab soup, and perfect fresh lump
crabmeat that I adored and that was a favorite of my Russian uncle when it
was made "Imperial." In New Orleans there was Commander's Palace, serving soft-shell turtle stew; Le Ruth with frogs' legs, oysters, and artichokes, and
French fried parsley long before it became a fad in the eighties; the Bon Ton
had its fried soft-shell crabs; and Maylie's my favorite fried oysters and soft-
shell crab po'boys. In Detroit there was the legendary London Chop House
with its menu of Americana, Continental cuisine, and English grills. In Boston, Locke-Ober, the scene of my twenty-first birthday dinner, had its famous
baked oysters, as well as a lobster dish from a century earlier in New York. The
Union Oyster House was where I had spent most of my college allowance on
scrod, codfish cakes, clam chowder, and oysters.

This was all very appealing, but you couldn't get these ingredients except
in their locales, and even then they were often frozen. The age of airline ship-
ping of fresh food would not arrive for at least a decade.

I had brought along one of my favorite books, a 1958 *Picture Cook Book*
from *Life* (Time Inc.) that listed the great American city restaurants of the day.
Of the nineteen selected, we saw that only five served American-ingredient-
driven menus, and they were all in either San Francisco or New Orleans. Of
the photographed specialties from eight "America's Inns," only one, "devilled
crab," was American, and only southern and Texas restaurants had menus
derived from regional ingredients. We decided that, seventeen years later, the
two notable American restaurants (rather than Americanized European) were
the American Restaurant at Crown Center in Kansas City, Missouri, and the
Four Seasons in New York. Jim had consulted on both. We laughed about
the former's Swiss German chef, who could just not resist the old European
sauces (Grand Veneur) and garnishes on indigenous American ingredients.

Jim asked me if I had read Frank Crowninshield's 1939 book, *The Unof-*

ficial Palace of New York: A Tribute to the Waldorf-Astoria, for the Sert murals, the chapter by Elsa Maxwell, and the American menus with Diamond Back Terrapin, Chicken California Style, Roast Mountain Sheep, and Basket of Lobster, all at one dinner in 1899. And especially for the 1937 menu for an "Idaho Dinner," which then called out the origins of the ingredients: Snake River, Twin Falls, Sawtooth Range, Jerome County, Boise Valley, and Lone Pine, Idaho.

I told Beard of my obsession then with Rex Stout for his food-loving private eye. In Stout's *Too Many Cooks* of 1938 there was wonderful food in praise of America: Creole Tripe from New Orleans; Missouri Boone County Ham—cooked with vinegar, molasses, Worcestershire sauce, cider, and herbs; Chicken in Curdled Egg Sauce—almonds, sherry, Mexican sausage; Tennessee Opossum; and Philadelphia Snapper Soup. Or the *Nero Wolfe Cookbook,* one of the first books I read that made me want to cook.

Beard told me that when he, Joe Baum, and Restaurant Associates created the Four Seasons restaurant in New York, the menus were huge, and I should get one to study. Three days later I had one from the woman I bought menus from for my collection, Jan Langone in Ann Arbor, Michigan.

A dinner had eighty items, not including the twenty or so dishes listed "As a Dinner Accompaniment," which might include "Nasturtium Leaves," a "Beefsteak Tomato Carved Tableside," and "Broccoli Flowers." In block letters was written, "OUR FIELD GREENS ARE SELECTED EACH MORNING AND WILL VARY DAILY." Under the separate "Vegetables & Potatoes" it said, "Seasonal gatherings may be viewed in their baskets."

They were obviously mad.

I could not wait to carve a beefsteak tomato tableside.

I couldn't get mallard duck or Jersey poulardes, or frogs' legs. And I'm not sure how many of those ingredients were fresh and in perfect condition anyway. I called Jim in New York to pose that question. I could almost hear his lifting of what was left of his eyebrows in reply. (Those brows over the years did a lot of rising and falling.)

But the menu fascinated me. It was mainly in English and in its scope reminded me of an article called "Recent Menus" from an English publication named *The Epicure.* I had filed it years before under "Regional Dinner Ideas," and showed it to Jim. The article featured a banquet "recently given at the

California Hotel, San Francisco, the object of which was to prove the possibility of making up an extensive menu solely from the products of the State." No date is given for "A Californian Banquet," but a supper menu that follows, for three hundred at the National Skating Rink on London's Regent Street, is from 1896. Of the hundred or so dishes I had underlined Artichokes; Lettuce, Egg Sauce; Bear's Meat; Striped Eels, fried in butter; Spiced Pickled Cantaloupe; Black Halibut; October Strawberries; Frozen Watermelon; Figs White; Figs Black; Grape Fool.

"It's like Delmonico's," Jim said, "and from the same era."

"So how about an American restaurant!" we chimed in together.

AN AMERICAN RESTAURANT

I fell into his large arms and onto his even larger belly and gave him a big kiss before heading off to Panisse to cook dinner, proving Marion Cunningham wrong when she claimed that Beard was incapable of loving anyone. "And don't forget California wines!" he bellowed as I was once more going out his hotel room door. Apart from Panisse, the only restaurants I knew pushing premium California wine were the Four Seasons, the Wooden Angel outside Pittsburgh, and Bern's Steak House in Tampa, Florida.

Late that night on the ride home, I thought about the complexity of Jim's personality. He was like an erratic elevator car, one that could take you up fast but sometimes, when you stepped in, wasn't there. Like all the great men I had met, he had two parts: the big jolly one and the big-tempered one. One could never claim to know him until one had seen the temper-induced flapping and flying of his weighty and ponderous jowls, their quivering a preface to an even more serious seismic body event and a stentorian roar. I'd seen it for the first time a few weeks before in a restaurant on San Francisco's Nob Hill. I had finished bandaging his startlingly black and maroon legs, had massaged the even worse feet, rewrapped the bandages, taken tea, heard the latest gossip, seen on the coffee table the latest unreleased cookbooks and endorsement proposals, and listened to what was going on in the cooking world and its satellites. Then it was time to take him to lunch in the new restaurant of his choice. We were oiled to the table by the maître d'. The owner's prostration made Jim nervous from the outset. Nothing went well.

The food was mediocre, our guests fidgety. Jim's already pink face turned even redder, splotched with streaks of purple. Those jowls started to quiver, but he held himself back. When his espresso arrived the jowls went into full swing. "Who asked for lemon zest in the coffee?" he roared. The waiter looked as if he might make a puddle. I hid. Soon his cane was found and he launched himself, Robert Morley–like, into the foyer. "And furthermore, the coleslaw was terrible."

Thank God I was paying (he never did). I stretched to a new height and said, "Okay, Jim, but whose coleslaw is better? Your uncle Billy's or my aunt's?" The latter I had fed him a week earlier; Billy's was from one of his cookbooks, *The New James Beard*. Jim looked at me fiercely. His body stopped heaving and began to roll. Tears appeared and he roared again, this time in laughter.

A month earlier I'd had my thirty-third birthday lunch with Jim at New York's Maxwell's Plum. There was something coyly in the air, and it wasn't until after our hamburgers and a magnum of Dom Pérignon (I was paying) that he offered the usual advice: write a cookbook and take on the job of chef at Maxwell's—in no particular order. After lunch he called his editor, Judith Jones, at Knopf to set up a meeting about doing a Chez Panisse cookbook, and we looked at the kitchen at Maxwell's Plum. It was far too small to make all the dishes on the menu, and I could see why the chef wanted to leave. There were four-foot-high mounds of bus tubs packed with food oozing out of them and spilling down the narrow stairs. When I left I stopped to wipe my alligator shoes. "That's New York, my dear," he said. I gave up on the idea of moving to New York and redoubled my efforts to capture America. A few months later in 1976, I was hit with three bombshells, one professional and two culinary.

BOMBSHELLS

Willy quit after the glowing *Gourmet* review. He couldn't stand the idea of "food weenies or trendies" who float from restaurant to restaurant, like the lone diner who had a copy of that *Gourmet* open on his lap under the table in the dining room and kept demanding dishes we didn't have but had served weeks before when the reviewer had dined.

The first culinary bombshell was Jim Villas's article in *Town & Country* covering restaurants serving American food, titled "At Last, a Table of Our Own." It heralded "the possible existence in the United States of a slowly developing formalized American cuisine, a stylized native cookery that might one day rival the European and Far Eastern culinary traditions." That was what were trying at Chez Panisse. Villas mentioned the bicentennial "American Culinary Festival" that Hilton International was holding around the world during the summer of 1976: "Sea Bass with Ginger," which Jim described as Californian; "Berkeley Banana Fritters" in Tehran; and "Peanut Soup," "Black Bottom Pie," and "Shoo-Fly Pie" in Hong Kong! I knew the Hilton chefs were fishing in unchartered waters: bananas from Berkeley? Perhaps just menu alliteration. My notes from Villas's article read: "Duck with Quince Puree; Walnut-Macadamia Nut Crepes but make crepes with cornmeal; Sweetbreads with Crayfish Ragout; Oysters with Green Chilis and Meyer Lemon Vinaigrette; California Cheeses; think Thomas Jefferson." None of those dishes had been cited, but the article was so provocative I started making up my own.

The second bombshell was the Gault and Millau article summing up what French chefs were up to, calling it "la nouvelle cuisine." An account that immediately caught the imagination of all Western food chefs and writers. In their *On the Town in New York,* Michael and Ariane Batterberry explained what the term meant: All unnecessarily complicated cooking was to be dumped. In order to "reveal forgotten flavors," cooking times were to be reduced, and the new style was designated a *cuisine du marché,* cooking inspired by what is found in the marketplace and reliant on the freshest seasonal produce—a proposition that would lead to collaborative efforts between chefs and breeders of livestock, cheese artisans, and vegetable and fruit growers to secure the finest. Domineering sauces were to be discouraged, especially any thickened with flour; game was to be served fresh and not high from hanging; regional dishes would be reexamined; technological breakthroughs like the food processor were encouraged in the interests of convenience, speed, and virtuosity; long menus, once the hallmark of "grand hotel" or "Continental cuisine," were to be discouraged.

Our less formal in-house printing job at Panisse meant that we could finalize a seasonal market menu honoring the day's best fresh produce mere hours before the meal service. But I had still some work based in France and its great traditions that I needed to finish before I launched into new American cooking. I needed one last taste of what had started off my love of cooking decades earlier.

ONE MORE OLD WORLD TASTE

As 1976 opened Alice and I were starting to go in different directions. We were equal partners in the restaurant, and up to this point had avoided confrontations. I believed that revamping the upstairs of Panisse with a high volume, low-food-cost cafe would be its financial saving, as well as bringing in new, younger, and less affluent "starter" customers. And we needed non-reservation seating, since our fame had brought also the ruinous phenomenon of no-shows. But Alice didn't agree that great restaurants should have cafes attached to them.

The fact that I was living temporarily in her house made the arguments turn final. Alice had recently been assaulted there and didn't want to stay alone, and she didn't regard Willy, before he quit, living in the garage with his paintings, as protection. It was not long before the close quarters became claustrophobic. It had been a while since Alice and I had sat on the terrace of Venice's Gritti Palace in the moonlight sipping vintage Krug champagne, or stayed with friends on a romantic trip to Nice. Both were wonderful memories, but I was newly seeing, and in love with, someone else: a teacher, Gregg Lowery, the love of my life, with whom I was to live, if for not nearly long enough. One night I did not come home when I said I would and in the morning I had forgotten my house keys. Alice met me on the steps, screaming loudly enough to bring out the neighbors. "It's my house!" she shrieked (which was true), "my car" (not true), and my restaurant" (she owned 10 percent). It was such a preposterous lovers' tiff performance that all I could say was "May I have my toothbrush?"

I took "her" car to go buy fish.

The next day, while eating the last of the crystallized fruits that Alice and I had bought at Vogade in Nice, I decided to take a break and think. Or quit. But whatever: it was time to find myself again.

I sent a roomful of parrot tulips to Alice with an apologetic note. "Like Lord Henry's wife," it said, "she was usually in love with somebody and, as her passion was never returned, she had kept all her illusions." I told her she should write a cookbook called "A Matter of Course," the title taken from Max Beerbohm's *Zuleika Dobson:* "As the homage of men became for her, more and more, a matter of course, the more subtly necessary was it to her happiness."

PARIS

I fled to Paris, only to run out of money two months later and terrify myself with lots of nights alone in the Île Saint-Louis apartment above Marc Chagall, which I rented from Pavel Tchelitchev's former lover Charles Henri Ford. My thoughts turned to employment and therefore to California. In Paris, even though I no longer felt "a soul exhausted by concealed thoughts" as I had in Berkeley, I ignored Charles's guest, the young and godlike godson of the queen of England who said of the Bay Area, "It's a pleasant euphoria, but not for me," and planned to get back.

Alice felt abandoned by my leaving, but while I was away she had my wonderful sous chef Jean-Pierre Moullé, who had long since given up his first notions that if food was not French, lobster, or filet mignon, it did not make for a serious restaurant. The menus from the time I was away were mostly the dishes we had done in the past, leaning heavily toward Provence, the Brittany Regional Dinner menu, and the dishes that I had brought back with me from Richard's house in the South of France. Emotionally bruised by French bureaucracy and shopkeepers, I looked around California with a new glee, even a little love.

DADDY BEARD

I remembered all the conversations I'd had with Beard about my career, and all the doubts I had about California were transformed into a new focus as I reread Charles Ranhofer's cookbook from Delmonico's, *The Epicurean.* I realized I had been improvising for years, so why fret any longer about authenticity of French ingredients for French regional food? Why not just go shopping in Northern California and call that the region? I wrote a series of menus called "A Week of the Cuisine of Charles Ranhofer, Former Chef of Delmonico's," including a dish called "Crème de maïs à la Mendocino." What in the world, I thought, was the chef of New York's most famous 1890s restaurant doing thinking about dishes local to small regions of California? Once again it was the soup that kick-started my future.

I was all fired up with new plans for Panisse even if I felt I was numbering my days. I told my partners all the ideas I'd come up with in France: an à la carte menu for Panisse downstairs, including four menus starting at the low end of ten dollars to the high end of twenty-five dollars for a tasting menu with California's best ingredients, a cafe menu, and a list of "dishes available on command one week in advance." I wrote a statement for the menu: "If there is ever a dish on the menu that is not available, it will be because of the caprices of the weather, the fish themselves, the transport services, and our own limitations. We would rather buy sometimes scarce first-rate good ingredients and run out of them than compromise standards and disappoint ourselves and the customer."

Alice was dead set against the ideas, especially for the cafe. No one on the board had heard of a tasting menu either. Only the headwaiter, Jerry Budrick, and I were insistent on the need for a cafe. I decided to stay until the end of the year and let them all buy me out.

The Panisse board decided to sell the restaurant instead. On May 26, 1976, Herb Caen reported the price as $500,000, adding, "Now that the restaurant has made a big splash with the critics, the owners are tired." Perhaps. Certainly they had had enough with reviews saying that Panisse was becoming pretentious. I felt we were not pretending to do anything but actually trying and most of the time succeeding. A customer, the journalist Robert Scheer, complained that Panisse at ten dollars per person was "expensive" (untrue) and a "hangout for drug pushers" (true). I replied that Panisse was a victim of his uninformed "radical-chic liberal veneer," but my partners were unnerved. They felt I was taking them down a path they didn't know, even more so now that the food was taken for granted and critics were focusing on things like us not having senior citizen discounts, or that Panisse was in a converted house. Another said we were not expensive enough to survive.

And on it went, making me more determined than ever to keep from being made or unmade by the press. I was a bit defensive about our old house, which I'd redesigned three times. We now had heat, a chilled wine cellar, a carpet, and a pleasant atmosphere. It was also "world famous," because the great chef Jean Troisgros had actually asked if his nephew Michel could work with me in the kitchen. I was aghast. Troisgros was one of my heroes—I said it was I who should be studying with them. "Au contraire," he said. "You may not know what you have here, but I envy you and admire what you are doing with the food. I am jealous of your freedom to do what you want, to make the customers want what you do. I have to cook what the customers expect, and if I were to do it again I would do what you are doing." And once more I was reminded of that Jim Morrison quote.

Michel Troisgros arrived and was part of the cooking team that took over from me with Jean-Pierre Moullé as their leader and executive chef. Mark Miller and Fritz Streiff, who had worked in Paris with Jacques Manière at Au Pactole, were the others.

Alice herself was now getting the hang of special festivals and events. Her main interest in 1976, others than friends' birthdays, was a benefit she did for Les Blank and his "Louisiana Playboys" to raise money for a film. Although I had a deft hand with gumbo and other dishes I'd learned in my culinary travels through Louisiana (our very first regional dinner at Panisse had been Creole), Alice imported a certain Creole "madame" to "authenticate" the food. She was hardly a madame, and she dealt a fair blow to that always "difficult concept of authenticity" when she boiled twenty pounds of beef lung in our big soup pot, without salt, producing a sludge-gray mess so stinkingly ugly that even our resident tomcat, Blackie, hissed at it. We threw it out, and at the last minute I had to cook another whole meal.

THE LAST OF THE FRENCH FESTIVALS

"Authenticity" took on less meaning after that, and we all now saw it as a verbal and mental crutch. Its kissing cousin, "purity," raised even more hackles in my kitchen. Whenever I heard a cook say, "I am a purist," I knew that bean sprouts were only a moment away, and that his or her pets were fed macrobiotically. Despite our using Big Sur trout and California pigs, no one challenged the authenticity of my menu for an Alsace dinner, which Alice called "one of the highlights [for her] of the last ten years."

Dinner for Alsace
Pigs' ears breaded and grilled, mustard sauce
Alsatian vinaigrette salad
Live Garrapata trout cooked in court bouillon, butter sauce
Munster cheese
Tart of dried fruit with a coffee cream

This was the last of the French festivals, since my mind was on America in my last year at Panisse. But I summoned up the energy for one final push, returning to the lessons of past masters in order to understand the forces that had shaped the current ones, even if only in reaction, to create a foundation for the future. I announced we'd be educating both ourselves and the public with menus to "celebrate a great master, a great pupil, and their followers." The "master" was Escoffier, the "pupil" Olney, the "followers" the young French Turks Paul Bocuse, Michel Guérard, and the Troisgros. Then I became caught up in the idea of educating the public and expanded the masters to include Carême (1784–1833; "I want order and taste"), Urbain Dubois (1818–1901; "a new order"), Prosper Montagné of *Larousse Gastronomique* (1865—1948; "Miracles? No, simply good food"), and Philéas Gilbert (1857–1934), who had persuaded Escoffier that Montagné was right in a "reform" of the classic cuisine and service. I wrote a two-page history and handed it out to the public and staff.

The regional French food "Curnonsky Week" at Panisse two years before had been a huge success and resulted in our first featured magazine article. But the roar of success from the Escoffier week—five days of my adapting menus from *Le Guide Culinaire* and *Ma Cuisine,* with a menu printed in side-by-side French and English—spread the word of what was happening at Panisse far and wide. Darrell Corti sent us a funeral wreath and a note that said there was nowhere to go except down after this little death moment of success.

That week was followed by two of the Olney menus, ending with one from Olney's Paris teacher, Georges Garin, that included a duck boned through the neck and left in one piece so it could be presented whole but sliced right through.

There remained one region: our own.

I was encouraged to take on America by an act of daring at the Four Seasons in March 1976, the "First Annual California Vintners Barrel Tasting Dinner." The menu was in English, with French terms only for those now accepted in American grand dining.

The dinner started with Snapper Tartare and continued with several more dishes including Quenelles of Shad, Velouté of Crayfish, Spring Chicken in Joseph Phelps Riesling, Emincé of Young Rabbit, and Essence of Fennel. The wines were Wente, Chateau St.-Jean, Freemark Abbey, Parducci, Mirassou, Phelps, and Beaulieu for these courses. The menu seemed wonderfully way over the top, but the language was elegantly restrained, a perfect combination. I wondered if any of the diners knew just how New York it was, in the Astor and Diamond Jim Brady grand tradition of twenty or so courses.

AMERICA'S SWITCHING POINT

I loved the daring of this menu and now wanted to have our own new region at Panisse. My menu, in English, was a celebration of our new sense of place, of where we lived and ate.

The Northern California Regional Dinner
October 7, 1976

Spenger's Tomales Bay Bluepoint Oysters on Ice
Cream of Fresh Corn Soup, Mendocino Style, with Crayfish Butter
Big Sur Garrapata Creek Smoked Trout Steamed over California
Bay Leaves
Monterey Bay Prawns Sautéed with Garlic, Parsley, and Butter
Preserved California Geese from Sebastopol
Vela Dry Monterey Jack Cheese from Sonoma
Fresh Caramelized Figs, Walnuts, Almonds, and Mountain Pears
from the San Francisco Farmers' Market

In his *The Last Days of Haute Cuisine: America's Culinary Revolution,* Patric Kuh predicted that this night at Panisse "would be one of the great switching points in American gastronomy."

I didn't have such high-flying sentiments then. I was trying only to finish the year and then do great things in the next and final year of my stint and ownership at Chez Panisse. To go out with a bang and no whimper. With only three months to go in 1977 I amused myself with a series of menus to amuse everyone else: one for the "Society of Grand Stomachs," one "For the Spirit," a "Black and White," and some old favorites that spanned a century or so.

The menu on what was meant to be my last night, New Year's Eve, 1977–78, was ambitious. Paul Bocuse's famous Élysée Palace truffle soup, roast fresh wild mushroom stuffed quail on a bed of watercress, California cheese, chocolate cake with in-house nougat ice cream, our bonbons, and a croquembouche made to order for every table (to keep the profiteroles crisp), all for twenty-five dollars per person.

At the end of the evening I was still making one-and two-foot towers of pastry-cream-filled profiteroles stuck together with hot caramel. I remember laughing bitterly at the irony that I should have my arms and hands burned by the hot caramel in order to fix this most festive of French desserts when American chocolate cake would have done just as well. My French-American schizophrenia was dead after that night, well gone by the time the burn scars had healed. But I did return once more to cooking at Panisse.

THE FINAL BOW

At the end of 1978, after I had worked at Big Sur's Ventana Inn for six months (much more about that later) and with Richard Olney at Time-Life Books in London, I took over from the chef Jean-Pierre Moullé. Alice wanted to take the last three months off and did not trust the kitchen team headed by Jean-Pierre to hold the fort, especially when she heard that Beard would be coming back after Christmas. The previous nine months of dishes had been pretty much drawn from my old menus, with more Richard Olney menus and an-other Alice B. Toklas dinner. Alice's menus had been ones like this one, later included in the 1982 Panisse cookbook: "Huîtres natives, crepes bretonnes, porc braise au cidre, salade ou fromages, fruits." Right back to France as the culinary region for Chez Panisse, leaving California as a memory. The menus she left me with to start off the ninety days' absence were "The Best of Chez Panisse." It was familiar territory, so I left most of the work to Jean-Pierre and the others while I busied myself trying to launch an American restaurant in San Francisco. I thought to write the last few weeks of menus and go out, again, with a bang.

There was a bit of tension in the kitchen, however, since I was there for no particular reason other than to soothe Alice's nerves. Sous chef Michel Troisgros wanted to show the latest *beurre blanc*; Mark Miller was inclined to think he knew everything already; and Fritz Streiff had never forgiven me for not showing enough sympathy when, during an important wine tour with Olney and a group of American journalists, he returned to our hotel room in Strasbourg with a bloody nose, having been attacked in a public men's room. Only Jean-Pierre was his usual steady as a rock.

After the Best of Chez Panisse menus were finished, I did a week in honor of cooks who had influenced Panisse menus the most: "Richard Olney, Prosper Montagné, Auguste Escoffier, Elizabeth David, and My Russian Uncle." Then, since Alice was now back, I asked the team to each take a night for the last week of the year and write their own menu. They all had so much difficulty deciding what to cook that I took over their menus. My Saturday night menu:

Fresh Select Tomales Bay Oysters on Ice with Lemon and Pernod
Poached Fresh Sturgeon with Caviar Butter
Capon Stuffed under the Skin with Truffles Lucien Tendret
(homage to Alexandre Dumaine)
Crepes Suzettes in the Original Manner of Auguste Escoffier at the
Carlton Hotel in London

What would be my very last Chez Panisse menu coincided with Beard's visit: "The Orlando Dinner: Following the Last Hundred Years," a four-course affair with Carême (ragout of vegetables in a puff pastry, which he called "Moderne"); Escoffier (his oyster "Favorites" with black truffles); Point and Dumaine (white veal loin with cream, truffles, and fresh noodles); and then "New and Future" (fresh tropical fruit with creamed chilled papaya yogurt and fresh macadamia nuts). But I never got to do it. When Alice returned and saw that Beard was coming to dinner on December 27, 1978, she condoned a palace revolt. She said that the chefs wanted to cook for Beard by themselves. And with a different menu. They wanted the usual duck.

I saw Jim at his hotel as usual that morning, and told him I would not be cooking. "I guess they don't want me to know you have been holding their hands." He giggled.

"Do you think I should force the issue?" I asked him.

"Jeremiah, you have already done that. If I were you I wouldn't ever go back. You should have never agreed to fill in for Alice in the first place."

The next morning he called me early.

"Well, that was god-awful," he bellowed, with just a tinge of accusation, as if it had been my fault.

"The duck was inedible," he said, then went on to scold me for every dish as if I had been there cooking it. "At least that reviewer Merrill Shindler said that the public noticed your food when Alice was gone, even if she called you 'oft-crazed.' But don't do it again."

I went to his room to kiss and make up, and then went home to reread Alice's farewell letter, which she'd written on a piece of yellow lined paper.

THE NEW EMPEROR'S CLOTHES

"Dear Jeremiah," it started, and then expressed how hard it was for Alice to accept the fact that I wanted to leave Chez Panisse. She went on to write that our relationship and the restaurant would never be so vital after I left.

I would not go so far to say, like Ford Madox Ford, that "there is no man who loves a woman that does not desire to come to her for the renewal of his courage, for the cutting asunder of his difficulties," but Alice had done some of that for me originally. Now this private Alice showed it was the same for her still.

But the public Alice after I left Panisse had another face. By my last year she had already begun circumspection with the press, editing where credit was due in the kitchen and for the success of the business. In 1978 I felt that if that was what she needed to do, so be it. What harm could it do to let her have the limelight? After all, we had been equal owners, and I had always given her credit and told her when photographers would be around, a gesture she did not return. I knew that there was plenty of room for everyone. But within the next few years I was beginning to be a bit edgy about the extent of her editing.

In interviews she said she was now the chef at Chez Panisse, and taking on the task of "flying in the face of old, conservative menus." Linda Guenzel, who wrote *The Chez Panisse Menu Cookbook,* wondered with me over the telephone about that comment, and agreed it was pretty funny thinking the Dalí menus and their leg of lamb "drogue et sodomisé" could be considered conservative. But Alice believed in her role so much that when an interviewer in a Bay Area publication wrote that Jean-Pierre Moullé was the head chef (he was), Alice called me asking me to fire him. "How could he say he is the chef?" she asked. I told her he was, and that I couldn't fire him even if I wanted to. I hadn't been his boss in months.

The press began to believe Alice totally. But later, when they said that the food and perhaps Alice were tired, that there were too many fingers in the pie, that Panisse was now just a case of the emperor's new clothes, Alice described herself not as the chef but as the "orchestrator." She lamented that it was very difficult to be so successful "and not have people upset."

When Jean-Pierre Moullé had gone back to France, and Bay Area restaurant critic Robert Finigan wrote in 1983 that dishes poorly executed and badly served were coming out of the cafe and main dining room with alarming frequency, Alice said he was nitpicking and just looking for something to write about.

The general press feeling was that Panisse had lost it. One article said that even though Alice wanted a one-star restaurant, by 1983 it had no stars at all.

But by 2001, the thirtieth anniversary party was a national event, lauded by everyone. Reading all those accounts of the party, I thought Alice could replace all those little lettuces in her arms with both arms full of awards—and sit back for a well-earned rest.

Paul McCartney summed up our relationship when talking in 2001 on American TV about his own with John Lennon: "We had a war in the newspapers."

CHAPTER 13

FROM DELMONICO'S TO DADDY BEARD

"Dear Jeremiah Tower," is how my second letter of employment read. "Your salary will be $22,000 gross . . . and the starting date will be July 15, 1977."

The Ventana Inn in Big Sur was a mess. Had I known how much, I would not have taken the job. But in that halcyon beginning, both the general manager, Lee Ivey, and I thought that a great American restaurant in the middle of several hundred California coastal acres—a wilderness of frozen vegetables and chefs salads—would bring us national attention and fill up the inn.

So I reread Beard's massive *American Cookery* and set out to write the Great American Menu.

THE GREAT AMERICAN MENU

I dug out plans for a fruit and vegetable garden I had made in the late 1960s on the farm in Prides Crossing, Massachusetts, then looked my collection of American menus. The first I found was from the September 1959 "Southern Pacific Special Train" that took "Nikita Khrushchev and Mrs. Kruscheva" from Los Angeles to San Francisco: Caviar Frappé, Omelet with Walnut Jelly, Strip of Bacon, Fried Young Chicken, White Wine-Flavored Au Sec [*sic*], and so on. No wonder there was a Cold War! This was boarding school food, not what I knew America could do better, and a long cry from America's first luxury train and its dining car, the Delmonico. I looked at a menu that René

Verdon, chef for the Kennedys, had given me from the 1962 White House. The language was compromised French, like "Pommes Chipp," but then I remembered the Kennedys and the day I was drinking Jack Daniel's in my Boston "Champagne Palace" when Jack was shot, and put the menu aside.

Perhaps further back in the past was the clue to the future. A 1936 dinner menu from Yosemite's Ahwahnee Hotel began with the usual appetizer, a flat glass dish of celery and olives, as well as the ubiquitous first course, Grapefruit with Honey, broiled or not. Then the standard prime rib "au jus," Virginia ham, "Broiled Half Spring Chicken," and "Spiced Blue Plums." It was a September menu with no hint of seasonality, so I put that aside as well.

A menu from the San Francisco Western Women's Club in the midst of prewar rationing seemed more promising, though not with "Lemon Ring Salad with Seedless Grapes and Stuffed Figs," which reminded me too much of my New England grandmother and her grape peeling. But "Sliced Avocado, French Dressing, Crab and Grapefruit Louis" seemed likely to please the rich ladies of Carmel and the Pebble Beach Club, and "Broiled Sweetbread au Beurre Noir, Crisp Bacon" would please the serious eaters.

A late 1930s souvenir menu from the SS *Morazan* of the Standard Fruit & Steamship Company (with my mother and sister aboard) encouraged me more with its Calf's Brains Vinaigrette and Sauté of Lamb Kidneys. But it was a 1961 menu from the Montecito Room at the Clift hotel in San Francisco that sealed my determination to update the future with a bit of grace from the past. The food was pointedly seasonal, "Fresh Cracked Crab Now in Season," and not a French word in sight. It included even "Grand Central Station Oyster Stew" ($1.75), for which I had always made a pilgrimage every time I visited New York. On the back it invited diners, "Mail this menu to a friend," and paid the postage. An eminently stealable idea.

That was the past. Now I had to look around at the present. When Cecilia Chiang, America's greatest Chinese restauratrice, told me that momentous things were afoot in Los Angeles, I knew I had to take the tour. It was early 1977, and her itinerary listed her new Mandarin, Mr. Chow, Le St. Germain, La Scala Boutique, Rex, Le Bistro, the Palm, Le Restaurant, L'Ermitage, Chaya, and Michael's in Santa Monica. The black-and-white decor at Mr. Chow's was daring; Rex was all homage to Art Deco; the Palm was interesting, but couldn't hold a candle to New York steak houses; there was nothing new about the Italians; and the French restaurants were new only in that their owners were young, ambitious, and of a generation not quagmired in preconceptions. What were new, and already resonating with the drumbeat of revolution, were the restaurants created by young Americans steeped in the traditions of France yet just beginning to express their California background and lifestyle in food, attitude, and decor.

The three restaurants that in the late seventies gave birth to the "California" look were the West Beach Cafe in Venice, Michael Roberts's Trumps, and Michael McCarty's Michael's in Santa Monica. The first was a single room, its bar featuring glass shelves that held fifty single-malt whiskeys and cognacs. It took my breath away, then breathed into me the courage to banish red plush "serious restaurant" forever. I loved the irony that the most avant-garde and trendsetting "first" hailed from that roller-skating little beach town named after an Italian city. I loved even more the stark white concrete decor that changed every few months depending on the arrangement of the sand sculpture around the dining room cornice. Sitting at its concrete bar waiting for my lunch guests to arrive, I felt immediately that this was going to be the new restaurant establishment look.

Trumps was pure Michael Roberts, insanely individual, almost uncomfortable in its concrete bunker style of cheeky chic, its menu in the new California colors of white and beige, ferociously spare in its English ("cold lobster pesto," or "grilled swordfish"), the whole place daring in everything from its lack of flourish to its new Italian glassware.

Michael's food was basically French bistro, but the interior and exterior were a new version of Mediterranean (Roger Vergé's Moulin de Mougins) that was a whole new California style. At my first lunch, I had a grilled chicken with pommes frites and watercress that was the perfect spirit of French bistro cooking, but better than most in France could do it. The chef was the young, bushy-haired American Jonathan Waxman. Out front was Michael McCarty, in azure tie, slicked-back hair, and Susan Bennis–Warren Edwards ocelot loafer-slippers. The waiters, the umbrellas in the open garden, the curtains, the walls, the tablecloths, were the color of Michael's suit—off-white toward cream. We sat at a garden table. Marion Cunningham was along and chattered away, but I could barely talk. Cecilia knew why: I was choked up by seeing and sitting in the future. These were the Young Turks of the moment.

I knew what I had to do, but jobless, first I had to make enough money to eat.

ON A HILL IN PROVENCE

Richard Olney had written that he'd been hired for a Time-Life series called *The Good Cook*. The twenty volumes were to be heavily illustrated with how-to photo spreads, and to keep the costs down the recipes had to have been previously published and in the public domain. That meant surfing the last four centuries of cookbooks for material. The French and Italian recipes had to be translated, and all the recipes had to be usably formulated: Would I come to the South of France, look after his house whenever he was in London, and translate the old texts? I called him when the Ventana negotiations bogged down, and by April I was living with Richard, surrounded by dictionaries, lexicons, chickens, and an old Corona typewriter.

While translating old French cookbooks into English in his little farmhouse in Provence, I reveled in the local ingredients from the markets and the garden, cooked, ate out, and continued to plan the second great American seasonal menu. The first had been the Four Seasons' in New York in 1959. So when I took a day off for lunch at Roger Vergé's Michelin three-star Moulin de Mougins, it was one thirty on a boiling hot French Riviera Sunday. I was with my great Harvard College friend, John Sanger, and after some cool white wine we stared at the huge menu card and felt ill, amazed at the lack of attention to season. It was, in effect, a dinner menu for February. Was there nothing light, cold, refreshing, we asked? The waiters stared. Not even a salad? *Non.* John and I shared a grilled lobster because it was the closest thing to something cold. A chicken and foie gras terrine was superb—but foie gras should be outlawed in the South from May to September. After seeing the bill of $140 for two, I could not blame the poodle at the next table for biting the waiter when he served it a $40 lobster salad under the table.

The next morning, back at Richard's house on the Solliès-Toucas hill, despite the insanity of the Mougins chefs putting sugar in their sauces, I felt unexpectedly nostalgic for the restaurant business. Since rumors were afoot that Richard was up to something and, for the first time in his life, in the chips, a flurry of the famous came through the little house on the hill an hour from Toulon. Naomi Barry, at the top of her form in *Gourmet* and the *Herald Tribune,* told me over a dinner of zucchini flowers stuffed with green fresh almonds, and the first bottle of Cheval-Blanc 1948, that I should go to New York to find my fortune. A week later the collector Mary Guggenheim, with the writers Édouard Roditi and Philippe Jullian, suggested Paris. The novelist Sybille Bedford, over several bottles of Krug, said I should try London. Over a lunch of oysters and "pourpres," Michael James of Robert Mondavi Cooking School fame and Julia Child's *Mastering the Art of French Cooking* coauthor Simone "Simca" Beck said nothing that wasn't petulant. Julia was without any advice at all. I wrote the general manager of Ventana and said that I was hot, tired, and mentally exhausted after two days of Simca, Richard, Julia Child, English writers, unbelievable Côte d'Azur rich lesbians, and U.S. Cuisinart salesmen, but ready to return. Then Richard said I should forget the whole terrible nonsense of running a restaurant and live with him. I said I might have if I were not already in a relationship with Gregg, whom I was desperate to get back to. I was going back to California and to Gregg. "First," Richard said over the phone from London, "join me here in London, meet the Time-Life editors, and apply for the job of creating *The Good Cook* with me."

LONDON'S GOOD COOK

In London, my pal Rudolf Nureyev said I should live with a dancer, which was the only sane if impossible advice I received until Elizabeth David advised me to have another glass of white wine. "Oh dear," she said, "oh dear," her voice trailing off into memories of when she was young and beautiful. "If you must" (go back to restaurants), she went on, "let's go and look at Boulestin's. Perhaps you could revive that. And the original Dufy's murals, even if a bit faded, are very pretty."

I have hardly ever been as happy as when having lunch with Elizabeth. Not so much because of the restaurants of choice, in which anything could go wrong and the hours could be filled with more "Oh dears" than eating, but because the conversations, which would come to life after the second glass of wine and continue until she'd called it quits in her Chelsea kitchen at around seven in the evening, were spectacular.

Mention of James Beard elicited two further "oh dears" before a long pause and the observation, "He could be very sweet, but what about all those rather louche boys?" Certainly there had been enough queens in her life—that was not the point. It was more about Jim's scholarship: could he really concentrate on the culinary matters at hand, she wondered, while obsessing about rent (as she saw them) boys? Was there perhaps just too much of Oscar in Beard?

Of Alice she said, "She *does* mean well," while wondering aloud why, if Alice regarded her as the first inspiration for Chez Panisse, she'd never actually bothered to contact her? But Elizabeth was flattered that someone should pay her such homage for so long. She was far from ungrateful, and a couple of years later, while visiting her friend Gerald Asher, the wine writer for *Gourmet* magazine, in San Francisco, she met Alice and became very fond of her.

Before Elizabeth came to know Richard Olney well, his name would provoke an "Oh dear" and a very long silence. In the beginning she thought Richard a bit bombastic and a snob about wines. She hated his restaurant scenes, when invariably he would call the waiter over and ask him to ice down the red wine. One Sunday summer afternoon in the London Ritz dining room it was a 1947 Cheval-Blanc. He was quite right to, since its temperature was of the too-warm dining room rather than hotel's cellar. Later, when the great wines flowed and flowed, she became more tolerant, but did stop going to restaurants with him and insisted we cook for her at our apartment on London's Conduit Street, across from Hermès.

After a long Saturday lunch at that flat, I would take Elizabeth home at five and we would dig into quite a lot of Chablis to reestablish her sense of reality. Both of us would feel a tiny bit guilty as I got up to open the third bottle, but Elizabeth would inevitably sigh, "Well, if we must." Then we would continue talking about whatever latest scholarship possessed her. Perhaps how the Romans transported ice to chill their creams, and did I know anything about New England icehouses? Did Richard as a boy really have chilled oysters brought in by train as late as May in Marathon, Iowa?

I adored her.

It was time to go only when we both got teary-eyed over some past and improperly forgotten glory—such as restaurant service in the fifties, or how a real sole Colbert or côtelette Milanese should be cooked. Then she would wipe away the ever-rebellious strands of wispy gray hair, her Garboesque former beauty now glorious only in its suggestions of past magnificence, and lift to my face her robin's egg blue eyes, now clouding over with fatigue and old age. As I kissed her good night, my heart would break at the delicious sadness of her brilliant mind in a body so gracefully tendered into frailty.

Back in Richard's house in France, alone and consoled with a twenty-year-old Côte Rotie and whole fat-encased lamb kidneys, flavored with wild thyme from the Provencal hillside above the house, and cooked very slowly in earthenware in the embers of the kitchen fire, I thought sadly of the ingredients I had been used to. Nothing in California could match the South of France, and the best was in Southern California. Could I live in Los Angeles? I thought not.

The next morning, over a plate of Tunisian oranges sprinkled with sage-flower sugar, a double cafe au lait, and a baguette tartine slathered with Normandy butter and wild fig jam, I wondered why I would ever leave France. But I wrote a list of food to serve at Ventana, even if we had to grow our own.

Suggestions for a Big Sur Lunch Menu

Virginia ham with California fruits

Smoked local Big Sur trout

A devastating green salad with our own fresh herbs, and herb flowers

"Fruit salads" with sauces like watermelon vinaigrette

BBQ Monterey Bay jumbo prawns

Chicken and pheasant hash

Paso Robles peaches in local red wine

Shad roe on toast

Chicken pie Delmonico

Wild boar, walnut vinaigrette

Scrambled eggs with sweetbreads

Macadamia nut cream pie

Cathy Simon's Blackbottom pie

It was mid-1977, and California was calling. I missed Gregg and had to get back to get on with my life. My French life of old Rhônes, a perfect butcher in the village owned by the "Mouton" sisters, five-dollar white wine made by local priests, original Piaf records at four in the morning as the mistral blew through the terrace's cork-beaded curtains (each cork a memory of a perfect meal), Richard in sweat-soaked and revealing gardening bikinis—none of these could delay my return. Back in Berkeley I packed up Alice's old house where I had lived and filled the car with wine and cat. Gregg and I drove to Big Sur.

BIG SUR'S VENTANA INN

The three of us moved into the little cabin on the highway, the hundred-year-old Pfeiffer homestead, of an original landowning Big Sur family. From the beginning it was filled with the feelings of Big Sur, which, stories of UFOs and ghostly magnetic fields aside, is one of the most magical and spiritual places on earth. No matter what horrors happened up in the restaurant, the mornings on the back porch with my Earl Grey tea in the light of the rising sun reflecting on the honey-colored hills, looking at my usually spooky Abyssinian cat now cross-eyed with contentment, were as happy as any this side of France. If up at the restaurant I felt like a UFO myself, in the cottage I never felt more at home.

My Mexican restaurant staff was a godsend, their *jefe* a dream. But even then I needed help. Ventana's restaurant in the summer was a seven-day-a-week 250-seater, serviced by a three-man cook team. The bad habits that had set in after a long period of neglect could hardly be eradicated by one person. Then there was the U.S. Immigration and Naturalization Service's habit of rushing in at the busiest times and sending the Mexican cooks scattering into the fields below, their white hats high in the air and aprons fluttering after them—all very amusing to the guests, until they figured out the relationship between disappearing cooks and nonappearing food.

In addition to preparing the menus, I oversaw the inn's and the store's baked goods from our shared pastry shop down the hill. This little fiefdom, like the rest of the operation, saw me only as a disturber of the old ways. Nothing I could do would convince the pastry chef to get rid of the cream fillings that needed no refrigeration for months on end. I was desperate. Marion Cunningham, in a break from washing Beard's feet, offered to help. She sent me three ideas on a piece of foolscap paper: rhubarb with *crème anglaise*, a rhubarb ring with strawberries, and baked bananas. The American public then wouldn't touch rhubarb, and I hadn't gone near the smell of cooking bananas since my time on that Italian ship from Australia. Hearing Marion's ideas, Beard snorted, "Well, my dear, she's great at cookies." From then on Marion would be known to us as "Cookie."

I called Panisse and a few friends and begged for help right after I started. To my surprise, everyone showed up, with Alice leading the caravan. Then the sensible ones decamped after a week. Only my old pal and sous chef Willy remained. He had as much disdain as I did for the man who claimed to be the owner, but Willy stayed on.

After one of Pebble Beach's richest women refused anything but chef's salad made with the frozen canned ham loaf and cheese muck that I had inherited from the previous kitchen administration, I had a talk with the general manager. Not from this chef, I told him. But my confidence was shaken. Together we reviewed the rest of my original menu ideas:

Excellent steaks (a ranch connection in Santa Barbara)
All grilling to be done on wood or real charcoal
Vodka in a block of ice—small individual bottles
Aquavit the same way (do our own herring)
All fruit and vegetable juices done to order at the bar
Lillet with champagne
Juleps
Fiuggi water only

I was getting carried away, I told him, so went back to the grilled food:

Roast duck with Big Sur blackberries and green walnuts
California real chicken with Napa Valley olives
Braised beef cheeks finished in the wood oven
Charcoal grilled tuna steaks with our fresh herb butters
Live trout from Garrapata Creek
Oysters out of our tank, on a bed of ice, with our own lemons
Deviled venison ribs
A wonderful boiled dinner, beef, chicken, and duck, vegetables, pork belly, little cornmeal dumplings
Parsnip cakes with watercress salad
Pigs' feet or sheep trotters on johnnycakes
Whole fish grilled over wild fennel branches and rosemary
Smoked Big Sur lamb

Bread and butter pudding with pears
Syllabubs
Turtle Cay bananas in rum with mango ice cream
Tangerine sherbet served in the fruit

"And let's change the menu every two months, and do the breakfasts with everything raised on the property—the honey, the jams, stone-ground flours, Indian cakes. And espresso machines in every room. I realize this is only a list and not menus. It's New American food, and sometimes Californian."

"Let's go for it again," Lee Ivey said. We did, and almost everyone hated the food. I lasted less than a year in 1977.

But there was one menu left in me before I took my American menu on the road again. Beard was in San Francisco, and I invited him down for a dinner in his honor.

A Dinner for James Beard, at Ventana, Big Sur, California
January 7, 1978

Perrier-Jouët "Flower Bottle" 1971
Seafood Service with Crayfish
Paiusnaya Caviar Blini
Consommé of Big Sur Chanterelles
Petaluma Pheasant Salad
Chappellet Chardonnay 1974
Steamed Whole Fresh Périgord Truffles and Potatoes
Chateau Haut-Brion 1970
Wild Herb-Roasted Wisconsin Veal Loin
Chalone Pinot Noir 1971
Fresh & Aged Lafler Canyon Goat Cheeses
Troisgros "Opus Incertum"
Monterey Vineyard Botrytis Sauvignon Blanc 1974
Entrance of the Mandarins
Delamain Très Vieux Cognac du Grande
Champagne Corti Single Vintage Cognac Selections

Among the group of twelve were Alice Waters in Victorian black lace, a black ribbon at her throat holding a gardenia; Marion Cunningham in denim;

an impeccable Cecilia Chiang in Mandarin clothes, pearls, and emeralds; and Darrell Corti in English tweeds. Jim loomed large next to Emile Norman, who, I had told Jim, had introduced me to the glories of drinking great wine, naked, in the countryside of Big Sur.

The tables were set with big glass globes full of water holding goldfish and sprays of cymbidium orchids. The "Entrance of the Mandarins" was an homage to Cecilia Chiang. To the overture of *Coppelia* we wheeled in a live orange tree covered with mandarin oranges hanging from gold wires. The waiters snipped the wires with fruit shears, and presented each guest with an orange filled with a sorbet made from its own juice.

The gesture caught the breath of the guests, and the eyes of Ventana bugged. Now they thought I was truly mad. Later, when I posted the gushing letters of thanks from the famous, Lee and I were heroes.

No letter was as warmly written as the note from Alice.

"I will never forget a single moment," she wrote. She told me that every moment of the meal was unforgettable, and none so much as the moment when Darrell Corti read from my copy of the Lucien Tendret book the story of overindulgent nuns and their craving for crayfish. Alice loved the sea urchins, the taste of the sea in the mussels, and the fact that the caviar on the blini was so thick she could hardly see the little pancakes. She loved the entrance of the mandarin tree, and wondered, looking into what she said were my "sad, Escoffier eyes," what that look was all about.

I hoped Jim Beard would do for Ventana what he had done for Panisse, but we both knew it was too late. The ship had started leaking badly before I got there, and then a few weeks later a fire burned most of the countryside and nearly the inn. As the huge walls of flame approached over the ridgeline, Gregg and I packed, the car engine running, the cat screaming at the prospect of leaving paradise. But the flames stopped on the ridge a few hundred yards above the cottage. When the rains followed the fire and washed out what was left of the village and our supply route from Carmel, the charm of the countryside turned to nightmare, given the inn's nonexistent cash flow and unpaid bank loans.

I knew it was time to go.

Four days later Richard Olney called from London and Time-Life. He could not handle both the photography studio cooking and the writing for *The Good Cook* series now that a book was due every two months. Would I come to London to cook? I felt that travel itch again.

CHAPTER 14

THE GOOD COOK

Richard and I lived in the center of London, above the food photography studio and around the corner from the Time-Life offices on Bond Street. The seven-day schedule was rough but no worse than at a busy restaurant.

At seven every morning we'd review the day's shooting and the next day's writing. At nine I would start cooking in front of the camera and do so until 7 P.M., crawl upstairs to nosh on leftovers, drink some Lynch-Bages '66 until midnight, and plan the next day's shoot. The late-night Scotches were soon relegated to Saturdays devoted to finding and translating more recipes, outlining and writing the next books, and reviewing what we had done the previous week. Sundays, if not devoted to more of the same, meant lunches at the studio with writers, publicists, journalists, and friends. I made sure to put the sexy food on Friday's studio shoot. There's nothing like a little leftover goose or suckling pig with a pumpkin and black truffle gratin for keeping the soul together.

I cooked for all of my London writer heroines, including the very English, large, and wonderful Jane Grigson, whose presence in a room made one feel like taking off for a country cottage and cooking there forever. She was the woman whose book on charcuterie had helped me put Chez Panisse and later Stars on the map. I had been dying to meet her. This lunch as recorded in my notebooks must have come during the making of the "Beef and Veal" volume, since the loin of veal was already roasted. And paid for.

Lunch with Grigsons, Elizabeth David, Sybille Bedford,
Richard Olney, Jill Norman (Penguin Books)
Chez Nous, Conduit Street, London

July 9, 1978

Smoked Salmon
Chablis, "Mont de Milieu" Pic 1975
Cold Loin of Veal Stuffed with Montpelier Butter
Château La Pointe 1971
Château Lafite 1962
Cheddar
Château Rieussec 1975
Gooseberry, Red Currant, and Almond Fools
Château Filhot 1969

It must have been the superb Sauternes, because somewhere at the end of
lunch it was decided that we would all go to Bordeaux for a weekend. After
Richard spent an hour on the phone the arrangements were made and the
Comte and Comtesse de Lur-Salaces invited us to lunch at their Château
d'Yquem. Within days Richard and I were off to France with Sybille Bedford
and the ex-wife of the director John Huston. Elizabeth did not go, thinking
that more than two on the road was too much. The Yquem lunch lived in
all our memories for all the obvious reasons, but two stood out: the taste of
Sauternes with a crayfish sauce and the subsequent story of the Sauternes
dinner at Panisse a few years before; and the red wine served in a plain carafe in the middle of the table but never offered. For years afterward we all
wondered what one of the greatest men in the white wine business would
offer for red wine in Bordeaux. I was restrained from asking by Richard, so
we never found out.

We started the meal with Pommery & Greno champagne, a very old-
fashioned gesture.

Lunch at Chateau d'Yquem
Filets de Sole au Coulis d'Écrevisse
Château de Fargues 1970
Caneton Farcis

Vin Rouge en Carafe
Jardinière de Legumes
Fromages
Château d'Yquem 1969
Frangipane
Château d'Yquem 1937

The frangipane was a puff pastry stuffed with almond butter cream. Perfect with the 1969 d'Yquem, which, though not as famous as the '67, had more guts and held up to the cooked flavors of the puff pastry. The 1937 seemed older than expected with a very deep color, but it was still bright. "Polite" and "round" were the words the others used. For me it was almost too polite. But it did have the infinity of a great Yquem.

After a tour of Latour, a tasting at Mouton with every wine from 1971 to 1976, and a lunch with the director of Lafite, it was back to London. I was reminded again how magnificent it is to taste wines that have never left the places they were born. Then my sister, Mary, rang from San Francisco with two pieces of news. One was a devastating closure of the past; the other blew open the future. My mother had just died and Mary had found a site for my new restaurant.

I was devastated that I would never share with my mother a grand hotel suite overlooking the Quirinale Palace, the Mount Lavinia beach in Ceylon, or see her face seized in frozen politesse when a young plover was brought to the table at London's Connaught hotel smelling more like ripe Pont L'Evêque than perfect game. The huge and great parties in Sydney with people dancing until dawn after staggering buffets, wonderlands of fresh pineapple, shops full of rubies and Egyptian gold necklaces, deep-carpeted Roman couture houses, and sea-urchin-filled seafood restaurants floating on the then clean Bay of Naples. My mother had shown me how to live.

CHAPTER 15

ON THE STAIRS TO STARS

Back in San Francisco I went to see the site, that of a very run-down restaurant called Bacchini's in the scary Civic Center part of town that only we believed would be great again. The owner of the space was polite, if skeptical because I wasn't Italian, and was, he seemed to think, too young to be taken seriously. Never mind that when I walked into the restaurant on its last day of business, it was so dark after the strong California sun outside that I tripped over the potted plants and fell into a jungle of plastic leaves and fronds. As I picked myself off the floor, a covey of Sicilian "businessmen" rolled off their bar stools and turned to me, eyes rock still. The only noise in the vast room was the sound of the owner's artificial leg scraping against the once-plush carpet, now slick with decades of grime. No expense had been spared when the restaurant was built in 1961, but it took a starry-eyed optimist to see even a trace of that grandeur now.

Yet I was breathless, and not just from the air, which hadn't been clean-filtered in twenty years. It was the perfection of the setting. When my eyes grew used to the dark interior, I saw not the swarms of cockroaches eating the grease in the kitchen or the dirt-encrusted walls, but a perfect stage setting for a grand American brasserie. I envisioned a place evoking the staying power of Delmonico's and Rector's, the food of Le Pavillon, and the ease and comfort of San Francisco mahogany-lined restaurants like Jack's, Sam's, and Tadich, but with new air tinged with the cordite smell of the California food revolution. I saw it all as I dreamed of how to make again the powerful synergy between restaurants and freshly harvested ingredients, just as Delmonico's had done with its own truck garden in New Jersey in the nineteenth century.

I signed an option on the lease to lock it up for the six months it would take to get money and get it going. Two years of wooing, gaining, and losing investors in places as far-flung as Alexandria, Virginia, New York, Boston, and Florida followed. Wherever I went I asked for money. I took any job that came along, continuing my stint with the *Good Cook* series. Along the road I gave parties for Eartha Kitt and Geoffrey Holder's rich friends and sponsors, for the younger sons of mainland Chinese warlords laundering money in the restaurant business, and for anyone else. To pay for the lunches and dinners, I said yes to any invitation to do cooking classes. The most lucrative were at Carol Steele's cookware store in Scottsdale, Arizona; the most fun with the bored of New York in Nantucket; and the best with Ken Hom in Berkeley.

"EAST MEETS WEST" IN HOT FUSION

In 1978 Ken Hom was a long way from the *Independent* magazine's 2001 description of him as "a Buddhist monk in Gucci shoes." He was no monk, not by a long shot, and was barely getting by, totally unrecognized as one of the best cooks in America.

To make ends meet, he gave cooking lessons in his Berkeley house. We used to cook together, his Franco-Chinese and my Franco-Californian food side by side. In 1977 he began teaching at the California Culinary Academy, from where some pupils went on to great success, among them Chicago's famous chef Charlie Trotter. Ken was a Chinese traditionalist, "fresh" meaning killing chickens in the kitchen, but a modernist as he combined other cuisines' principles with his Chinese. In 1979, when Belle Rhodes, involved in public relations for Robert Mondavi and Joseph Phelps wineries, suggested that we do some classes together in Napa, we agreed with enthusiasm.

She named the four days "East Meets West," an oft-used phrase now, but a first and original at the time. She invited local and national press, a few bankers (for my new-restaurant fund-raising), cooks from Panisse, and the cream of Napa Valley "society."

The first dish started off as planned, but then I coveted Ken's Asian ingredients. And Ken coveted my Western ingredients right back. I took some fermented Chinese black beans for the wilted curly endive salad. He took my fresh herbs, vegetable purees, and extra-virgin olive oil. By the end of the first day, we were filching each other's mise en place at a furious rate, and the students were as fascinated as we were.

The second-day menu morphed into cooking that no one had seen before, unless one had been to Richard Wing's surreal Imperial Dynasty in the Central Valley town of Hanford, where the menu featured things like tripe consommé garnished with various glandular parts of slaughtered-to-order Chinese frogs. Ken and I kept to the dishes on our list, but the printed recipes were virtually useless except to see the variations on our themes.

Fish and Shellfish

Jeremiah	Ken
Fish Stew with Artichokes	*Sweet and Sour Cod with Fruit*
Sea Urchin Soufflé	*Scallion Steamed Fish*
Bouillabaisse	*Sizzling Rice Shrimp*
Zephyrs of Perale Sole	*Blue Crabs*

My bouillabaisse turned into a fish stew with whatever was on the table, adding a flourish of Ken's sizzling shrimp. Ken set my artichokes and foie gras on his steamed fish, and some of the strawberries ended up in the sweet and sour cod. And so on it went. The next day he put his squab in puff pastry and I found a use for his noodle cakes. At the end of the last class, Belle said, "Jeremiah, something amazing happened here. Something really has now changed forever."

One student spoke for all: "There was a time when I would have been totally intimidated because I didn't have a specific recipe to follow. Now it's just a pleasure to watch them work and learn new rules." The *San Francisco Examiner*'s Harvey Steiman opened his account with a boxing ring metaphor, with Ken in one corner and me in the other: "At the sound of the bell, Tower starts applying the techniques of Carême, Escoffier, and the French housewife. Hom uses the centuries-old methods of Chinese chefs—and housewives." It was an exploration of a spur-of-the-moment "market-basket" approach to cooking and menu making. In "the battle of the ducks, no winner was declared."

FINDING MY TEAM

My foie gras was not covered by our rather minimal food budget, so after the Napa event I was broke again. In the nick of time came a call from my friend Ron Batori, dean of the California Culinary Academy. Would I provide an antidote to their usual European classical recipes and worn-out techniques? I would have total freedom. Ken had horrified the students by blowing up chickens' butts before killing them in the open kitchen. After that precedent, he said, anything goes.

After I toured the academy's kitchens, I called Ron back, shocked by all the carts piled high with five-gallon tins of Maggi stock and powdered sauce bases, as well as the frightening canapés covered with industrial gelatin, made Tuesday to be served on Friday. What was that about? I told him the air was thick as a skunk's den with old-guard Swiss and German professional jealousy and suspicion when I walked in. Perhaps, I said, he didn't want me making trouble.

"That is exactly what I do want," he said. "Just don't kill any chickens!"

As far as I knew, the students were satisfied with their old Swiss masters and their mummified canapés. An obvious place to find out was to start with ingredients and their benchmarks. In the first class I explained that new techniques in air transportation guaranteed arrival in the marketplace in good condition, and that these changes were a challenge to completely rethink the concepts of "fresh," "local," and "quality." Fresh fish in San Francisco had always meant from the bay or outside the Golden Gate. Now, I told them, after local storms keep the boats at sea, that fish is three days old. At that same time, Norwegian farm salmon could be only eighteen hours from their water to our kitchens. So "quality" had new boundaries now that "local" did not now always mean "fresh."

I took them to a new San Francisco import company that with my encouragement was now bringing in fresh European ingredients such as mascarpone, buffalo milk mozzarella, and real Reggiano Parmesan. Next were blind tastings of beer, rum, chocolate, whiskey, cheese, pepper, coffee, bottled water, dried meat, smoked fish, and every possible oil coming in from France, Spain, and Italy. Each student had a form on which to grade each product according to appearance, color, odor, taste, and overall quality. All were astonished by the results. Before we blind-tasted the beers, I asked them to name their favorite. "Budweiser!" came the resounding cheer. Not when they couldn't see the label. Much to their horror, 85 percent preferred the Czech Pilsner Urquell and put Bud last.

At Panisse I showed them dessert wines and taught them that the dessert must always be less sweet than the wine served with it if the wine is not to taste sour. With Darrell Corti we tasted single-cask cognac and whiskies against blended ones. With the *Chez Panisse Menu Cookbook*'s author, Linda Guenzel, we tasted chocolate. That became the ultimate lesson in quality and why one shouldn't mind paying more for it. The differences between Hershey's and Lindt was profound. The Swiss chocolate was "conched" 40 percent more than its American counterpart, making it smoother, richer, and much more satisfying. And clearly worth the extra cost. When the students found they could easily taste the difference between a mass-produced product and a hand-crafted one, they were willing to accept that excellence is not just a personal "matter of taste," that one can commonly perceive and measure a standard that can be agreed upon as "the best."

Now that we were ready to cook I imported the ingredients I needed, all new to the commercial marketplace: extra-virgin olive oil, nut and grape seed oils, cured meats like bündnerfleisch, gravlax, and smoked salmon, real Roquefort, goat and Val d'Aosta fontina cheeses, red and green peppercorns and real saffron, fresh herbs, salad greens, white veal, haricots verts, snow and snap peas, radicchio and Treviso, American caviars, fresh paprika, Belgian endive, fresh ginger, fresh Asian vegetables and spices, ripe heirloom-variety tomatoes, Jerusalem artichokes, sherry and balsamic vinegars, fresh tuna, yellow bell peppers, foie gras, wild mushrooms, truffles, or fresh and great quality dried pasta. With these ingredients in hand at the beginning of 1980 we cooked the following dishes for the public at the academy's restaurant:

1980 California Culinary Academy

Salmon tartare with deep fried salmon skin and chive flowers
Tricolored bell pepper salad with crayfish sauce and tails

Baby green bean salad with Treviso, whitefish and steelhead caviars
Buckwheat pasta with goat cheese and onion flowers
Bayonne ham with ripe farmers' market figs
Provimi veal carpaccio with fresh ginger, salted anchovies, and Key limes
Grilled squab with fresh raspberry vinegar
Sole "fingers" with Muscat Beaumes-de-Venise
Salmon stew with Szechuan pepper, artichokes, and kombu
Grilled duck with blackberries, cloudberries, blueberries,
and Jerusalem artichokes
Duck with mangoes and fresh lychees
Fresh albacore with Mexican limes, avocados,
and grilled red torpedo onions
Santa Barbara white peach salad with basil and rose peppercorns

Unlike at Ventana, the food we cooked was a big success with the public and, more important for me, with the academy's main benefactor. When I accepted the job I was not unaware that Cyril Magnin was also the Bay Area's richest and most influential man. Would this legendary food lover fall in love with the idea of a great American brasserie? Ron Batori thought so. He made the introduction, and Magnin was taken with the proposal. He especially loved the thought of saving millions in labor costs by using CCA students in the kitchen. I chose twenty of my best students, made them my executives, drew up a staff list, and called the bank with the good news.

Then Cyril Magnin died.

Once more I was staring unwilling bankers in the face.

And more teaching.

FROM UDDER, TO BUTTER, TO CHEESE, TO THE FINAL DISH

In October 2015 I was fascinated to read on Facebook a posting by Randy D. Adler: "I have [Tower's] memoir [but]. . . . so many don't realize how much he contributed to the farm to table/locally sourced movement. His book *California Dish* is must read. . . . You go Jeremiah Tower." But in 1979 I was still looking for a farm.

And fascinated to read a letter to me on the Fourth of July of that year from John Ronsheim, a professor of music at Antioch College in Yellow

Springs, Ohio. "Richard Olney has suggested that I contact you. Finally I got the faculty to accept that I prepare the College for a new program to give a B.F.A. in the Culinary Arts. It will be the first."

It took my breath away to think one could get a degree while working on a farm that provided ingredients for a college dining room: what a departure from the diet of bread-margarine-marmalade at my English boarding school, the chipped beef in flour sauce on Wonder rusks at my New England prep school, and the lime Jell-O with bacon and marshmallows at Harvard!

I knew this Antioch idea could be the beginning of a national awareness about food in all parts of our lives, and I was convinced that school food, no matter how young the students, was the place to start. Since Panisse, America had learned that California no longer meant a Pebble Beach Club Salad of canned peaches and cottage cheese, and the press had trumpeted the idea that the movement had meaning for the whole country and its national culinary identity. Restaurant work no longer needed an apology. After the Young Turks of France found international fame, and soon the young ones in California, it was not much longer a second-class profession. Now it would have a place in serious academic thought as well as being the foundation of training for the trade in grade and high schools all over America. Students could summer intern at Antioch, learning to grow what they cooked and ate.

I called John Ronsheim and told him I had visions of my favorite eighteenth-century architect, Claude-Nicolas Ledoux, who spent his life designing the "ideal town" of Chaux. Perhaps we could have a modest "ideal town" of our own, with working farms where students could track a single ingredient—say, milk, from udder to butter to cheese to the final restaurant dish. Ohio would become just as prolific in perfect ingredients as the Ile-de-France. Perhaps, I went on, we could do everything from reproducing Thomas Jefferson's kitchen garden and vineyards, or Louis XVI's private dining room to teach service, to serving thousands of students three times a day. Even mad John was quiet on the other end of the phone.

"Couldn't we just start with making wine?"

The Antioch staff was scared half to death, but I wrote everyone in the United States, Italy, and France who I thought would be interested enough to raise money, drew up the board of advisers, and created a budget. I set up files on experiments such as the new Picart Snail Factory in Santa Rosa, California, and Aquatic Farms for oysters raised on land in Maui's Waihee Valley.

In February 1980, John's letters to me struggled with questions such as "Does Mimi Sheraton pose a problem?—call Jim Beard." I did. He said she did. "Madeleine Kamman—great response. Has Alice Waters asked Coppola?" At a West Coast meeting, Janet Trefethen gave a dinner and I presented the board of fifty-one I'd recruited, which included Jim Beard (reluctantly), Joseph Baum (founder of Restaurant Associates and the Four Seasons restaurant in New York), Craig Claiborne (*New York Times* restaurant critic), Darrell Corti, Elizabeth David, Sybille Bedford, M. F. K. Fisher, Gael Greene (restaurant critic for *New York* magazine), Pierre Franey (partner with Craig Claiborne), Barbara Kafka (cookbook author and restaurant consultant), Jane Grigson, Robert Mondavi, Richard Olney ("The art of the table will be very much at home with the Humanities, and this program cannot help but rapidly influence and humanize the food of America"), Joseph Phelps (of his Napa winery), James Villas (*Town & Country)*, Chuck Williams (Williams-Sonoma), Hugh Johnson (English wine writer), Cecilia Chiang, and Sri Owen (English cookbook author). Jane Grigson wrote, "I think your idea of connecting the source with the final dish is admirable."

John and I organized the 1980 East Coast Meeting at the "21" Club for the board. The meal was to have been sponsored by the club, but ended up as a two-thousand-dollar tab handed to me by the headwaiter. Now my funds were as exhausted as I was. I told John that we could not keep up the pace and money required to get this off the ground on one coast, let alone two. But the idea had been launched. The Antioch East and West fifty-one-member Culinary Arts Advisory Board evaporated, but it soon reentered existence as the American Institute of Wine & Food, a name that took at least a case of Dick Graff's (founder and chairman of Chalone Vineyard) Chalone chardonnay for a small group to decide whether it should be "food and wine" or "wine and food."

There is a moment in all revolutions when the bureaucrats take over. With Robespierres on the horizon I decided to bow out. I handed over the reins to Dick Graff and Julia Child, both of whom had a great deal more tolerance for such bureaucratic perambulations than I did. And sources of funds.

Dick had the machinery to get a business going, including Chalone's San

Francisco offices and a private Cessna to fly south to meet Julia and the provost of the University of California, Santa Barbara. Julia had convinced the
provost to donate some campus land to the institute near her "winter headquarters." The site we picked smelled of the crude oil spillages just offshore,
but it was free and on the beach. As I enthused about bringing La Jolla's
Scripps Institution of Oceanography into the organization, some of the board
members began to look at me the way John Ronsheim had the year before.
When my negotiations began in earnest in 1978 for a San Francisco restaurant site, I was relieved to be out of the world of food politics and back in the
familiar territory of cooking.

Enough people did stick around to keep the organization alive, especially
the wealthier wineries of Napa Valley, led by Lila Jaeger of Rutherford Hill
Winery. The institute went on to promote and celebrate American gastronomy, and was a necessary first step for two formations: the James Beard Foundation (a center for showcasing emerging chefs in the United States) in New
York, and the Robert Mondavi culinary center in Napa.

SERENDIPITY (AT FIRST)

In 1978, while I was teaching at the California Culinary Academy, Mark
Miller, who had been one of my sous chefs at Panisse, opened the Fourth
Street Grill in Berkeley with the former Panisse hostess Susie Nelson. It was
a smash hit. Heady with success, the pair opened another restaurant up the
road in the old Santa Fe Railroad Station and called it the Santa Fe Bar &
Grill. Another hit at first. It's Bar & Grill name was a bow to traditional San
Francisco restaurants like Tadich and Sam's, but its location was an area more
comfortable for prostitutes and drug dealers from Oakland than for Volvo
drivers from the upper Berkeley hills.

One night right after the opening, I was sitting at the Fourth Street bar
trying out their margaritas and lamenting the paucity of investors for my
restaurant when Susie—whom I had once approached to be part of the new
restaurant but who had grown tired of waiting for me to get the financing—
gave me a lead. "Why not talk to Doyle Moon, our new partner in the Santa
Fe," she said. "He has money and knows the bar business," she added, referring to his once hugely successful Balboa Cafe in San Francisco.

The Balboa was located in the singles bar battleground off Union Street called the "Bermuda Triangle" after so many customers' girlfriends had disappeared into the arms of other men (or women). But now the Balboa had reached a state of neglect where no one cared who disappeared, gone from being packed with singles to being half-empty with people who always would be. I called Doyle Moon. He said if I wanted access to his bankers and credit line, I would have to give the Balboa a quick fix.

THE BERMUDA TRIANGLE

The Balboa Cafe had been one of the first "fern bars" after the legendary Henry Africa's years before, and I found the look and smell of vintage testosterone stuck in dark corners. The food was somehow hamburgers and Iranian food operator. The bar was stale and tired. The "fix" obviously meant freshen, so on the first day, in 1979, I showed up with my car full of flowers. Within an hour I had free-form English "country" arrangements now seen everywhere but then had the few die-hards at the daytime bar immediately proclaiming "sissy" and "faggoty." No worries, I told them, wait till you see what's next! I installed women bartenders ("treason," "queer," "they must be dykes"), white tablecloths on the tables ("too fancy"), and long white aprons on the waiters ("effeminate").

Soon the disapproving bar hounds were gone, replaced by the likes of socialite Ann Getty and her friends eating hamburgers and pasta next to actors, real estate moguls, and restaurant workers on their day off. On any afternoon, you could hear the two or three regulars who refused to decamp giving anyone who'd listen their admiring appraisal of the day's flowers and taking credit for the idea of female bartenders. We'd succeeded.

After nine months, just as everyone was getting bored, things came to a boil across the bay. Doyle and another Balboa partner were owners of half the Santa Fe Bar & Grill. Known to Doyle but not to me, the Santa Fe Bar & Grill was broke as well as under surveillance by the Alcohol Control Board. Oakland dealers were ensconced at the bar drinking free Baileys Irish Cream and selling drugs and firearms. Loss of liquor license, foreclosure, and arrests were imminent.

Within minutes of waring calls from the bank and another from the con-

trol board, Doyle and I were in his new BMW speeding across the Bay Bridge
to Berkeley. My queries about our destination and mission were answered
with uncharacteristic coyness by this Apache in Hugo Boss. When Doyle
pulled off the freeway into University Avenue, on which I had driven for years
to Panisse, my stomach turned. But when he pulled into the parking lot of
the Santa Fe, I knew it was another fixer: save it or kiss the bankers good-bye.

I nearly threw up in the parking lot.

THE SLIM CHANCE

My horror yielded to mixed emotions as soon as I walked in. My fatal attraction to underdog, once-beautiful spaces kicked in. Like that of Black Beauty,
the restaurant's body was racked by neglect and cruelty, but the soul was still
there. I was charmed. Just as I had never been able to resist the allure of a
neglected but once-great garden, I was challenged. Tired and unfiltered air,
walls and carpets stained with grime, peeling paint: all could be easily dealt
with. As could the coke dealers at the bar. They were not like the first rather
jolly dealer at Panisse's third birthday party, who took to my rose champagne
like a fish to water. These guys were grabbing shot glasses of Goldwasser and
Amaretto in hands heavy with gold.

There was no time for pleasantries. The Balboa was making money now
with my makeover, and Crocker Bank had confirmed to Doyle that if I cleaned
up the Santa Fe, we'd get a $350,000 loan for the new restaurant. Crocker was
calling the shots. As we stood in the bar surveying the situation, Doyle told
me Crocker wanted the place redone ready for the Berkeley-Stanford football
game, and its guaranteed cash flow, four days from that moment.

"Get them out of here," I told the bartender, nodding my head toward
the gold.

How had I gotten here, on the end of yet another banker's strings? Every
moneyman I'd ever cooked for had so far told me I had "no track record"—
including the ones who'd wanted special favors at Panisse, or the married
banker staying at Ventana Inn who wanted discretion regarding the young
men in his free suite. That day at the Balboa, thinking of clearing out the
restaurant, was one of life's lonely moments. Would I instead do the healthy
thing and walk out the door? Or stay, following my troublesome preference

for the slim chance? It was midafternoon in a near-empty restaurant: a good time to act, if I was going to. My gut told me I was dealing with the Devil & Company, but I was willing to make that bargain if I could just get on with my own San Francisco restaurant.

"We'll have to close the restaurant now!"

"Fine," said Doyle.

I told the thugs at the bar that the restaurant was now closed. Then I told the staff to be out in ten minutes and to come back the next day to reapply for their jobs. Then I called a locksmith. I called my best students at the academy. I opened a bottle of champagne Grande Dame. Within an hour we had new locks and keys, and my students had assembled. "We have a date with destiny," I told them—a better line than the one I was actually thinking, which was "Welcome to the final circle of Dante's hell."

That was the Tuesday in November before Saturday's game, Berkeley's biggest day. Ideally we would reopen on Friday to catch the first wave of fans.

The next morning at the staff meeting, after an all-night setting, suddenly I couldn't walk—muscle cramping, brought on by the tension of having to come up with the outline of restaurant and bar menu and philosophy. The cooks made a massage table from the bar tables. From there I addressed the wide-eyed new staff.

"WE OPEN IN THREE DAYS"

"And I want to finish what I started at Ventana, continued at the California Culinary Academy, and lay the foundation for a great American brasserie."

"What about the Southwest?" someone piped up. "We have the name 'Santa Fe' and an Indian Santa Fe Superchief logo. Won't the public expect chilies?"

Thank God for my mother, I told them, and all those Sunday morning huevos rancheros and chiles rellenos. If she could, in the thirties, drive from Connecticut to Mexico City with my two older siblings in a Model A Ford, I could conjure up all my childhood Mexican food and barbecues in Australia at my parents' friends' hacienda.

The allusions confused everyone.

For the food, I told them to remember the dinner that Mark Miller had done for the Académie Internationale du Vin and Richard Olney a couple of months earlier at the Chalone Vineyard. That meal, cooked outside and served on white-clothed tables on top of a wilderness mountain, was southwestern-infused yet truly Californian in style, the next generation after my California Regional Dinner of 1976.

"And we," I said, "will create the generation after that."

As for the facilities, they could be surmounted, I told them, feeling a bit like the commander of the fleet in *Sink the Bismarck* who encouraged his staff in the face of impossible odds.

"Is it going to be that bad?" they asked.

I recounted one of our most delirious moments: when my Balboa cooks and some CCA students had prepared an elaborate dinner in San Francisco's de Young museum without any facilities at all. It was a fund-raiser to create the Philharmonia Baroque Orchestra of the West. The museum had promised us a back room and kitchen, then made us work on the floor of a corridor filled with priceless twelfth- to fourteenth-century triptychs. I got the go signal a half hour ahead of schedule, when my cooks were all in the parking lot taking a last-minute break before service. It fell to me to make 250 salads by myself. I was madly tossing the contents of four twenty-quart bowls when I heard a gasp from three cooks who'd just walked in and looked up to see leaves of baby lettuce and rivers of vinaigrette rolling down tens of millions of dollars' worth of Flemish altar paintings.

"Get a towel, say nothing, and plate the fucking salads *now*."

The seventeenth-century dinner was a triumph, and we hadn't, somehow, altered the course of Bay Area art history.

I hoped that this sermon would inspire the staff and give the hosts a sound bite for the public when they came in the door for the first time. But it seemed to be making things worse. Finally my star pupil, Mark Franz, said, "Let's just cook good, simple food, and not make fools of ourselves." That put a lid on my ramblings. Everyone understood and knew what to do.

Lawyers representing other partners showed up the next day, but I told the staff not to bother with them. We had menus to write. And since the reality is always determined by the layout of the kitchen, we set about analyzing the setup, how many people it would allow to cook at one time, and what kind of food we could do in quantity without compromising quality.

CHAPTER 16

RE-CREATING THE GRILL

The kitchen layout was the kind that came from the original owners' initial budget of close to zero: nowhere near enough space to plate cold first courses, and there was an obstacle course to run with the hot ones. This was not going to be pretty. The grill was a monster, six feet long by three feet deep, guzzling twenty-five pounds of mesquite charcoal at a time. If you were slightly crazy and a firebug, you could cook fifteen or twenty orders of fish and meat at once. Steven Vranian was the man to do it, unfazed by multiple burns along his forearm flesh from being sizzled on the grill's front (a sound you could hear over the noise of the kitchen), and sanguine about the .22-caliber bullets that occasionally exploded in the charcoal and shot his way. The waiters became adept at ducking without dropping plates—the knowledge that bullets travel faster than sound perhaps mercifully repressed.

We all felt charmed. Young and untouchable.

There was neither time nor space for advanced sauce making, so we opted for salsas and simple compound butters that took no time to do and could be made at the last minute. Their beauty was that if we ran out of Key limes for a lime-cilantro-cumin butter, there were always tangerines or mandarins or Meyer lemons, dipped in mint oil and rolled around on the grill to toast the oils in the skins before throwing them into the food processor with butter, salt, and chilies or pepper. As for salsas, we started with the fresca of tomatoes, red onion, cilantro, lime juice, olive oil, salt, and sometimes garlic, which was always chopped by hand. When this ran out we'd invent salsas based on whatever was in the walk-in refrigerator and easily assembled.

There was another reason for our reliance on salsas and butters. The majority of the main courses at the Santa Fe were grilled, and it makes no sense to create a crisp skin or surface and then douse it with something that leaves it a soggy mess. So out of one restaurant's necessity came, after the Newport Astor mansion lunch, a national fad. Eventually salsas would be one of the cliches of California cuisine. In 1981 they made total sense.

We never made the Friday evening as planned because I was still on the massage table and the utilities inspectors hadn't signed off. But the day of the big game we did—to great success. Within days the drug dealers had found greener pastures, replaced by the usual free-spending foodies and the critics, including Robert Finigan of the infamous Panisse lamb incident. He'd been about to publish a scathing review (with the restaurant business as soap opera, using an account of the fallout between Mark and Susie), but in the face of the new regime, he changed his mind. "Enter Jeremiah Tower's team," he wrote, "all dressed in chef's whites and fresh from transforming the Balboa Cafe into one of the city's most popular bistros." The Santa Fe, he continued, is "much cheerier now . . . and there is a comfortable air of informal elegance about this place and the seriousness of the kitchen is immediately evident." He praised the smoked Oregon trout and sturgeon, the wild Bélon and Pigeon Point (Sonoma) oysters, the black bean soup and cake, the squab marinated in raspberry vinegar, bay scallops, Rex sole, and other local ingredients. "Tower delights in devising and executing menus like this one, emphasizing freshness of ingredients prepared with that extra twist of inventiveness which distinguishes the great chefs from the useful ones. See to what levels apparently simple conceptions can be taken in the hands of a master."

I was ecstatic that our first review was so positive. But I'd have to spread the word if we were ever to get back over the bay to San Francisco.

MORE AMERICAN CULINARY REGIONS

I had moved from Berkeley to San Francisco in anticipation. One night, early in the Santa Fe era, I was sitting in Gregg's and my Bernal Heights rose and vegetable garden, drinking champagne with my college friend Philip Core. He had just finished his paintings for the restaurant's walls of famous people who'd traveled the Santa Fe Railroad, and had then rendered the likes of Escoffier, Marlene Dietrich, Richard Olney, Gary Cooper, Johnny Hard-On, Clare Boothe Luce, and Truman Capote on my dining room ceiling. He was bored. As we moved from champagne to a bottle of 1927 Taylor from the cellar under a trapdoor in the dining room, he said, "Let's do a TV show. Or a book. We'll call it 'Stars in Your Eyes'"—I guessed from the stars on the room's ceiling— "and it will be all about the food and culinary regions of the Americas. We'll travel around on the Santa Fe Railroad and have them pay for it."

Into the second bottle of Taylor we did an outline, with topics like "Combination of heritages—roots of American eclecticism; Reworking tradition—the bounty of nineteenth-century America; Harvest as menu—the new eclecticism as the garden and market come full circle; European principles established in America; The American outdoors—localization and ease of preparation, the directness of Texas, redefining the frontier." The symbol of the show or book would be a dining car with people looking at a menu while the American landscape speeds by.

I couldn't cope with all this inspired madness while opening the Santa Fe. But he did give me an idea of how to promote the new American Bar & Grill. I would restart the regional dinners we had done at Chez Panisse, but using the culinary regions of America.

I started in March 1983 with a benefit dinner for the American Institute of Wine & Food:

Florida State Dinner
March 1983

Tarpon Isle rum cocktail

Salty dogs

Florida backwoods biscuits

Gulf stone crab claws with Key lime "Old Sour" sauce

Palm Beach crabmeat salad with avocados

Key West conch stew

Roast Appalachicola oysters

Tarpon Springs fish and shellfish soup with salt cod dumplings

Cross Creek French fried eggplant with "Guspachy" sauce

Pompano en papillote

Grilled rum-spiced Gulf shrimp with creamed onions

Turtle Cay bananas with mango ice cream

Guava pecan pie

After the dinner a *Metropolitan Home* editor asked, "Is this really Florida food?"

"No," I replied. "But it should be—and with your help it will be." This dinner was such a hit that we followed it immediately with another at the Santa Fe, this time inspired by memories of my visits to San Antonio spice-vendor friends.

Texas and Spanish America Dinner
April 1983

Grilled Appalachicola oysters with 1883 Catsup
Broiled Spanish onions cowboy-style with BBQ sauce
Gulf shrimp and bonita in escabeche with avocado
Rabbit chili with mole sauce and peppered mangoes
Smoke-grilled red snapper with fresh sea urchin roe sauce
Goat stew with hominy, cilantro salad, and smoky chili sauce
Hot pecan pie with chocolate ice cream

The national press was now paying attention, so when we did a "Michigan and Midwest" dinner, the governor of Michigan actually attended. His presence did nothing to ameliorate the hurt pride of my friends in Napa and Sonoma, who were aghast that I'd do regions of America with no indigenous winemaking. I promised we would do them next. Again.

In an article in late 1982 in San Francisco's *Focus* magazine called "Withstanding the Taste of Time," Liz Lufkin said that "until recently, no one paid much attention to California cooking." Although Spanish Jesuits had planted orchards of pears, peaches, plums, apricots, cherries, and oranges, a variety of anything other than fruit was nonexistent, and the accounts of miners and settlers about California food in the 1830s are famous for their enthusiastic disgust. It made me laugh to read that Liz felt sorry for a priest who "back then lunched on only an ear of corn roasted over coals," as we were making our living to re-create those haunting flavors not interfered with by an over-enthusiastic chef. She went on to say that cooking in California was coming into its own: "Indeed, some think it's a trend that will sweep the country and change the face of American cooking." Six months later, in the spring of 1983, our Newport lunch proved her right.

CHAPTER 17

CALIFORNIA CHANGES AMERICA'S FACE

New American Cuisine, springing out of "California cuisine," might never have been discovered if it weren't for a bunch of pushy French chefs.

In the spring of 1983, the ad agency for Ocean Spray was charged with placing cranberries at the forefront of American gastronomy. Their idea was a weekend headlined "Innovations in Food" for one hundred syndicated food journalists at Beechwood, the Astor mansion in Newport, Rhode Island. The main event would be a dinner showcasing the "innovative sauceless cuisine" of Paris's Guy Savoy, with my crew from the Santa Fe Bar & Grill in Berkeley preparing a little lunch to keep up the strength of the writers for the all-day workshops on culinary trends.

I didn't mind the supporting role. In the three years since Savoy had opened his own Paris restaurant, the New York food press had fallen in love with his originality and dash. I had profound respect for the French and especially for the Young Turks of nouvelle cuisine, as well as for Guy himself.

If it was obvious why Savoy had been invited, it wasn't clear why I had been. Although the two celebrated Jameses of the food world, Beard and Villas, had lavished praise on my cooking at both Chez Panisse and the Santa Fe Bar & Grill, only one restaurant (Panisse) had as yet become a national sensation. But I didn't press the agency for a reason. I was grateful for the opportunity to put the Santa Fe in front of the national food press and, since I had no formal training as a chef, eager to see a master at work.

Beyond that, I could never resist a challenge. I was sure we could do it—I just wasn't sure what "it" would turn out to be. We'd fake it as we went along.

My assignment was to provide a simple California lunch using cranberries. It was an odd request for April, but I could see one of the agency's points: demonstrate that you can cook with cranberries all year. Top it off with a famous French chef including them in three-star Michelin food, and the press would go wild. Perhaps it was just an agency budget waiting to happen. Whatever the reason for the cranberries, I decided to use them to marinate racks of lamb, ignoring the fact that traveling with my crew from San Francisco would make it the most expensive marinade in history.

THE FIRST CHALLENGE

The first challenge was to get the cooks and food to New York from California. What kept me up at night was how to get past the airport check-in with fifteen hundred pounds of food and luggage. Airport check-ins back then were familiar with the demands of first-class traveling socialites with mounded Louis Vuitton hat boxes and toy poodles, but when the five of us arrived pushing a long line of carts filled with coolers and bags of charcoal, we looked like anything but first-class passengers. Airports in 1983 were as yet innocent of chefs and their entourages. Up to that point road shows were the purview of rock bands and circuses. Chefs soon came to resemble both, as only a year later one could see toques on famous chefs in every major airport in the United States, blue and white ice coolers dominating the luggage carousels, and fans lining up for autographs in the passenger lounges. But that morning we were a shock.

The list of our "bags" was staggering: 125 individual California goat cheeses, two hundred grape leaves (in April that was like asking a winery to give up a whole vineyard), five gallons of sauce essences, and twenty-five California lamb loins. Everything was packed in four enormous coolers, one of them full of noisily scratching Bay Area Delta crayfish, another full of fresh coconut ice cream. It was for this trip that I developed an elaborate traveling system: vacuum-packed foods stacked with the blue ice in coolers and, in two huge suitcases on wheels, a massive on-site support system that held everything from cheesecloth to extension cords, food mills to pepper mills, first-aid kits to baling wire and clip-on lights.

The greatest of my nightmares was getting eight fifty-pound bags of mesquite charcoal, whose purpose in life was to spew fine black dust onto everything in its path, on a plane to New York. All that charcoal seemed a bit obsessive even to us, knowing that the chances of finding a foodie in the grim faces behind the ticket counters were less than slim. But mesquite was one of our "innovations," and no mere gate agent was going to stand in the way of our publicizing it. Halfway to the check-in window I saw the agents whispering. The face behind the window in front of us was pure bulldog; at the Westminster Kennel Club, she would have taken best in show. Our eyes locked. "Nothing doing" was her unmistakable look. I could see she was focused on the coolers, no doubt convinced they were full of dry ice that would blow up the plane.

COMBAT

As we both braced for combat, I searched for another window. The staff had seen the bulldog look and were cowering behind their carts. A whispered "Oh shit, no" was all I heard from them. I raised an arm in a full-speed-ahead gesture and then, feeling like Patton in the lead tank, swerved with the team toward the check-in with the long red carpet, crowd-control ropes, and their guard wide-eyed with shock. I remembered that my PR folder had a very complimentary James Villas *Town & Country* article on the Santa Fe Bar & Grill with a full-page color photograph of me. So before the customer relations agent could say a word, I whipped out the photograph and launched into a spiel about "local kids" on a mission to show those easterners how to cook. Impressed, she unhooked the first-class rope and took us to the window. Nothing could describe the look on her face as she tried to understand the scratching of hundreds of tiny claws against the cooler walls, but minutes after my explanation, the five of us had first-class tickets and increased luggage allowances.

"Kids," I said as the plane left the runway, "this is just the beginning."

The plane ride is a blank. I must have gone through the shopping list over and over again, wondering where in New York we would find California-quality vegetables and fruit at their peak of perfect ripeness and flavor, let alone restaurant-quality fish and shellfish.

It was not going to be easy, so to reward my staff for their work so far, and to get them in the mood for going that extra mile in the days ahead, I decided that a lunch at the great Four Seasons, my home away from home, was just the ticket. It was my idea of America's finest restaurant, created by people I adored and admired—James Beard, Joe Baum, and Barbara Kafka—and now the realm of two great restaurateurs, Tom Margittai and Paul Kovi, and one of the nicest chefs in America, Seppi Renggli. It didn't hurt that the building I had studied at architecture school involved my two favorite architects, Mies van der Rohe and Philip Johnson.

I wanted my team to experience perfect service in a perfect room, and ogle the enormous silver chariot of desserts crowned with the pastry chef Albert Kumin's famous cake, shaped like a half cantaloupe turned upside-down, covered in chocolate, and topped by a foot-high chocolate version of a scarf Loretta Young would have tied around her head. None of us could figure out how Albert had spun chocolate into this couture shape of silk settling in a light wind. Now, ten years after I first encountered this creation, I told Albert I had waited all that time to ask him the secret of his gossamer construction.

"I would have told you anytime," he said with a huge grin. "It's simple: I use a hand pasta machine. Of course, the chocolate has to be the right temperature and it's only that way for a minute or two."

Yes, I thought, time enough for a master who knows all chocolate's intimate secrets, and for the rest of us to screw it up completely.

The next morning, full of fine memories of our magnificent lunch and the spectacle of New York seen from the bar on the 107th floor of the World Trade Center, it was time to return to earth. We picked up an enormous van from our uptown hotel and headed downtown to Balducci's, the only place where I thought we could get the quality of produce we were used to in California. As it turned out we could—at five times the price. We shopped for boxes of red and gold bell peppers, leeks, zucchini, red torpedo onions, ripe mangoes, and passion fruit. At the meat counter I saw beautiful coils of fresh fennel sausage; they turned out to be a last-minute inspiration for a snack with drinks. The veteran Balducci's staff was as impressed by the mountain of crates on the Sixth Avenue sidewalk as I was by the proportionately small mound of cash left in my hand. Later, the ad agency told me I was crazy to buy food for one hundred at what was then New York's most expensive boutique grocery. But the quality was worth it, even if I did end up having to split the tab.

My sous chef, Steven Vranian, was thin, wiry, and pale-skinned to the point you could see the blue veins pumping an intense energy. He had dropped us off in front of the store with the intention of circling the block. After an hour standing behind the pile of crates and boxes on the sidewalk looking anxiously for the van, we realized it really was gone. We still had to buy fish and shellfish before finding our way through the nightmare of parkways and bridges out of New York to make it to Newport on time. With no van, no food-filled coolers, no clothes, and no money or directions, we had no way of getting to Newport. Our California boy had disappeared in the maze of alien West Village one-way streets. Since this was before cell phones, he was truly lost and we truly in the dark. He finally showed up, red-faced, sheepish, his shoulders in a shrug, giving us the "shit happens" both- palms-up gesture. If I hadn't needed him so much I would have killed him.

I had planned to buy the fish at its source in Newport, but now the team overruled me with "Let's have it in hand." Perilously off schedule, we raced to the Fulton Fish Market for an aquarium's worth of live clams, mussels, crab, and shrimp—leaving only lobsters and oysters to purchase live the next day— then barreled up the New England Thruway.

OUR NEWPORT

We drove around Newport searching for our lodgings, expecting something grand (given the mansions we saw), but the address on the slip of paper I was clutching turned out to be a motel. Not a bad motel, but a motel nonetheless, and that meant no room service. Since chefs never eat at normal times (defined as when we're cooking for everyone else), we survive on room service. My staff knew I could put up with just about anything provided I could get a chicken club sandwich and champagne twenty-four hours a day, so two of them peeled out of the motel driveway for the makings of club sandwiches and a case of bubbly. As my all-time heroine, Madame Lilly Bollinger, when asked "Why champagne?" replied, "I drink it when I'm happy and when I'm sad. Sometimes I drink it when I am alone. When I have company I consider it obligatory. I trifle with it if I'm not hungry and drink it when I am. Otherwise I never touch it—unless I'm thirsty." I would add the wonderful words from the Pink Panther: "Champagne is a minimum of alcohol and a maximum of companionship. It takes care of all extremes." And this was going to be an extreme weekend.

I wanted my staff in tip-top shape in the early morning, so I grabbed a bed by the door to ensure that no one would slip out during the night, but the boys were too quick. Newport had been the stomping ground of Brad Barker, one of the cooks, and he decided to give Steven a tour of his old watering holes. Oxsana Czuczman, another cook from the Santa Fe, stayed behind to watch over my nerves. Staff legend has it that she sacrificed her entire stash of pot to calm her nerves while I paced our little room and fumed, waiting for the errant boys. They staggered back in the middle of the night drowned in Coors, but at least without the companions they reeked of.

The next morning was quiet, tense, and hot for April, even in those early hours. The heat made the shaky staff even shakier, and I felt worse than they did—grimly low on adrenaline and nourishment. The sunlight was already far too bright, so I stopped off in town and bought a pair of large fire engine red, Doris Duke or Barbara Hutton plastic-framed Ray-Bans as much for me as for any photographic moment.

Pulling up to the venue's (Beechwood estate) gates we drove up an endless, impeccably tailored gravel driveway to the mansion—a two-story Palladian house with Doric columns set a few feet above a lawn that stretched for a mile or so down to the water. I saw an open porch around two sides and the back of the house covered with the as-yet-unset tables for the lunch. It was all very impressive, and I expected a kitchen of comparable grandeur with space for two teams of cooks, mine and Guy Savoy's.

It was not. It was the size of a large closet.

THE FRENCH CREW

The French arrived just as we had figured out how to make it work and started to cook. I had heard Savoy was a decent bloke, but I never had a chance to find out. His crew preceded him, and they were armed with attitude. At first they ignored us, but packed into that small kitchen it wasn't easy, so they asked us to leave. Their needs took precedence, they said, because the serious meal—dinner—was theirs.

All was quiet for a moment. I don't know what made me keep silent, my English-schooled manners again, or possibly my status as a guest in someone else's kitchen, but all I could think of was keeping our focus. Every moment of energy had already been spoken for, and realizing that a pissing match at that moment would get us nowhere, I stepped aside.

"All right, girls and boys," I said. "Grab everything and follow me."

I had read Sun Tzu for years, and stepping aside was my first *Art of War* move. By not making a scene, I let the force of the French arrogance fire up my cooks and give them a powerful sense of purpose and determination to show these guys what they could do. In an instant, they forgot their throbbing heads, and we searched for a new place to cook.

"This," I told my team, sweeping an arm over the landscape in front of all the tables, "is the place for us, right in front of the bloody press."

I pushed the red sunglasses up on my sweating nose and got to work. We lined up four five-foot grills just far enough from the press to keep the smoke from their eyes but close enough so they could see the color of ours. The grills were meant to have been kept out of sight; now they would be the focus of everything—a great stage and the center of our entertainment. I insisted that only the most beautiful things should show, that all the mechanics be stowed away under the tables, so the food would "appear" seemingly effortlessly.

Two hours later, the press materialized. Their schedule gave them thirty minutes to wander around with glasses of wine before sitting down, so we served them a snack that I could cook and talk about simultaneously: the fresh fennel sausage from Balducci's, coiled into large rings, skewered, and grilled whole, then cut into bite-size pieces on large wooden planks. They were served still sizzling from the grill with the juice from our newest exotic ingredient, Rangpur limes, and sprinkled with a salt we flavored with ground, oven-dried peel of lime and cumin seeds. On the side were bowls of grilled tomatillo salsa.

A hundred food journalists took one look at us and one bite of sausage, raised their eyebrows with expectation, and away we went: salsa, grilling, and California were suddenly it.

"CALIFORNIA CUISINE": GRILLING IS IT

We played up grilling as essential to the California style and mesquite char-coal as the only one we used because it burned very hot and added a slightly acid taste to the food. We didn't mention that it was the only non-briquette kind we could get. It was perfect for fish, but in the cooking business every perfection has its flaw, and mesquite's was the occasional unspent .22 bullets put there by Mexican baggers as revenge against the gringos. A bullet blasting off and whizzing by inches from a cook's head was not something I needed journalists to see, so the press watched us sort through a huge black mountain of the charcoal before setting it in the grills. "Just the choice pieces," I lied, while keeping an eye out for bullets.

Luncheon on the Terrace
April 28, 1983

Grilled Fennel Sausage with Rangpur Lime & Orange-Cumin Salt
Grilled Mixed Shellfish with Grilled Garlic & Ancho Chili &
Herb-Shellfish Butter Sauces
Cranberry Puree Marinated Grilled Lamb Loin
Mixed California Vegetable Salad
Cranberry Chili Relish
Grilled California Goat Cheese with Garden Greens
Tropical Fruit Compote with Coconut Ice Cream

The first course was shellfish, the lobsters cooked initially on a bed of fresh seaweed (to give them maximum ocean flavor), then finished off on the charcoal fire, which also pushed all the flavor of the shells into the lobster meat. Each guest was served a big white plate with two ramekins: one for the warm lobster butter sauce made from the crushed shells and mussel stock, the other with a sauce made from my secret dried ancho chili puree and sour cream laced with mayonnaise. Warm towels scented with fresh tarragon and Meyer lemon gave them all the confidence to eat with their fingers.

We decorated the guest tables with vegetables instead of flowers—huge platters of leeks, red and gold bell peppers, yellow zucchini, and red torpedo onions. The vegetables were oiled, to glisten and reflect the sunlight as well as to marinate them for the grill. As soon as the shellfish was served, the waiters removed the table decor in unison, then marched over and emptied the platters onto the grills to create the illusion of vegetables cooked to order when, of course, we had the ones we were to serve already done.

Next came the lamb loins marinated in the juice of crushed cranberries with thyme, bay leaf, and olive oil. To our astonishment, the berry juice worked beautifully, making a sweet-sour caramelized glaze that was a perfect counterpart to the richness of the lamb fat and the slightly musky flavor of the meat.

So far, so good. But we had planned, while the lamb was on the grills, to use the kitchen ovens for the Sadie Kendall California goat cheeses, which were sandwiched between two thin pounded-out slices of oven-dried tomatoes (a new product in those days), a sprig of fresh flowering wild thyme on each side, and wrapped in fresh grape leaves. Only in that way could we achieve a seamless transition between the courses and hold the lunch to ninety minutes. But one last pleading at the kitchen door was like Oliver Twist in the orphanage asking for more gruel—a firm *Non.* The little cheeses came back to me on the rebound, so we stoked up the fires, furiously brushed off the grills, and laid out the cheeses. If we didn't have the journalists in the palms of our grillers' hands by then, the sight of all of us coolly turning (and turning) 125 individual goat cheese packages certainly did the job.

But they weren't totally floored until we grilled the dessert.

By now high on fatigue and adrenaline poisoning, I pushed the red sunglasses up on my head and commanded each cook to down a glass of champagne and pick up two huge sauté pans. On a signal from me, they filled them with mixed tropical fruits, raspberries, and passion fruit sugar syrup. Then all of us in unison tossed the fruit compote up in the air like master omelet makers. That got a standing ovation. We plated the tropical fruit ragouts, scooped fresh coconut ice cream into the center of each plate, added shortbread cookies—and we were done.

THE FRENCH WERE NOT SO LUCKY

At the end of the lunch the cooks collapsed on the lawn, while I went from table to table. I remember a flood of journalists blaming me for nearly killing them with food, but all were smiling. I kissed the cooks—mine, not the ones standing around on the sidelines stage-whispering furiously in French. Assuming we couldn't understand them, they scourged us for our "nonculinary" herbs like lemon thyme, and our lack of chefs' hats and names embroidered on our jackets. Any hint of admiration in some of their voices soon reversed when they saw me help my cooks clean and pack up. Not a chef's work. But that's where the chilling champagne was, and it was a good point to make that it should be.

I took a bottle of champagne and went down to the water. I was numb. I knew that I had to attend the dinner in four hours' time, coherent, with a smile, and acting as if everything the press had seen had been carefully rehearsed. In truth, I could never have planned that level of success. In those days we would have been declared insane if we had announced a meal cooked entirely outdoors on an East Coast early spring day. And to have grilled dessert? Certifiable.

The press had no preconceptions of what we would cook, but Guy Savoy was not so lucky. The journalists had been told to expect no sauces, no flour, no cream, and no butter. But this is what they saw:

Dinner at Beechwood
Potage de Homard aux Airelles
Saumon au Persil
Rillons de Ris de Veau aux Truffes
Bavarois aux Airelles

Savoy didn't use flour, but sauces, cream, and butter were everywhere. There was cream in the lobster soup with cranberries, cream in the salmon with parsley sauce, and the Bavarian cream with cranberries was exactly its name. Packed. The sweetbreads had a flourless veal stock and truffle sauce. To say the least, we were confused. The advance press from the agency had likened Guy's innovative cooking to that of the famous Paris restaurant l'Ami Louis. That was a laugh. A normal dinner there was an eighteen-ounce slab of goose liver, a whole chicken, or entire leg of baby lamb served with a potato pancake cooked in butter and duck fat, and pastry crust and butter-sugar caramelized apple Tarte Tatin for dessert, all of it weighing in at around seven thousand calories.

Actually none of my team cared whether the food was sauced or not—it was delicious. But the press still didn't get it. The *California Union* explained that what was meant by sauceless cuisine was actually "sauces that are done at the last minute." Having told everyone it meant no sauces was not an especially good PR hook for Savoy unless you understood the sauce tradition against which he and the other Young Turks had rebelled.

People who rail against traditional French sauces often mean the *Espagnole* or advanced version of the flour-thickened "brown" sauce that has been screwed up for decades by hotels, luxury resorts, and the majority of French restaurants, all rendering a muddy, opaque brown sauce, the color in the jar a child is left with after painting for hours with watercolors. A true *Espagnole* takes three days to make, including the initial stock, and demands a monogamous relationship: full devotion from a sauce maker who never abandons his charge. Each day there has to be a rest period so that the fat on the top and the detritus on the bottom of the jellied mass can be easily removed. Then it sits on the edge of a burner for several hours finishing, cooking at such a slow rate that it barely shimmers—it merely "smiles" at the cook skimming off its last traces of fat, scum, and skin.

This accomplished, and poured over a few bones and carcasses of whatever creature it is meant to enhance, then strained and made to "smile" again, it becomes a sauce so easy on the body that four hours later you're ready for the next meal. And the flour? Transformed like the silk cocoons that become an Hermès scarf. The fat? Not a drop. The stock-becoming-sauce has never vigorously boiled, and so the fat, unincorporated and removed, can neither ruin the diners' plumbing nor mask the true flavors of what is being sauced. And the clarity—like looking though clear amber.

Even the revolutionary Turks Paul Bocuse, the Troisgros, and the great unsung Jacques Manière knew that this great basic brown sauce could be magnificent and a test of a truly great kitchen. But when you're starting a culinary revolution, it's easier to blame the sauce than the saucier, to guillotine the aristocrats instead of overturning the regime. It was the restaurant critics and guidebook writers Gault and Millau and then their following in the American press that lined up all the figures of classicism and beheaded them indiscriminately. Gone were the creamed crayfish-sauced quenelles of the master Fernand Point at La Pyramide in Vienna; drawn and quartered were the butter-based sauces of Henri Soulé at New York's Le Pavillon; rack-

and-pinioned were any flour-thickened meat essences. Fat was now labeled treason and its eaters, traitors.

Un-American.

OUR "MAGIC GRILL" DAZZLES

All these crazy thoughts pounded through my exhausted brain as I sat at Savoy's dinner in the ballroom at Beechwood. Everything seemed to move in slow motion, the sounds coming out of the writers' mouths like a tape at half speed. I was so tired that I could not remember anyone's name, barely even what I was doing there. I knew this was Guy's night, and these journalists were professional. They wanted to give him equal time, even if they could be in no possible way as physically interested as they were before lunch. But with nine powerful journalists to my right and left at our round banquet tables, I sat just waiting to hear about my party and which way the thumbs were pointing, up or down. I knew right after lunch that we had pulled off a success, but now, at the evening table, doubts crept in. It was my first big public performance, and I wanted praise strong and constant enough to overwhelm my fears, of both failure and, oddly enough, success.

As it turned out, the French handed the event to us on a platter. Not that their event wasn't wonderful; one just couldn't *feel* it. The *Christian Science Monitor* gave France its forty words, California two thousand. "Berkeley Chef's Magic Grill Dazzles Eastern Experts at Al Fresco Lunch," one headline trumpeted. Phyllis Richman in the *Washington Post* made our lunch one of the first full-page color cover sections, writing of a "far from down-home barbecue, with white tablecloths . . . and a hushed silence." In the *Boston Globe* on July 6, 1983, Nina Simonds quoted Ruth Reichl, then at *California* magazine: "Tower's cooking is a brand of California cooking that is instantly recognizable. It is understated and depends on local ingredients, unusual flavor combinations and impeccable timing." Simonds then quoted me, making a first stab at a characterization. I said that nothing had changed as far as the fundamentals. What was new was the marriage between "the aesthetic chasteness of nouvelle cuisine and the hearty, robust hominess of bistro food: New American Cuisine." Within weeks of the Newport event, that term was repeated widely.

The press had France on their minds when they arrived, but they left with their hearts in San Francisco—or just across the bay. The love affair between the American food press and California had begun.

Another affair began, too—with me. "Tower is a photographer's fantasy. He stands tall and regal, cool enough to tame the fire," wrote one reporter. I ate this up, of course. It would have taken a stronger person than I was not to see this as a way to get our message across and make money doing it.

Great success is supposed to be followed by great elation, but with me a great performance has always brought on that "little death" feeling. The greater the success, the more devastating its successor. I didn't have it as bad as my pal Rudolf Nureyev, who would vacuum down a bottle of Stoli in the wings right after the last curtain call. But almost. As W. S. Gilbert (of "and Sullivan") puts it in the wonderful film *Topsy-Turvy,* "There is something inherently disappointing in success."

My California kids felt they had "kicked French butt." The next morning, as we loaded up the van, I felt as if I had been kicked in the head. As soon as the road was a clear shot out of Newport to JFK Airport in New York, I crawled into the rear of the van to find a sleep that never arrived. While my cooking team raved with delight and was filled with pride in the front of the van, I ended up in a fetal position in the back. I felt sorry for myself that I was going to get everything I ever wanted because I knew at that moment that some part of me didn't want it. I felt an awakening pain of the old adage of being careful what you wish for, and I was fairly certain that my life would never be the same again.

Would we lose the un-selfconscious "anything goes" exuberance of my little band of outlaws that had made our triumph possible?

Steven Vranian wrote a note afterward describing his feelings about the event. He said that the staff felt that the sight of my moving from table to table, face still flushed from the grill, revealed something new and vaguely disturbing: "The half of him that he pretends to be, and the half that others expect him to be, merged together and created the new Jeremiah." I had chosen, Steven said, "a path that would consume and redefine" me.

Did I want to be redefined by success? In my youth I'd been defined by the lack of it—first as a "Yank" in Australia, then as an "Aussie" in England, and then in the United States, where everyone assumed I was English. The truth is that I was a bit of an alien wherever I was. But at Newport I learned that my vision—of a new, serious simplicity that could change the way people thought of fine dining—had power.

I was learning that people who are best at keeping their huge success are somehow detached from it, able to regard it as something outside themselves. Only then can one stay focused, both when being lionized and then, inevitably, when being torn down. If the press loves first to proclaim "Long live the king," they love just as much to cry, "The king is dead!"

As I slumped in my seat, tears falling, in the plane headed westward, Steven noticed me and leapt over the back of his seat—somehow not spilling a drop of his gin and tonic. "Are you all right?" he said, a note of panic in his voice.

"All right," I said. "Quite all right."

At that moment I knew I would go for it, whatever the ultimate cost. I knew that what was coming wasn't an occasional ride on the tiger's back but a life living on it. I decided to go for the crown, in full view of the guillotine.

———

Grilled Garlic and Ancho Chili Sauce
Serves 4–6

2 dried ancho chili pods	1 ripe lime, zested and juiced
1 head fresh spring first-crop garlic	½ tablespoon fresh oregano leaves, chopped
2 sprigs fresh thyme	4 ounces unsalted butter
½ cup mild extra-virgin olive oil	Salt

Grill the chilies over a charcoal, wood, or low gas flame until they puff up, or about 3 minutes. Put them in a bowl with enough warm water to cover them. Weight them down with a small saucer, and soak for 2 hours. Drain, saving the water, and remove and discard the stems and seeds.

Meanwhile, wrap the head of garlic loosely in foil with the thyme and a tablespoon of the olive oil. Cook over low fire or under a broiler until the garlic is tender, or about 20 minutes. Remove the stem and rough outer layers of the skin and discard. Put all the cloves in a food processor and puree the garlic with the remaining olive oil. Pass through a sieve and discard the residue.

Puree the chilies with just enough of their soaking water to make a smooth puree. Sieve. Clean out the food processor.

Put the garlic and chili purees in the processor with the lime zest and juice, oregano, butter, and a teaspoon of salt. Puree until soft and smooth. Add more salt if necessary.

Serve on top of grilled fish and shellfish.

––––––––

Tropical Fruit Compote

Serve the warm compote either with custard, vanilla or coconut ice cream, mascarpone, or English clotted or heavy cream. Add cookies of your choice, like shortbread or warm gingersnaps five minutes out of the oven.

Serves 4–6

2 ripe mangoes, peeled, cut in ¼-inch slices

1 ripe papaya, peeled, seeded, cut in ¼-inch slices

2 ripe passion fruit, cut in half, pulp and juice saved

½ cup medium sugar syrup

1 basket raspberries

1 tablespoon unsalted butter

Salt

Put the mango and papaya slices in a medium-size nonreactive frying pan. Whisk the passion fruit pulp with the sugar syrup for 1 minute to break up the pulp, and add to the fruit.

Warm the fruit over medium heat until just heated through—about 3 minutes. Add the raspberries, butter, and pinch of salt. Turn up the heat, and swirl the pan around until the butter is just melted.

Serve immediately in soup plates with the cream or ice cream in the center.

––––––––

CHAPTER 18

THE CUISINE GAME

We honed our skills with the help of another journalist. In a 1982 issue of *Cuisine* magazine, Pat Brown and her "Cuisine Game" gave a group of chefs a market-basket list of ingredients and asked them to come up with a menu and recipes.

Ingredients
Lamb shoulder
Trout
American caviar
Coconut
Asparagus
Salt cod
Rhubarb
Pine nuts

I decided to serve the pine nuts toasted with champagne, then continue the champagne with a tartare of trout with asparagus. The rest:

Menu
Raviolis of Salt Cod with American Caviar
Braised Lamb Shoulder with Garlic Cloves

Fried Goat Cheese with Shredded Romaine Lettuce Salad
Rhubarb Soufflé with Coconut Custard

When the contest was published, the Santa Fe customers immediately wanted that food. Once more a restaurant that had started simply was pushing its limits to live up to what had been promised in the food press. In August, we cooked a menu for the birthday in 1982 of *Gourmet's* wine columnist, Gerald Asher, using local wild salmon we smoked ourselves, served with Sacramento River sturgeon caviar processed by Narsai David, another Berkeley restaurateur. Following the salmon were:

Birthday for Gerald Asher
Santa Fe Bar & Grill, Berkeley, 1982

Garden Herbs, Flowers, and Black Truffle Soup
Ravioli of Brain Puree with Sweetbreads
Mesquite-Grilled Partridge with Chervil Butter
Laura Chenel Sonoma Goat Cheeses
Figs Poached in Sauternes with Rose Petals

By the time we cooked a dinner called "Future" for a promotion for Berkeley's sportswear company The North Face a few months later, New York was watching. I began with trays of champagne and pills—a joke on the futurist idea that all food will one day be in pill form. But the courses that followed were "real" and included melted Sonoma cheese in a ramekin lined with Meyer lemon leaves and Lunar Free-Ranging Rabbit Stew with Crazed Mushrooms.

But it was another menu that whetted Jim Beard's appetite.

1982 Napa Valley Wine Symposium
Fresh Berkeley Hills morels stuffed with duck livers fattened for the
Santa Fe Bar & Grill
Poached wild striped bass with chervil butter and
nasturtium sauce
Sonoma squab smoke-roasted over cabernet vine cuttings
Warmed goat cheese dipped in violets
Winter fruit compote in Napa Riesling

The squab's breast meat was served in its juices, the leg and thigh meat chopped into a puree with sage leaves and served on grilled garlic toasts. "If that is not new American food, my dear, it should be," said Jim, impishly parroting my Florida dinner line. The food seemed awfully French to me, but I kept that thought to myself.

CALIFORNIA CUISINE

By mid-1983 the word had spread about "California cuisine." Wolfgang Puck had given up his job at Patrick Terrail's very French Ma Maison and opened Spago on Sunset Boulevard in 1982. It picked up on the theme set by Michael's a few years earlier: simply done, all white, great lighting, and a bedazzlement of highlighted flowers, a style now known as "Californian."

Word had spread as far as that hotbed of trends Hong Kong. The Mandarin Hotel wanted to transform its old-boy Mandarin Grill. They called to persuade me to introduce Santa Fe Bar & Grill's "New California Cuisine" at the Grill. As I talked to them, I could feel the starched heavy linen sheets in the suite with its own butler. I needed a rest. I sent them a list of 150 dishes, some of which were:

Anaheim chilies stuffed with California goat cheese, Chinese black bean sauce

Warm avocado salad with shiitake and lobster mushrooms

Palm Beach crabmeat salad with pomelo

Duck prosciutto with pear and spiced pecan salad

Grilled oysters with barbecued duck skin

Gumbo with crayfish, smoked duck sausages, fried pork belly

Grilled sweetbreads with sea urchin cream sauce

Buffalo steak with BBQ sauce

Cranberry-glazed lamb loin

Turtle Cay bananas in rum with durian cream

Tropical fruit compote with coconut ice cream

Cornmeal blini with three American caviars

The Mandarin's press release said, "Inspired by the superb natural produce and wines of California, and fresh Pacific seafood, Jeremiah Tower is leading a revolution in American restaurant kitchens with a highly inventive, highly personal style of cooking, giving new flair to ethnic and regional dishes, whilst maintaining their basic simplicity. Dishes are brilliantly eclectic blends of wholesome 'country fare' and exotic imported ingredients such as blood oranges, Maui onions, Oregon morels, nasturtium flowers, stone crabs, quail eggs, American caviar, and garden tomatoes." I thought garden tomatoes were going to be a challenge in Hong Kong, but the Mandarin assured me their import company didn't know the meaning of unavailable, that we could get whatever we wanted in Australia.

I burst out laughing. The land of flathead and carrots fit for pigs would supply us?

"No way, mate," I said.

"Check it out," the supplier replied. "You'll be surprised by what's going on down there."

All I knew about Australia was that anyone who could live somewhere else did. My childhood playmate Brett Whiteley was now Australia's most famous painter, and he lived in London, as did all his Australian pals. I knew the names of Tony and Gay Bilson, who would open the amazing and Panisse-like Berowra Waters, in Sydney; of Phillip Searle, Neil Perry, Peter Doyle, and Serge Dansereau at the Regent, all of whom were said to believe that California chefs lived by the motto "If we can sell it, someone will produce it." Serge told me that in Australia restaurants had to drag, cajole, and coax their suppliers into producing anything other than mass-market ingredients. I was not optimistic.

But the ingredients from Australia turned out to be marvelous, and I made a note that I must soon return to the land of my culinary awakenings—both wonderful and horrible.

In Hong Kong I ruined two pairs of Italian loafers running up and down the stairs in the multilayered hotel kitchen, wowed the local press, and filled the Mandarin Grill with locals loving California food. The night we finished I took my Santa Fe crew to the floating fish market restaurants. The next morning, due to leave for mainland China, I could not get out of bed. The train left in four hours. The Mandarin doctor was called. He knew what to do, pumping my behind with an enormous amphetamine–vitamin B–antibiotic cocktail such as only Hong Kong could provide. In an hour I was up. In two hours I was on the train, where I revived myself with a bowl of goose and of fresh pink ginger soup. In the Canton (Guangzhou) markets I saw that "freshness" and "local" still held their original relationship: everything was alive, and in its skin (including for my morning pick-me-up of cobra blood mixed with Chinese wine). Giant salamanders, eagles and owls, civet cats, puppies, and snakes were in abundance, if menu challenging, but the richness of choice was an inspiration.

The success of the Astor mansion event a few months earlier had made the Hong Kong promotion easier, and I could hardly wait for the next one. So when I got a call from Jonathan Waxman and Larry Forgione (of New York's River Café, and later, of An American Place) saying they were organizing a charity dinner, in either New York or San Francisco, using American chefs, I felt another great moment could be upon us.

CHAPTER 19

THE REGION CALLED AMERICA

When the list of chefs arrived I saw it was made up of East and West Coast friends of Larry's and Jonathan's, with no one new and no one between the two coasts. I pointed out that if this were to be a truly American festival, we should cover the geography of the nation. What about Paul Prudhomme from K-Paul's Louisiana Kitchen in New Orleans? What about Bradley Ogden of the American Cafe restaurant in Kansas City? Or Jimmy Schmidt of the London Chop House in Detroit?

The list was finally decided, and the dinner was held at the Stanford Court, then owned by James Beard's West Coast angel (in every way), James Nassikas. My copy of the menu for the 1983 dinner is inscribed top and center by Dick Graff: "Hooray! The American Institute of Wine and Food." Barbara Kafka wrote, "Laugh a Little."

This menu celebrating regional America says it all.

An American Celebration
San Francisco, 1983

Cultured Olympia Oysters from Puget Sound, Washington
Bélon Oysters from Tomales Bay, California
Portuguese Oysters from Vancouver Island, British Columbia

****

Terrine of Three American Smoked Fish with their
Respective Caviars
Larry Forgione, River Café, Brooklyn

Red Pepper Pasta with Grilled Scallops
Jonathan Waxman, Michael's, Santa Monica

Garden Salad
Alice Waters, Chez Panisse, Berkeley

Blackened Redfish
Paul Prudhomme, K-Paul's Louisiana Kitchen, New Orleans

**Marinated Grilled Quail with Poblano Chili, Cilantro, and
Lime Sauce**
Mark Miller, Fourth Street Grill, Berkeley

**Roasted Rack of Lamb Stuffed with Missouri Greens
and Hazelnuts**

**Gratin of Wildroot Vegetables, Fiddlehead Ferns, and
Cattail Sprouts**
Bradley Ogden, American Cafe, Kansas City Jimmy Schmidt,
London Chop House, Detroit

American Cheese Selections

Pecan Puff Pastry with Chocolate and Sabayon Sauces
Jeremiah Tower, Santa Fe Bar & Grill, Berkeley

Balboa Cafe, San Francisco

After-Hours Party

Spago Pizza
Wolfgang Puck, Spago, Los Angeles

Tripe Gumbo
Barbara Kafka, Star Spangled Foods, New York

The donated wines were the best of Napa and Sonoma: Schramsberg, Jordan, Beringer, Iron Horse, Acacia, Robert Mondavi, Joseph Phelps, and Domaine Chandon, with a little South Coast—Chalone and Sanford—thrown in.

Prudhomme was banished onto the hotel fire escape because his blackened redfish cooked in white-hot black-iron skillets would produced thick clouds of impenetrable and eye-stinging smoke. Out there he wouldn't set off the interior alarms. But the hundred-foot-high pillars of fish and spice smoke were just as impressive on the outside. Soon every street fire alarm had been pulled by awestruck onlookers and every hook and ladder in the city was on its way to save the Stanford Court.

Photographs of us all eating Wolfgang's pizza after the main dinner show faces filled more with relief than with awareness of a momentous occasion. The look of slowly forming elation that history is being made, that the burgeoning American food movement had come together for the first time, is on only a few faces, but we had just made American cooking history.

Bill Rice from *Food & Wine* wrote to me about a panel discussion we had all participated in before the event: "As Barbara Kafka said, it's too bad Julia [Child] couldn't have been there to realize there really is an 'American' cooking/cuisine." Harvey Steiman in the *Examiner* wrote that Alice was not sure it was an amazing event, that she suggested it was more about novelty than about the actual quality of the food. But most of the enormous amount of press that covered the event agreed with the headline in *Revue West*: "American Cooking Comes of Age."

Jimmy Schmidt wrote to thank me for the opportunity of participating, as did Bill Wilkinson from San Francisco's Campton Place hotel, for inviting Bradley Ogden. They met at the event and Bill offered Bradley the job as the hotel's executive chef. Bradley arrived to take up the job at the same time two other chefs new to the Bay Area were starting: Masa Kobayashi at Masa's and Hubert Keller at Sutter 500 with Roger Vergé. I gave a lunch for them at the Santa Fe Bar & Grill to welcome them and meet the local press, restaurateurs, and my suppliers.

THE CHANGES WERE ALMOST COMPLETE

I resigned on December 1, 1984, from the Balboa Cafe. I no longer had time for it and to keep the Santa Fe going. I gave notice to myself there a year after that. I sat one last time at the Santa Fe bar, where I had asked the drug dealers to leave years earlier, and wondered at how far we had come. Halfway through a bottle of 1971 Dom Pérignon, I let the kaleidoscope of memories pass in front of me in this restaurant that had launched us to national fame, it seemed, without our even knowing it. For my part, it was a fame nearly cut short when the local restaurant union decided to use me as a springboard for recruiting new members. None of my staff was inclined to join their lines, especially after someone from the crowd on the sidewalk shot at me through the windows. I was used to flying bullets from the Mexican charcoal, but someone trying to kill me because I was famous did rouse a few worries in my head about the path I had chosen. I then used state police (regulars for free hamburgers and coffee) to bust the picket line, making everyone realize what I had known for years—that Berkeley was just not for me. Other, more warming memories filed through my head: making sandwiches for the firemen who left after a kitchen fire holding hands; the lunches I gave there for chefs like Hubert Keller, Masa, and Bradley Ogden to have them meet local personalities like Alice Waters, Mark Miller, Cecilia Chiang, Jim Nassikas, Gerald Asher, and Barbara Tropp.

But what I thought would be six months had turned into nearly five years, and it was time to go to San Francisco.

THE SAUCE FOR BEING SERVED UP

To receive from someone happiness—is it not to choose the sauce in
which we want to be served up?
—Colette, *The Pure and the Impure*

My first professional menu writing had been a daily-changing task for each
lunch and dinner. Foie gras and "turtle fat" in 1973 couldn't feature on those
$6.50 per person menus, but I still needed to let out the Cecil Beaton in
me, so I loved cooking outside the restaurant. I could splurge at home or at
friends' houses. Sometimes the menu was over-the-top (even if the food was
simply prepared), and sometimes the wine.

One dinner was both.

An Alice B. Toklas Dinner at Fern Canyon for
Von Thurn und Taxis
May 29, 1974
Ten people, ten bottles.

I cooked this menu for some friends at their palatial Mill Valley, California, house, on top of Mount Tamalpais. The menu was written mostly
in French, because in 1974 that was the language of Chez Panisse, and the

friends wanted a Panisse, Alice (B. Toklas) inspired, menu. The dinner was a big success despite the guest of honor, the Prince von Thurn und Taxis, declaring as he looked at the first course, "All you need in life is birth control pills and hundred-year-old cognac." I agreed about the cognac.

The prince turned out to be a fake, but no one and nothing else was.

Pâté de Foie de Volailles
Lillet
Quenelles de Saumon, Sauce Nantua
Champagne René Lalou 1966
Pigeoneaux Rôtis
Richebourg, DRC, 1959
Glace d'Asperges
Gigot de la Clinique
Purée de Topinambours
Château Montrose 1932
Brie de Meaux
A Tender Tart
Château Suduiraut 1955
Château Suduiraut 1928
Nitrous Oxide
Cocaine
Champagne Roederer Cristal 1966

The cumulus-cloud-light salmon quenelles with a cream crayfish sauce were followed by plain roasted pigeons stuffed with herbs because, after the quenelles, I wanted something not too rich but substantial enough for the great big rich Burgundy. I don't like a sweet fruit sorbet intermezzo between courses (the sugar spoils the palate for anything else), but a nonsweet sorbet of asparagus was the perfect precursor to the very rich lamb, which had been injected every day over a week with a mandarin-orange-and-spices concoction and cooked for seven hours. A wonderful Brie finished off the rest of the red wine, even if my choice would have been for a big white. Finally the rich but not too sweet "Tender Tart" from Toklas's cookbook was accompanied by two aging Sauternes. Nitrous oxide sent all to their "postprandial pleasures" on a high and me back (now uncaring) to my little one-room apartment in Berkeley.

A DELTA DINNER

Another dinner for eight people was for Ron Batori, the dean of the California Culinary Academy, who had invited first Ken Hom and then me to teach there. He invited Ken and me to cook at his large old farm mansion along the Sacramento River Delta. The wines were brought by Darrell Corti from Corti Brothers' wine and food emporium in Sacramento. My notes say that the wines showed Darrell's wonderful madness and deep knowledge of great wines as well as his willingness to share it by the shovelful.

Darrell Corti, Ron Batori, Ken Hom, Gregg Lowery et al.
February 15, 1980

Champagne Jeanmaire Brut en magnum
Smithfield Ham
Champagne Pol Roger en magnum, 1973
Tokaji Furmint 1975
Tokaji Szamorodni 1973
Tokaji Aszú 3 puttanos 1973
Tokaji Aszú 4 puttanos 1973
Grilled Delta Sturgeon
Joseph Phelps Chardonnay, en magnum, 1977
Duck Breasts and Legs with Kumquats
Chateau Margaux, en magnum, 1960
Chateau L'Evangile 1971
Cheeses
Chateau de Pommard 1972
Reserve de Chèvre Noir 1934
Pear Tarte Tatin
Tokaji Aszú 5 puttanos 1973
Tokaji Eszencia 1969

Ken and I decided it was important to keep the menu as clean as possible across from the almost (but not quite) overwhelming lineup of wines. Particularly the progression of the very heady and rich Hungarian Tokaji, going from the driest to the beginning-to-be-sweet (three puttanos) to the sweetest at five puttanos and then the Eszencia itself. I love old Malmsey Madeira, or semisweet sherries with ham, so to taste the progression of dry to sweet Tokaji with the Smithfield ham (soaked, poached, cooled, very thinly sliced) was an education in the level of sweetness that was perfect with salty, rich ham.

Ken cooked the duck Peking-style for the breasts with seeded kumquats stewed briefly in duck stock and red wine, and we poached the legs in duck fat to make confit before grilling them to be served with endive salad.

A NAPA WINERY DINNER

For a dinner at Joseph Phelps Vineyards to celebrate Joe having amassed a huge cellar of wines from auctions in London and the arrival of a lot of new fresh products onto the California marketplace, I wrote and cooked this menu for Joe, his then manager, Bruce Neyers, and a bunch of visiting chefs, like the great Frank Stitt from Highlands Bar & Grill in Birmingham, Alabama.

Dinner at Joseph Phelps Vineyards
Friday, October 10, 1980

Beluga Caviar
Champagne Billecart-Salmon, en magnum, 1975
Great Lakes Whitefish Gold Caviar
Chicken Breasts with Fresh Oregon Morels
Château Gruaud-Larose 1962, 1937, 1934
Rack of Lamb Grilled over Vine Cuttings
Château Gruaud-Larose 1945, 1929, 1926, 1918
Autumn Vegetable Stew
Basket of California Goat Cheeses on a Bed of Vine Leaves
Coulommiers
Salad of Warm Fruits, Guatemalan Cream
Steinberger Riesling, TBA 1959
Roasted Italian Chestnuts
Cockburn Port, vintage 1950
Unknown Port, perhaps Warre, vintage 1920

I don't remember what the Guatemalan cream was, but at that time I was very excited about the newly arrived fresh tropical fruits. I think the cream was all about fresh guavas.

I was stunned to be able to taste a sequence of one of my favorite red wines, Château Gruaud-Larose, over a forty-four-year period, let alone to taste one harvested at the end of the First World War. But my excitement was to convince everyone to serve a white wine with the cheese, a crusade that to this day has been only partially successful but that I still fervently believe in as a better pairing than cheese with red wine. With white wine one can taste to their fullest both cheese and wine; with red, the flavors of both cheese and wine are dulled. Better rich cheeses with a high-alcohol, high-extract California chardonnay served after the red wines.

A DINNER FOR CHEZ PANISSE FRIENDS

May 19, 1981

The superb Martine Saunier, of Martine's Wines, in the Bay Area, shared a passion with me for the wines of Burgundy's Fixin, as well as for the wines of Leroy and the Domaine de la Romanée-Conti, which she represented in California. So when I wanted to cook a dinner at my house for Alice and some of the staff from Chez Panisse (including Pat Curtan, who later did all the drawings for the Chez Panisse cookbooks) a couple of years after I left the restaurant, Martine supplied the wines. So much for the so-called Alice-Jeremiah feud.

Salad of California Smoked Sturgeon

Bourgogne Blanc, Rene Manuel 1978

Chassagne-Montrachet, Chateau de Maltroye 1967

Spaghetti with Sun-Dried Tomatoes

Hermitage Rouge 1976

Sadie Kendall Goat Cheeses

Fixin, Clos La Perrière 1964

Platter of Indian Mangoes and Strawberries

Chateau Doisy-Védrines 1964

THE SOUTH OF FRANCE

In 1975 Richard Olney wanted to introduce me to the Bandol wines of Domaine Tempier, owned by his friends Lucien and Lulu Peyraud. He knew I would be bowled over by the kind of hospitality that the Peyrauds offered, and would want to introduce their wines to California. When I returned I did through George Linton of Connoisseur Wine Imports.

Lunch at the Peyraud Family Table

Rosé 1964

***Fresh Striped Bass with Fennel Grilled over Vine Cuttings and
Sauce of Its Roe and Liver***

Rouge 1973, 1972, 1970, 1960

Tomates Provençales

Lamb's Lettuce with Garlic Oil

Fromages de Chèvre

Rouge 1961, 1968, 1964

Fruits

Coffee

Marc de Tempier 1961

I didn't need notes about the food because I knew it would be forever etched in my memory. The wines, though, were a challenge since Richard, Lucien, and I had tasted twelve or so from the casks before lunch.

While sipping the rosé before lunch I saw Lulu stocking up a fire of vine cuttings and dried wild fennel branches outside the back door of the kitchen for cooking the bass. I had not seen her making the off-white sauce that appeared on the table in an off-white sauceboat. But when tasted it was one of those few life moments. She had ground up the liver and roe of the bass with a mild, fruity extra-virgin olive oil and lemon juice, a bit of fish bone stock, and lots of freshly ground white pepper. It did not look like much, but spooned over the moist, white, flaking flesh of the perfectly fresh and perfectly grilled fish, flavored by fennel and the lemon-like acid of the smoke from the vine cuttings, it was heaven on earth.

BREAD AND WATER WITH RICHARD OLNEY, 1975

After all that wine, the coup de grâce of the marc (think French grappa), and a two-hour drive over the mountains back to Richard's hillside house, I was more dead than alive but, oddly enough, a few hours later a bit peckish, as one can be after a long day of food and wine. Casually and with sleight of hand, Richard produced a dish that, for the second time that day, created a memory that is perhaps even stronger now than the moment, perfect for its time, when I ate it. We went out into the garden in the fading light of the evening and picked potatoes, onions, and thyme.

Soup of Water, Potatoes, Onions
Puligny-Montrachet 1971

We added chunks of stale bread and French butter to the soup, salt, and ground pepper. A lifesaver!

COOKING FOR JAMES BEARD

The guests were Cathy Simon, Michael Palmer, my Special Forces or "Green Beret" brother, Gregg Lowery, and James Beard. His command had been to keep it simple, but that he felt like some great French wines (he had heard I had a decent cellar). Also that he was pining for the fresh and chemically untreated bay scallops I had been bragging about as now available in San Francisco.

I knew he would love the caviar and would understand my serving the pressed, or *payusnaya*, apart from the fact it was all I could afford. And beef was always safe when served with Lafite.

Dinner for James Beard, My House, San Francisco
October 19, 1979

Caviar Paiusnaya and Toast
Champagne Jeanmaire, Blanc de Blancs
Tagliarini with Bay Scallops
Córton-Charlemagne, Louis Latour, 1970
Roast Beef, Jerusalem Artichoke Puree
Château Lafite 1955
Cheeses
La Tâche, Domaine de la Romanée-Conti 1953
Fruit Compote
Wehlener Sonnenuhr Auslese, J. J. Prüm 1950
Cockburn 1950

Jim wouldn't hear of putting a white wine with the cheeses. After a precautionary tasting of the old Prüm, the comments were "faded from opening, should have been aperitif, overpowered, badly placed," so we put it with the compote and drank the La Tâche, which turned out to be truly a great one, with the cheeses.

Two months later I cooked another dinner for him at my house, a menu to revive tired palates after a season of feasting.

POST-CHRISTMAS BEARD DINNER, FOR TIRED APPETITES
December 27, 1979

The guests were Cecilia Chiang (of the great Mandarin restaurant in San Francisco); Marion Cunningham (Beard's San Francisco factotum and minder in those days); Robert Finigan (restaurant critic and wine writer, now speaking to me after the lamb incident at Chez Panisse several years before); Alice Waters; my great love, companion, and rose grower Gregg Lowery; and Ken Duprey, my host in Nantucket. I must have found some money from somewhere to pay for the Sevruga.

Champagne Pol Roger, Cuvée de Blancs de Chardonnay 1971
Caviar Sevruga Blini
Pol Roger, or Aquavit Frozen
Smithfield Ham in Old 1950 Madeira
Pol Roger, or Malmsey 1920
Salad "Alice," Chinoise
Compote of Tropical Fruits
Pol Roger, or Rieussec 1975

The salad was adapted from Escoffier's *Ma Cuisine* (curly endive, lemon juice, walnut oil, olive oil), which I made "Chinoise" for Cecilia by using fresh water chestnuts. The fruit for the compote was mangoes, papaya, and stewed quinces, flavored with an essence of roses from Gregg's garden.

COOKING FOR LOVERS

There is nothing like past and present relationship tensions and appreciations to spice a meal with friends. Alice Waters cooked this dinner at her house in

Berkeley for two pairings: hers with Robert Finigan, and mine with Gregg Lowery.

I brought the wines from my cellar. The wine everyone was poised to taste was the sweet white wine made by Beaulieu Vineyard from botrytis grapes in the thirties. It was the gold color of a middle-aged Chateau d'Yquem, stunningly good, but turned out not to be sweet. It was more like a Chateau Grillet, or a *vin de paille,* a bit oxidized, but beautifully, if you have that English taste. My notes say it "would have been perfect early in the meal—with fish. Memorable, *haunting* wine."

As was the evening. Mine with memories of Alice with me in the moonlight at the Gritti in Venice, of her coping with Gregg's existence, and of several stories Bob related about Alice visiting three boyfriends in one night, funny only by the time we got to the Mount Veeder.

Dinner with Alice and Boyfriends
May 26, 1980

Baby Lettuces
Meursault Genevrières 1970
Grilled Lamb Chops
Beaulieu, Georges Latour Private Reserve Cabernet
Sauvignon 1974
Mayacamas, Cabernet Sauvignon 1969
Mount Veeder, Cabernet Sauvignon 1973
Asparagus
Coulis of Strawberries
Beaulieu, "Chateau Beaulieu" 1930s

DINNER WITH ALICE AND NEW BOYFRIEND
October 27, 1980

This was a meal I cooked for Alice Waters and her new boyfriend to celebrate their being together. He was a wonderful guy, very good-looking, not yet twenty-one, and very complicated. They both were very nervous about the occasion, so I invited old friends in common with Alice, Cathy Simon and Michael Palmer, as well as Gregg Lowery, to show that we were not against the new one just because our common good friend Bob Finigan had been at the altar before him.

Vouvray Mousseux, Brut 1970

Veuve-Clicquot, Brut NV

Fettuccine with the First Fresh White Truffles

Chateau de la Maltroye 1967

Mixed Green Salad

Sonoma Goat Cheeses

Les Forts-de-Latour, en magnum, 1970

Dried Fruits and Nuts

Gonzalez & Byass 1970

Abundant white truffles have a way of conveying that all is right with the world.

Balance may be everything.

CHAPTER 20

THE FUN OF AMERICAN FOOD

"Eat American!" was the opening line of a 1985 *Time* cover story called "The Fun of American Food." The cover image was the Renaissance-style head of a chef with an asparagus neck, romaine lettuce shoulders, a sea bream forehead, tangerine cheeks, and shrimp lips. On his head was a star-spangled chef's hat.

Two years earlier, just after the American Institute of Wine & Food's "American Celebration Dinner," the *San Francisco Chronicle* asked some of the personalities involved for their idea of "an elegant meal." Sautéed foie gras and fresh truffles with asparagus and Madeira sauce, said Julia Child. "Fresh rabbit cooked étouffé style," said Paul Prudhomme. Michael McCarty, always the up-to-date showman, said first caviar, followed by pasta, then "quail grilled over mesquite coals, served with a salsa of fresh cilantro, jalapeños, and triple virgin olive oil." Alice Waters wanted Chinese food from Cecilia Chiang's Mandarin restaurant. Larry Forgione cited the menu he was cooking for the Brooklyn Bridge's centennial: "Sixteen courses based on American recipes from 1880," among them soft-shell crab glazed with beach plum jelly and "oysters and sea urchins sharing a shell." I wanted American woodcock, black walnuts, southern white peaches, and wild strawberries, although not together.

We were all over the map. So what was American food?

That same issue of *Time* said it started on the West Coast and was more or less interchangeable with "Californian," with its "dedication to lightness and freshness and its celebration of vegetables, herbs, and fruits." A *Life* article of the same period agreed that California had a profound effect on the new cuisine, and named Chez Panisse as the formative influence, crediting me as "the innovator" who still dreamed of a farm-restaurant that would produce its own "butter, honey, jams, vegetables, chickens, trout and hams. Tower is already trying out tastes newer than radicchio, miniature vegetables, and fruit vinegars, and pushing the next trend: Southeast Asian flavorings like lemongrass and fermented Chinese black beans."

The writer wondered if that mix was un-American. "Nope," I was quoted as replying. "The cuisine of the United States, like its population, is an amalgam, taking ideas from abroad and, in pure American style, mixing them all together."

Jonathan Waxman added, "You can fool around"—only this time he didn't mean sex and drugs.

Whereas the necessary culinary pilgrimage in recent years had been to France for the latest three-star food of Paul Bocuse, Michel Guérard, and the Troisgros brothers, now it was a summer trip "with equal zeal" through the United States. The *Life* article reads, "Sample the highly publicized creations that make up the new American cuisine." As the restaurant becomes "the new American theater," said *Life,* even the reigning Francophile Julia Child is courting young Americans. Travelers sought out Paul Prudhomme, Larry Forgione (An American Place), the Ivy in Los Angeles, Chez Panisse in Berkeley, and me at Stars in San Francisco. In Boston, America's best woman chef, Lydia Shire, believed that "the average diner was very much aware of 'new American cuisine.'" For her that was the creative cooking of good simple food, using American products while infusing some kinds of classical preparations, an example being her smoked Massachusetts partridge under a cloche.

Almost as important as ingredients, said *Life,* was the new esprit de corps. Waxman credited Forgione with giving him so much help with suppliers that his restaurant Jams should have been called "Another American Place." A full-page *Life* photo shows Jonathan looking embarrassed in a pond full of ducks, Top-Siders hanging over the edge of his dinghy. How I agreed to get into jodhpurs and Hermès riding boots for my photo I don't remember, but I do recall hauling myself and a goat to the top of a hill above Paso Robles, California, for a reluctant kiss with the goat.

Waxman's Jams was a shock to New York, if a delightful one. The prices were electric, and the decor an eye-opener for New Yorkers who hadn't seen Michael's Trumps or the West Beach Cafe. How could a "serious restaurant" with a "famous chef" be so plain? None of the "frog-pond" great French restaurants had white walls. And the elegance of the Four Seasons (the only other American restaurant mentioned) was indeed very formal. The co-owner of Jams, Melvyn Master, explained: "I hate the theatrics of pseudo haute cuisine—the kind where you need a torch to see the menu." He opted instead for bright walls with works by modern artists and a kitchen open to public view—where diners could watch Jonathan prepare his trademark dish of "free-ranging" chicken cooked over mesquite charcoal and served with french fries.

Time claimed that the new cooking was in "an intellectualized, even esoteric style, characterized by the use of fresh native ingredients." Now I would add that, since one cook's esotericism is another's poison, the term *California cuisine* was brought to its knees by overenthusiastic combinations of ingredients known only for their newness. Kiwis were piled on top of blueberry vinegar-infused reductions that were loaded into squirt bottles lined up in front of restaurant cooks just waiting for some poor squab to come along, probably paired with foie gras, scallops, and balsamic vinegar–drowned baby lettuces.

But that was later. For now California was the media darling: it had the freshest ingredients in the land.

FROM CHEF TO RESTAURATEUR

With that Californian cornucopia, conceptualizing the food for my new restaurant was the least of my worries. Panisse was all about food, as was the Santa Fe Bar & Grill. But now I wanted to make a restaurant statement, about the greater challenge of being a restaurateur rather than just a chef. On my mind was whether Americans were ready for a new take on the brash elegance of old New York and San Francisco. I loved the callused-hand-with-a-manicure elegant roughness of Tadich and Sam's. I loved Clark Gable in a gold-paved San Francisco with Jeanette MacDonald. I worshipped the photograph of Gable, Gary Cooper, Van Heflin, and Jimmy Stewart in white tie at Romanoff's in Los Angeles and hung it wherever I went. As in someday it will be regained. I wanted a place where the young princes of Ken Russell's *The Music Lovers* could rub elbows with bankers and dancers and musicians from the arts center a block away, where fur coats could be flung aside with the seeming carelessness of Dietrich onstage. In short, a place that was chic, with cheeky panache.

In early 1981 I had sent my Green Beret brother a letter that included the proposal for the restaurant, telling him it would be a brasserie like Flo, Lipp, or Pharamond in Paris, but modernized and adapted to San Francisco. My sister had found the location in late 1978, and I wrote that in mid-June we'd finally close with the bank and start construction. My two partners, I said, had experience and assets, and seemed "normal and honest."

Stars would not open until July 4, 1984.

It had been a maddening six years. The promised group of ten investors had come and gone like dance partners at a dateless prom. The owner of the ghostly old Italian restaurant had panicked several times, forgotten to renew his lease twice, and died once. After our lease was signed and various lawsuits settled, my partners decided to savage each other. One of them, an accountant, had distinguished himself by delivering Balboa's annual report on a cocktail napkin. He was soon history. I should have known to leave for New York then, to take glamorous offers from Windows on the World or Le Plaisir, or with the head of Air India to buy the Royal Palms in Scottsdale. But my sister, who had seen firsthand my experience with equal partners, advised me not to worry, that unlike Berkeley, I'd be working with grown-ups in San Francisco. Since I had never trusted grown-ups, that should have been my clue to run.

In March 1981 I led James Beard, Barbara Kafka, James Villas, Jim Nassikas of Stanford Court, Danny Kaye (fresh from an affair with Laurence Olivier), and several awestruck investors on a tour of the deserted site. I warned them to pause just inside the front door to let their eyes adjust to the interior's deep gloom. The fixtures had been removed and the place was gutted. Only two remaining forty-watt bulbs responded to my flipping on the circuit breakers to illuminate the five thousand square feet. The hushed group tried not to notice that Jim Beard had taken a swing with his cane at a large rat. A little bit of light was worse than the darkness. Now they could see the remains of the gold-flecked black mirrors on the walls and the grimy plastic flocked-red plush wallpaper. Dominating the view was a geyser of water spewing eight feet above the kitchen floor. My friends tiptoed gingerly through the mirror shards, damp-eating fungus, and rat droppings.

"Jeremiah, it's a disaster," cracked Barbara Kafka.

"Really, my dear . . . ," began Jim. Words uncharacteristically failed him. His huge gold-bedangled hand waved limply in a gesture of hopeless dismissal.

Danny Kaye gave his usual glass-shattering whistle to test the echoes.

It was all so awful that I had to fight off a fit of giggles.

Jim Nassikas saw only expense and privately withdrew any thought of investing. All I could see were pale lemon walls, mahogany wainscoting, shiny brass, huge Chinese tubs holding oversize flowers and entire wild rosebushes, and a deep, star-covered Wilton carpet, from which the restaurant would take its name.

Everyone emerged from the site quite shaken. Perhaps worse interiors had been successfully remodeled, though doubt hung heavily in the fetid air. My choice of site was thought downright suicidal. Although the restaurant was in the heart of the Civic Center, itself the political and cultural heart of San Francisco, the area was a mess. Drug dealers, criminals, and the homeless moved amid the blowing garbage. The only visitors by day came to beg or bribe for building permits. At night the visitors getting out of cars held their noses against the smell of urine as they hurried out of the Civic Center garage to the opera or symphony. But no one was as shaken as my partner Doyle Moon, because the answering machine for days recorded messages he didn't want to hear: the site is hopeless, the facility a mess, and "that man [Doyle] downright dangerous."

THE KIND OF STARS

I saw a different future, but with doubts. Breaking the rules at Chez Panisse and the Santa Fe had been lauded, but would the public understand our choice of site? I saw a restaurant to which you would drive up, give your car to a valet, come in for a drink or oysters, walk a block (escorted by my staff) to the performance, walk the block back two hours later with the crowds, have dinner or a snack or dessert, then pick up your car at the valet and leave. I knew people would come to see beautiful dancers or famous opera or ballet stars, so I would subsidize the young dancers and court the stars. I wanted people to feel as if they owned my restaurant, as if it had everything for them rather than something for everyone. San Francisco didn't need another "special occasion" restaurant, it needed a great "regular." A home away from home, a place one could casually drop into for a glass of champagne, a business lunch or dinner or meeting in the bar, or a four-hour gourmandizing meal. I had visions of a place full of lawyers and city politicians selling us all down the river at lunch, afternoons at the bar full of glad victories or unhappy defeats from the law courts next door, the cocktail hour with all the office workers in the area, the pre-theater crowd, a full house for dinner, and then after 10 P.M. the restaurant full again with the stars of the performing arts eating oysters and drinking champagne, the fans coming by to ogle the lithe young bodies of the corps de ballet. Filling the place four to five times a day was the dream. Reality was the pro forma at the bank that said three, and a "best possible" gross at $3 million a year.

Meanwhile, there was a restaurant to build.

Pushing aside the lawsuits against my partner as thick on my desk as the rats had been on the floor of the abandoned restaurant, I got to work. The sheer weight of our press (from the Newport Astor mansion, the American Institute of Wine & Food festival, and many other Santa Fe national and international events) was enough to convince the Crocker Bank to set a meeting to sign loan papers. Then our banker left Crocker, sending us into a scramble to find another who would hand over $350,000. Our ace in hand was the very favorable and valuable lease I had negotiated before I met Doyle. Then a lawsuit from one of Doyle's partners forced a public auction of the lease, our only asset. Few showed up to bid, and those who did were scared off by the Apache Doyle in his Eddie Bauer sunglasses, which he wore throughout the session. His expression in victory was not one of joy but one of bloodlust. "If we ever have a problem," he assured me, "I am more than willing to step aside or buy you out." His long list of victims, he promised, would stop at me.

The problems began at once. Doyle evidently had no use for my master's in architecture from Harvard or my successful remodeling of Chez Panisse, Santa Fe Bar & Grill, and even his own Balboa. He insisted on managing the project himself, which would have been all right if he didn't habitually show up on the site an hour before the workmen left for the day, which made the pace of reconstruction painfully slow. My taking over some of the decisions caused one scorching battle after another.

Looking at the mess of construction every day, I would have to remind myself of the wonderful dignity of trains like the 20th Century from New York to Chicago, of what it was like to dine in those mahogany-and-nickel cars as they flashed through the countryside of the United States. I'd think of the great ocean liners; of the grand old restaurants of New York, New Orleans, and San Francisco; and of Lucius Beebe, my hero since college days, who had dropped dead in his Turkish bath a few miles south of San Francisco only a few years before I arrived. His column in *Gourmet,* called "Along the Boulevards," described a life I wanted to re-create, and the terms on which I wanted to re-create it. "If anything is worth doing," he once said, "it is worth doing in style and on your own terms—and nobody goddamned else's." I wanted to be as James Villas described him in a *Gourmet* article called "Lucius Beebe: The Last Magnifico": the randy and dandy boulevardier, the "eminently polite, generous, witty, and kind gentleman, who was not out to impress anybody and simply relished a civilized evening on the town over 'a hot bird and a cold bottle.'"

Eventually the spirit of this millionaire bon vivant prevailed. But the opening of the restaurant was a nightmare. The stakes were vastly higher than they had been at the Santa Fe Bar & Grill, and I was about to be hoisted on my own press petard. The staff and public actually thought I knew what I was doing, so I had to act like it.

The sound of Birkenstocks slapping across the bare boards of the old Victorian in Berkeley, or up the tarmac drive to the Santa Fe, was to be replaced by the sound of Manolo Blahniks swishing across a soft and star-filled Wilton carpet, but there was no carpet. A week before we were to open the restaurant, it wasn't finished, not by the stretch of anyone's imagination. So I turned the previously scheduled press lunch into a tongue-in-cheek "construction" one. We couldn't let the workmen stop, so we made them part of the scene. Remembering Jean Cocteau's playful tables for one of Picasso's lunches using toys from the boulevard hawkers outside, we set a long, plywood-and-sawhorses table with nails, colorful electrical wire, hammers, and drills in the carpetless dining room. The only other decor was a massive bouquet of flowers in the one completed corner so *Vogue* could photograph the "finished" restaurant, in the tradition of the great Dorothy Todd, who changed fashion magazines into lifestyle when in 1924 for English *Vogue* she photographed my other hero's revolutionary new London restaurant, Boulestin's. Barbara Kafka reminded me how thin a limb she was perched on by writing that the restaurant was already a great success. She said she'd kill me if that wasn't the case by the time her *Vogue* lifestyle article was published.

The press was poised to be enchanted, but their Caesar-like thumbs hovered between up and down. When I told the champagne-swilling crowd that the menu might veer from their printed ones because the gas had not been turned on, they looked around to see if I had been smart enough to invite the president of the utility company. While the cooks fired up the grill and I prayed there were no bullets in the charcoal, I told the story of the grilled dessert at the Astor mansion lunch a year before. I downed a glass of champagne and relished the adrenaline of the moment.

"Right," I said to the cooks who had been with me at Newport. "Line me up eight sauté pans." Hearing the cheers of the press as I juggled four pans for each hand over the fire, I wondered why I hadn't thought to stage the whole thing. I relished the thought that events beyond my control always seemed to produce the most powerful results.

NEW-OLD FOOD IN A NEW-NEW SETTING

On opening night the public was less forgiving. And who could blame them? Bare bulbs were still hanging from the ceiling because Doyle's chandeliers were still in Napa. He had been promising to deliver them the next day for the last six months. We had promised glamour, and here was only gloom and confusion. What customer in those first two months could be expected to know, walking in the doors for the first time, what the place was going to be?

On opening day, the hostess ran up to me just minutes before the doors opened and urgently inquired: "When the customers ask what kind of restaurant it is, what kind of food, what shall 1 tell them?"

I tried to think. "Tell them . . . American brasserie. Whatever that means."

"Oh," she said. "That's fine," as if I had said "Italian bistro."

After lunch I asked her what people had made of the "American brasserie" tag.

"Oh, no problem, they got it."

Which was certainly more than we did at first.

But soon we did get it, and as we all pulled together as a team, we felt that Stars could be what the new American restaurant was all about, more than just a California style.

Not that I thought Stars would ever win the best food in America contest. It was too big, and I couldn't supervise it all, all the time. What Stars did best and uniquely was measured in the breadth of the food, offering everything from lobster with veal marrow or scrambled eggs with black truffles in a buttered and baked brioche "box," to what the *San Francisco Chronicle* columnist Herb Caen called a "superb $3.50 hot dog with sauerkraut or the $7.50 hamburger which is probably the best in town."

Robert Finigan had wondered what we could do that we hadn't done at the Balboa Cafe and Santa Fe. He wrote that the food "resting on its raw materials is at once harmonious with Tower's latter-day style, familiar from Santa Fe and Balboa, and yet more exploratory and adventurous. Once you glance at the Stars menu, you will see how far the offerings range beyond 'California cuisine' clichés (sun-dried tomatoes and goat cheese), even those which seemed so new when Tower and his colleagues developed them." His favorite dishes: the Iced Oysters with Spicy Lamb Sausages ($6.75), which "are truly sensational in the truest sense of that overused word"; the hollowed-out Brioche with Marrow, Lobster Sauce, Poached Garlic, and Chervil ($7.50); the Blanquette of Veal with Summer Vegetables and Crayfish Sauce ($15.00); and an "exquisite" fattened Duck Liver on Grilled Bread ($12.50). He loved the huge champagne list, the long list of innovative cocktails, all the flavored frozen vodkas, and urged his readers not to miss "being present at the creation of something very special indeed."

The kitchen was but one element in the overall experience, but its aesthetic and work ethic pervaded the overall experience. We were maniacal about the quality of green salads and how its ingredients were treated.

THROWAWAY ELEGANCE

As San Francisco's version of Walter Winchell meets the *New York Post*'s "Page Six," Herb Caen wrote in his column the morning after I introduced him to my pal Rudolf Nureyev and his "date" Natalia Makarova: "Thank God for Stars, which honors the city's legendary reputation for kick-up-your-heels liveliness." He found Stars "the perfect place" to wind down after a show: "Stars looks terrific," Caen wrote, going on to describe the fifty-two-foot bar, the illustrations and posters crammed on the walls, the various eating locations, the cafe effect in the center of the room, the chandeliers and paneled walls, the wide-open kitchen, and the grand piano presided over by San Francisco's favorite, Mike Greensill. "And then," he continued, "there's the energy and electricity. You feel it the minute you walk through the doors. It's enough to light the city of Bakersfield." A couple of years later, Herb gave me an even more sparkling quote about Stars' "unique mixture of fun, vitality, throwaway elegance, and wide, beautifully done choices." Then he said Stars blessed San Francisco as a world-famous hangout. "That puts Jeremiah Tower right up there with Coit Tower as a beloved landmark."

Whether you came in for Herb's beloved hot dog or a sixty-five-dollar truffled three-pound lobster cooked in the wood oven, you arrived in Clark Gable–in–San Francisco style, up the steps from the alley into the pulsing main room filled with three hundred guests, sixty of them at the fifty-two-foot bar in the center of the space along a wall facing the oyster bar and the open kitchen with its ten cooks.

Finigan said the kitchen, bar, and patrons were the principal decor, while dishing the namesake carpet, which looked to him as if it belonged in the office of the president of Paraguay. He was right about the powerful punches that created Stars' ambience. It was not just that we didn't have money to spend on expensive fixtures. It was also that I didn't believe (and I still don't) that a restaurant should outdress its customers.

On Jim Beard's return visit he immediately got that Stars had "caught the spirit of its time." He loved its welcoming informality, comparing its look to a "quality that one sometimes finds in a nineteenth-century restaurant that has lived on" and its hustle-bustle to Paris brasseries like Le Vaudeville and La Coupole. Those favorites of mine had been my part of my inspiration.

Caroline Bates in *Gourmet* got it, too. She remembered my telling her that Joe Baum's motto "new-old food in a new-new setting" would be Stars' and reported that the food was provocative and satisfying. The feeling of the restaurant captured "the times so surely that someday it may be looked back on as the restaurant that best defined the tastes of the eighties."

"THE ONLY TRULY DEMOCRATIC FAMOUS RESTAURANT"

I told the staff on opening day that the Stars motto was "Everything from black tie to blue jeans," that it would be dining for people of all incomes, all in one place. Everything for someone, as well as something for everyone.

In Stars you could see the mayor, Dianne Feinstein, looking better now that she had let her hair turn from basic black to gray, squeezing in next to diners in jeans like the Nicaraguan left-winger Daniel Ortega. Everybody getting along just fine, the way San Francisco was meant to be. One magazine caught the crowd in amber: "Tuxedoed men and ball-gowned women from performances, students and stockbrokers and Sacramento car dealers, old money and borrowed money." R. W. "Johnny" Apple Jr. of the *New York Times* called Stars the "only truly democratic famous restaurant" he had ever seen. Stars was Paul Bocuse's favorite, "the kind of restaurant that every Frenchman envisions an American restaurant to be." It was not surprising then, that for Jacques Pépin, Stars was "the most exciting place in San Francisco."

Within four months *Travel & Leisure* recognized that "le tout San Francisco" had adopted Stars, and we were soon filling it my envisioned five times a day, doing three times the bank's best-case scenario. *Metropolitan Home* used the word *Superchef* for the first time and gave six full pages to photographs of the food. The articles were great for morale and business, but my favorite response to Stars was written on a cocktail napkin: "Dear Jeremiah, Ahhhhhhhhhhhhhh!! We've been to Paris, England, Berkeley, Germany, Yugoslavia and Livermore etc. and this is #1. Thank You."

Needless to say, there were dissenters, not all of them lipstick limousine liberals like the ones who told the *Boston Globe* that California cooking had started when Alice Waters built her pizza oven. Some distrusted the story of where the restaurant got its name, some felt uneasy with all the signed photos of stars on the walls, and some Berkeley critics just decided to build a wedge between Alice and me.

Trouble was in the air.

In the *Chronicle,* the Birkenstock-clad old hippie Stan Sesser, with whom

I had much-publicized rows, hated everything about Stars and, of course, me—a stance later inherited by a restaurant reviewer for the same newspaper, Michael Bauer. Sesser repeated his peeve: "Tower's weakness has always been a lack of consistency, an inability to control the kitchen so that everything comes out just right." How unable, or not, the years would show.

At the time, however, I listened more to the averages than to Sesser. I knew that in feeding six to seven hundred people a day there might be casualties. But most of the complaints turned out to be of the "high" prices–"small" portions variety. And then there were those who felt that a superstar chef should "always be in the kitchen."

My "patrician" accent and stories of storms with a soon-to-be iconic Alice turned up in a few East Bay reviews. One important national review opened with me hearing an airline promo in my car on the way back from Napa and capriciously jetting off. "Seizing the moment Tower thought 'why not' and twenty-one hours later was lunching at Alain Senderens' Lucas Carton in Paris and then, after shopping for supplies for the restaurant, in less than forty eight hours was back cooking in his own restaurant." On the flight back I had read all these reviews. What I read made me want to head right back to Paris—and to decide never to read anything but constructively negative reviews again, and then only the ones about Stars itself. Wide open to the press, who were either fawning, lapdogging, or on the attack, I felt that Stars and I were getting too vulnerable for comfort.

But nothing made me feel as vulnerable as assassins at my door.

CHAPTER 21

WHO'S KILLING THE GREAT CHEFS?

Around four on a Tuesday afternoon five months after we opened in 1984, my dining room manager gingerly handed me an envelope, apprehension on his face.

"Another fan who wants me to father her child?" I asked.

"How did you know?"

THE POISON PEN

The writing on the envelope made me recoil and drop it on the floor. The contents were even more scary: details of a murder of Masataka "Masa" Kobayashi, the fabled chef and co-owner of San Francisco's Masa's. Then, in what sounded like acid-fueled rantings, it spoke of our taking the insurance money, getting married, raising kids, and sailing off into the sunset.

"Call North Station in case this means something later," I said. "And put the case number on file as usual." The police were used to these threats and loyally sent an officer by to pick up the letter. He had his usual hamburger and coffee and left. Two hours later the front-desk phone was for me.

"Stay right where you are," a captain's voice said. "Do not move. Don't leave the building, we'll be right there." That sent me to the bar for a fast champagne. A second glass was cut off by the sight of flashing police car lights in the Redwood Alley entrance.

The captain and two officers made a beeline to me.

"Jeremiah, we want you to get out of town, and don't pass go. Be gone for four or five days and tell no one but us where you are. Here's the number for a private line to the mayor's office and to North Station."

"What the hell is going on?" I asked.

"Masa's been murdered. We found his body today, but he was killed, probably on Sunday."

The captain handed me the envelope with my name on it. "Look again," he said. "Note the postmark."

I looked: It had been mailed on Friday, two days before the actual murder. I dropped the letter again, this time in the captain's hands, and had another glass: a double Polish vodka.

The officers were to see me to the airport. But I knew I would stick out a mile at any Los Angeles resort, whereas there is nothing so anonymous as being at a local hotel under a false name, cash deposit on account, and making sure to be in the bathroom when room service shows up.

While one officer got my car and another took keys to get things from my house, which would be off-limits to me for at least a week, I called a pal who managed the city's most luxurious small hotel. I told him that I'd have to enter anonymously, that no one could know I was there, and that I'd be using cash. I told him nothing else, but the tone of my voice upset him. He said no. I went anyway, and let the police take me there. After a club sandwich and bottle of La Tâche, I calmed down, thought the whole thing ridiculous, even if the coincidence that the night before Masa was killed was the end of the season run of *Who Is Killing the Great Chefs of Europe?* gave me pause. Not long enough to stop me going home. After ordering a sophisticated alarm system to be delivered in the morning, I watched horror movies all night with my cat, Boy Burma. The cat had never shown fear of anything.

After an alarm with a silent panic button to signal the police station was installed, I finally slept. The next evening police, very angry at not finding me at the hotel, found me at Stars. A van had been discovered at the base of my street in Bernal Heights, the interior soaked in human blood with hundreds of little pieces of paper, torn up from larger ones with my home telephone number written on them, stuck to it.

Boy Burma and I got out of town, to a friend's house in Inverness, a place so quiet at night that the cat growled at every sound and scared me half to death.

BACK TO BERNAL HEIGHTS

Two days later, still alive, I returned to the house in Bernal Heights and went back to Stars.

The night of the second day at home I heard a noise downstairs. Burglars, as it turns out, are like sharks. You might think you see one, but when they are there you know it. When someone is actually in the house it's unmistakable, no matter how much you try to wish that realization away.

I wondered why the intruder was talking to himself.

Then it hit me: there were two of them.

I swallowed my fear and guessed that once you cry out and turn on the lights, burglars will run away. So I yelled that I knew they were there and turned on the lights. They didn't run away. Now they knew where I was. Now they could see where they were going. I hit the silent panic button along with the horns that would wake up everyone for miles.

As the men came up the stairs, I threw on a pair of briefs, even at the time thinking that hiding nakedness was a stupid reason to die. I searched for a weapon and found only my twelve-inch seventeenth-century sterling silver English letter opener. I grabbed it and tried to scoop up Burma. He had taken a bulldog stance at the top of the stairs and was growling a banshee wail down at them, his raised hair making him look three times his size. Urging him on, I ran through the guest room and out a window on top of the front-entrance roof.

"Freeze!"

There were policemen everywhere. Guns pointed directly at me. Later they told me I had been an immeasurable moment from being blown away, because all they could see was a silhouette against the lighted window holding what looked like a huge knife.

The kitchen at the back of the house was under construction, so the two intruders dove through the plastic cover, fell into my vegetable garden below, dashed down an overgrown gully into the projects at the base of Bernal Heights, and disappeared.

It was time for more late-night television, expensive Burgundy, and cigars with the two handsome cops, who stayed with me until dawn. They left, saying I should tell no one of the incident. Or their staying.

"OH REALLY, JEREMIAH?"

The next day I called a real estate agent and explained my needs for the next place I would live. She showed me various plush apartments but had the same reaction to my security concerns that people have when they read about rock and roll or movie stars and their "necessary" bodyguards. "Oh really, Jeremiah!" was all she could muster. Sure enough, the gossip columns a few days later had me arrogantly demanding security that no chef could possibly need, no matter how famous. The next night another chef, still clad in his white jacket, was ambushed as he got out of his car nearby and fatally stabbed through the head with a large chef knife. His murder shut the real estate agents and gossip columnists up for a while, at least about me, although one columnist did speculate that I might be next.

Wishful thinking.

Meanwhile, there had been a funeral and lots of newspaper coverage about Masa's murder, the fact that he had no money, and that his widow and children were penniless because Masa had died four months before his life insurance policy would have automatically reverted to him (and his wife). The principal beneficiary was rumored to be his partner Bill Kimpton, then in a heavy expansion mode. The newspapers and police were fascinated that the murderer(s) had shown up when Masa's wife and children were out of town, on his night off—and that they'd evidently been welcomed, since there was no sign of violence, other than Masa's being dead. So it looked as if the murderer was no stranger. I had a personal investment in knowing the motive. Would I be next?

The list of people Masa knew and trusted was small, and no, I told the police, he did not have boyfriends. Find someone who could benefit from his death, I said. I could see the list going through the captain's head, processing the list of potential suspects. A few weeks later, I checked in as usual at the private number at the mayor's office. The woman on the other end said she had no idea what I was talking about. I cited the case number and got the same response. There was no record. Someone had gotten to it.

I felt a connection with Masa. In early 1985, Herb Caen had reported I was about to put Santa Fe and Stars up for sale and open a place all my own in New York. I had planted that story, and had even gone to New York to look at sites, to get my partner Doyle's attention. Certainly nothing else did, unless it was time for his lunch or a cocktail waitress. During this period I turned down the job at Stephen Spector's Le Plaisir, despite Jim Beard handing it to me on a plate. Why not use the sous chef Masa, I had said. Then, when I turned down the job as chef of the Auberge du Soleil in Napa, Claude Rouas, whose top San Francisco restaurant, L'Étoile, was put out of business by Stars (some said), hired Masa. He and I thought we were stalking each other. So when I learned his widow was penniless, I decided to act.

I gave a fund-raiser at Stars one Sunday morning to send Masa's widow and children home to Central America or, as her thank-you note to me said, to "ensure a stable future for my children." When Bill Kimpton showed up for the event he approached me. "Why would you bother to do a thing like this?" he asked. I was speechless.

Later I decided the attacks—except for Masa's—were all what Lord Peter Wimsey or Hercule Poirot would call a "red herring," that the idea of serially killing chefs had been borrowed from a famous book, movie, and TV series. I meant nothing—and neither, probably, did the chef who was knifed in the head in the Sunset. Nothing like leaving too many clues to get away with murder.

THE KING IS DEAD. LONG LIVE . . .

Soon after Masa, Jim Beard died, on January 21,1985. At the age of eighty-one, he was a testimony that if you stay vitally interested in life, it does not matter what you eat. Or how much.

He managed to leave this planet to go organize another with most of his dignity intact, and a life full of pleasurable culinary moments. His body had not kept up with his desires, and there were long hospital stays. Vast quantities of animal fat eaten in his life tended to stick around.

A few months before he died he called me to New York. The instructions over the phone were vague, but his voice held no room for refusing. I arrived at his house on West Twelfth Street in Manhattan around ten in the morning.

He offered no coffee or anything to eat, so I knew the business was serious, even when it took him almost ninety minutes to get to the point.

"Jeremiah"—his voice steely velvet—"you know you still have an enemy out there."

Stunned, but not surprised at the statement, I waited to reply, thinking, Only one? And one so important he had to say it personally and in private?

"Of course it's not Alice, because that would be stating the obvious. And not worth the plane ride. You wouldn't have called me all the way here to tell me that." After a silence I added, "You're not going to tell me who, are you?"

He snorted his agreement.

"But it is someone whom you consider a close friend."

Then silence again. A long one.

"I guess I can't buy you lunch," was all I could muster, especially since I knew the conversation and visit were over. How could any digestion follow that?

We were in the downstairs library, him sunk into a huge chair. It all seemed so formal. I leaned over him and didn't avoid the old-man unevenly shaved, bristly wet lips.

"Good-bye, darling," were the last words he ever said to me.

CHAPTER 22

FIGHTING FOR STARS

On the plane back to San Francisco I had a premonition that I would never see Jim again. I had thought I had found safe home ground in the Bay Area by opening Stars, but Jim had said I had enemies, and not ones I could keep close. And I always listened to what Jim had to say. I liked my enemies out in front—this one was obviously more of a terrorist hiding in the gloom.

What I thought of Jim was best summed up by one of Australia's greatest impresarios. Leo Schofield was a critic and food writer for the *Sydney Morning Herald*. A year later his article "California Cuisine" in *Australian Gourmet Traveller*, a magazine I read religiously, said Beard was the person who "liberated American cooking from Gallic shackles." He mentioned chefs whom Beard had influenced, among them Wolfgang Puck ("combining European traditions with chutzpah," photographed in Spago drinking champagne with Stevie Wonder), Bradley Ogden ("the wunderkind from San Francisco, via Traverse City, Michigan"), and me. Puck told Leo that Beard was more important than the *New York Times'* French classicist Craig Claiborne, "who thought one had to go to France for ideas." Schofield mentioned that my link with Beard was particularly strong because of my love of nineteenth-century regional American cooking. When I told Leo my favorite story of a nineteenth-century Cape Cod picnic ending with sun-ripened cantaloupe melons filled with hundred-year-old Madeira that had been chilled the day before down a well, Leo pronounced that I "combined a romantic streak with extraordinary practicality."

I told him he had it the wrong way around, for me and for Beard, that American cuisine, like Australian, was all about straightforwardness of personality and that attraction for the slim chance. "Americans have never been ones to hold back. They go at something, and if that's lemongrass in a sauce, the next thing you have everywhere is Lemon Grass Beurre Blanc. It may not work, but at least they will have a go."

Sometimes this American quality was lauded. In me it was increasingly seen as the "arrogance" of a "megastar."

"ONE LITIGIOUS BITCH"

The king was dead, but dreams needed to go forward.

When asked by a reporter in early 1985 about my future plans, I said the first thing I would do was raise my salary. My disputes with my partner in Stars had turned into a full-scale war of litigation, and my salary was frozen. I was still paying myself fifteen thousand dollars less a year than my chef. But my ambition was to retire as soon as possible with as much money as possible. And that had been my thought from the day I started. Then I could open a restaurant in Monte Carlo like the one half in and half out of the water I had designed for my Harvard School of Design thesis.

Before we opened Stars, Doyle and I had agreed that if the partnership was not working, we would just have to say so and one of us would buy the other out. He delayed and delayed signing the buyout contract. But we had an eye-to-eye handshake. By the piano one afternoon thirty-six days after we opened Stars, my throat, guts, and heart in a tangled mess, I sat down with Doyle and his wife for that chat and our promise to part amicably.

"Tough," was Doyle's reply. The two of them smirked at my astonishment while the bartenders leaned over to hear why I was so alternately red and white in the face.

Our differences were no secret. The previous night Doyle and his wife had come in at prime time to a packed Stars. He complained to me that he had been waiting for two hours for a table. "Let them [the walk-ins] wait" (rather than "let them eat cake," I guess). I knew then that we were truly different animals: I could no more have commandeered a table that night in my own restaurant than have told the cooks to burn the food. Owning a restaurant meant one thing to me, another to him. The next morning I looked at my Gault Millau travel guide filled with photos of the Côte d'Azur and wrote in my daily notebook: "Plan the way out, a coup, or just sell out."

The following night Doyle pulled his own coup.

It was a Sunday evening, and the only reason he was in town on a weekend was for the first benefit we were holding, for AIDS research, one of the first in the United States at which world-famous stars and socialites thought it safe to be seen in public for such a then socially unacceptable cause. Terry McEwen, director of the opera and a grand queen of great style, had the idea of bringing the world's top musicians and singers to the San Francisco Opera, with our very chic mutual friend and mentor Denise Hale ensuring the social turnout and its press. The musical evening brought tears to all but the most hard-bitten, and the after-performance party across the road at Stars was both triumphant and socially safe. Suddenly raising money for AIDS at social gatherings was fun—and acceptable. The only fly in the ointment was my partner.

The mayor and guests were surprised to see Doyle in his Napa farming clothes for a black-tie affair. None of the staff were surprised to see him sitting at the bar downing drinks. I could see that Apache chip on his shoulder slowly growing back into a tree as the more and more famous and bijou-bedecked socialites assembled around the bar before dinner. It did not sit well with Doyle that we were giving away the evening, "losing" probably fourteen thousand dollars in gross sales. It never occurred to him that the staff were donating their time and that the food and wine had been donated as well. The next day our headwaiter, Rick, who was gay, was incensed when he described Doyle's reaction to the event and his comment to him.

"IF IT WEREN'T FOR YOU FAGGOTS"

As I remember, and according to Stars' headwaiter Rick, Doyle said something like, "If it weren't for you faggots, we would not have to do things like this." That was shocking enough for Rick, but the fact that the comment could easily have been heard by the opera director (gay), the mayor (straight), and a major opera star (gay), all standing within earshot, was even more damaging. Rick said that since Herb Caen, San Francisco's gossip columnist, hadn't heard Doyle, he told him.

The next day Herb called to ask what I was going to do before, the implication was, he told the entire city. Two days later the story was out, on the *San Francisco Chronicle*'s most-read page. The staff, outraged, assembled in the alley outside the restaurant after calling me at the Santa Fe. They would return if I insisted, but they wanted my assurance that I'd do something, and fast, about my partner.

I drove into the alley at Stars and persuaded the staff to go back to work. I asked the managers if they wanted to work for Doyle. The answer was a resounding "No!" It was obvious that he should now manage the Santa Fe and I, Stars, so I posted an announcement that I'd be taking over 100 percent of the operations, and that Doyle and his wife would no longer be coming into the restaurant except as equal owners, with all those carefully defined privileges. Within the hour, the staff of the day at the Santa Fe showed up at Stars. I sent them back, and then several of San Francisco's most expensive lawyers began working overtime.

A superbly ruthless attorney understood my predicament.

"You want me to put his neck in the gutter and stamp on it."

With his help I kept my partner and his wife out of Stars long enough to calm the restaurant down. But I knew that the trouble was just starting. I had Stars to myself now, and decided to go for the big deal. Fight for it. But there was still the Santa Fe Bar & Grill.

On New Year's Eve 1985 I was supervising dinner at both Stars and the Santa Fe—alternating one hour at each. Hurtling back and forth over the Bay Bridge without a driver on New Year's Eve, I wondered if my divided loyalties and responsibilities would get me killed. On top of that, Santa Fe was in chaos under Doyle's control. He had promoted a mediocre waiter to manager, where he was even less competent, and when I arrived at 6 P.M. on the biggest night of the year, he was having a leisurely dinner in the office. The staff looked lost, and Doyle was nowhere to be found. No one knew if he'd show up at all.

When my attorneys filed a suit to appoint a receiver for the Santa Fe, Doyle countersued. When asked by a reporter for his take on all this, Doyle said, "The restaurant business is intense and complicated and often inspires disputes." I laughed when I read that, since if Doyle had known as much about the restaurant business as he did about intensity and disputes, we wouldn't have had a problem. I publicly shrugged off the countersuit: "I don't own anything personal in California except a cat, some clothes, and a lot of cookbooks." And I made sure of that the next day.

But I was worried. This was much more dangerous than Alice standing on the steps of her house and screaming, "It's my house, my car, and my restaurant!" A lot more than the tensions inside her Panisse kitchen as described by one of the staff: "We were told that we were a family, but it was more like we were the ugly stepsisters and Alice was Cinderella." More than Jonathan Waxman saying you could never really know fear until you'd heard Alice's footfalls on the stairs. This was Doyle's last stand, and he had a pit bull lawyer.

After too much money spent and time wasted, we agreed finally that the Moons would run the Santa Fe and I would run Stars. It was a big "Duh" for me, but that created a management vacuum at the Santa Fe. After a kitchen fire that was the direct result (or so one of the kitchen staff told me) of no one having set maintenance schedules, Doyle alleged to me that the staff had left the flues dirty to make him look bad. Feeling he was sociopathically paranoid, I suggested we sell the Santa Fe.

ONE PARTNERSHIP DOWN, ONE TO GO

In 1986 I listed Stars with Sotheby's real estate. I knew no one would buy it without me or a noncompete clause, but if the opening bid of $5 million was met, so be it: the Côte d'Azur hadn't gone anywhere. Of course no offers were made, the realtor telling us that without me, why would anyone buy it? Doyle and I entered the next phase, in which we could bid against each other for 100 percent of Stars.

We needed to be at the attorneys' office first thing on a Monday morning with a down payment of $50,000 in cash. The remaining balance from a successful bid would be due in ninety days. I didn't have anything more than a Mercedes payment to my name, so I had to go to the bank. As it happened, however, a manager, Steven Vranian (from our now-famous Newport lunch in 1983), had missed the three o'clock Friday bank closing, so I took the cash from the restaurant. I was later sued for fraud for that ingenuity, but it worked, even if all weekend I was terrified of the illegality. Fortunately, I had much to distract me that weekend, including a celebrity appearance at an Orange County March of Dimes gala and an article to finish for *Vogue*. On Sunday night I opened a magnum of vintage Krug and looked for a bad movie on TV to put me to sleep. The only option was *Attack of the Killer Tomatoes* and that seemed somehow quite fitting.

At 9 A.M. sharp on Monday we were in the attorneys' office, ready for more drama than a high-stakes craps game in Vegas. As usual, Doyle was half an hour late. To save a few bucks, he'd searched for a parking space instead of putting his $60,000 car in the building's garage. After the Moons arrived, it took six hours to set the rules. The bidding started at three thirty. The Moons' attorney tossed the 1889 silver dollar, the wife called, and I won. My opening bid of $500,000. So nervous I forgot the agreed-upon floor and wrote $550,000. Doyle immediately topped it. The poker game had begun.

PHILIPPINES TO THE RESCUE

One had to have the money in hand. I didn't. What I did have was a secret weapon. Tapping a San Francisco source would have given Doyle a shot at finding out how much I had to spend, so I'd gone to my international contacts again. Sitting in the foyer was a man whom I had not introduced. But he could never have been mistaken for poor. Benjamin Bitanga, a friend from the Philippines, and I had an understanding. He would guarantee me up to $1,250,000, over which I promised not to bid.

As the bidding reached $1,000,000, rivulets of sweat rolled down under my shirt. I could not remember how to write the numbers that add $50,000 to a million, and after almost bidding $1,500,000, I pulled the note back and told my lawyer, "Here, you write it, you know what I mean."

What was the restaurant worth? While there are mathematical formulas for working this out, the spread of multipliers is so great, the variables so numerous, and the psychological and emotional forces so powerful, that establishing the monetary value is more art than recognizable science. Commonly understood practice is to multiply the annual net by a number ranging from three to eight, depending on the intrinsic values of the lease, the location, the staff performance, and the goodwill of things like the central figure staying on or not, or anything else that will affect the future viability or earnings. So to Doyle the restaurant was worth a good deal less than it was to me. If he bought Stars, it would be without me, goodwill, or the top staff. But this was poker. Bluffing would get me to pay him more than I wanted to spend.

When the bidding hit $1,250,000, Doyle, his wife, and attorney left the room. Because I was used to his tactics, his rigor mortis smile meant nothing to me. The sweat pushing out from the armpits of his Hugo Boss suit did. I had him, but I was at my ceiling, so he had me, too. He returned with another $50,000 deposit, which I topped with money I didn't have to reach $1,350,000.

Doyle shot out of his chair and said to his lawyer, "Let's take a walk"— which I took to mean they were walking away from the game. Lose his fifty grand to me.

Champagne bubbles floated in front of my eyes. I called the restaurant and told them to put the cases I had in my car (in the event I lost) on ice, and to serve them to the hundred or so regulars in Stars waiting for the outcome.

"You have not bought anything yet," my Asian friend said coolly.

He was right. I called back to tell the restaurant to put the champagne on hold, but I knew from the uproar on the other end of the phone that I was too late. The chefs had had their resumes ready in case of my defeat; now they were ceremonially tearing them up. I told my attorney that if the Moons returned with another bid, I'd have a choice between slitting my wrists and jumping out the office's thirtieth-floor window. Doyle came into the room and spoke.

"YOUR ACES BEAT MY KINGS"

Doyle looked pointedly at my ace Filipino friend. I called the restaurant and confirmed the outcome of the shoot-out. When I returned to Stars, I saw that the evening's menu bore the inscription "All Our Love and Support." I was going to need it.

The opposing attorney later said that Doyle had been "very much a buyer." I wondered where he'd gotten the money—if he had it at all. We later heard an eerie rumor that it was Bill Kimpton and his group. In any case, it was by no means clear who the "winner" had been. The Moons had put only their initial $57,000 into Stars. I thought their getting $1.3 million would satisfy their appetites (2,300 percent annual return should satisfy anyone) and whatever sense of honor they had. But how hurt was their pride? With my first partner I had ignored the power of a woman scorned. Now I had denied the power of a dishonored Apache.

CHAPTER 23

STARS IN OUR EYES

Now that I owned and had Stars all to myself, we had to really face running it. My typical day started at six in the morning. I would stop at Stars for a coffee and to check how many of the flowers had to be replaced. I was doing the arrangements myself because flowers and the flower market brought me peace and sanity. Also I wanted to find out how much labor and cost it took to install the five arrangements: two six-foot-tall and four-foot-wide beauties that reached from on top of each end of the bar to the eighteen-foot ceilings, and three other restaurant-size ones.

A DAY IN THE LIFE OF STARS

That day the espresso machine fouled my cappuccino, so I left a note to the opening bartender wondering what it was in his job description and checklist that he didn't understand about flushing the machine every day with cleaner. Of course my note was written in state-of-the-art California human resources language rather than mine. I didn't want a pouty and whiny bartender when I returned for my next coffee.

I bought twelve-foot-long wild rose runners, massive magnolia and just-fruiting fig branches, and twenty dozen cut flowers. After a fast gossip with a couple of the less discreet vendors about which restaurants were not paying their bills, I stuffed all the flowers in the Citroën Deux Chevaux

ve back to Stars. As I walked through the doors, the bartender
a smile and held out a new cappuccino. As soon as the flowers were
done I visited the basement and greeted the Latino-Tibetan-Vietnamese
prep crew. These were my favorite employees, and twenty minutes with
them could have been the last really good moments of the day, depending on what I would hear at the morning managers' meeting at ten. So I
savored the time talking about washing lettuce by hand and showing them
again how to peel fava beans (never blanched) and peel and cut the cardoon
for a lobster dish slated for one of that night's private parties. Without these
little teaching sessions (which worked both ways), and sometimes despite
them, the day—which could last until two the next morning—could go
really bad.

I checked on the toilets, the homeless outside, the basement pumps, the
carpet, the "take" from the day before, and sat with my chef, bartender, assistant, private dining manager, dining room manager, sous chef, and book-
keeper. We knew it was going to be a rough day, so I canceled my daytime
once-a-week bartending and called in the spare.

The mayor was in for lunch with a new girlfriend and so was his old
one with someone else, so seating in the preferred section was going to be
delicate. Our most regular couple, and also our most demanding, hated the
mayor and, when drunk (every time), would go over and tell him why his
lack of Irish ancestry left him less than a man. They too were booked at the
same time as the mayor. Joan Collins and Barbra Streisand were booked at
lunch for the same time and the same table and, knowing restaurateurs never
have the benefit of coincidence, I wondered aloud if one of them was for
the same time the following week. Either way I would be asked to sit with
both after lunch, cutting into my time to prepare for dinner and the private
parties.

Herb Caen put the pressure on with a note saying he hoped we would
do our "usual eleven out of ten" for "Baby Denise" that night. *Parsifal* was
opening at the opera, which meant starting an hour earlier. Lunch would
be frantic to end early. Denise Hale's party for Zubin Mehta would leave us
a little more than the usual fifteen minutes to turn "the Club" from regular
seating into a fairyland of special decor that would have strained London's
Ritz when there were four staff members for every two guests. Carol Chan-

ning was with that party, and her anti-allergy lunch box had to be taken from her the moment she entered and kept at the maître d' stand so she didn't worry it would be contaminated. Godfrey, Denise's chauffeur, was to be there at 5 P.M. with her pink lightbulbs, the candle stands, tablecloths, and napkins. All the special plates, glasses, decor, and flatware would have to be polished by 5 P.M. and put nearby in the hallway out of sight for the minutes we had to set up her party. I told the bartender to make new special ice cubes with Evian for Denise's husband and San Francisco patriarch, Prentis Cobb Hale, and to leave a note for the evening bartender to have his Waterford glass, little tray, and two pieces of bread ready for his arrival by 7:45.

"It's your neck," I reminded the dining room manager, and continued briefing.

The security guards for the jewels worn would have to be fed. The piano had to be moved and tuned in place for the reception, then moved back for the later bar crowd. That took eight people and me. Chilies had to be crushed for Zubin Mehta no earlier than 8 P.M., and cookies set aside for the chauffeur. The North Station guys alerted us that Danielle Steel was wearing her two-million-dollar-each Graff twin diamonds, one on each hand. The dining room staff alerted that her Dior dress cost $150,000, that no waiter was allowed near her, that the red wine would have to be poured only by the manager, and that she needed a special stool because she couldn't sit down in that dress. Our insurance company had to be alerted about the jewels and the dress. There was to be a special cake, which Mrs. Mehta had arranged to arrive by private jet from Los Angeles by six o'clock. An alert was to be sent out to me and the pastry chefs if no one had seen it by then.

There were two private dinners that night other than Denise's, one for twenty-five in the Grill Room and one for forty in the "JT's" room. The chef reported all the food was prepped. The late-arriving wine steward said he'd checked the wines and one selection of the parties' wines was missing.

"Find it!"

The flowers were being supplied by the hosts of the parties. I reminded the manager about our 10 percent service charge for that, and to make sure Denise was not charged for the cake Mrs. Mehta was bringing.

"Whatever you do, if I am busy, make sure the security guards have the homeless out of there by seven o'clock." I heard a shout from the men's room as one of the bookkeepers ran into a particularly scrofulous homeless man taking a bath from the sink. We threw him out, and the dishwasher cleaned up the piles of wet old newspaper that had been used as underwear. With concealed rage I reminded everyone to keep the front door locked until 11 A.M. and told them to reclean the room. Then I went up to my office.

The first meeting was about the ever-mysterious and always emotional annual health insurance policies, the monthly financials, the bank loan payment now at $35,000 a month, cash flow, and the cash for my trip. The second was with my assistant about my seven-day round-the-world press trip in two days' time.

DENISE AGAIN

The phone rang. Denise would be late for the afternoon decor meeting because her red dress being flown in by Gianfranco Ferré had not yet arrived. But the new fragrance presents for her guests, Fendi, had. Her driver would drop them off.

I told my assistant to copy the letter from Wolfgang Puck's wife, Barbara Lazaroff, after we had launched Wolfgang and her frozen desserts in San Francisco, and put it on the staff board for all to see: "For my darling adorable *talented* #1 boyfriend—it was fabulous. See me for the other list of adjectives in private!" And to post BBC's famous chef Ken Hom's letter saying how "fantastic" we all were.

The other letters to be answered included one from Frank Stitt at the Highlands Bar & Grill wondering if he could come and observe the kitchens for a couple of days; from Diana Kennedy with "abrazos" suggesting a trip with Alice Waters and Dick Graff (of the Institute of Wine & Food) to see her in Mexico; thanks from restaurateur Danny Meyer for his "fabulous" dinner at Stars and offering jobs in New York to any of my staff; from chef Jasper White loving the Stars excitement; from chef Jan Birnbaum scolding me for not offering him a job, forcing him to take the Quilted Giraffe job instead; from Bill Rice at *Food & Wine* saying I was one of the first to be nominated for the "Dining Hall of Fame"; from Willy Bishop, now in the North County Jail, saying, "I don't know what the fuck is happening here . . . but I need money"; from *Cook's* magazine's Chris Kimball saying he needed by the next day my nominees for their "Who's Who" (I wrote in Joe Baum, Marion Burros, the Chino Ranch, M. F. K. Fisher, Judith Jones, Diana Kennedy, John Mariani, and James Villas); from Bruce Neyers at Joseph Phelps Vineyards saying the previous week's trade tasting at Stars "was quite simply the benchmark against which we will undoubtedly compare all future tastings"; and from the chef Michael Chiarello, then at Toby's in Miami, saying that the Stars crew was the "most intense, totally committed group" he had seen. He wanted "to be just like you when I grow up."

I answered those and letters from the Soviet ambassador about my proposal for a culinary exchange between "our two countries"; from *New York* magazine's Gael Greene saying how beautiful our fish had been at the Citymeals-on-Wheels at Rockefeller Center and asking me to do another; from Martha Stewart about her supper at Stars after we judged a March of Dimes together; from March of Dimes director Elaine Whitelaw asking me to do an event in Houston; and from amfAR's (American Foundation for AIDS Research) Mathilde Krim and fourteen other organizations inquiring about donations.

I dictated letters to the chefs Alain Ducasse and Gerard Besson (always my first lunch stop in Paris) to thank them for coming to Stars; to Jacques Pépin and Madeleine Kamman for saying Stars was their favorite restaurant in San Francisco; to Julia Child for our breakfast together; to Terry Durack and Jill Dupleix, my favorite Australian food writers, who wanted to fly to Stars from Sydney for the night; and to Coudert Frères, from whom I hoped to make arrangements to buy the Grand Restaurant Colbert in Paris. Then there were the hate letters.

One woman was "very angry" at having spent ninety dollars for five people in Stars Cafe, which had butcher paper on the tables. She accused me of "fraud" for calling a salad of mixed greens with oil and vinegar a "green salad," a dish she said was defined as having vegetables in it. And she said that if a steak could not be cut with a fork it was not a steak. She called me a "cheat," so I penned in return very politely what a salad was, what made up a great New York steak, and advice that she should get new teeth. Another letter hated the noise and the color of the walls, and insisted I was a "screwup." All possibly true, I replied, but give us another chance.

LUNCH

Then it was time for lunch service. I blew up a page from a profile on James Beard in *Gastronome* in which he was questioned on food fads ("Chacun a son mauvais gout") and hung it on the cooking line. There were three appetizers, seven salads, one soup, four sandwiches, seven grills and main courses, and six desserts for me to taste—a teaspoon each. After that I just wanted to go home. Six hours into the job, and ten to twelve more to go. After the lunch service was over and I had said hello to half the 225 guests, I sat down to my own—a salad. The fork was about to enter my mouth when I heard an urgent, if not desperate, "J.T.!" My chef, Mark Franz, had arrived and was gesturing from the kitchen door down to the basement, where there were offices, wine, food storage, and the sump pump.

"The drains again—backed up big-time."

There was a scream from the ladies' toilet as something gray and uninvited came up through the floor drain. I looked into the kitchen and saw the same. If it was not stopped in a few minutes, Stars could be closed for twenty-four hours by the health department, and they were fifteen feet across the alley from our entrance. The opera started in three and a half hours, and Denise was due in twenty minutes for the third of many meetings about the lightbulbs to be changed for her party.

I ran down the stairs, back into the farthest reaches of the basement. The water was an inch deep, around the large-oil-drum-sized, five-foot deep hole in the floor, now overflowing with what looked like the bottom of San Francisco Bay. Two dishwashers, two sous chefs, and some prep crew were gawking. The faces turned to me signaled a silent but very clear "do something." It was clear that this was something they could not be asked to do. It was a job for the one at whom the buck stopped.

I flipped off my now-soaked Italian loafers, peeled off my Hermès blazer, and jumped in. Having to not breathe underwater meant I had less than a minute to save the day. I bent over double in the confined space filled with sewage water and pulled out a cook's towel that had been sucked into the pump. The group hauled me out, and burst out laughing. A tampon was lodged on my shoulder, and a piece of onion skin was stuck to my forehead as a third eye. They wrapped me in garbage bags so I could get home without ruining the Connolly leather in my car.

Back in Stars an hour later, pink-skinned from all the scrubbing and disinfectant, I found the bar-hound regulars bowing to me. A few curtsied. For a moment I thought I was a sewage hero. It turned out that San Francisco's most important magazine, *Focus,* had come out with its annual awards, including "Classics of San Francisco," which included the Opera House, M. F. K. Fisher, Levi Strauss, and Jeremiah Tower, "self-proclaimed monarchist who overthrew the ancient regime of Continental chefdom, ushering in a new era of endless experimentation, American regionalism, and California cuisine." After the ribbing I needed a tetanus booster shot from a customer who was also our Stars doctor who, alerted and bribed with a glass of champagne, plunged the needle in while suggesting we reroute the sewage away from the sump.

AFTERNOON

In the hour before the bar filled up with operagoers, we had the afternoon managers' meeting to go over the details of the rest of the evening again. The topics other than the night's events and its overtime costs were Halloween: no leather chaps with bare asses or nipple rings this year; the policy again that managers may not take employees home with them when they already have someone there; the ongoing and never solvable problem of staff meals; the annual January closing for cleaning; the location of the thirty-three bottles of Leroy wines, back then valued at $1,000 each, for Lalou Bize-Leroy's tasting in two weeks and where to store them; and the right message to the managers about the details and extravagance of my press trip. They knew already that, like James Beard, I was "born with an airline ticket in my mouth."

Then I tasted wines with the Joseph Phelps manager Bruce Neyers, who always showed up around martini time; with the liquor salesman "Fast" Eddie Cayson to change the house vodka; with the wine rep Madeleine de Jean, to change the champagne by the glass from Billecart to Clicquot; gave a lesson to the staff on what "corked" wine really is and tastes like; met with the ADA inspectors and refused to talk to the Channel 4 TV crew, who were checking measurements in the men's room again; heard with deep shock a favorite (five days a week at the oyster bar) young customer tell me he had AIDS and ask if I could pay for his AZT; still reeling from that, was therefore not shocked when a naked streaker ran from one door through the restaurant; greeted the public utilities inspectors at their usual bar stools drinking so many Sapporo beers that I was practically a Japanese national hero.

At five thirty the flowers for one of the private parties had still not been arranged. The dinner was at six. I ran to my office and grabbed the flowers, made four centerpieces, and delivered them to the tables as the hostess walked in. "Just checking them myself to see they are perfect," I lied. She adored the lie. For the other private party thirty minutes later, one of the reserved wines had not arrived. I took the host to the wine cellar and let him pick wines from the right side of my private collection. The wine was on me. The Mehta cake had not arrived, but I got a call from the pilot of the Lear: they were about to land. I checked on the homeless at the front door. It was raining, so they hadn't moved. My nemesis was shouting he wanted to kill me and chased me inside Stars. I hit the panic button at the podium, and when the North Station guys showed up and moved the homeless down the street, some of the customers cheered and some called me a fascist.

EVENING

Right on schedule our most regular customers arrived. The O'Deas were already smashed, telling me they were not moving from the table until they got to see the Mehtas, to whom they were going to give several pieces of their now-blurred minds about the Three Tenors.

Denise arrived and, bathed in the light of the hastily installed pink lightbulbs, wondered aloud if they were the right color.

"Well, here comes Zubin, so they had better be," I said.

"Remember," she whispered in my ear, "the Haut-Brion is for me and Zubin. All the others get the Jordan."

At that moment, Sally Jordan walked in and asked what wine we were drinking tonight. I told her the usual, and the usual: hers and the bottles wrapped in napkins. She looked at me, and the corners of her mouth twisted into an unspoken "That Denise!"

"I guess I'll have to have the Jordan."

The menu:

Dinner for the Zubin Mehtas
Scallop Hash with Lobster Sauce
Black Truffled Braised Beef
Cèpes Mashed-Potato Timbale
Passion Fruit Stars Cream with Raspberry Sauce
Jordan Chardonnay 1988
Jordan Cabernet Sauvignon 1987

Halfway through the dinner I saw that the waiter had let the napkin fall off the mystery bottle. I couldn't have Denise busted, so I raced to the table and told everyone that the Haut-Brion was my gift: I just wanted to see if the host and hostess liked it before I offered it to the group.

That really cost me.

The cake arrived in the arms of a chauffeur.

Meanwhile I ran between the two kitchens attached to the private rooms to cook and help serve. Since I was cooking also for the Mehta party, the three menus became confused in my head, and I directed one of the dishes to the wrong room, though, thank God, not to Denise. I went out to the hostess and lied that I had not liked the fish I had recommended a few days earlier and changed it at the last moment. Of course I would not charge her for the dish.

That cost me more.

She loved that I was cooking.

I was summoned over to the edge of Denise's party. One of the guests, almost as smashed as the O'Deas, who were now glowering at the Mehtas, told me that her Oscar de la Renta (he was at the head table) had been ruined by water in the ladies' room, and that the "water" was not water. I would have to pay for the dress ($3,500). On checking out the cause of the dampness, my maître d' whispered to me that perhaps the woman had peed herself since there was no "water" on the floor. I sent a note to her on my card saying Stars would be happy to pay for the dry cleaning—even when, as she informed me, it would have to go to New York.

The day was becoming expensive. I wondered if I could send the dress in the Mehtas' plane to New York.

The wife of a famous local rock star grabbed me on her way back from the ladies' room.

"Darling, the light in there is bright enough to sear the makeup right off a whore's face!"

I tilted my head at the manager to check out the lights.

"And, furthermore, the counter is wet, so I lost all my fucking coke."

That I didn't have to pay for, thank God.

The bathroom bulbs were indeed white. The dining room hosts had forgotten to change them to pink. I hoped that Denise didn't have to pee before I could get one of the staff to find the bulbs so I grabbed a busboy and the spares at the podium and put them in.

The dining room manager then told me that Denise was ready for dessert, but that Mrs. Mehta did not want the planned forty wild strawberry soufflés we were about to put in the oven. Only the cake.

That cost me several hundred dollars in ingredients and lost revenue, since it was now too late to put the soufflés on the supper menu or offer them to the private parties and charge a supplement.

The waiters hauled the cake to the table draped and ready. Denise and Mrs. Mehta came over to the cake. Then Mehta handed me the knife and asked if I knew how to cut cake.

"Use this," she said.

Visions of sinking it into her head instead of the cake temporarily unbalanced me, but a quick "excuse me" before I did and a nip of champers at the bar put me right. Back at the cake table, sticking the knife into the cake nearly broke my wrist. Halfway in it was solid. Trying to pull it out nearly dislocated my back. The cake was still 50 percent frozen. Now I was standing there in front of forty of America's finest with Excalibur in my hand. The look on my face brought a couple of managers running.

"Get Mark [the chef] now!"

Somehow, and against the adderlike whispers of Mrs. Mehta that it had to be cut right there and right now, the cake was removed to the kitchen and sawed into pieces. I retired to the end of the bar farthest from the party for a breather before they left. Then I shook hands good-bye with the sixty-odd private dining guests after a speech in each room and went back to the bar. My stomach felt as if the sump pump was getting its revenge, so I pushed the champagne away for a Fernet-Branca.

ALMOST MIDNIGHT

I shook hands with everyone from Denise's party and saw her glare. After all had left and the flowers were being put in her car, she showed me her bill. She never paid them at the moment but always wanted to see them. The computer had automatically added a cake charge even though the waiter had written: "Cake—comp JT."

"Frank," I said loudly to the dining room manager, who had been at both meetings, "come over here and kill yourself." This was one rap I was not going to take. But the party had been a success because her tycoon trophy hunter and patrician rancher husband had the last word. As usual.

"Well, what do you expect from a chef? They're all goddamn cheats," roared Prentis.

"If I were, Prentis, I would be as rich as you."

He shook with repressed laughter and went down the corridor on his cane. "And don't forget to get the goddamn ladies' room fixed." I saw them into their car and waved good-bye. I had earned some oysters and Montrachet. Then a little voice behind me.

"J.T.?"

I recognized one of my favorite people at Stars, my Ethiopian head valet, Solomon.

"J.T. We have lost a car."

I was then momentarily distracted as Gianni Versace walked in with some of San Francisco's socialite switch hitters, and I showed him to the best table in the house. He had just come from the opening of the opera, for which he had designed the costumes.

At the bar, someone male, young, Asian, and handsome motioned me over. "Would you tell Mr. de W. with Versace that I would like to meet him? My name is Andrew Cunanan."

I did, and he sat at their table.

Meanwhile, it seemed to Solomon that I had forgotten his valet problem. "It's not just any car, J.T. It's a new Mercedes 560 SEL."

I went to the front door and saw a couple standing there on the sidewalk. Had Solomon looked everywhere? With no sign of the car except for the owners' valet parking stub, I told Solomon to give them my keys. I told the extraordinarily patient customers that my 560 would be there in two minutes, and did they mind it was silver, and could I have their telephone number? I gave them Solomon's number and prayed my car had enough gas in it.

Solomon drove me home, and I told him to leave a note on the opening chef's desk to say that I might be a little late in the morning. And for no one to call me if the customers in my car ran out of gas in Mill Valley!

The author, 1947

The author's childhood home in Sydney, 1947

At a resort in the Great Barrier Reef,
Australia, 1948

A school portrait at age six

The author's family home on Trodds Lane in Merrow, Guildford, in Surrey, England

The author at age twelve, 1955

The author with his class at King's College School in Wimbledon, London, 1957

Portrait taken just before the
author attended the Loomis
School in Connecticut, 1959

The author played on the Loomis soccer
team at age seventeen.

The author in Newport,
Rhode Island, after graduating
from Harvard College, 1965

A notice advertising an opening in the kitchen at Chez Panisse in Berkeley, California

Drawing from Willy Bishop, sous chef at Chez Panisse

CHEZ : PANISSE

REGIONAL DINNERS

7 : October : 1976

The dinner that started the revolution in American cooking

Northern California Regional Dinner

October 7, 1976 $20.00

Spenger's Tomales Bay bluepoint oysters on ice

Cream of fresh corn soup, Mendocino style, with crayfish butter

Big Sur Garrapata Creek smoked trout steamed over California bay leaves

Monterey Bay prawns sautéed with garlic, parsley, and butter

Preserved California grown geese from Sebastopol

Vela dry Monterey Jack cheese from Sonoma

Fresh caramelized figs

Walnuts, almonds, and mountain pears from the San Francisco Farmers' Market

x

Wine offered by the glass $1.50

Schramsberg Cuvée de Gamay 1973

Mount Eden Chardonnay 1973

Beaulieu Cabernet Private Reserve 1970

Ridge Zinfandel, Fiddletown 1974

Mission Del Sol, Harbor Winery 1974

Tawny Port, East Side Winery

The menu from the Northern California Regional Dinner at Chez Panisse, "the dinner that started the revolution," 1976

The author with Julia Child at her birthday celebration, 1982

The author cooking lunch for one hundred food journalists
at the Astor Mansion, 1983

The author at the front doors of his Stars
restaurant in San Francisco, 1986

Colorful menu art from Stars

NEW YEAR'S EVE 1986

CHOICE OF FIRST COURSE

Six Native Oysters on the Half Shell
Six American Belon Oysters on the Half Shell
Stars' Gravlax with Grilled Herb Brioche
Mark's Muscovy Duck Breast Prosciutto
Beef Tartare with Shaved Black Truffles
Jeremiah's California Warm Vegetable Salad in Truffle Oil
Truffled Brandade Gratin with Lobster Hollandaise
Mixed Fish and Shellfish Fry with a Truffle Black Pepper and Lemon Sauce
Galantine of Boar's Head Stuffed with Pistachios
Belgian Endive, Watercress, Hazelnut and Duck Crackling Salad
Polenta with Wild Mushrooms

CHOICE OF MAIN COURSE

Grilled Whole Dover Sole with Fried Artichokes and Lobster Butter
Poached Red Snapper with Two Risottos and Normandy Butter-Chervil Sauce
Chartreuse of Pheasant with Truffled Duck Neck Sausage and Marrow
Grilled Saddle of Rabbit with Foie Gras, Radicchio and Chilies
Roast and Confit of Mallard with an Artichoke, Celery and Truffle Salad
Roast Rack of Lamb, Perfumed with Sage, Served with Celery Root and Black Truffles
Grilled Filet of Beef with Foie Gras and Madeira Sauce

CHOICE OF DESSERT

Caramelized Pistachio Cream
Individual Pippin Apple Tartlet
Poached Pears with Passion Fruit Sabayon and Raspberry Sauce
Bittersweet Cake with Chocolate Sauce
Chocolate Bread and Butter Pudding with Mocha Sauce
The Stars' Paradise
Alice B. Toklas Nougat Ice Cream with Caramel Sauce
Mango, Papaya and Passion Fruit Compote with Italian Cream

$100.00 Per Person Plus Tax

The three-course New
Year's Eve dinner at Stars,
1986

The author opened another
branch of Stars Cafe in Oakville,
Napa Valley, California.

The dining room at the
Peak Cafe in Hong Kong,
which opened in 1990.

By 1988, Stars of San
Francisco had been an
international sensation for
nearly five years.

The signed menu from SF Chef's 2012 Dinner Party Project: Stars Realigned

Scuba diving in Turks and Caicos, 2014

The author testing food at Foreign Cinema's tribute to Stars in San Francisco, 2013

CHAPTER 24

THE JUDGES PRONOUNCE

The next morning I was to leave on the trip I had put off for Denise's dinner, but I decided to hang a right to some tropical island first. I took my first extravagant, nonworking vacation since I'd started at the Santa Fe, four years previously. I went to Bora Bora. Ever since that glass of pineapple juice in Fiji forty-six years earlier, tropical air and food had always been a guaranteed way of nursing myself back to life. Extreme hotel luxury helped. While I was sitting on the white sand with my understanding companion Charles Thompson in front of the azure waters, sipping a forty-year-old Calvados after a lunch of still-kicking rock lobsters, the future of owning Stars on my own came into focus: get back to the real business of running restaurants, and back in the biggest possible way.

FOLLOW THE MONEY

I had taken eighty-six of the allocated ninety days to come up with all the money for Doyle, and now I was committed to a killing payback. It was going to take a lot of grilled fish and hamburgers to pay off the $5 million of principal and interest that would accumulate after the buyout. At least, I comforted myself as I wrote my new cash-flow projections from my tropical villa, I was free from the thousands of dollars a month in attorneys' fees I had been paying for the last four years.

When I returned from vacation, there was a huge stack of "discovery" demands on my desk. Sued again. The shock was as big as my delusion that everything was going to be mine, and mine in peace. Leaked to the *San Francisco Chronicle*'s Herb Caen, the Moons' new lawsuit made headlines. To the press it seemed I was incapable of letting a year go by without going to court. And they were right: in the past twelve years I had spent almost a million dollars on attorneys and costs for the privilege of being a partner in restaurants and then a sole owner. One column quoted someone calling me "a litigious bitch." Only my long-suffering but well-employed attorney, Richard Collier, knew that I had actually initiated just one of those lawsuits—the Santa Fe one that moved Doyle to the negotiating table.

Now the Moons wanted to see every receipt, guest check, letter, and memo that had been generated since the day we opened, totaling several hundred thousand documents, including some 800,000 guest checks. The cost of compiling those records would have choked a billionaire. The only, if extremely painful, answer was to let the Moons back into Stars to search and do the copying themselves.

Doyle knew better than to waste his own time, but his wife was possessed. Now she had a more significant role to play than being locked up in their country house by her husband. She would be the Sherlock who'd find evidence of the $985,000 they claimed I had stolen from Stars and Santa Fe.

After a year of this, we ended up in binding arbitration. But that meant once again putting the restaurant on hold. Now the ninety-hour weeks I had slated to resurrect Stars were filled with amassing the answers to the Moons' hundreds of allegations, and searching through the dusty basement storage area for documents now in disarray from their blind gropings by Mrs. Moon.

It was time to head over to the arbitrator. He turned out to be a white-haired septuagenarian of the old school. Definitely someone to relate better to me than to Moon, and his shiny new and ill-fitting suit. But the list of accusations was so vast that, if only a quarter of them proved true, I should have been thrown in jail and the key thrown away.

As sins going back ten years to Santa Fe were recited, I would reach down and pull out a folder of explanatory records and put it on the table under the gloating eyes of the Moons. At first the judge was enthralled. On the third full day of their accusations and my comprehensive answers, he fell asleep—a good sign, given the vividness of my alleged crimes. When, across the polished rosewood table, the burly and bellowing Moon attorney failed to rouse him but my patient and quiet response did, I knew we had won, but for how much, I didn't.

THE JUDGMENT

On my way back from Napa to Stars one afternoon, I called my attorney Richard Collier for any news from the judge. First I told him about the little cafe I had just seen in Oakville with a "For Sale" sign outside (later to become Stars Oakville Cafe) and then remembered to ask if there was any news.

Out of the nearly million dollars the Moons claimed I hoodwinked from under their noses, they received nothing but the price of my ticket to Tahiti. In my shock upon returning from the beach to find the foot-high stack of lawsuits on my desk, I had forgotten to reimburse the travel agent, who had then billed Stars. This was the only time in eight years I had not kept perfect records, down to my smallest reimbursement, a personal check for $1.75, which so inspired my white-haired justice.

The results of the hearing were not publicized, so I remained a crook in the old-boy capitalist eyes of my richest customers. But to reassure the staff, all capitalists themselves, I walked up Van Ness Avenue and returned forty minutes later with a new silver BMW 750 IL.

Now I could finally turn to the business of Stars.

Ann Bramson, one of America's greatest cookbook editors (then at William Morrow, but she had done *Jeremiah Tower's New American Classics* for Harper & Row), described Stars better than anyone: "It has an energy and spirit and a come-hither quality that makes you feel just plain better the minute you walk through the doors. It's a high to be there. Unlike any other place I've ever been."

Now I just had to keep it that way.

OTHER JUDGES AND JUDGMENTS

Herb Caen reported my vow "to give Stars my best shot now," saying I should be encouraged by the framed letters from famous lovers of Stars on the walls. The one that amused him the most was from his pal in crime Harry de Wildt, the man who had asked fifteen years earlier to be moved from next to me at table when he found out I was a chef. His note saying how wonderful Herb's seventy-seventh birthday had been reprimanded me: "Next time, you must join us and *Sit Down*." My favorite was from someone not massively famous. Yet. "You looked great, and so did my favorite restaurant in the world, Mario Batali. PS. Barbara Kafka won't come into my new restaurant [1993] without you, so get out here [New York] soon!" Others were already famous: "Still fresh and exciting, as if it has always been there," from Jasper White; from Georges Blanc a postcard said his French chef pals wished us "très fidèlement a bientôt"; Robert Parker thought his Sonoma rabbit loins wrapped in pancetta better than any in France; the "Lettuce Entertain You" genius Rich Melman from Chicago thought Stars "wonderful"; Australia's wine guru Len Evans adored Stars because Ernest Gallo had fallen in love with him there; and a message from the Archbishop of Canterbury said Stars was his favorite restaurant in California. The great Johnny and Betsey Apple loved the buzz in Stars that was just like his favorites and mine. "La Coupole, Bibendum in London, George Lang's in New York [Café des Artistes]"; Anne Willan got right to the core, saying Stars' "sophisticated good eating reminded me irresistibly of a picture of the Savoy in London in Escoffier's time—and now Jim Woods in [the *San Francisco Examiner*] tells me you were brought up in the Savoy shadow—so perhaps it's not just an accident"; and from Julia Child: "You have such a flair. Gastronomy is not dead chez vous."

Now that all these compliments were in print and in view, we had the public challenge to live up to them.

My managers and I outlined a battle plan at the same time that the press heaped new attention on the restaurant. Germany's *Die Welt* spoke of our "kalifornischen Meisterkoch." *People* magazine had a full-page victory photo of me lounging on the star-covered carpet stairs, a glass of champagne on the upper step. *Members* magazine, for the rich and famous, named Stars one of the world's best brasseries, with Harry's Bar in Venice, Bice in Milan, and Le Caprice in London. The mayor of San Francisco, citing the restaurant's community and charitable work, declared a "Stars Day" in 1988. What to do to pay off our debts seemed clear: more of the same.

I told the managers that success in the future meant building press away from the melodrama and hubris of the "Superchef" to focus on the restaurant. We had not strayed irretrievably far from that priority, so now we could go full steam ahead without diversions.

CHAPTER 25

"THEY ROLL INTO TOWN LIKE ROCK STARS"

One of the best tactics for the restaurants promoting themselves in the eighties was their role as fund-raisers and providers of high-profile press coverage for national and local charities. Our first AIDS research fund-raiser and the 1983 American Institute of Wine & Food "American Festival" dinner had proven that a lot of money could be made by giving the rich an amusing time while they ate and the press watched. A cover story in a 1987 San Francisco's *Focus* magazine explored this increasingly big business through the prism of an event called "AID & Comfort." A thousand people paid $250 apiece to attend. According to the article, Alice Waters charmed her way through the crowd, "lending her glamour, her name, her star appeal. Back in the kitchen, as Jeremiah Tower was quietly putting the finishing touches on one of the evening's culinary triumphs—tuna carpaccio—one of the local restaurant mavens cracked, 'That's the way it's always been, Alice out front, getting all the glory, and Jeremiah in the background, cooking great food.'"

But most of us felt it was about teamwork, with enough publicity to go around for everyone. We all made out splendidly from the new charitable bashes. In addition to the Meals-on-Wheels extravaganzas, there were various other AIDS fund-raisers, Open Hand, Share Our Strength, and more. My personal road show was Elaine Whitelaw's March of Dimes or, as the *Washington Post* called it in 1988, "The Munch of Dimes."

The Stars team learned a precious lesson on our first extended road show.

When we arrived at the site of an event in Maui, we found the Austrian chef in a severe depression, sitting alone in his glass-walled office high above the empty kitchen, chewing the end of a three-foot raw kielbasa coiled in his lap. The first bad moment was when I realized he had no idea who we were and why we were there. The second was when the promised team of six cooks never appeared. The third was when the equipment ordered weeks before was a no-show. We got to work. After staying up all night cutting five cases each of red, gold, and yellow bell peppers into very fine slices by myself, I swore on my bleeding hands that I would not be dependent on any chef or restaurant not controlled by us ever again.

I doubled the number of staff on the road show team and insisted they be put up in the same hotels as me. When this was viewed as "demanding," I had a momentary lapse of resolve. But after landing in New York in the middle of an ice storm that delayed our arrival several hours, the limos gone, and arriving at the Hotel Pierre to find our donated reservations nonexistent, I decided a different future was starting that night. These were pre–cell phone days and, as we stood in the Pierre lobby with our mountain of luggage, equipment, and supplies, the person behind the front desk masquerading as a man finally agreed to let me use his phone. I called the manager of my favorite hotel, the Plaza Athénée, and explained I needed four rooms and my usual green suite—this on a Friday night in the beginning of New York's holiday season.

"Really?" Gasp and a long pause. "You'd better come right over."

Once I was in my suite and the staff bedded down, I wondered how I would explain this expense to a judge. The trip was just before the last arbitration with the Moons. As I sank into the Irish linen sheets and watched the snow falling outside the greenhouse on my penthouse terrace, I didn't care. I vowed we would now pay for everything, and to hell with the ever-evanescent donations and freebies.

Some of the disasters, of course, were of my own making. I thought it would be cold for one October Meals-on-Wheels in Los Angeles under a tent in the parking lot of Wolfgang Puck's original Spago, so I decided to do suckling pig with a white truffle sauce (one dramatic food and one expensive) to show us off and grab press attention. As one of the longer lines gathered in front of our Stars sign, I realized the first gasps were of not pleasure but disgust. Most of the guests were Jewish. Some asked, how could I have been so stupid? Even my usually loyal staff were shaken at my naive miscalculation. The turkey-necked and pearl-throated squawks from some of the older matrons in orange Capri pants finally unnerved us all, so we left early to get back to the Westwood Marquis. Over the first Ladoucette Pouilly-Fumé, we discussed our next road show. I promised that we'd serve "safe" food, and that the only drama would come from the props. "You will notice," I said, "that none of the chefs is doing anything to decorate their booths. That's our way to glory."

The next Citymeals-on-Wheels was a year later at Rockefeller Center. This time we were ready, arriving well in advance to get a prime location on the rink across from the steps down to the fountain. I had noticed at past events that no one could see the food once the sun had gone down, so that was my focus, and we had our travel pack (lights, tools, electrical equipment, French tablecloths, first aid kit) with everything we'd need to be independent of the local support staff.

On this June night at Rockefeller Center we set up a ziggurat of ice behind our well-lighted front table (also ice) for a huge shellfish bar. I lit the ice from behind, using the same colors as in the huge golden-figured fountain beside us, and when the guests arrived at the top of the stairs, they saw first the fountain and then us. It helped that we were spit-roasting a whole head-on tuna over an eight-foot-long mesquite-charcoal grill, something no one, including us, had seen before. When the cameras for the TV show *Lifestyles of the Rich and Famous* arrived, the fish caught the camera. With that publicity, the five thousand mid-eighties dollars it cost us to do the event would have been cheap at ten times the price.

A Ruth Reichl story in the *Los Angeles Times* about a Meals-on-Wheels on the terrace of L.A.'s Pacific Design Center, aka "the Blue Whale," was called "Chefs as the Star Ingredients." The lead photo shows me arriving with my crew and hauling my private rolling "Travel Pac" full of some of the tools we would need. Wrote Ruth, "They roll into town like rock stars, roadies in their wake. They stay in the best hotels, are wined and dined in the finest restaurants, and when show time finally comes they are interviewed, photographed, and besieged by autograph hunters. They are 'The Celebrity Chefs.'" She went on, "Chefs used to send a check, a recipe, or a dish to charity. Now they send themselves with such regularity that some of them have regular road crews." One of the guests said she came more for the show than for the food. "I just wanted to come and look. I guess you could call me a food groupie. But isn't he handsome?" Another fan passed up our tuna. "I've never heard of him," she sniffed, and went searching for whoever was being filmed by *Entertainment Tonight*.

A RUSSIAN GENERAL

I was already a victim of the travel bug, but all this touring and cooking had such an invigorating effect on the staff and the tourist business at Stars that I rarely turned down an invitation to any exotic or educational spot. And I thought up a few on my own when morale was sluggish. Several times I took deserving staff to Paris or London for the weekend, most memorably for the famous breakfast at Paris's Crillon hotel. The hotel alone cost seven thousand dollars, but it was worth every penny, inspiring changes at Stars that became trademarks. The traditional European seafood service stands, the round paper covers imprinted with a star logo that covered the butters on the table, the little copper pots for sauces and soups.

But as much as the road-show promotions brought new press and new customers, any restaurant has to look after its locals and regulars if it is to survive. So I installed brass name plates at the regulars' tables and on the bar, giving them a recognition for which others would soon fiercely compete. Eager wannabes were soon smuggling in screwdrivers to remove a plate or two to make room for their own. I formed a "Brassplate Society" and held annual lunches for the original members, whose deaths were anxiously anticipated by those who wanted in. Everyone knew my list was the only thing at Stars that could not be influenced by money, power, or politics. I loved the fact that there were local shopkeepers and lower-level bureaucrats drinking my champagne and Cognac while rich socialites looked on wondering how such a mixed crew got to be such stars in Stars.

But this showy democracy did not cause as much ruckus as the three-day event in the summer of 1989 we held to welcome the Kirov Ballet to San Francisco. Jeannette Etheridge of the famous Tosca Cafe, and her mother, Armen Baliantz, who had been Nureyev's all-forgiving mother figure since he first landed in the United States, suggested we do it.

This was before perestroika. The dancers were still surrounded and contained by KGB and my job was to get them out on the town. First there was a party at my brand-new Stars offshoot, Speedo 690. I had been warned that the dancers were coming by bus and, always hungry, would want to eat right away. So I created a buffet that featured a stack of twenty wooden farmers' market boxes of ripe peaches, melons, grapes, figs, and apricots. The hundred people arrived at the door with military precision. The young dancers gasped at the sight of the food, while we gasped at their beauty.

They all sat down, but then nothing happened. It was totally quiet. I went over to the male star, Andris Liepa, a twenty-one-year-old of world-challenging magnificence, and asked what was up. He pulled my ear down to his mouth and whispered, "KGB." The head honcho was a porkpie-hatted Brezhnev look-alike who introduced himself through an interpreter as the minister of the interior of the Soviet Union. With that kind of authoritarian rank in attendance I knew I was in trouble. So I called Armen, who rushed over. The hulking senior men had resisted any of my frozen vodka tactics to jump-start the party, but a few moments after Armen had ensconced herself at their table I heard the old guys shout a toast in Russian, knock back their vodkas, and yell for food. Instantly the ninety dancers and Kirov staff plunged into the food.

I asked Armen what she had done to get the old geezers off their cheap-suited behinds. "You see this pin I am wearing?" she asked. "Well, it's a Soviet army medal. The minister asked me how I had got it. I told him I had to fuck a general." The roaring laughter of the generals had been the noise that launched the party.

I was bowled over by the natural style and the elegance of the young Russians, who came from a society described as "impoverished." Each table made a fruit centerpiece of a plate stacked on upturned glasses, a spontaneous table decoration that would have done Maxim's proud. Just so they could eat the fruit with their eyes before devouring it. The magnificent star pulled me onto his lap and told me he'd seen a peach or apricot or any fruit like this maybe twice in his life. Dodging the KGB, I managed to steal him and five of the dancers for a spin in my new BMW.

The car phone grabbed their attention, so each called his boy or girlfriend in Leningrad or Moscow. Except the star. He gave me his hotel room key, a palliative for some heatedly disapproving local press accusing me of loving "Rooskies." They weren't far wrong.

CHAPTER 26

RIDING THE PRESS TIGER

The twentieth-century American novelist and historian Louis Auchincloss, America's expert on its polite society and old money, said of Ruth Draper, "You can get away with absolutely anything, if you are a success." So the carping of the right-wing press had no effect on my social local standing after I was seen with the blond Russian superstar on my arm. A lesson I had learned with Malcolm Forbes was that two celebrities are exponentially mightier than one. Surrounding myself with the famous was both armor against the media and oil for our business machine. "Tower promotes himself and his restaurants tirelessly," said one article. "'It is bone-crushingly exhausting,' he admits, 'but it certainly is much better for the business to be constantly in the public eye.'"

That was certainly true once Denise Hale adopted Stars as her venue.

For friends like Jim Beard, whom she once tried to hire as her private chef; for Italian friends like Gianfranco Ferré, French friends like Givenchy and Frédéric Chandon, Hollywood friends like Billy Wilder, Kirk Douglas, George Christy, Dominick Dunne, and the Reagans, and New York friends like Oscar de la Renta and the Kissingers, we were "it" at Stars. Everyone else came to watch. Denise's list extended to the Gettys, Rex Harrison, David Brinkley, and the king of Spain. All feted at Stars. The laconically flamboyant Berkeley critic Charles Perry wrote that I was paying too much attention to fame and not enough to food: "It's too bad that celebrities can't be eaten, because the way many California restaurants are going these days, the promise of hobnobbing with the wealthy, famous, and powerful is almost as big a drawing card for them as their menus." He had been to Spago as well.

Charles was early Berkeley, so David Webb paste or real diamonds around surgically enhanced necks would have been difficult for him to swallow. Especially since he couldn't wear them. But he had a point. At a party for the U.S. ambassador to Mexico (the toweringly handsome John Gavin), such was the power of Denise that tout San Francisco came out on a rainy Sunday night when they would usually be home in their TSE cashmere sweats secretly watching *Tales of the City*. All the newspaper barons were there, the Hearsts and the Thieriots, Danielle Steel with a few million in Rajasthan jewels studded into her gold maternity jacket, corporate giants from Syntex, the incomparable helicopter-flying Al Wilsey, the gloriously beautiful and impeccably dressed Urannia Ristow, the Safeway Magowans, and the winery Jordans. It was heaven, gushed the gossip columnists, and the three hundred others who came to have dinner and watch agreed. All except Charles Perry. Stars was proof that if you open such a place, all the world will come to see each other. He would rather they came for the food. He reproached me with early days of Chez Panisse. He was reliving them. I was not.

Gerald Asher from *Gourmet* gave his view of my appetite for the press. "The press, especially the Eastern press, loved Alice—this little girl who'd started a terrific restaurant with no experience was a good story. Why should she argue? It would not have helped if she had been a shrinking violet. When she was cast as the Joan of Arc of California cuisine, Jeremiah probably felt like the Dauphin."

Now I was ready to be king.

Constantly in society's eye, chefs now moved from socially unpresentable to socially necessary. I had never been comfortable telling my old-school grandmother (with her staff of domestics) that I cooked professionally after all that money my grandparents spent sending me to Harvard college and graduate school. Now working in a restaurant kitchen became not only respectable (sort of) but glamorous. "Talking to Tower," one reporter wrote, "you realize the days of the semi-literate hash slinger are over, and that the men in white hats are, well, white collar as well." But when *Time* magazine said I was receiving "as much press as Meryl Streep," damaging controversy started to rule as much as door-opening fame.

The end of the eighties saw the maturation of the chef as superstar, until it picked up again around 2000 with TV shows. But the first seeds of discontent were sown, and not just from Berkeley writers who had not been invited to sit with the likes of the king of Spain or America's best-selling romance novelist. I had stopped reading about myself, but the regulars at Stars never resisted the latest silliness in the columns, like my "Ronald Colman" voice and "Ivy League" airs, or being called "the Cary Grant of the cuisine scene."

NOUVELLE NAPOLEON

I particularly loved *Focus* magazine calling me a "nouvelle Napoleon spreading the revolution." But most went beyond the food. When a paper as far away as the *Maui News* reported that I looked "like an Americanized Michael Caine, curly blond hair and skin flushed from the tropical heat," it was obvious that more than food was involved. Which came first in this love affair, I wondered, and who will be blamed when it falters? One reporter talked of my "auburn" curls, another of my "blond" ones, and yet another of my "long English locks." I vowed to get out of the business while I still had hair.

When the reporters got to my old friends, I knew it was time to reassess my love affair with the press. They found my Harvard roommate Michael Palmer in the late 1980s. "Were the stories of flying blancmanges true?" they asked.

"It never came to blows," he said. "Jeremiah does have a temper and doesn't hesitate to make demands. He does have a certain verbal outrageousness."

Asked if success had tainted his old Harvard cooking buddy, Michael laughed. "No, he's the same old perverse Jeremiah."

Yes, I had done more than my share of wooing press attention, but even as I worried that my obsession would backfire on me, I found it impossible to resist saying yes to almost every promotional offer, whether national magazines or billboards as a Dewar's poster boy.

The one erected outside Spago on Sunset Boulevard annoyed Wolfgang Puck with its huge caption "Jeremiah Tower: Chef to the Stars." He said *he* was.

In 1988, USAir's in-flight magazine exaggerated that I was "arguably America's best-known chef-restaurateur." What was more true was the statement that Stars (I would have included Spago) "has introduced diners to a new way to appreciate dining out." In an article called "Drugless in L.A.," the blowup quote beside a photo of Elizabeth Taylor said, "Most people would just as soon meet a chef like Jeremiah Tower as Warren Beatty." The next day the story went around that I had been at the Betty Ford Clinic with Warren and Liz. A *Chronicle* piece called "Jeremiah Tower: The Star Behind Stars" noted gratuitously, "He is not insufferable." And if I couldn't get into trouble enough by myself, some reporters started currying favor by taking sides that were not even there. One said that Wolfgang Puck, "the over-hyped proprietor of Spago . . . couldn't pull it off. His bars are little more than overpriced queues for patrons praying for a power table, whereas Jeremiah Tower . . ." and so on with more rubbish.

I wondered how long it would be before a writer unable to get a table at Stars would turn on me.

A Carmel newspaper wrote: "Some call Jeremiah Tower aloof, a snob. They say he doesn't take telephone calls." I wondered who had not reached me on the four phone lines at my desk, my car phone, or my cell phone, on which I was available seven days a week. Who had I jilted without knowing it?

With all this, I again made a vow not to read favorable publicity anymore. I knew that disaster was the only possible result of believing it. I would have my assistant hand me only the negative items, things that we could do something about. There was nothing I could do about the fawning and swooning and lapdogging. I knew I had to build a buffer against the press or else go mad.

Or maybe it was time to get out of Dodge.

I made a plan to sell Stars a year after the $1,350,000 buyout of the Moons, now with interest more like $5,000,000, was paid to the bank by 1992. Without shoveling money into the bank, cash flow would be great enough in one year to set me up, and the sale would let me live well. By 1993 I would be back in Sydney with a house above Bondi Beach near Neil Perry's Blue Water Grill.

I didn't hear God laugh until the earth shook.

CHAPTER 27

GOD LAUGHS

I had rented a house in Sea Ranch on the Mendocino coast north of San Francisco for a much-needed week away from everyone. I had been there an hour and had just popped an ounce of beluga in my mouth to chase a large shot of bison-grass vodka when the phone rang. I thought of not answering, but it had to be Stars since no one else knew where l was. I looked at my watch. It was 5:19 P.M. It was Stars' chef, Mark Franz.

"J.T.—there's been an earthquake."

THE EARTH QUAKES

It had happened fifteen minutes before.

"Stars seems fine, and the windows are still in Speedo [my new restaurant around the corner from Stars]. At a fast look it seems we have lost only a few bottles of liquor. But the power is out, and everyone wants to know what to do." I told them to turn off the gas and water, lock up, and leave. That was my first mistake. There was no earthquake business interruption insurance then, so we should have left the gas on. We did have fire insurance. My second mistake was trying to get on my motorbike after two vodkas, thinking that the bike would be fastest not only on the winding coast road back to San Francisco but through any backed-up traffic leading into the city. After the first hairpin turn along the Highway 1 coast road, however, I went back to the house for the 750 Beemer. I told it gently that somehow it had to get me back to San Francisco in record time and in one piece.

I set off with visions of a Beirut-like scenario of fires in the city and police barricades at the Golden Gate Bridge but not a patrol car was in sight. Now quite sobered with adrenaline and fear of what I would find (the radio did not work on that mountainous coastal road), I arrived on the bridge to see that there was nothing out of the ordinary except for a total lack of traffic. And a plume of smoke over the Marina area at the San Francisco end of the bridge.

The Marina itself was blocked off with motorcycle cops, so I drove up into Pacific Heights and down into the Civic Center. On the way the only people I saw were gathered at corners, just standing in silence. I stopped the car for a minute and listened; the city was totally quiet except for distant sirens. After the telephone call, it was not a surprise that the huge storefront windows on my restaurant Speedo 690 were intact when I passed it around the corner from Stars, but it was a relief nonetheless. I had expected the sights we had all seen from Afghanistan, or China, or South America, with buildings down everywhere and bodies in the debris. It all looked normal, though the silence was powerfully eerie.

I tiptoed gingerly into Stars, and sure enough, there were the five broken liquor bottles on the bar with a note to me saying that everything else was intact. Incredibly relieved but somehow still very worried, I went over to Speedo 690 to find some gathered managers waiting for me with cold champagne. At least the ice hasn't melted yet, was the first in-shock thought that came to mind. We laid out a plan of action for the next day and went to our apartments to see what was left of them.

My house, even the dining room's painted ceiling, was intact, although Barbara Stanwyck's already lined face had a few more cracks. As I looked at the newspaper I saw it was October 17, and at the irony of having opened Speedo 690 five months earlier to the day, I felt superstition sliding into my unease. Every day closed would cost Stars thousands of dollars in profits, and I wondered how much we were going to lose. I knew Speedo's infant but successful cash flow could not take a big hit.

Nineteen eighty-nine had been normal until that day in October. We poured the new slab for Speedo on April 1. We had picked up our usual awards from the *San Francisco* magazine; we had already served about 150,000 meals at Stars, including hosting several winemakers, like Masteroberadino, Gaja, Maurizio Zanella of Ca' del Bosco, Jordan, Bernard Hine, Pierre Lanson; had hosted an Open Hand charity dinner; had greeted the usual Australians like top food journalists Jill Dupleix and her husband, Terry Durack, who flew in for the night from Sydney for Jill's birthday; had hosted Condé Nast, the Gunds, Bronfmans, Sotheby's, *Newsweek, Vogue's* Grace Mirabella, legendary Italian designer Gianfranco Ferré, and Rose Marie Bravo for Saks Fifth Avenue; the Kirov Ballet and its KGB shadow; *Vanity Fair's* editor Carter Brown; Liza Minnelli, Danielle Steel, and Watergate chef Jean-Louis Palladin.

I had finished a two-year court case brought by a cocktail waitress who allegedly misserved some customers and then sued me and Stars; had ended up in court with the Speedo corporation when they sued me for using a diver logo for our new restaurant's, Speedo 690, with Bondi Beach and surfer theme decor; had survived Denise Hale's birthday week of at least twelve parties; had seen Stars on *Lifestyles of the Rich and Famous;* had snuck the annual case of Stoli to top columnist Herb Caen for his birthday; had attended world championship boxing with San Francisco's mayor; had cooked at the Meals-on-Wheels in Los Angeles again.

I had got a call from Hong Kong saying we had very surprisingly won the government lease tender for the old Peak Cafe (and had started commuting there in late July); had made a video of life at Stars; had taken a private jet to Bangkok with the Hales; had yet again fought off rumors that I had AIDS when Philip Core, my great college pal and painter of my dining room and the 150-foot "beach" canvas at Speedo, had died of AIDS; had done a photo shoot at Denise Hale's for the Tiffany *Entertaining* book. All of this before the earth quaked in the longest ten seconds anyone could remember.

At 5:04 on that Tuesday, the city had shut down.

SAN FRANCISCO UNHINGED

I had a gut feeling that for a while nothing was going to be normal. Had I known then that those few minutes would end up costing me a million in expenses and nearly $12 million in lost sales, I would have taken that match down into the basement of Stars during the aftershocks and happily gone up with it to more heavenly stars. All I knew then was that the city was without electricity, that the gas was off, and that the president of the utilities company, a great customer of Stars for whom I had done favors, was not taking my calls. We had Paul Bocuse coming in for dinner in a few days, the *Aïda* cast party on Sunday, the Special Olympics dinner on Monday, a *Cook's* magazine shoot on Tuesday, a Nissan convertible commercial on Wednesday, a trip to Hong Kong Thursday, and an International Wine & Food Society dinner at the Hong Kong Hilton and press lunch at the Regent Hotel a few days after that.

By the next day it was clear that when we would have utilities again was quite unclear, so we took the perishable food down to the Red Cross and Open Hand headquarters in the Marina Middle School. Finally the PG&E president took my call, and four days later we were up and running again. Before most. My purchasing agent stopped me on the kitchen stairs and asked me if I wanted anything special since Julia Child was coming in the first day.

"We're open, that's enough," was all I could say. And open just in time to greet Julia and serve Bocuse his usual meal of steak tartare and large New York strip steak.

Stars recovered, but we did have to close Speedo a year later, since pouring more capital into damaged San Francisco seemed not a very good idea to my investors, who had all seen the endless television coverage of the fires and broken bridges. The Civic Center damage doomed it, its cash flow a year later not enough for its payables. I fire-sold my shares in the young but fabulously cash successful Peak Cafe for $500,000.

Now that I was without the restaurant where I could cook using the new fresh Asian and Indian ingredients, I was tempted to change the food at Stars. I did replace the pizza oven with a tandoor, but other experiments just confused the public. It was time to take stock of what kind of restaurant we were going to be in the nineties. As the decade opened, America was still looking back at Chez Panisse and California for clues.

DINNERS FOR STARS

By the time Stars was well under way with private parties, it could be said of the San Francisco's gilded set's pet, Jo Schuman, that "the best thing she makes for dinner is a reservation at Stars." And that the food had to be good, but most particularly small, chic, not too odd (no feet, eyes, scales, or feathers), and sit easily on the stomach. After all, one's guests might have just arrived by plane from eight time zones away, just had a four-hour lunch with the same people they were about to eat dinner with, and did not want to bulge out, even in the tiniest way, of the unique, made-for-the-evening Ferré, de la Renta, or Dior.

THE UGLY BUSINESS OF BEAUTIFUL WOMEN

Jo gave a dinner for Michael Gross, who was on the road for his book *Model: The Ugly Business of Beautiful Women*, a tricky business with Ann Getty, Carmella Scaggs, and Jeannette Etheridge at her table. To soften any assumed message she ordered an expensive wine. "Will everyone know how expensive it is?" Jo asked of the Chateau d'Yquem. "Not fifty thousand dollars for the 1787," I told her, but they will know. The 1967 was famous enough to distract them all from the scattered standing ovations given to Joan Collins, fresh from *Private Lives* across the street, and the opera star Samuel Ramey, as they arrived ten minutes apart.

No food could be riveting enough to keep heads from snapping up when Nureyev walked in on the arm of the magnificently fabulous Kenneth Jay Lane jewel–covered Dodie Rosekrans for the party given for him by producer Carole Shorenstein Hays after the opening night of *The King and I*. One did excuse oneself for staring at the couture babushka on Natalia Makarova or the Cossack sable on Danielle Steel, especially after Rudi pulled at the baggy pants of his Kenzo and told Dodie they made "his bum look big." One had to look somewhere.

Sometimes the conversation was so fast nothing else could keep up. Nan Kempner opened one lunch, when asked about her travels, with "Well, one cannot live by blood alone." She was referring to an impoverished member of royalty she had met at Valentino's party in Rome—or maybe she had met him at Malcolm Forbes's birthday party in Tangier. Both events were all anyone could talk about—as well as about who from San Francisco had been invited. Denise had, and everyone knew it.

With moments like that I knew the food had to be serviceably delicious but uncompetitive for attention. Saks Fifth Avenue's Rose Marie Bravo's lunch for the impeccably groomed Georgette Mosbacher dropped the bombshell that her new perfume cost fifteen hundred dollars an ounce. That brought silence to the table and, for an endless minute, the food was the center of attention. After all, Vicky Tiel's perfume, launched at a Stars dinner the night before with the same guests, was only three hundred dollars, even if she did call it "Nudes All Around." Denise Hale's Jungle Gardenia from Walgreens cost only twenty dollars! No one knew which one Jimmy Galanos was wearing, or how much it cost, but the sweet smells of success were definitely in the air and overpowering the aromas of food and wine. If it wasn't perfume it could be smoke. So for George Hamilton, fresh from introducing me to Imelda Marcos in Manila, and now introducing his line of cigars, we served lobster and champagne and finished with peaches and cherries soused in ten-year-old Old Weller bourbon.

SOCIAL FOOD

Raw garlic or onions were never served. Social food by the eighties and nineties had to service jaded if always appreciating palates but never distract from the real business at hand: chat and people summing up while the other diners in the room watched. The young people, as Ann Getty called them, paid a bit more attention. Viscountess Serena, in a very un-English comment about the food, adored her chicken at Denise's dinner for her and her husband, David, Viscount Linley, in town to show off his new book, *Classical Furniture*. With guests introduced with names like Prince Alexandre de Borbón-Dos Sicilias y de Habsburgo-Lorena, one could not eat with one's mouth full of complex food. And with the "young people" I could be more in charge if I had to be. Billy Getty and Gavin Newsome always knew what they wanted, but not all did. And since Stars donated the food at the fund-raising dinner for 180 guests of the United States Holocaust Memorial Museum organized by Auschwitz survivors and by Gay and Lesbian Campaign leaders Tyne Daly and Mark Leno, I chose chicken. "Banquet chicken was raised to new heights," raising $150,000 that night alone. Even though I cooked the chicken myself, I knew it was really Michael Tilson Thomas sitting at Stars' grand piano and playing "Fascinatin' Rhythm" that covered up the fact that it was only chicken, after all.

By this time I had told my chefs the menu rules for special dinners at Stars many times: by all means remember that there might be guests too polite to disrupt the evening by saying they had the flu, that their jet lag was worse than a crash from carb overdose, that they were on a diet, that they were really vegetarian, that they were allergic to shellfish, that they had just arrived from an inescapably late lunch, that this would be their eighth social meal in a row, that they hated lamb, or that they couldn't look rabbit in the face.

A Dinner for Sophia Loren
March 31, 1995

Mushroom Timbale
Fava Beans and Purple Asparagus
Smoked Pheasant
Oven-Roasted Vegetables and Lamb's Lettuce Salad
Ginger Mousse
Warm Ginger Cookies

The idea of the timbale was its small size so that guests could pick at it and make it look as if it were mostly eaten—just in case they hated mushrooms, or cream. Then they could eat the fava beans and push the color-coordinated asparagus around if they were nervous about it, as some people are. The pheasant was breast only, delicious but innocuous in its way, and once again, one could pick at it and eat the vegetables or salad instead. As for the ginger mousse, small again (everyone is allowed to pick at dessert), and no one can resist cookies four minutes out of the oven.

The Italian consul general and his wife said this dinner was the highlight of Sophia's and Carlo Ponti's visit to the Bay Area, even when Herb Caen had announced in advance the menu and the fact that the dessert sounded like the name of a Tenderloin stripper. In this case, everyone ate everything. I was nervous because I had been told that Sophia ate only pasta for lunch (I was not going to cook pasta for an Italian) and sandwiches for dinner. Admirable. Me too. And what food could compete with those lips (signature "Coral Nude"), those eyes, that hair, cheekbones "so defined you could hang laundry on them," and "those, um . . . that poitrine." More worried than I were some of San Francisco's beauties. As Cynthia Robins of the *Examiner* said, they were "in a swivet" and grabbing their cleavages every time Sophia swept by. All except Daru, whose own famous poitrine held up perfectly. Bob Colacello was worried only about his Neopolitan Brooklyn family Italian or, in his own case, Bensonhurst. Everyone agreed with San Francisco's greatest beauty (here unnamed) that Sophia at sixty was "the most glamorous woman in the world."

DINNERS FOR COUTURE

Dinners for couture were the most difficult because one had to assume each of the guests was as figure conscious as anyone could be, and that having to wear a Calvin Klein (in town for a fashion show at I. Magnin and Denise's dinner for him at Stars), for example, that had not been worn since the beginning of the season and now many dinners later might not fit, could leave a bad taste in the mouth no matter how good the food.

For Vicky Tiel it was beluga and potatoes washed down with magnums of 1983 Roederer Cristal; for Jil Sander ("She's fantastic, the female Armani," I had said to the press) grilled Nantucket scallops with tomato basil sauce; for Bill Blass, grilled wild Pacific salmon with sweet corn and heirloom various-colored tomato salad with peach cobbler to follow; and for Oscar de la Renta with Danielle Steel in a Ralph Lauren military tunic (she had checked her Oscar coat) and Nan Kempner ("I just love Stars") and New York's Rose Marie Bravo ("You outdid yourself; I can't tell you how much I miss Stars") it was Japanese eggplant timbale with chilied crab ("now Oscar's favorite dish").

When Gianfranco Ferré came to town and Denise gave a dinner or lunch at Stars, I could rev the food up a bit. After a few weekends at the Hale Ranch with Gianfranco, I knew him well enough to know he would have been disappointed if I hadn't. It was a dinner for "stargazing and grazing."

Dinner for Gianfranco Ferré
Celery Root Gratin
Scallop Hash and Lobster Vinaigrette
Grilled Lamb Medallions
Artichoke Bottoms Filled with Chickpea Puree
Wild Strawberry Soufflé

Gianfranco dined on plain rice. "I'm not well," he said. "It must have been the caviar on the Concorde."

PURE SAN FRANCISCO

It was a typical Saturday night. The time quoted to walk-ins was one hour and forty-five minutes, with everyone waiting for the opera crowd to leave at 7:45. Paul Pelosi had just incapacitated the dining room manager into a fit of giggles by telling the valet parker Solomon, "Park my car in her trunk," as Jo Schuman pulled up in a stretch limo. The giggles left five reservation lines blinking with a promise of more scenes if those diners ever showed up. A gossip columnist was on the phone wondering what I would serve for the *Harper's Bazaar* editor Liz Tilberis's dinner (curried crabmeat soufflés) to promote her new book, *No Time to Die*. Mayor Willie Brown had a reservation for eight o'clock and didn't show. Danielle Steel did show up with her matched Graff "D" flawless diamond twins, and I had not alerted the security or insurance companies. Francis Ford Coppola was there for drinks only (had to get back to work) but after a drink decided "to stay for starters," making a scramble for the staff to set another place at Denise's already tight table; then the great Escada-tiger-print and rhinestone-covered Charlotte "Tex" Swig kissed her husband, George Shultz, good-bye, so he wasn't staying. Bob Colacello lost his pen—then it was found with Francis signing autographs. Peter Coyote lost his diamond ear stud, so Dodie Rosekrans's otherwise *very* conservative husband borrowed Frances Bowes's gold bead ones, first trying them on himself and thereby reducing the rather fey maître d' to yet another fit of incapacitating giggles.

There was a birthday party in the Grill Room and a bat mitzvah in the other private room that needed his attention. Matthew Broderick was competing with that year's gold medalist downhill skier from the Bay Area for the ogling of women, and leaving not a few of Stars' cooks serving the oyster bar slack-jawed and weak-kneed. The Fat Boys across the dining room were showing ogling diners their necks and arms, heavy with more Los Angeles gold bling and New York diamond-district bracelets than all the socialites put together.

A cockroach had found its way up from the basement, despite the weekly bombing, and was doing a Rockettes routine along the wainscoting next to a particularly fastidious and now hysterical prima donna. The Stars doctor was dining on the edge of the Ferré party and drinking a twenty-five-year-old Petrus, which I was hoping no one in the party would see and then ask for. Regulars Jim and Jo O'Dea were at their usual table and alcoholically itching for a fight. Or Petrus.

"It's pure San Francisco," the O'Deas told Pat Steger of the *Chronicle*'s "Social Scene" column.

"I couldn't care less who's here," said another patient customer. "I just want a table."

DINNER FOR WHAT GLITTERS

Particularly close to the metaphor in my heart was the dinner we did to help launch *Faking It*, Kenny Jay Lane's book about what was not real but still glittered. I repeated the menu we had just done for hostess Denise for her gold-plated David Rockefeller dinner, though without the 1983 Dom Pérignon *en magnum*.

Black Truffle Custard
Prawn Vinaigrette
Capon Breast with Lobster Sauce
Fava Beans, Wild Asparagus, Garden Peas
Passion Fruit Soufflé
Warm Ginger Cookies

Kenny was dressed in a double-breasted glen plaid suit and yellow tie, long before they became powerful, and had a warm cookie in each hand as he regaled the table with stories of Sophia Loren, Judith Leiber's objets (he did the first ones using dime-store plastic bracelets), the Duchess of Windsor, and Jackie Onassis (she couldn't find any faux cabochon jewels of poor enough quality to copy the $250,000 "piece of junk" that Ari had given her).

Not junk, glittering, and definitely not fake was Dede Wilsey's diamond the size of an iceberg, and almost the same color, though not below the water-line. It was so large that when Nancy Pelosi saw it, she literally stopped talking in midsentence, not an easy feat for a politician (someone wagged). Denise's diamond-and-sapphire David Webb necklace shone like a stand of Christmas lights, and Sally Jordan's watermelon-slice Judith Leiber minaudière looked more delicious than the soufflé (someone else wagged).

Others raved about the soufflé with gossip columnist Pat Steger, saying that if most of the jewels were not real, at least the real J.T. was there, but wondered about the two matching diamond rose brooches on Ann Getty's left shoulder.

Definitely always real were Connie Wald and Princess Genevieve "Geni" di San Faustino, as were the gorgeous pink ranch roses from Denise's country garden: "I talked to my roses for a week and told them not to let me down." Some of them did, so Ray Reddell had to step in with a few hundred of his own old-fashioned ones, and so started a real revolution in which roses—old or new—were considered chic.

At a party for the Hale's anniversary, David Pleydell-Bouverie, who owned the Sonoma ranch on which M. F. K. Fisher lived, said the decorated dining room looked "quite chic." Everyone knew that he knew. Five hundred candles in pink-lined (more flattering to anyone over forty, as most were) shades were set among every white lily available strewn across the green-moiré tablecloths sprinkled with little gold stars. H.R.H. Prince Alexander of Yugoslavia wondered all night if the stars were real, until Constance Towers (married to John Gavin) plastered a few stars across her décolletage before getting up to sing "My Romance," really meaning "yours" (the Hales'), so that wasn't real. But Mitzi Gaynor's response to Carol Channing calling out that she couldn't hear her singing was real enough: "Tough."

The night went on longer than the premiere of *War and Peace*, playing that same night at the Opera House, and definitely real were the thousands of dollars lost to Stars (we had closed Stars that Saturday night for Denise) by not having the hundred or so people coming over for champagne at the end of the performance. For the lesser thousands in tips lost to the staff, I reminded them of Dodie's remark when looking at the crowded dance floor: "Don't dance with anyone you don't like."

MUSICAL CHAIRS

Some people, no matter what we did, were never happy where we sat them. But all was forgiven if they liked to eat. A trim (in grand opera terms) "superstar" Luciano Pavarotti in 1994 could not find a place that made him happy, or at least we could not. No drafts were allowed (understandably, given what a cold could do to his performance), and no one was permitted to walk behind him. But he wanted to sit in the center of the room, where everyone could see and greet him.

I put him near the kitchen and was the only person allowed to walk behind him. He rather liked the dinner ("un grande complimento—una cucina grande")—or just loved Stars because we used to sneak him ice cream onto the cafe table onstage during *Bohème* when he was supposed to be on a diet.

Un Grande Complimento

Timbale Golden Oyster Mushroom with Mussels,
Nasturtiums, Sage Flowers

Wild Turkey and Rabbit-Filled Pasta "Pillows" with
Truffled Celery Root

Braised Beef Cheeks with Ramps, Carrots, Red Mustard Gremolata

Warm Apricot, Hazelnut, and Pear Tartlet

"The beef cheeks were a hit at the dinner," Pat Steger reported in her column, "but before getting down to the beef, Luciano got around to hugging and kissing a few cheeks." Of course the O'Deas were there, getting ready to try to top Patty Rouas, who, clad in the latest Hervé Leger, looked disapprovingly at Pavarotti and said in a stage whisper, "The waif look is out. Full figures are in."

LUNCH FOR A PET

Not all celebrities were two-legged. Some four were Stars regulars. Like Bentley, a famous seventeen-year-old basset hound.

The San Francisco journalist Rob Morse reported, "On Tuesday Warren Hinckle [journalist extraordinaire himself] threw a touching wake at Stars for his beloved Bentley, who had to be put to sleep. Actually, it was a pre-wake, because Bentley attended. Chef Jeremiah Tower served Bentley magnificently. We'll miss him, but maybe not his fleas." The meal was attended by San Francisco's district attorney and sheriff in case anyone became stroppy about dogs at the bar. Jack Davis, the man who made mayors in that town, had arranged the postprandial transportation to Pets Unlimited, a wide-load and superlong-bedded open truck, onto which a kennel had been strapped in place of the usual bulldozer.

Bentley's Lunch

Grilled Ground Chuck

with bacon

Evian in a Silver Dish

"His ashes," said Hinckle, "will be delivered to Art Agnos, who, when he was mayor, once kidnapped Bentley and threatened to do away with him." Not everyone likes dogs lapping up spilled Bushmills at the bar.

DINNERS FOR MEDIA

"With your fingers. Just tear them apart," said Martha Stewart. And she should know, as "the elegant expert on entertaining." She was talking not about the fawning reporters but about the quail.

White Oregon White Truffled Salt Cod Puree
Lobster and Oyster Vinaigrettes
Quail in a Brioche Nest
filled with foie gras, black truffle sauce
A Mere Trifle
Wild Blackberry Sauce

Actually, for this, another Jo Schuman dinner at Stars in 1994, the quail were boneless, so a single swipe with a knife would have done quite well.

Denise Hale ("San Francisco's most gracious and successful party giver") had helped Jo plan the party, and it was a perfect time for Martha and Denise to compare notes on what makes for perfect entertaining. The men at the dinner (even Denise's husband and another who kept his private jet on hand for their trips to Hong Kong) could have heard "There are so few interesting men," but they were too busy looking at women to listen. Martha was signing their copies of *Menus for Entertaining* even though Denise had predicted no men would be interested. "Even empresses can be wrong," wagged a guest.

But if you have a very attractive man, like the Comte de Chandon de Briales, as guest of honor, then surround him with ladies. Martha agreed. So did all the men with Denise: "Always have on hand some very attractive girls who are amusing, very beautiful," because the most important ingredient for a successful party is the choice of people.

Especially the unattached: "You have to have single people. You can have couples and it's a quiet dinner, but it's not a party." Denise knew this well—she had once asked the advice of the greatest party expert before Martha, Elsa Maxwell. "My child," replied the diminutive and rotund trouser-roll Elsa, "be ruthless whom you invite."

Both Denise and Martha agreed with Dodie's dance advice. Invite only the people you like, and never bores.

"A bore is a bore is a bore."

Choose from the many walks of life, and choose people as different as possible as long as they are interesting.

"Whatever they do they have to be the best at it."

CHAPTER 28

SURVIVAL PLANS

A big part of accepting the Peak Cafe in 1990 was to have the cash reserve for Stars given the earthquake-destroyed Civic Center surrounding Stars restaurant.

The city government took a year to assess the damage and announce plans for its future. Some buildings, such as the state building next door to Stars that produced for us about $600,000 a year in bar and food business, never opened again after that fateful afternoon. That was bad enough. Worse was news from the mayor's office that the Civic Center would close in its entirety in 1994. The government would be moved elsewhere; the opera, ballet, two other performing arts halls, the library, the museum, in short 60 percent of Stars' business would be gone. Stars had brought life to the center of San Francisco in 1984. Now the Civic Center was going to suck the life out of Stars.

CAFES

A ray of hope appeared in the form of developers who wanted to raze the block on which Stars stood and turn it into a 6-million-square-foot city offices and law building right next to a huge new courts building. So when I realized that a spot around the corner from Stars was coming available, and that it was the only corner in the Stars block that was not going to be razed,

I held a meeting of the restaurant's board. We could wait it out in total chaos while they built around and above us, or we could sell Stars to the developers for their proposed $3 million in cash, void the current lease, write a new one with the city, and come back in three years to operate Stars as the major tenant in the new city office building, the restaurant designed and fitted out at their cost. I proposed the way to keep the Stars name operative in San Francisco while waiting for the new Stars to open was to franchise and move the cafe to that corner, then look at moving Stars as a franchise to the up-and-coming Silicon Valley. It was a whole new concept, with 70 percent Stars Cafe and 30 percent Stars instead of the other way around. That formula, I told them, would survive any recession.

And high six-figure cash coming in from Hong Kong would be gravy.

I told the board that the reconstruction was backed by my pal the mayor, that the only snag would be the Board of Supervisors. They had said they were in favor, but I knew what a nightmare that board could be. I had just seen the current president, Angela Alioto, as she presided over the highly emotional smoking ban hearings, flipping through a magazine, berating smokers, and then in the corridor bumming a cigarette from Tosca Cafe's Jeannette Etheridge and me. In San Francisco anything could happen, and if it was self-righteous enough, it usually did. So all faces were turned silently toward me in the Stars boardroom after I asked them to make a decision. Perhaps the silence was because of my closing remark. I said that if we were to proceed as planned with our project at the mercy of the supervisors we could be screwed. "Royally!"

San Francisco government resists change. It took another twenty-seven years for the development of the Stars site on Golden Gate Avenue, seventeen years after I sold it. But at that time our business plan was to have a building with a main restaurant and a cafe, each with its own kitchen, but with the old formula for space allocation reversed. Stars would have fifteen line cooks and ten prep cooks, a large menu, and serve sixty seats. Stars Cafe would have five in the kitchen, a small menu, and serve two hundred seats. Stars would have the cachet and reputation, a training ground for all the cooks. The cafe would be the cash flow, kept full by Stars' reputation and recognizable value. We would have gross sales similar to those we'd had before, but with a million shaved off our currently $3 million annual payroll.

We decided to go ahead and move both Stars Cafe to the corner and take Stars to Palo Alto, where a local developer, Jim Baer, wanted the franchise. He had lost Wolfgang Puck as a first choice—a piece of news that I listened to since I was pretty convinced that Wolfgang didn't do bad deals. I called Wolfgang to ask about Baer. He said nothing was amiss. When I heard the Napoleonic-size Baer say in a meeting two weeks later that "I have never made anything less than a perfect decision," I should have headed for cover. But by that time the franchise deal and management contract had been signed.

It didn't help that I was traveling a lot.

TRAVEL BUG AGAIN

The new decade had opened with the Peak Cafe in 1990. I began commuting to Hong Kong, not only to operate the cafe, but to look around in Southeast Asia for someone to buy Stars, in case the plan for a closed Civic Center Stars and later a new one didn't get signed.

Stars was still very profitable in the early nineties, so why not find someone to pay me $8 million? Then pay himself what so far had been a guaranteed 15 percent return on $10 million (1990 dollars) annual revenue? I looked at a site on the river next to the Oriental Hotel in Bangkok and in Sydney on the way out to the Opera House. And I stepped up all the public relations I could get my hands on, no matter how much it kept me away from Stars. One such trip in 1996 was a true PR marathon. I flew to Saint Martin in the Caribbean to join the maiden voyage of a Viking Line ship that was to host two hundred American food journalists on a three-day voyage to Miami. I gave a lecture on my plans for Stars. First I did a demo for some press at Cap Juluca in Anguilla, then caught the ship, survived the press dinner the first rough night out, did cooking demos the next day, gave the lecture, and managed to cook the press dinner the night before docking in Miami. From there I went straight to New York to see the Michael McCarty's new-new Michael's on West Fifty-Fifth Street, before getting on a plane that night for Berlin for the three-day In Flight Catering Association conference. There in front of two thousand delegates I gave a talk on California cuisine, and looked for a buyer, setting off a small flood of German press, like *essen & trinen* magazine calling me the voodoo priest of American cooking, and talked to *Die Welt* about

Stars' plans for the next five years. There was no buyer in Germany, so I flew on to Hong Kong. I cooked a press lunch the day I arrived at the Regent Hotel. I had dinner with Australian food magazine press to excite any would-be buyers there, and flew that night to San Francisco. The evening of the day I arrived, we cooked for the Academy of Friends. Three days later we cooked a lunch in Napa for a hundred of Beaulieu Vineyard's friends and press, and the next day I went to Las Vegas to check out an offer from the Howard Hughes Corporation.

So far no bites on Stars.

Then there was.

One involved the plans for reconstruction of the Civic Center. Just as I was lining him up, San Francisco changed mayors. Our deal was dead. We would have to survive the emptied-out Civic Center after all, in isolation except for the hordes of homeless, mentally ill, and drug dealers who poured in to fill the unsupervised void. The area was no longer civic, and it was the center of nothing. What was to be a wait for our 1997 triumphant victory march return now turned into a long wait for that year to arrive. I had thought I could sell Stars to a Japanese group, perhaps to the new Stars groups forming in Singapore and Palo Alto, or at least to Canadian Pacific Hotels, for whom I was consulting. But now the dangers of the Civic Center would be obvious to all. When the San Francisco old guard's Prentis Cobb Hale died, the inner part of me that lived happily in the old order vanished. With Prentis gone there was no one to tell me how full of shit I was, when I was. I started to make real mistakes.

In an attempt to understand the changing times, the first ones came from listening, not to my instincts but to my handlers who ruled the times: publicists, personal assistants, insurance companies, and human resources experts. I continued my international search for a buyer for Stars. My business card, which in 1990 read Twinkle Inc., the Turk Street Group, and Free-dragon Ltd., in Chinese as well as English, in 1996 had a single name, Stars, in English only, and even that was soon being fitted for the emperor's clothes.

CHAPTER 29

JUST DESSERTS

For ten years my team at Stars had been my soul mates, but now there were signs of hairline cracks in the bonds that had held us together even through all the early partner disputes, the drama surrounding our meteoric rise to success, and the lawsuits.

It didn't help when, in 1993, we were sued (again) for wrongful termination.

"Oh, that," I said carelessly.

And AIDS discrimination.

"Oh, dear."

When I first met the lawyer who had trumped up the charges against Stars, Kafka's *Trial* and *Metamorphosis* somehow combined into one. He had the same kind of black-eyed greed as the sewer-loving bugs I saw in the garbage left by the homeless in the urine-filled parking garage of the Civic Center. But the charges could hardly be taken seriously, and thinking the usual exterminators would do the trick, I called the lawyers.

The plaintiff had been terminated a few years before when I was out of town. Human resources and the dining room manager, Tony Angotti, had called to say that a waiter had lied to some customers, given them what they said was compromised service, tampered with the guest check to cover up his errors, and lied to his supervisors about the incident. My final permission was required to help protect us against wrongful termination suits, and to prevent any ganging up by the managers against one of the staff. I asked if they had processed this potential firing by the book: were there a minimum of three documented discussions and counseling in his file? More than three, they assured me, with witnesses, and signed by the waiter himself. They insisted the action was deserved, just, and, with respect to the labor board rules, watertight. I consented, and then double-checked the file when I returned.

Three years later the waiter was hospitalized with full-blown AIDS and the family needed money. So who better to sue than the perceived closest, easiest, and, they thought, deepest pockets?

There was always someone around trying to extort money from Stars. This case was thrown summarily out of court. And thrown out again at another hearing. And then again. When after the third time the judge had had enough and told the waiter's attorney to desist, the attorney sent me a letter. It said that he knew he had no case, but that if he ever got me in front of a San Francisco jury, he would destroy me.

Some months later he did his best.

During that time the California Supreme Court ruled that all wrongful termination suits had to be heard in front of a jury. Retroactively. That meant me.

I was told on a Wednesday that a trial was set for the following Monday, rushed because the plaintiff was dying.

My hastily called deposition was no good: I simply could not remember a three-year-old incident that had taken ten minutes of my time on the phone from Hong Kong and a quick staff file search. As for all the staff, customers of Stars, and most of my best friends who had died of AIDS since we opened in 1984, those memories were well buried. Unearthing did not come easily.

I got my initial whiff of danger when, on the first day of the trial, a large photo of the dying waiter with tubes up his nose was left in the courtroom for all to see. Sitting in the courtroom were two attorneys, my regular protector Richard Collier and regular customer Jim O'Dea, himself a legal hit man for Boston's more dubious Irish politicos in older and rougher days. Having him defend me would have been like having Mayor Daley as an attorney in Chicago, and I considered asking him to take over the case. But a sense of fairness to my insurance company attorneys handling the case tripped me up, and I didn't switch.

The list of my alleged sins was long, saying I had cared nothing for any

START THE FIRE **273**

of the staff and had brutalized them, particularly the gay staff, for years. I was flabbergasted that the opposing attorney was allowed to spit out these lies in court. Both his scribbled note admitting to me they had no case and the previous judge having dismissed the charges three times were inadmissible.

I sat for four days as the waiter's lawyer hurled insults and charged me with arrogance and an "uncaring" attitude. To an extent the charge was true: I *didn't* care about this at best mediocre waiter who was now trying to extort $13 million out of me. I'd barely known or talked to him—a fact his lawyer twisted as proof that I cared for none of the staff. Why would I care to pick on a waiter, I wondered, if I did not care for any of them? And there was a catch-22. I was accused of illegally looking in an employee's private file, but of not looking long enough to discern that his serial absences were the consequence of AIDS. I must have known he had AIDS, they said, because he was gay. In my eyes discrimination in itself, but what would I know. It was in fact illegal for me as his employer to have concerns he was gay!

Called to the stand, I was a terrible witness, overwhelmed by the long list of gay male waiters I had allegedly pilloried, starting with our first fatal cases of AIDS. Both I had supported privately, paying two thousand dollars a month or a quarter of my salary for AZT. I was hoisted on my own petard of old-fashioned English manners. The American part of me didn't come out of me in time when accused of sending these men to early deaths. I broke. A month earlier a close friend and loyal Stars customer had actually died while on the phone with me from his hospital bed as I was telling him I would be right over with his Stars hamburger. I choked at that memory and rose to leave. I saw the gloating smile from the opposing attorney, the approaching bailiffs, the understanding judge, the incredulous faces of the people in the courtroom, and the mixed looks of believers and unbelievers in the jury box. I wondered how I could have let things come to this.

THE BILL IS FINALLY DUE

The bill was finally coming due for every sin I had ever committed. Every sarcastic remark, every hour not spent counseling an employee who had broken the rules or screwed up, every flashbulb moment not shared with one of my chefs too late for the shoot, every huge bonus that was not big enough. One ex-employee prosecution witness after another testified that I had not taken them to New York or London or Paris, that I had played favorites. And that I never had taken employees who were on probation or consistently late for work. Only in San Francisco would this make sense to a jury, and it did.

The trial started on my fifty-first birthday and went for two weeks. My friends botched their best efforts to protect me, and others, who had done very well out of Stars and gone on to big jobs in the United States and abroad, exaggerated and outright lied in front of that impressionable jury. Sitting and hearing that, I felt cut off from everyone and everything. All I could think of were my Burmese cat and my BMW motorbike. Give me a tank of gas and I would be out of there with only a saddlebag of cash on one side and the cat on the other. No wonder the jury felt I was "distant."

Herb Caen had taken care of the verdict the week before the trial when he printed that I was getting my "just desserts." Only in San Francisco could political expediency take precedence over years of personal loyalty. The politically gay activists, who for years had been fed by my hand, joined Herb and were now ready to bite it. Suddenly I was political death in San Francisco. After the prosecution lawyer opened the trial saying that the million dollars I had raised for AIDS research and hospices had been to hide my alleged anti-homosexuality politics, a rumor went out that ACT UP was going to come in and trash Stars. No one knew where to hide, but it certainly was not behind me. I called my pals at the North Station, all good Italian and Irish cops. They knew what to do. The moment the ACT UP clowns started brownshirt tactics in Stars, the police were there to arrest them. Now I was even more a pariah.

The closing arguments were on the Monday before Thanksgiving. Everyone knew a verdict would come in Wednesday afternoon since the jurors wouldn't want to be back in court on Friday. While they were out deliberating, I attended the punitive damages hearing with the judge and the smugly confident opposing lawyer, who doubtless had visions of moving from his Tenderloin (very seedy part of town) apartment-office to a downtown suite, where he could put out a brass plaque commemorating the destruction of Jeremiah Tower.

Then he went ballistic when he discovered that I owned nothing. Nothing worthwhile to him, that is, and nowhere near the punitive $13 million that he saw in his dreams. Stars without a noncompete clause and still paying off the bank was worthless. The cat wouldn't have him. The apartment was rented, the cars leased. My cookbooks, worth a hundred grand, seemed like too many *Joy of Cooking* to his eyes. I gave them all the records. Now he was speechless. My best Cheshire cat smile drove him over the top. The judge's similar smile didn't help. A sweet moment.

The jury filed in and sat down without looking at me. That moment I knew for sure, as I did when my pathetic insurance attorneys moved one step back and to the side of me.

"We find for the plaintiff."

GUILTY

Who else could they find for.

As the verdict was read out, all the jurors but two only gave me looks of hate. I had nothing to say to them or to my counsel. I reached into my jacket pocket and caressed the first-class one-way Cathay Pacific ticket to Hong Kong that I'd bought the day before. I wondered if I could get out of town in time to use it. I expected a sheriff with handcuffs and an orange jail suit for me, but no one appeared except the reporters, whom I had kept fully employed for two weeks. The room seemed weirdly still immediately around me, but outside that cocoon-like realm there was a chaos of camera lights and microphones on gaffs shoved into my face. Finally a reporter's yell got through my daze: "Any comment?"

"No, thank you very much," were my only words—ones widely reported the next day as evidence of my unrepentant arrogance. More petard hoisting.

On the jury was a Presbyterian spinster minister who had frowned on me with disapproval for ten days. When the award came in far less than demanded—approximately one four-hundredth of the $13 million requested—it was because of this woman, a caretaker for transgenders with AIDS. Only in San Francisco could I have been so reviled and then so oddly saved. From bankruptcy. It turned out that the jury was split ten to two, the other dissenter being Penny Alexander, an executive search consultant. She later told the *San Francisco Chronicle*, "I was amazed at how ineffective the system is. I always assumed that it worked, that it was fair. But it's amazingly unfair and in no way gets at the truth of anything. There is no such thing as a trial by your peers."

I was hissed at by my peers at an ARC (AIDS-related complex) benefit a few days later. Later, the San Francisco AIDS Foundation would withdraw my selection for the Community Service Award, bestowed on an individual "who has made hastening the end of the HIV/AIDS epidemic an urgent priority in their life." They wrote they were sure I would understand.

I did perfectly.

"You are so dear to us," they added. The "so" suggested not dear enough.

A month after the trial the California Supreme Court revised the decision that had landed me before a jury. The previous retroactive was now unconstitutional.

One of my first post-trial crisis management acts was to take down from the wall in the VIP section of the dining room all the photos of fading stars and put up new ones of younger, cooler, and hipper ones. Gone was the large photograph of Robin Leach and me engaging in the sport of champagne drinking because it was captioned "The mediagenic master of faux familiarity has fashioned a career out of celebrity voyeurism." The line referred to Robin but was printed on top of my image—an irony I'd enjoyed until people believed it of me.

But I knew I had to keep up the front that I was still functioning and that Stars would be the same despite the exodus of all Civic Center arts and governmental functions. I walked up the street and leased a shiny new and very big Mercedes.

THE EMPEROR'S CLOTHES

We kept up appearances, but nothing was ever the same again. Confidence and loyalties had been stretched to the limits, and the original team started to fall apart.

Mark Franz had been my star pupil at the California Culinary Academy and, after a stint cooking for fishermen in wilderness Alaska, had run the kitchens at Santa Fe Bar & Grill and Stars. Mark was the one who knew my palate, and no one could see inside the soul of my food the way he could. Also Mark was one of the boys, and the leader to whom the testosterone-driven young cooks could relate when my role to them may have sometimes seemed other-planetary. Steven Vranian (the one who got lost in Manhattan in the van on our way to Newport in 1983) had been our great grill chef. Now he was in charge of buying and storing the food. No one could organize a storeroom or walk-in refrigerator as maniacally, or knew better that a restaurant's food could never be truly great without those controls, and that keeping track of and properly storing newly arriving perfect ingredients was the only way to prevent them from turning into ordinary ones. Noreen Lam, also from the CCA, was in charge of Stars Cafe. Like Mark and Steven she knew the food I wanted. And no one could set the standards with prep cooks as she. Her infinite patience and willingness to take the time to teach and create perfection never lagged.

Others had come and gone, but these managers were the core, the conscience of Stars' philosophy and its quality standards. They were the ones who trained any newcomers, managers, or line staff in what it was all about. For a long time we all got along swimmingly.

I am not sure which came first: their doubt that they wanted to go on managing Stars, or my doubt that they could manage Stars with their conflicting emotions about staying. Money was not an issue since I had been paying them generous sums for the time. It would have been deserved and practical to make them partners in Stars, but before 1988 the stock was not mine to give, and after that, at least until 1993, its ownership would have been encumbered with lawsuits, potentially huge punitive damages, and enormous capital gains taxes.

In my heart I knew that different bones thrown to them probably would not work, but I still hoped they would. Mark had always said that he was in my shadow, a place we both knew he found, at least for a while, more comfortable than being on his own. I hoped a good compromise with him was a country restaurant that he could call his own. Feeling guilty about not making him a partner, I bought and gave him Stars Oakville Cafe in Napa and my BMW 750IL to go with it. He probably didn't want either, so things became even more complicated. With those kinds of emotions the year before he left, we often passed like ships in the night. A few years later Mark told a reporter what it was like working for a man who he said was unpredictable, moody, and an unrelenting perfectionist. "You never knew if you were going to get your ass kicked or what. You could really get roasted for doing the wrong thing, but he was always a gentleman with me."

Steven had always said that he wanted for his children the same kinds of advantages that he had had as a child, while traveling around South America, so I hoped that Stars Singapore would be what he wanted. I knew that Noreen's hometown, Honolulu, was calling strongly to her but hoped that she would want first to travel among the new Stars, including the Peak Cafe in Hong Kong, to teach her dedication to perfection to new staff.

As I had never let personal relationships stand in the way of adventure, I missed an increasingly important point. Single when we bonded at the Santa Fe Bar & Grill, the team members were now married, soon to be, or in lasting relationships. They needed a stable future, and one that shed its own light on them. When they realized that the kind of drama that surrounded us at Stars was not inevitable, they looked further than the light shining from it, a light still visibly shining, but originating perhaps in the past, as if from a now-dead star.

I knew Mark was in trouble when one Sunday afternoon, as I was setting up to cook the menu I had chosen for Jacques Pépin that night, Mark more or less demanded that I step aside because he wanted to show Pépin that he could cook without me.

I should have said no.

I knew that there was something more wrong than just this dinner as I saw him bring out more and more bottles of Sapporo. He was well into the beer by the time Jacques arrived. Without me he could cook magnificently, but that night he self-parodied both in his choice of menu and in how he served it.

After the Pépin dinner, Mark and I were a bit leery of each other, wondering how two people who trusted each other with their lives could find it so difficult on any given day just to sit down and say the situation was *merde*.

First to quit in the mid-nineties was my great dining room manger, Tony Angotti, who had held the service staff together with a sympathetic but iron fist before heading off to Las Vegas. After he left, the remaining team members started vying for each other's reputations and salaries, given that it was plain that we could not go on paying flush-times salaries in the downturn days of the Civic Center. After Tony, Noreen left, and then Steven. Finally, a year later, Mark came in from Napa to the boardroom when we were all actually discussing the problems in Napa and quietly told me, as a gentleman, that he was through at Stars.

That was the second time I should have gone down into the basement, turned on the gas, and lit a match. My beneficiaries were the core team members, and they would finally have owned Stars, or whatever was left of it.

BREAKING UP

After the team broke up I changed my will to benefit a home for retired donkeys of Calcutta—showing what I thought of the endless stream of new managers who came in. They were impressed with the reputation, the honors on the walls, and the superlatives lavished on me and Stars, but they had never lived them. Now Stars had no one apart from me who knew fact from legend. Dressing these new people up as consorts was a challenge as big as showing any interest in the process myself. To find a way out, and to recover from the exhausting holiday season, I took off for my spiritual home: Paris, and a large, luxury hotel room. In January 1996, after my obligatory walk in the Tuileries Gardens outside the hotel, I went to find solace at Rudolf Nureyev's grave on the anniversary of his death, where I laid an enormous bouquet of white lilies for this friend who had died of AIDS. As I stood there in the rain, the television cameramen asked me to pick up the flowers and put them down again. And again. I politely refused. Something in me snapped when they became angry. I now look back at that moment as the birth of my growing realization that I was as little interested in the sacrifices of being a star as Rudi was before he died. After weeping into a couple of dozen Bélons at La Coupole with a Brazilian picked off the Avenue Foch, and realizing the beautiful flesh at the table with me held no emotional support for me anymore, I canceled my visit to Guy Savoy's new concept everyone was talking about: that all famous restaurants should have a cafe. Oh really! And called Air France. Given my history with Guy and with this cafe concept, even back to the days of Panisse, I realized all the ironies at play. But it was time to gird my defenses and set off for New York, where I was to get up onstage and accept an award without noticeably looking around to see who was still throwing stones.

CHAPTER 30

STARS FOR GRABS

At any other time I would have turned down anything as patently self-serving as an organization like Chefs in America. But they had managed somehow to get Carnegie Hall, an Oscar look-alike statuette, and Lee Iacocca to present it. No one outside the community of chefs would know that it meant nothing, and it was good for at least temporary emperor's clothes, hiding the fact that the year looked like it would be very naked indeed. Full dressing occurred, however, when a few months later I received my real Oscar, this time for the Outstanding Chef in America from the James Beard Foundation. It was a very much bigger deal, and invitations to donate money and services flowed in, as did customers.

We did the usual benefits and dinners to much acclaim (cystic fibrosis in Florida, International Association of Culinary Professionals for Julia Child, at Stars for Pavarotti, Placido Domingo, and Martha Stewart). But the Citymeals-on-Wheels at Rockefeller Center that summer was a grim wake-up call. I didn't want to spend the usual ten thousand dollars on the trip, so decided to do a new brand of tomato stand and have the Florida growers pay for it. The tomatoes showed up an hour before the event, unripe and ordinary, and, for the first time ever, the event was rained out. If I had trouble grasping large-scale disasters, I certainly knew a small one when I was standing in the middle of it. When I suggested to the new team members that we cut our losses and split, they were confused. The old team would have had us packed up and out of there before even I realized we should go. Standing there in a location that was not our usual the center of the rink, and with bad supermarket tomatoes, I just wasn't interested in summoning up the old bravado. It was a mess, so call it a mess, and get out. The new staff expected miracles from me, and I was running out of them.

Right after the tomatoes and Mark Franz's dinner for Jacques Pépin, I answered the phone on one of the nights I was working as maître d' at Stars. It was the Pacific Grove, California, police. My brother had been killed moments before. This several times wounded Green Beret, Special Forces, and 101st Airborne soldier with three tours in Vietnam at the height of the war was killed getting on his ten-speed bike on the grass verge of a park in the center of town. He was on his way to celebrate his birthday with his family when some kid ran him over.

I walked over to the bar, had a glass of champagne, and considered my options. I picked up the phone and found the people I wanted to talk to at their offices in Tokyo.

"Right," I said to Sapporo and Sony in separate calls, "if you are still interested in Stars, let's talk."

The next morning, feeling the false resolve of unrealistic decisions, I made the list of potential buyers. Japan was at the top, then my friend in Thailand (even with rumors of a palace coup confirmed when I called and the queen, in hiding, was sitting next to him), followed by Golden Harvest Films in Hong Kong and the developers in Palo Alto.

I was ready to sell.

FRANCHISED STARS

The first Stars franchise with its promise of big returns was in Palo Alto.

But things started to get strange right away in Palo Alto after the meeting, when I told the head of the investor group that he, with no experience in opening a restaurant, should not be project manager. Perhaps his having different sets of architectural working drawings and not being able to coordinate them was an indication that I was right. That's when he told us about his perfect record in decision making. Having just finished with Doyle Moon, I felt I was perhaps yet again in the company of another sociopath and should have walked out of the room. But we needed the money to support the Civic Center Stars.

The project took on an unreal glow.

Stars Palo Alto finally opened in 1995, to a *San Francisco Chronicle* rating of three stars out of four. But when the inevitable cost overruns from Baer's disorganization became known, Jim put all the blame on us. The investors, just as inevitably, took his word. Trying to get a grip on the difference between the project's fact and its fiction, I took an afternoon off with perfect margaritas at Zuni restaurant and waited for a call from Jim to tell me not to come back. Or to make one myself. Over the third cocktail I wondered what it was about me and the kinds of people with whom I was involved.

First there were the Jesuits in Australia, then the sexual predators of English schools, though I'd more or less outrun them all. So far so good. My great friend and lover in freshman year at the apartment on Boston's Beacon Hill turned out to be purely psychotic. Alice could be actually quite adorable, but hostile when threatened. My original Stars partner, Doyle Moon, was rough-diamond charming and a lot of fun for a few lines of coke and some wonderful drinks, but dangerous when someone threatened to come between him and what he wanted. I found his killer instinct a bit fascinating (as long as I was not on the list of his victims), and I envied his single-minded strength in destroying his friends, once his fondness, loyalty, and often endless tolerance for them were replaced with paranoia and greed.

I found nothing to admire in Jim Baer.

When the entire franchise fee from Palo Alto went to floating Stars, I answered with interest a potentially lucrative call for a consultation from the owners of the Hotel Vancouver. They wanted to redo its dining room. After my first visit, I was hooked. Not only did I like the regional general manager and his wife, the migrating whales, and the otters on Vancouver Island competing with bald eagles for salmon; I fell in love with the region and its ingredients. When I attended a festival of British Columbia foods and for the first time tasted cloudberries and the wines from the Okanagan Valley, I knew the region was in the same phase California had been when I started at Chez Panisse. I loved the enthusiasm of the chefs and the farmers who were supplying them, and the very unjaded way in which they appreciated what they were trying to do.

A new development opportunity became available in Seattle in 1997, in a building that was to finish off the revival of the new downtown. I jumped at the chance. Since 1981 I had been telling the press that Florida and the Northwest were the only two culinary regions of America that were left to develop and received only raised eyebrows in response. But by the mid-nineties it was obvious to all what we had known in California for years—that the best berries, mushrooms, pinot noir, and fish were now from Alaska and the Northwest, not California. And no psychos.

Following my culinary nose, I decided to open a Stars five blocks up from Seattle's waterfront market—a Stars that would help make America's newest regional food. I told the architects I wanted the same kind of huge bar overlooking the dining room as in Stars San Francisco, but that we'd hide most of the kitchen with a big oyster and seafood bar for casual and single diners. It would be a celebration of local seafood, a visual statement of where we were and what kind of food we would be emphasizing. I wanted a big fireplace separating the bar and the dining room to give the feel of a Northwest lodge. I knew that anyone coming up the escalators out of the Seattle rain and seeing a hearth with a roaring fire would not be able to resist coming in.

But that was two years before the opening, and before an old friend in Hong Kong's film business called and said we should meet. He was developing a team to open entertainment restaurants in Asia and then in the United States. They wanted a Stars franchise and to pay for it. Always one to travel at the drop of a hat, I flew to Singapore to meet his group, where I would be dealing with three very civilized and ethical principals: the owner of Golden Harvest Films, the chairman of the board of the city's biggest investment house, and the minister of tourism, who, very usefully, was also in charge of Singapore's work visas. To the extent that I could feel secure with any human beings at this time, I warmed up to the appearance of successful, rich businessmen, well liked in their community, and a government that ran a state as well as any ever had. I accepted. My Hong Kong friend introduced me to the young California team who he thought could lead and operate the projects.

My slightly criminally minded publicist took one look at the team leader and warned me not to trust him in or out of my sight, saying that there was more snake in him than man.

I didn't see it then.

I could see that he hadn't much experience with money unless it was someone else's, spending like a kid given the keys to a billionaire's cash. He made me nervous when he talked about budgets, blithely skipping through a three-year projected budget awash in projected red ink. He signed a lease the restaurant could never afford, and talked about losses as inevitable, even part of the plan. I had never *planned* to lose money in my life, but nothing I said fell on open ears so I kept quiet. The owners of Stars Singapore were very big guys in finance. I figured they knew something I did not.

All doubts flew momentarily from my brain when I climbed up the ladder and put my head through the hole hacked in the floor of the hundred-year-old building across from Raffles in the heart of Singapore.

I gasped in joy.

"THE MOST BEAUTIFUL RESTAURANT IN THE WORLD"

It was a room I had waited a lifetime for: a hundred-foot-long Palladian rectangle with a row of Doric columns five feet away from each of the long walls, a big shuttered window centered between each column. Here was classical, grand colonial, tropical architecture at its best. When I learned it had been the dormitory for the boys of the Sacred Heart orphanage, I could almost see the same lineup as my school in England, with its long rows of bed-chair-bed-chair.

The other possible locations—an old Chinese spice shop, a government building on a hill—were beautiful, but this city-block convent with its little cathedral that would be our banquet hall was unique in the world. And after seeing the outdoor fast-food restaurants and the exotic food markets I knew all my fantasies from my upbringing—of tropical fruits and verandas filled with elegant white suits and cool gin and tonics—could come true here. Who could resist creating a new cuisine with California inspiration behind eight kinds of mangoes, huge baskets of rambutans and mangosteens, of headily fragrant pineapples, and sugary finger bananas stacked in small mountains next to bamboo baskets filled with thirty-pound red snappers, octopus, garoupas, and exotic striped moray eels? It was a world to which I was happy to escape. Over drinks at Raffles I signed the franchise contract, holding back a desperate eagerness to say, "Why not buy Stars instead of merely franchising it?"

The finished Stars—with its pizza oven and rotisserie oven at one end of the dining room and huge bar at the other, a spiral staircase in between joining the cafe below with the upper main Stars—was magnificent. Drew Nieporent, a man of many famous restaurants on both American coasts, said Stars Singapore was "the most beautiful restaurant in the world."

I thought about buying an old chophouse and setting up shop in Singapore, letting a management company operate all the restaurants. But after a few months, when the young California team failed to get even to first base in how to operate a Stars, were seemingly more loyal to each other than to the owners, and were more interested in glamorous special events than in everyday operations, I knew we were marching to different drummers. Their music was more Pied Piper than victory march. After helping them open the restaurant I returned to San Francisco to find the Civic Center in a morass of demolition.

I was determined to get a grip on the operations and to build the restaurant back up, but as construction of the new courthouse across from Stars' entrance began, huge barricades went up that isolated the area even further.

Since there is never a better time to strike successfully than when someone is down, the bottom feeders appeared, first with little bites, then in a wholesale frenzy.

BLOOD IN THE WATER

First was the FBI. A telephone call. How well did I know Andrew Cunanan? Gianni Versace had been murdered in Miami Beach a few days before, and Cunanan was the suspect, along with anyone who "knew" him. But because the real contacts were customers of Stars, I told them my lips were sealed.

They didn't like that.

The next day it was around town that I was mixed up in Versace's murder.

I got on a plane to Singapore and returned a week later.

I saw it on the evening television news the night I got back. An attorney in a wheelchair had invited a news camera crew into the men's bathroom at Stars and had filmed him bashing backward and forward, "trying" to get into the toilet stall, which, no surprise to anyone, he could not. Soon there was a lawsuit on my desk. The press howled in righteous outrage, and more inspectors,

TV, and activists showed up across the street at Stars Cafe. They objected to the marble bathrooms, installed at vast expense a few years before, inspected, and passed as conforming to the Americans with Disabilities Act.

It turned out that the perfectly accessible stall openings were one-quarter of an inch short of what was required by the newer regulations.

We ripped them out.

I had to give interviews in the bathrooms when they were finished. So this is what it has come to, I thought to myself. I really am in the toilet. I thought of Singapore, the strictest city in the world, where this would have been done via a letter in a dignified way instead of with barbarians at my gates.

The only people embarrassed by all this other than me were the fifty representatives of the Japanese Hotel and Restaurant Association, who had been my hosts in Japan and were now visiting Stars. They had come to California to see Napa and buy wine for the five hundred hotels and restaurants they represented. But our visit to some of Napa's most prestigious wineries ran aground on the new grandeur spreading through the valley. The Japanese were snubbed. I cajoled my pal, San Francisco's mayor, Frank Jordan, who gave them the key to the city and declared that day theirs. His presenting the signed parchment in person to them at Stars helped smooth their feathers. But they suggested between very polite Japanese verbal lines that I move to Kyoto. It was my favorite Japanese city and I couldn't have agreed more. Buy Stars, I told them above the lines.

My efforts to sell Stars to Sapporo and Sony came to a civilized nothing after the Japanese experience in Napa and their interested tour of the Civic Center area, now falling into the fetid laps of the homeless.

Moving on, I turned the old cafe space in Stars into JT's and a cigar room to show what I thought was the next trend: comforting, sensible, unadorned, single-ingredient-driven food. That approach was a few years premature: the new hires for it had no idea what I was talking about when I said that a great chef knows when not to get in the way of perfect ingredients. They had heard of the new postmodernist trend in food just then starting, and which would end five years later in a glass bell jar filled with smoke over an eighteenth-century Marie-Antoine Carême presentation of a caviar blini at New York's Eleven Madison Park. As if Chez Panisse, the Santa Fe Bar & Grill, and Stars had never existed. My telling them that a piece of impeccably fresh turbot needs no more than a made-to-order shellfish sauce, into which a sprig of tarragon has been infused for ten seconds, fell on puzzled ears.

There was no extra money to take the new managers and staff to the Crillon in Paris to see how breakfast was done, to Lameloise in Burgundy or the Four Seasons in New York to see how service was done, or to Maguy Le Coze's perfect Le Bernardin to show how perfect unadorned fish was done. At a lecture at the Culinary Institute of America in the fall of 1995, I begged the first graduating class of the bachelor's program to have a little humility. I said that spending all that money to become chefs was really only the beginning of the journey. The stunned silence that followed told me I should never have left Hong Kong, where the staff knew I knew more than they did, and would listen as long as I made them money, and as long as they could call me names in Chinese under their breath that would have stripped the paint off the culinary walls of fame in America.

Back in San Francisco, things became worse with the new mayor: the deal to buy out Stars and build one at their expense was revived, but it never seemed to be either in or out of favor. The cupboard was empty.

THE CUPBOARD IS BARE AGAIN

Denise Hale and I drank the last of the Cristal champagne in Stars' cellar on New Year's Eve 1996.

Her husband (with Al Wilsey one of the last great San Franciscan tycoons with any style) had just died. While he had been in the hospital we would sit every midnight in Stars, drinking and feeling nothing, not even the alcohol. We made a vow to be out of San Francisco for the next New Year's Eve. I told her that it should be in Hong Kong, and that I would show her the wonderland of Singapore, where nothing bad ever seemed to happen. Or Manila, from where I was hoping something good in the way of money would arrive.

Benjamin Bitanga, that cheery Manila pirate who had helped wrest Stars from Doyle, had always thought of it as "our" restaurant. Now he had been back to the rescue, agreeing that I should sell part or all of Stars to keep it afloat until the opera and ballet came back in the fall of 1997. I had already been to Manila earlier in the year and met the group who adored Stars and continued negotiations. When rumors that Stars was broke started, they were scared off.

At the end of 1996 I was easily persuaded to spend New Year's in Singapore, though it was a toss-up what needed my attention more that evening: Singapore Stars for its first December 31, or San Francisco Stars for its twelfth. When I decided on Singapore I knew I had cut most of my emotional ties with San Francisco. I took Denise Hale and my other two favorite San Franciscans, Brunno and Urannia Ristow, on a Christmas cruise on the Regent Hotel's yacht (the general manager's gift to me) around Hong Kong and gave them a champagne lunch. In Hong Kong I felt truly at home. I had sold my shares in the Peak Cafe for $500,000 to cover my earthquake-closed Speedo 690 and faltering Stars. And I had not been back to the Peak since 1993.

The staff cried when I walked in. The at-home feeling was intensified in Singapore, when at 3 A.M. on New Year's Day, Denise and I walked a mile back to the Ritz-Carlton, she bedecked in a lot of Bulgari feeling completely safe. The streets smelled of jasmine not urine, and there was not a homeless person in sight, let alone a thief. Neither one of us wanted to return to San Francisco and face the music. Her lawsuits were piling up from her stepchildren (other than Liza Minnelli), and I was wondering what was going to happen if the cash from my pending Manila, Hong Kong, and Bangkok deals didn't come through. Or cash from the franchises didn't start to flow. The Thai connection was proving elusive, potential deals with Hong Kong–MCA and/or Disney seemed far off, Manila was in weekly contact but agonizingly evasive, and Stars Singapore, with its impossible rent, was hemorrhaging money and percentage fees for Stars San Francisco.

Then Andrew Yap, the new owner of Stars Singapore, was arriving in San Francisco supposedly in a buying mood. The word was he needed something to go with his newly acquired famous Italian "cigarette" boat brand.

PROMISES, PROMISES

Andrew Yap was due at the Stars management offices at three thirty one afternoon in early 1997 to sign the letter of intent to buy Stars. By four forty-five he had not shown up or called. At five he did show, explaining that the San Francisco airport weather had held him up and that he now had only a few minutes to talk before his plane to Singapore. I knew all the airlines' schedules to Asia by heart and knew there were no planes to Asia until later that night. I knew what he was up to. I was used in Hong Kong to dealing with Chinese and he was only half. But just to check I excused myself and called the San Francisco airport. There had been no fog or delays in two days. I walked back and listened as Andrew explained that the original offer of several million dollars could now be no more than one. I rose, told him I was grateful for all the work he had done, and said I did not want to be responsible for him missing his plane. His mouth sagged slowly open, then quickly shut. He stood up, buttoned his coat, and instantly dropped the fatherly tone with which he had broken the news of our ruin. I escorted him politely to the door.

Back in San Francisco there was no end to the mounting bills. Only the Christmas holiday season private parties, each of which I was forced to guarantee to cook myself, saved our cash flow, if nearly destroying me.

Back in the Philippines after the season I met the investment group again, who were now excited (having seen the recent San Francisco cash flow) about opening a Stars in Manila. I phoned my comptroller with the great news of more franchise fees, but his news was less good. On my desk was another employee complaint about the new business manager of Stars. Because of the impending sale, we took to confidential mediation.

The mediation judge was a Stars customer, but since I had never talked to her, she didn't have to disqualify herself from the case. She took me aside and said the whole thing was "pure extortion." But did I want to settle or face another lawsuit?

I didn't. I knew I hadn't the money to fight a protracted battle, but was horrified when I realized I didn't have the desire to either. Or lose pending deals. Twelve years before, a settlement would have been $3,500. The trial of the waiter dying from AIDS had cost hundreds of thousands. Now just a down payment on a discrimination case was $150,000. At a break in the hearing negotiations, the two employees had dragged me into the ladies' room, their tear-filled eyes suddenly quite dry, to assure me that this was not personal, nothing to do with me.

I tried to remember that it was nothing personal when I left the judge's chambers to write a check for the 150. The last of the Peak Cafe share sale cash was gone.

When I drove off, I laughed. I was in a new Mercedes 560 SEL, and now seemed as if I wouldn't have a dime to my name.

CLOUD COVER

Stars' vendors had been held at bay by promised of Asian funds. So far at the end of 1997 and beginning of 1998 nothing had appeared. Then a check for $350,000 from the Stars Manila franchise came through from Bitanga's group. The money dented the vendor bills but we couldn't hold out for long. On my first morning in Manila in March, to see the Stars site, a call came through over breakfast in my room at Makati's Shangri-La hotel. It was Andrew Yap. He said he was downstairs and would like to talk.

I could barely breathe.

We met in the enormous foyer lounge next to a garden of royal palms. I told him that I still had plans to refurbish Stars to bring it back to its former glory for the reopening of all the Civic Center in the fall, but that I would need financing. Andrew looked at me with barely concealed cunning and told me that if he were to refinance Stars he would have to own it. I paused delicately, for as long as I could.

"Fine."

Hoping he would not hear the trap snapping shut, I named the price. He didn't want me to stand up and leave again so we shook hands. After mine had stopped shaking.

As I wandered into the garden, I wondered if the shaking of my hands was from sadness or relief. But now, assuming the deal went through, everyone would get paid.

After a stop in Singapore to check on its Stars, and a promotional tour on Crystal Cruises, I returned to San Francisco to put on our best face. We cooked again for the Meals-on-Wheels, for the fifteenth anniversary of the American Institute of Wine & Food, held at Michael's in Santa Monica, and with gritted teeth, for the AIDS Emergency Fund. But my mind was on the sale and what would happen if it fell through. Then Andrew and his team finally believed me when I advised them to hustle to be ready with Stars' new appearance by the opening of the 1998 performing arts season in September. The due diligence ended on June 3, 1998; the money was due on the twelfth.

On the fourth I cooked a big dinner for Shafer Vineyards; on the seventh I flew to New York for Citymeals-on-Wheels at Rockefeller Center. I made two appointments on the twelfth: one for an overhaul at my favorite salon, and the other, tempting the gods, for the movers to come and get my papers and personal goods from Stars.

The money was due by noon, so I made a spa appointment for eleven thirty. Whatever the outcome, I was going to need a massage. When my cell phone rang, I felt my heart miss several beats. It was the office at Stars saying they had given my cell phone number to the bank, but had no news. Of course I had already given the number to the banker, so the second time the phone rang I was calm, thinking the bank would not bother to call saying it *wasn't* there. It was. All delicious several seven figures of it.

The next day we handed Stars to its new owners. Then I headed to the airport for the closest tropical beach that was at the height of its mango season.

At Rosewood's Las Ventanas al Paraiso in Cabo San Lucas, Mexico, I had an ice chest of ripe mangoes put next to the hammock on my roof garden, and stocked up it with champagne and fresh pineapple juice.

Paradise indeed this was.

At last it was over.

I put on the earphones and listened to Gregg Allman's "I'll Be Holding On."

I did.

Sixteen months after I sold Stars (and I never set foot in it again), the new owners closed it "for remodeling." Journalists and some of the old crew sniffed an ending and went for a last look. Its former chef de cuisine Mark Franz was quoted as saying it was like being at your ex-wife's funeral. Both he and the wonderful Stars Cafe chef Loretta Keller, who had gone on to open her own cafe, Bizou, laughed with *Gourmet* magazine's Ruth Reichl, and her evaluation that the prevailing Berkeley attitude, "'Oh, it's OK, it's good enough,' was never good enough for Jeremiah. He brought this amazing style into the community and everybody—men and women—were in love with him. He was like a character in a movie. We were all walking around in Birkenstocks," said Ruth, "and here he comes this English gentleman."

LUCKY

In *Lucky Peach* magazine, Mario Batali summed it all up. Up until the late '70s/early 80s, he said, the general eating-out public took restaurants probably not "as seriously as going out to a game or opera or the movies." But when California chefs started making noises it all changed.

Reichl described "the California cuisine revolution, where Californians realized they had the same bounty as France and Italy, and that if they paid attention and made goat cheese and grew baby lettuces, they could have something that was similar to going to a two- or three-stars restaurant in Europe without all the travel," especially when "Wolfgang Puck made it very hip to go out to dinner in Los Angeles—not just to eat, but to be seen."

Then there was Stars in San Francisco. "I still consider Stars to be one of the greatest restaurants of all time. This is a place where you could wear a tuxedo, or you could be dressed like me with dirty shorts and a golf shirt. It was luxury—but not overpriced—for the masses. It was very fresh every day. It was all very vibrant. It had piano players. It was this giant restaurant." And one that made a "compelling" star of its chef and owner. "He's like James Bond. . . . Jeremiah would walk in and people—boys and girls—swooned."

Must have been the drinks.

CHAPTER 31

CULINARY AMERICA'S MIDLIFE CRISIS

The *New York Times,* in an eighties "Living" section cover story by Marian Burros, called us all "Disciples of Chez Panisse," saying that if Henri Soulé at Le Pavillon "can be credited with igniting the explosion of fine French food in America in the 1950s and '60s, then Chez Panisse deserves similar recognition for revolutionizing American cooking in the 1970s." The chef photo was a face behind the veil of Alice's antique hats.

DISCIPLES OF CHEZ PANISSE

When Adam Nagourney interviewed me for the *New York Times* in 2002, he quoted me saying Alice didn't know a little vegetable from a rotten one. I did for once regret not having handled the interview in sound bites even if that comment was supposed to be "off the record." What I had told him was that the true story of her enormous contribution has not been told, and that he should interview her to get it. I said that her real contribution didn't have a lot to do with the early revolution, that in the beginning she didn't know commercial vegetables from truly great ones, but that she had learned. Much of her story came later, especially after Sibella Kraus came onto the scene in the early eighties and planted those little lettuces in Alice's garden. That was the beginning of her actually great contributions, things like her advocacy for farmers' markets, for sound and sustainable agriculture, for supporting Carlo

Petrini's Slow Food movement, and for the Chez Panisse Foundation, which underwrites the Edible Schoolyard as well as the Garden Project at the San Francisco county jail. Ask her about all that, I said. Not about a perfect peach.

Mark Peel, chef of Campanile, in Los Angeles, had another view of Panisse. "I wanted to work at Chez Panisse in 1980 because it was a major force behind the return to our culinary roots. But it was not highly organized. There was never-ending confusion." Jonathan Waxman, at Panisse in 1978, was quoted while still chef at Michael's in Santa Monica as saying he applied at Panisse because of Alice's reputation, but "quite frankly I didn't understand what it was all about. But I learned that you don't serve a dish unless it's perfect." He lauded the use of fresh herbs and of "going through sixteen cases of fresh lettuces to find the finest." Mark Miller was inspired by Panisse to use "native ingredients," and Judy Rodgers of San Francisco's Zuni Cafe credited Panisse with the "obsessive pursuit of perfection" in raw ingredients. Judy said that Alice was "the kind of cook who is visceral instead of one who quantifies" but that she "used to get three cases of green beans in order to find enough tender small ones for a single meal."

At least I taught Alice and the restaurant something.

The *New York Times* went on to say in the early eighties that Alice acts simply "as a consultant to the restaurant and spends only two days a week there, one cooking and one working in the dining room." Alice mused to Burros in 1984 that she might go back into the kitchen—"I'm curious to cook up coq au vin right now"—and mused further about the difference between her and my kitchen styles: "Jeremiah was not hesitant. His cooking is more elaborate than mine, more flamboyant, and I was fascinated by his combinations, things I wouldn't have thought of." And my comment? "'Mainly,' Mr. Tower says, 'we had fun together. Alice has a wonderful sense of how to eat,'" as I well knew from our travels alone together.

I told the *Detroit News* I remembered an evening in September 1980 on the terrace of the Gritti Palace in Venice, under the moonlight, drinking Krug with Alice, when she admitted "that without you, there would be no Chez Panisse or me." I didn't mention that Alice and I, enjoying our on-and-off-again affair, on our way to lunch the next morning at Harry's Bar had sent a telegram. It was to her new beautiful boyfriend back in Berkeley for his twenty-first birthday:

funghi, uccellini, gritti;
seppe, fritti, harry's—
a hardonna! madonna (pardonna)!
krug '59

After I left Chez Panisse, it was undeniably still an unquestioned influence, and would be even in 2001, when the restaurant garnered first place in *Gourmet* magazine's "Best Restaurants in America" issue. After reading that piece, I wondered what made a chef of America's best restaurants. At 1990's so-called disciple dinner of former Panisse chefs, held in Los Angeles honoring Alice with the Robert Mondavi Food and Wine Award, the chefs made it quite clear that no such across-the-board real "teaching" had gone on during their tenure with Alice since I left. Even Alice, now as "co-chef" of Panisse, admitted she hadn't cooked in eighteen years. When she told me she was now "emeritus," I asked what it meant and she laughed. That night I asked the on-and-off Panisse chef Jean-Pierre Moullé what the term *co-chef* meant. He was not sure it was even true. We laughed about the night in 1978, while he had taken over from me as chef, when Alice had called asking me to fire Jean-Pierre because he had been mentioned in the press as "chef of Chez Panisse."

If it was true that Alice had not been cooking since I left in 1978, what was the lesson or lessons here about the nature of a chef, great, famous, or otherwise? How was it done? As Alice said in a 1986 interview with *Restaurant Business,* "It's hard to balance your own feelings as an owner with the necessity of putting someone else in charge" of the kitchen. Looking back on our equal-owner status, she in the dining room with me in the kitchen, I wondered if that was how she had always felt with me.

ROLLING STONES

By 1998 there was a backlash. Was it the twenty-eight-dollar price of chicken at New York City's California restaurant temple, Jams? Did the public agree with *Rolling Stone* that what we were doing was really "ambitious gardening followed by crude mixology"? One classically trained French chef called California pretentious. "Its cuisine consists of things you don't normally hear of going together, like alligator fritters with a parsnip sauce. The alligator tastes like chicken, and the parsnip tastes like turnips. It's frightening."

The revolution starting in air transportation and quick delivery of national and international fresh ingredients meant that in 1985 the list of local was becoming worldwide, increasing the quantity of choices we could cook with. For New Year's dessert was Satsuma mandarin orange, Meyer lemon, and Australian fresh young ginger and pineapple sorbets with ripe passion fruit sauce. We could celebrate three fresh American caviars for a dinner at the Imperial Bank in San Diego. At the California Wine Perspective dinner, after we had survived the evil treatment at the Hotel Pierre's front desk, we could serve braised sweetbreads with fresh Côte d'Azur violets, nasturtiums, and sage butter.

In the hands of a hack, the results were indeed very often frightening. But in the hands of a classical-principles-inspired new chef, the mixology was not jinxology, but "new" without being solely for newness's sake. Some visionaries looked forward, saying that the new tradition would be remembered not for certain dishes like the ones made famous by the previously established cooking—tournedos Rossini or chicken cordon bleu—but for our "attitude."

Rolling Stone had Alice Waters put the background of this new cooking into a nutshell: "At first we wanted things to be like in France, and we called everything by French names, then all of a sudden straining to, like 'Huîtres de Bolinas' instead of 'Bolinas Bay oysters.'" She was talking about the reason for my "road to Damascus" moment in 1976 when I saw the turn from France to regions of America, specifically California. Both Alice and the reporter pointed out that my 1976 California Regional Dinner at Panisse began Berkeley's second revolution, the first having been the political one of the late sixties. *Rolling Stone* thought Alice was still stuck in the first one, even if the Volvos parked outside Panisse were new and the bumper stickers no longer rooted for the Black Panthers but for the lifestyle of "Living well is the best revenge," a suggestion from the reporter that left Alice on the defensive.

The same magazine could not help but be fascinated by the difference between the clienteles at Panisse and at Stars. "Jeremiah is equally comfortable with the rowdy Beastie Boys and Run DMC who Tower shooed successfully out the door just as the baroness de Rothschild from Chateau Mouton-Rothschild showed up with a reservation for the same table." The article made the point that, whereas I had kept evolving my style, the one at Panisse had stayed the same, and that this "split" in styles had created two camps and an atmosphere on which the new young chefs were "neatly skewered."

Nowhere was the conflict between choosing whether to be a private or a public chef more evident than in the institution of the chef-driven benefit banquet, the proliferation of which the reporter blamed on me. The motives for participating were under suspicion. Were they self-promotion or charitable concern? "There is something that sticks in the craw about the average gourmet benefit," said *Rolling Stone.*

Only if the food is bad, I replied.

I added that for me, they were publicity opportunities waiting to happen. At a Rockefeller Center Citymeals-on-Wheels, Robin Leach was looking around for material more interesting than Wolfgang's spit-roasted ducks in flames, or Bradley's lamb chops on the grill in the interior kitchen threatening to burn down the tallest building. He spotted Malcolm Forbes and me spotting each other. As Forbes walked over and put out his hand, I introduced myself. "I know perfectly well who you are" was the reply caught on tape by *Lifestyles of the Rich and Famous* as Forbes quite snugly took my arm. All this intrigued the gay Robin so much that he later filmed Stars for a show that aired for years afterward all over the world, one in which the public remembers Leach saying that "Stars is the best restaurant in the world," even when he said no such thing. After that event any chef who did not have a publicist or handler got one. The relationship of the superstar chefs and the press was a symbiotic marriage made and consummated on the battlefields of charitable work, and definitely not in church.

NAKED CHEFS

The nineties was the decade when I sat on a cow for the Milk Board, Wolfgang Puck put his coffee in cheap hotels and did a bad raisin commercial, and there was lineup of naked chefs (even Jean-Louis Palladin) showing hairy bodies somewhat the worse for gravity and booze, hiding their genitalia behind food blenders, a reminder to prefer the real "Naked Chef," Jamie Oliver. All this made a clothed Jonathan Waxman ten years earlier, lying in a pond with ducks for *Life* magazine, look tame. *Rolling Stone* tried to define what kinds of chefs we all were: Alice was "Chef as Doyenne," and I the "Entertainer." André Soltner, the doyen of French chefs in America, in disgust called us all "soup merchants."

The eighties press had done its job, and the public was primed to eat new American, to see chefs as stars, to think that cooking was a new form of theater and part of the entertainment industry. So caught up was the nation in this new food fantasy pastime that there was hardly any dissent. The pendulum swing of disillusionment with this culinary flash dance wasn't to hit until 2015. A handful of writers used to identifying trends still in their fetal stage had already spoken out. *Town & Country's* James Villas in 1983 had said, "I am up to my neck with all the phoniness and abuse and elitism and celebrity. All this business is really getting out of hand." Perhaps he was still sore still at Alice having threatened to call the police over his smoking in "that military state called Berkeley." Or was it because Alice, now a celebrity, had once spent the end of an evening in his lap at Georges Blanc's restaurant outside Lyons before sliding to the floor? In his mind, she did not know how to behave.

But no one else in the now-fascinated public was fed up or thought anything had gone far enough. John Mariani took several pages to extol the "Regional Favorites" in his *Playboy* list of the nation's best restaurants, even if only eight of them served "regional" American food—interesting that regional America was now the measure. Those restaurants included Larry Forgione's An American Place in New York, Stephan Pyles's Routh Street Cafe in Dallas, Jasper White's Jasper's in Boston, and Frank Stitt's Highlands Bar & Grill in Birmingham, Alabama. Some reporters talked of the new "stars" of the culinary world, and some, like the "Question Man" in the *San Francisco Chronicle,* featured chefs instead of taxi drivers as "the regular Joe on the street." One can't blame the chefs for being a bit confused.

Gone were the days (momentarily) when a chef would be featured in German *Penthouse,* as I was in 1988, next to the naked centerfold, as a "Jet-set-Guru." Now it was much more an article in the *New York Times* about "how a celebrity chef of the '80s got his stove back," as Jonathan Waxman opened the Washington Park in April 2002 and had the confidence to put on the menu a dish that is seen as his signature from Michael's and Jams: the roast chicken with french fries and watercress from 1979. After years of being a media darling, Jonathan was no longer flying off to Paris's Taillevent for lunch, but was back in the restaurant.

The *San Francisco Chronicle* pointed out the irony in new American cooking in 1988. Hardly any chef in the country claimed to be cooking American food. Even if discovering America was what it was all about, each chef taking clues from California, how many cuisines were there in the United States? And was this new emphasis on regional cooking "a profound reawakening or another exhausting trend"? The always intelligent writer Jay Jacobs said it was a game of culinary star wars, with every chef grabbing his or her Warholian fifteen minutes of fame. The chefs who had been there at the beginning disagreed.

Jimmy Schmidt defended the superior flavors of any vegetables picked closest to you that went straight into the pot, adding that the celebration of regional food is merely recognizing food for "its true worth, rather than a marketing-created worth," and that some regional foods were so highly charged from childhood they would never be trendy and disappear. I thought of my Cape Cod family's clambakes with cantaloupe melons straight from the kitchen garden, filled with hundred-year-old Madeira and stuck down a cool well for the next day's lunch. It was an optimistic view of American childhood, but regardless, every chef agreed that when a vegetable or fruit is ripe, ready, in season, and in your own backyard, it's the best.

Larry Forgione of An American Place agreed, but cautioned not to forget new techniques and combinations. Most of the chefs voiced a vision that the pull of working with locally superior ingredients was so strong that regionalism was here to stay, that great cooking would always be ingredient driven. John W. Makin said from his restaurant in Napa Valley that the next great leap in regional cuisine "will be chefs moving out of urban areas and setting up restaurants in the countryside where farmers knock on their back doors with ripe products at the height of freshness." As the chef who had opened his kitchen back door to wandering amateur foragers sixteen years earlier, I loved the historically innocent freshness of that comment when it was wryly told to me.

Stephan Pyles and I were the lone voices of dissent in this vision, seeing an end to regionalism but not to the force of perfect ingredients, wherever they came from. We saw a sort of "culinary harmonic convergence," and I predicted that regional cuisines would exist for some time, but would result in a codification of a new American cuisine. Building on the tradition started at the Four Seasons in New York in 1959, fueled by its own foragers, and creating what Jeffrey Steingarten at *Vogue* forty years later called "a completely contemporary American haute cuisine," that's what happened. In 1979 Michael McCarty had to rely on his contacts in France to get the ingredients he wanted, but by the late eighties and early nineties he and every chef around America were encouraged by the spiritual, public relational, and financial rewards of encouraging local producers. The revolution became evolution in full flower.

The circle has been completed: restaurant guru Joe Baum's "new-old food in a new-new setting" all over again, driven, as always, by ingredients.

CONFUSED?

Trying to figure it all out, the Australian food and art critic Leo Schofield talked to the "megastars" of the West Coast chefs to find out what was happening, what "new directions" the revolution was taking in 1986. Leo predicted that chefs would be faced with a choice between two wells of inspiration—new ingredients or money. Was a chef to believe, as Bradley Ogden said he did of the Four Seasons in New York, that "style and decor are more important than food"? Which road was a chef to take? Another Australian, Jill Dupleix, knew why the nineties were not going to be the eighties, and wrote *New Food: From the New Basics to the New Classics*.

The food/decor question highlighted awareness of the tension between the now de rigueur philosophy of authentic simplicity and our steadily increasing bank accounts. This *crise de coeur* was nowhere more evident than in the 1986 cover story for *Restaurant Business* magazine titled "Chef Celebrities." The five cartooned chefs included Prudhomme holding his pan for blackening fish, Larry Forgione running after a chicken, and Alice Waters in overalls holding a rake. "Flashbulbs are popping and the videotape is rolling. Movie stars? No, chefs. Suddenly, working in the kitchen is a glamour occupation, and a new generation of aspiring chefs is entering the ranks, making American cuisine truly world class, as Americans have become food-crazy." In this same article I was held up as a prime example of the new dilemma facing chefs because of my maintaining a heavy schedule of public appearances, charity events, travel, and interviews with the press, my life reading, it said, like a script from *Lifestyles of the Rich and Famous*. Five years earlier, "Jeremiah Tower's appearances would have been limited to two choices: the front of his restaurant (dining room) or the back (kitchen)."

This picture was now not all about food. The chefs made their lives public like any major star in Hollywood. *Rolling Stone* warned of this emerging crisis in new America's cooking, incredulous that the *Los Angeles Times* devoted the entire front page of the food section to photos of the wedding vows not of a movie star but of the chef Michel Richard. The magazine notes that the epicenter of all this weirdness was Northern California (with its "edible flowers and homegrown snails"), where eating had taken over from sex as the preferred form of sensual gratification. "We can't have sex anymore because of AIDS, and we can't do drugs because of Ed Meese's [President Reagan's then–attorney general] storm troopers," said one of the chefs, "so what's left?"

But drugs were still around, and cocaine was still fueling the overtaxed schedules of famous road-running chefs. One night in Miami with the March of Dimes the guest chefs had been to a bizarre and huge estate patrolled by armed guards mingling with the guests. All that day had been TV and radio appearances for me, so by eight o'clock, when the curtain was ready to go up on our performance in black tie for five hundred of the Boca, the Beach, and Coral Gables classic swells, I was beat. After the reception I simply could not go on. In my hotel room for a minute to splash cold water on my face, I wondered whether all this was worth it and whether I would just rather be at home in the arms of a great white Burgundy. The telephone shrilled.

"Come on down to my room," a familiar voice drawled. "I have something for you."

A champagne thirst surged through my body as I hung up, but since the voice was that of a chef who had a reputation for cramming the divine white powder up his nose, my body waved with a certain peristaltic rush instead.

Sure enough, when I walked into his room's short corridor with its built-in dresser, the top ten inches below nose level, I saw four white powdery lines, each the size of a small python.

"Two are yours," he said.

And two I took. Within seconds I was myself again, or some newly energetic version of it, mentally fit for the press and all the smiling fans. The second round four hours later was laid out on the thick marble counter of the men's room, setting off a panic in me for a second as, my eyes only two inches from the counter, the white lines in the thick black Italian marble momentarily camouflaged the drug. We needed this round before going into the bar to face the event's sponsor's new vodkas being passed around in long-stem martini glasses the size of goldfish bowls. Glamorous "New Society" was embracing "New American Cuisine," or was it the other way around? Lucius Beebe, who had invented "Cafe Society" fifty years earlier, would have looked around the room for Cole Porter and the Murphys and seen only chefs courted by gun runners, drug dealers, and slinky trophy wives in Armani beaded couture.

TOO CLOSE TO THE FIRE

The benefit that *Rolling Stone* really choked on was for a whole new cause, held in San Francisco in 1987 and called "Aid and Comfort." AIDS had hit the California restaurant industry as early as 1984, just as Stars opened. Two of our best dining room staff fell fatally ill within the year, both events that ten years later would turn me from local hero to San Francisco pariah. At this time, however, the charity-going community was fresh and the party a huge hit, if a bit staggering, and foreboding. I was quoted at the after-event party for the volunteers as saying I thought perhaps we were flying too close to the flames, but no one else seemed worried or even noticed. After all, we had raised a lot of money for AIDS research and hospice support in a town where a thousand waiters had died of AIDS since the early eighties. The evening's very success bred a proportional amount of hype, and what some saw as en-thusiasm was already being seen by some press as opportunism. By the end of the food service, Alice Waters said she had no control, "as she was relegated at that point to picking up cigarette butts off the floor of the wharf, and no less than fourteen HYC [Hot Young Chefs] had muscled their way into the kitchen, as the whole thing had come to look like the biggest photo opportu-nity of the season."

These chefs weren't stupid.

CHAPTER 32

THE HOT YOUNG CHEFS

"The hot young chefs have arrived," screamed the *San Francisco Chronicle*'s food section a few days later. André Soltner (Lutèce in New York), the dignified and beloved older chef of the profession, who was seen (quite oddly) as having no penchant for public relations, was interviewed about all these carryings-on. "I blame you . . . the press," he said. "If you glorify a young guy at twenty-four, good for him, beautiful, but if you don't help him at the same time, you spoil him. We cannot forget, even if we are celebrities, who we are. We are cooks, but soup merchants too." Soup merchants with heads too big to see the soup pot beyond the latest press clipping.

VIS-À-VIS

The new chefs felt the first part of the American food revolution was the realm of legend. Of myth. They were too young to remember JFK: "The great enemy of the truth is very often not the lie, deliberate, contrived, and dishonest, but the myth, persistent, persuasive, and unrealistic."

This new group knew the origins of the changes in culinary America only from the press. Hardly any had been present at the revolution and they weren't grounded in what inspired it, either. This new generation had only the terminology of *fresh, organic, local,* and *California.* How many of them had ever gardened or been on a farm? Or did the essential meanings of these concepts live only in the press, cooking magazines, and the floodlights of fame? The question was not answered until the end of the century, when the new chefs and their sous chefs found and held their own true ground and the entire revolution reached its full farm-to-table and nose-to-tail fruition.

PAYING THE BILLS

Every chef in the industry adored and revered André Soltner, judging from the reception he received for Lifetime Achievement at the James Beard Foundation awards when he retired in 1994, and even if many of the new chefs on their feet may have been wondering why. Not even Julia Child ever got that kind of standing ovation. Between accepting this fame and his saying we should not forget that all chefs are cooks and soup merchants, too, and the seminal backlash in the national culinary press, any chef attuned to the pulse must have thought about which path to take. The restaurant business was a lot of work, and if fame alone as a payback for all the exhaustion seemed not enough, who could have blamed any chef for looking beyond the glamour for something else? A big bank account seemed the obvious answer, since it was now clear that fame only indirectly paid the Visa or MasterCard.

A good way, your publicist told you, to be taken seriously and make more money was to have your name on a cookbook. This trend escaped no one's attention. The success in America of promoting a whole new style or presentation was obvious. French publisher Laffont's late-seventies illustrated editions of the Young Turks helped make nouvelle cuisine world famous. Everyone saw the legitimization of Alice as a chef instead of restaurant owner in 1982 with *The Chez Panisse Menu Cookbook* even when she hadn't written it. Or the kind of publicity I received for Stars with the 1986 *Jeremiah Tower's New American Classics*. When it received a James Beard Foundation award I got to be seen, heard, or read in multimedia by likely more than 15 million Americans. Creativity of the menu across America was temporarily halted while every famous chef wrote a book.

Or had it done for them.

MYTHMAKING

At the tenth birthday party of Panisse in 1981 Alice gave me a copy of the manuscript of *The Chez Panisse Menu Cookbook*. The next day, as I looked at the manuscript, I noted with shock the lack of acknowledgments. Alice had taken sole credit for the most important events in Panisse's history, among them the Gertrude Stein dinner, the blue trout of the Champagne and Alsace dinners, the Louisiana dinner, the whole Escoffier festival, and even the California Regional Dinner. When I read on page 297 of the manuscript, "For some ten years now, I have faced, every Thursday, the weekly dilemma of planning" the menus, I nearly fell off my deck chair. That claim was unconscionable. Did she think she had done the menus all those years because she had typed them? I reached for my Beverly Hills Hotel cabana phone to ask the author, Linda Guenzel, if Alice thought I had never existed.

"I asked Alice about that," Linda replied. "She said it wasn't necessary to include your name everywhere after you had been mentioned once in the credits as having been the chef there."

I called Alice.

I told her the approach was beneath her or anyone else, and downright dangerous to her reputation if the book were published without some important changes. I made a detailed list and sent it to Alice, who said, "Before anything happens, I really do want it to be right with all my friends; I hope you believe that. I should have sat down and talked to you first, but it was such an afterthought to do it." I wondered if "it" was doing the right thing or trying not to. I told her, at the risk of sounding condescending, that giving proper credit and telling the truth could only reflect more credit on herself, that all the book had to do was "to honor all those people involved in the history—most of all yourself. Though a scandal might be fun, it is probably best avoided."

At the end of the letter I asked her to destroy it—to show it to no one—saying no good could come of anyone seeing the letter and knowing what she had done.

When the book appeared in print, I saw that some menus and events that were so obviously mine had been removed, and that the "for some ten years now" had been changed to "for some years now."

The lure of the myth was just too strong.

On the back cover, Richard Olney's quote characterizes the book as "wonderful—funny, instructive, and rich with common sense," which describes Alice's contribution to Panisse, and "eccentric and passionately serious, full of an air of celebration," which describes mine. The woman who actually wrote it, Linda Guenzel, was all of that. She told me that she had done the book out of love for Panisse and Alice, but also so that Alice would introduce her to the Random House editor Jason Epstein, for whom she wanted to write a book on chocolate. At the book launch party at Panisse, Linda reminded Alice of her promise. I had not been invited to the party, so I called Linda the day after. She was in tears. Alice had introduced her to Jason as "the typist."

Obviously typing in some cases was more important than in others.

OR TRUTH SHALL TRIUMPH?

On the inside cover Linda inscribed my copy, "For Jeremiah—The inspiration, the raison d'etre, the *creator* on these pages—without you, there would be no Chez Panisse, no cookbook. Truth shall triumph. Much love, Linda. August 10,1982."

CHASING OUR CULINARY TAILS

If you couldn't or didn't want to write a book, there was always the world of cooking magazines, even with its danger of who exactly was the tail and who the dog. It was one thing for a chef to be inspired by Jean-Louis Palladin's food from original material like his 1989 *Jean-Louis: Cooking with the Seasons,* since it looked exactly as it did in the restaurant, but another when the chef's food in a cooking magazine was prepared by stylists who had probably never met the chef, tasted the food, or been to the restaurant. When aspiring chefs, creatively stuck ones, or students would look at the magazine photographs, they thought they were seeing the chef on the page.

Within a week of a magazine featuring a famous chef, his or her food was being reproduced three thousand miles away in a manner light-years from the original. Charles Palmer's fantasy of caramel at Aureole in New York looked like Indian astrological temples, and was soon all over America. The only problem was that most of his imitators, experiencing it only from glossy photographs, had never tasted it, and thought it was all about architecture and not flavors. Imitations of these imitations were soon imitated in their turn, leaving Charles's new pastry chef trying to stay ahead of the field and imitating himself. All this could take just a year, putting the eighties right back into the arms of nineteenth-century staged foods and *pièces montées* from which we had all fled so righteously in the previous forty years. And without even knowing it.

CHAPTER 33

LETTING THE DICE FLY HIGH

Stay where you are, was one kind of advice. In your first restaurant, redo it and take care of business, or take care of business by opening some more was the second. Many might have thought that a single restaurant was a beast insatiably devouring one's life, so how much more could another be? Many were to find out, and some, like the great Mario Batali, even succeeded in handling more than one restaurant. The big dilemma was the food. Could the same food that made the chef famous in the first place be offered in multiple locations? Did it matter? Maybe that's what publicists and handlers were for: to publicize the food in ways other than how it was cooked in the restaurants.

Books paid the MasterCard and helped fill the restaurants, but they couldn't do it alone. The press had to be fed in order to keep one's restaurant full, and the cost of a publicist and a personal assistant to deal more and more professionally with the press seemed best amortized over more than one property. Whether to concentrate on increasing the quality of one's only restaurant while trying to squeeze more profits out of it or to open more was the single biggest decision facing the leading famous chefs in America in the second half of the eighties and into the nineties. We had seen a few amazing flops. Wolfgang Puck's brewery restaurant closed after less than a year, and I wondered with marvel how Jonathan Waxman could open Bud's and Hulot's in quick succession after Jams without even being there except (it was said) on opening night. So it was claimed years later, when the *New York Times* said his absence at his own restaurants was because he was too busy attending the openings of other people's, but no one questioned the quality at Jams while wondering what had happened at the other two.

Lack of quality in a restaurant was not as simple as a chef just not being there, although we hoped that our presence in the restaurants was what made them good. And until Las Vegas came along, one could fairly accurately predict who would stay with one restaurant, and who would go out and make more. I looked at Las Vegas as early as 1988 at the request of the Howard Hughes Corporation, and when Wolfgang opened his Las Vegas Spago and my sous-chef joined him there as chef, I looked again. After a couple of trips with my dining room manager, Tony Angotti, who was dying to take on a restaurant in Vegas (and later did), I knew that I could never stand to be there more than three days, so I called Wolfgang about my problem. "What do you care? You don't have to be there," he replied. I was elated, then remembered the brewery, though not for long enough. Nor did others.

Michael McCarty came a cropper over a hotel project in Santa Monica, a disaster he overcame with true grit even with forest fires burning down his beautiful Pacific Palisades house and earthquakes shaking his confidence.

Jimmy Schmidt and Michael tried the Rattlesnake Club in Denver, its initial huge success soon turning to a closing.

Paul Prudhomme went on a road show that left his New Orleans operation strung out enough to serve compromised (as I experienced) and smelly crawfish étouffé at one of Wolfgang's Meals-on-Wheels, and to have cigarette butts floating in the andouille "cooling off" in the iceless water of the bus tubs on the floor of his cafe above K-Paul's.

Larry Forgione soon realized one restaurant was enough after some attempts at multiple ones.

Some, like Texas's Cafe Annie chef and owner Robert Del Grande, stayed local and flourished, as did Scottsdale's Robert McGrath.

Some stayed single: Alice Waters (well, there was her Cafe Fanny) and Jean-Louis Palladin (sort of).

When Danny Meyer opened Union Square Cafe in Manhattan and soon was able to open others, my penny dropped. Maybe it was only famous expansion-minded chefs who were hoisted on their own petard of fame. No one but regulars expected to see nonchef owners in the restaurant or would even know who they were. No one else knew their names or faces. The fabulously successful Rich Melman in Chicago could open one wonderful restaurant after another, and no tourist even knew his name or asked him to come to the table. Had anyone ever seen the other restaurateur genius, Keith McNally, at Balthazar or Pastis? Other successful groups like the Bay Area's Real Restaurants were also faceless to the nation, as was anyone from New York's Restaurant Associates or the Flo Group in Paris.

When I received an offer to redo the Peak Cafe in Hong Kong, I thought it would be a perfect and safe absentee owner situation. I looked at the 12 percent labor costs and the one-time 14 percent income tax, and drooled. Stars Cafe had been a huge hit, so when the telephone call came in 1990 saying that the governor of Hong Kong had awarded me the lease, another cafe seemed a natural move. I was on the first plane.

Like a lot of restaurateurs around the world, I had lusted after the old Peak Cafe since I first saw it in 1983 at a lunch after the Santa Fe Bar & Grill promotion at the Mandarin Hotel. I had joked with the general manager that if the lease ever came up on the cafe, we should do it. Several years later, we did.

It became my favorite restaurant of any I had ever done, and not only because its 150 seats generated well over a million dollars of distributable cash a year. It was also because I was able to continue the "East Meets West" culinary exploration that Ken Hom and I had started eleven years before, in 1979. I added Indian food to a local menu as well as some Thai salads, some Chinese dumplings, California salsas, and some a fusion of all these.

The Peak Cafe was one indulgence that paid off handsomely, paying back its loans in ten months.

CHAPTER 34

A CRISIS IN IDENTITY

A crisis of identity was looming in the growing community of flashbulb chefs and their mostly adoring press. But what about the food? What was American food, really, as we searched our way in 1990? I agreed with Marian Burros that it embraced "the principle of simplicity and impeccably fresh ingredients that you must be prepared to highlight, rather than mask," but not everyone did. Menus were to be "not too esoteric, not too intimidating. Sort of straightforward and, at [their] best, surprising." These were the lessons established twenty years before and made into a philosophy picked up by the press and therefore the rest of the country. But had it still been inspiring a new generation of chefs?

By the mid-eighties, California and America had embraced the values and philosophy of Chez Panisse, but the food had moved on, evolving under the influence of both the tradition of Japanese, Thai, Chinese, and the Asian and Mexican-Spanish food that all chefs like to eat, as well as by the new products and fresh ingredients of these cuisines turning up in the marketplace. Chez Panisse stayed itself, marched to its own drummer, and the food stayed the same, a goal not to be sniffed at by anyone. But a leader in food, however delicious, Panisse was not. California cooking as "New American" bedazzled the American press, but in reality the change toward the national cuisine was led by most of the same people who had been at the Festival of American Chefs in 1983.

The lineup by 1990 was Lydia Shire and Jasper White celebrating New England and New America in Boston; Michel Richard, Wolfgang Puck, and Michael Roberts in Los Angeles basking in the riches of farms like Chino Ranch and L.A.'s amazing Farmers' Market; places like Mustard's Grill in Napa Valley under Cindy Pawlcyn; a few glimmerings this early from Joachim Splichal, who brought an amazing elegance to this emerging food; the ongoing festival of the French South at Commander's Palace in New Orleans (the divine Ella Brennan having brought forth Paul Prudhomme and now Emeril Lagasse); an extraordinary explosion of international foods and restaurants in Chicago by Rich Melman, king of American restaurateurs; Waxman's Jams and Forgione's An American Place in New York; Frank Stitt, of Highlands Bar & Grill in Birmingham, Alabama, who never forgot the tastes of the bounty of the rural South and the tastes of his mother's food; a huge Texas, Arizona, and Southwest movement led by Robert Del Grande, Stephan Pyles, Robert McGrath, Dean Fearing, and Mark Miller at the Coyote Cafe in Santa Fe. Add to these the Europeans Sirio Maccioni at Le Cirque, who presided over a strict casual elegance, and the great inspiration of Jean Bertranou of L'Ermitage in Los Angeles.

WILDFIRE

People have always cared for how food looks, but now the press made a national case out of it as they weaned themselves from the juicy stories about "nouvelle cuisine" and created the "New American Cuisine." Even the *Wall Street Journal* carried articles about cooking and food. "It's spread like wildfire," Larry Forgione told one of its reporters, "and the notoriety of the young chefs has helped fuel it." Some of the fires were fairly soon extinguished, as the public did not take too long to figure out that a single scallop on a white plate with a dollop of white sauce was not worth twenty-five dollars, or that someone was being made a fool of by the language of the menu, though whether that was the chef or the paying public was not immediately clear. The *Journal* lists one of John Sedlar's Manhattan Beach, California, restaurant dishes as a "Navajo Mosaic" of California vegetables, which must have left any Arizona or New Mexican Native American a bit confused.

What was contemporary American cooking after Panisse?

At Stars in 1984 we cooked for thirty American food editors, serving them Alaskan Pinto abalone with lime butter sauce as well as Portobello mushrooms in the center of which nested spit-roasted Gaspé ortolans, a dish I begged them not to talk about unless they wanted me in the fish-and-game penitentiary. For Pat Brown's *Cuisine* magazine we cooked a Virginia ham–stuffed saddle of rabbit with chanterelle-mushroom-filled pasta shapes, and for New Year's that year we served dishes like truffled salt cod ravioli with crayfish butter sauce, black truffle mascarpone-stuffed polenta with wild mushroom ragout, Muscovy duck breasts with chestnuts and persimmons, and California figs cooked in Zinfandel served with fifty-year-old balsamic vinegar cream. Whatever we cooked it had to conform to the list of food items available according to the month of the year that I handed out to all the chefs, a then cutting-edge list that included seasonal cheeses, edible flowers like violets, fuels like vine cuttings and fruitwoods, and herbs. The list was fanciful, given that the explosion of ingredients we'd started in the seventies was now in full roar and the months started to blend in with one another, but the list's variety does tell how much had changed since I was looking out the back door of the Panisse kitchen hoping some amateur forager would walk in with a huge salmon or basket of chanterelles.

We had started to make the things that we could not get, like duck breast prosciutto. The Stars chef, Mark Franz, built a special refrigerator in the basement (well out of the way of any health inspectors) for air-curing meats, and that is where we kept the game sausages, salamis, duck breasts, hams, and ribs of beef. By 1985 we served smoked Russian boar, our own gravlax, and smoked salmon.

These dishes and others, like wild boars' head galantine with truffled mushroom vinaigrette, or lobster risotto with monkfish, worried me that Stars had moved from California into a personal style that was made up of classical disciplines dressed up in new clothes. Did that mean we were looking fashionable? And if so, was it acceptable as a style? I compared it with what the other chefs were serving at the time: Wolfgang Puck's Gulf snapper with red onion sauce; Bradley Ogden's pheasant with smoked bacon vinaigrette. Certainly the sea bass carpaccio with lobster vinaigrette and caviar that I served to debut Wolfgang Puck's frozen desserts in Northern California was not classical. But by the time we got to wild boar ham with grilled sweetbreads, lentils, and foie gras in 1987 for the American Institute of Wine & Food, with Dick Graff, I thought perhaps I really had relapsed to the menu I had in Paris at Lucas Carton in 1965.

Dinner for the Retirement of Lucas Carton's Chef
Oyster
Minced Pike
Roast Lamb
Hare Pie
Woodcock
Cheeses

But when I remembered the dinner's radical futurist pairing of 1955 Chateau d'Yquem with the oysters, and the wild strawberries in the pastry for the hare pie, and drinking the 1929 Bollinger and 1911 Clicquot with the cheeses, I knew we still had a long way to go.

When the *Miami Herald* asked in early 1987 what the future trends would be in America, I said I had no idea, "But why not take Cuban cooking, easily one of the most mainstream of America's regional cuisines, give it a breath of fresh air, and turn it loose on the USA?" The reporter loved the fact that I answered my own telephone. "I would die to have time to do for Cuban and Indian food what nouvelle cuisine did for the grande cuisine of France. Rework it, make it smaller, lighter, more lively with less heat." When he asked me if this was Florida cuisine, I told him it should be. After saying this, I still needed to look around for a jolt of inspiration.

That's when the phone rang from Sydney.

AUSTRALIA AGAIN

The two-week California promotion Stars did in Sydney's Regent Hotel with its chef, Serge Dansereau, in 1987 was the jolt we needed. The perfection and abundance of the fish and shellfish that I had seen before only in the fifties in Italy, the seventies in France, and earlier at Neil Perry's Blue Water Grill right there in Australia brought a flood of ideas. A week on the Great Barrier Reef's Lizard Island beaches, after those two hellish kitchen weeks, brought sanity again, as well as time to contemplate Australia's new love affair with Asian ingredients and Thai flavors. I had picked up the scent of a new revolution about to happen. The genius of Australia's new chefs and their new casual style set my brain going, and rekindled my childhood Australian love of tropical and exotic. The photo we took of one of our dishes (mussels, Moreton Bay bugs or slipper lobster meat, fresh tiger prawns, and pieces of barramundi fillet on a plate sauced with shellfish–saffron butter sauce, with a drizzle of Thai basil cream and a tiger prawn head standing up proudly in the center of the plate) is still one of my all-time favorites.

As the press from this visit flooded into Stars from Australia, every regular customer, every food magazine editor, and every restaurant critic was the only one who knew what should be on the menu, and how much it should cost. We were stuck in the Stars fame rut with the fans wagging the menu tail, but I was raring to go. I built a private room at Stars so that I could cook for forty instead of four hundred and then, in another corner, a thirty-seater called JT's. There we could cook the kind of food I wished we had time for in the main dining room. The private dining room check could also be higher. In 1992 Stars' average per-person check with drinks and wine was forty-nine dollars; this with a gross just over $9 million with only two hundred seats, fifty more in the bar, meant the main kitchen was cooking as fast as they or anyone could. My JT's black-truffled salt cod puree club sandwich with lobster sauce and steelhead caviar would have raised screams in the main kitchen because of all the steps required. It was in these other venues that we could let our wings stretch out in the nineties.

Urania and Brunno Ristow: we served San Francisco's most wonderful couple and Stars' favorite customers white Oregon truffle custard with Jerusalem artichokes, chervil sauce, and more Quinault River steelhead salmon roe.

For another: capon breast stuffed with fresh Berkeley morels and steamed over lovage leaves, served in a lobster sauce.

Napa Valley's eminent collector Barney Rhodes's seventieth birthday: accompanying magnums of 1864, 1870, and 1874 Chateau Lafite, puff pastry in individual pithivier-like shapes filled with goat cheese and duck and goose cracklings.

And in outside venues:

James Beard Foundation House: Smoked sturgeon with deviled quail eggs and lobster rémoulade. Roast capon broth with ginger, foie gras, and Chinese fermented black bean custard.

The Florida Winefest: smoked wahoo carpaccio with grilled fresh Florida frogs' legs.

British Columbia's Mission Hill Winery: Arctic char with lobster mushrooms.

Barbara Tropp at Stars Singapore: lightly smoked sea bass with lentils, minced Chinese pork, lobster, and more duck cracklings.

CHAPTER 35

ALL OVER THE MAP

Charlie Trotter, at the 1993 Napa Valley James Beard Foundation benefit dinner, served hand-harvested sea scallops with olive-oil-poached tomato, artichokes, caramelized shallots, vegetable juices, red wine essence, and veal stock reduction.

Drew Nieporent and his chef from Montrachet, Debra Ponzek, served Pacific sea bass with chanterelles, spinach, and lobster "au jus."

Stars served a mussel-potato timbale with herb-infused huitlacoche shellfish sauce.

Ritz-Carlton's Gary Danko, for "A Taste of the Nation," offered a warm caramelized onion, goat cheese, and morel tart.

Bradley Ogden at the Celebrity Sports International event at Squaw Valley ski resort cooked a bit of England-California with Zinfandel jam on lamb chops, some Southwest with a black bean cake, and a taste of New England with his lobster and salt cod stew.

Wolfgang Puck had both Asia and California with Germany in his restaurant's Chinois chicken salad and apple-cranberry relish on foie gras.

Obviously we were all over the map. The country was inundated by famous chefs cooking in what seemed to the press like a dizzying spectrum of individual styles that were not easily legible as a single style, so they called it "New American Cuisine." Edward Carter's magazine of the best restaurants around the world said the Stars food "epitomizes what is now known as 'California Cuisine' by its freshness of ingredients, cleanness of taste, utter simplicity of flavor and texture that can't be faked and are unpretentious." I thought it was New American, but his analysis is not a bad beginning to define California cooking not fallen off its tracks.

A legion of frenzied writers and journalists in the late eighties threw the baby out with the dishwater, leading the public to think that California cooking could be defined by bashing the food.

Making fun of a few grains of corn on a huge white plate with some minuscule dollops of sauce is fine as long as one doesn't think oneself a dragon slayer, because there was no dragon, just a lot of enthusiastic mistakes. Paula Wolfert in *Cook's* magazine goes on about how her father used to cook tuna in his backyard, so doing it in a restaurant with a seasoned butter was no big "advance," pointing out that California cooks didn't invent coriander butter. On the defensive, she misses two points: that recipes do not develop in linear progression, but are historically cyclical, and that what "advanced" the United States from Continental cuisine was not her father. Not tuna, butter, or mesquite alone, but a vision that allowed a new simplicity to be recognized and welcomed as being as important as the temples of red-plush French, old Italian, and Continental American food and restaurants beloved by previous generations.

The new vision was strong, clear in what the food should taste like. Cutting edge and trendy as it was, it now had a purity and simplicity that indeed made it classic in the manner of Fernand Point.

DONE UP, NOT OVERDONE

One journalist scolded Alice. Throwing "a few aging pansy petals on a one-note salad" did "not make a cuisine." I told everyone at Stars that the food should be done up but not overdone. The debate whether there even was a styled California cuisine had raged since 1981, when the *Chronicle's* Harvey Steiman and a bunch of us gathered at the California Culinary Academy with Julia Child to debate its existence. She stopped all conversation with "When I first came to San Francisco, the height of gastronomy was cinnamon toast and artichokes," a mind-boggling statement until everyone realized she didn't mean together. Marion Cunningham said she thought California cooking existed in "fresh, pure, and seasonal." The academy's French chef said that it was all about regional cuisines that developed around the availability of the raw materials and the genius of the cooks working with them. Alice Waters said, "It's very exciting to be in kindergarten," meaning (I think) that we had "advanced" no further than that.

Harvey put up with everyone rattling on and said California was the only place in the United States with a great abundance of fresh ingredients. That was the point. When I reminded everyone that in 1973 there was no such bounty, I met only blank stares, as if I had said that the pope wasn't Catholic or bears never shit in the woods.

Of course it took someone outside Californian tunnel vision to nail it all down. When Sydney's Renaissance man and critic Leo Schofield walked into Stars, he wrote that he felt he was witnessing the death of the old culture, defined as an evening spent out with a three-course meal. Stars, he said, was not Old World dining but a new style that said, "Here it is, just pick out what you feel like eating and we'll get it for you—either just a salad or a five-course meal if that is what you have the time for." When the lifestyle caught on in the East Coast, he said, for obvious marketing reasons the food could not be called "California," so it became "Nouvelle American." Leo's last evaluation is a bit bitchy, but there is a hint of truth in that it was the East Coast press who determined first that California was the leader after the deluge of national press in 1983 when we did the Astor mansion lunch, and later that America was in the lead after the American Festival in San Francisco the same year. *Newsday* wondered where "America's Nouvelle" was headed and asked if it was "an evolutionary process." An evolution toward "Liberty Cuisine," the *Detroit News* called it. Alice Waters said, "There is no set way of doing things." Jimmy Schmidt was driven by his love of experimentation. Paul Prudhomme yelled, "Just freedom!"

Len Allison from Hubert's in Manhattan spoke like a true chef: "The challenge is to create a harmony, to be inspired by the past but allow it to be an inspiration, not a ball and chain."

REVOLUTION

In an interview in 2014, Chris Kimball from *America's Test Kitchen* asked me to define first a "revolution" and then what a food one was. And how it made changes in American cuisine.

First Kimball argued that all revolutions, "especially a food revolution, should be fun, counterculture, flamboyant, and full of the unexpected. That is what you brought to American cuisine but it was a moment in time that has long gone. Those heady years only occur, at best, once in every two or three generations." As in the French Revolution, the moment of Talleyrand, his clothes and food, and his encouraging his chef, Carême, to create a new style of a few perfect ingredients instead of the old compiled and complicated ones, I answered. But, he said, "you have been described as a royalist. How does a royalist co-opt a revolution?" I'm not really a royalist but I'm certainly no lover of mobs unless they are turning out the old with something new that is fabulous. Who else but someone who knows or has known privilege would know how to challenge it? And there is no hierarchy to perfection.

"Does a revolution have to be reckless?" he wondered. Without caution, careless of consequences, it's just chaos, but even the most carefully planned revolution needs some chaos or else it's just a committee meeting.

"What about that fire-starting seminal moment of the lunch at the Astor mansion in Newport?" Was that "a good quick definition of how California cuisine outpaced French cooking at the time?" I'd say not so much the food as the attitude, spontaneous improvisation, which is the same as making a menu from the market stalls in front of you, and not with preconceived concepts of what is "proper." "What are your rules for cooking for success?" Make it good, unfashionable, and cheap. "How long does a dish have to be around before it becomes a tradition?"

How long is a tweet?

CHAPTER 36

LONG LIVE THE EVOLUTION

The day started with a sunrise promising to radiate its desert red onto Scottsdale's Camelback Mountain. It was a perfect Arizona winter desert morning in January 2002, the temperature picking up, the air clear, smelling like clean dust and doused campfires. I was at the Roaring Fork restaurant with its owner, Robert McGrath, gathering material for my book *America's Best Chefs Cook with Jeremiah Tower* and filming the PBS television show *America's Best Chefs*, as recognized by the James Beard Foundation.

VICTORY FARMS

We met Gina Collins at her Victory Farms truck in the parking lot while she pulled out vegetables and greens picked in the cool of the early desert morning. Robert, Gina, and I decided on what mix of greens we would use on the show and for that day's Roaring Fork menus. The next farmer's truck had every kind of fresh and lightly dried chili I had ever seen or heard of, gallons of fresh cream, and its butter, which made my mouth water.

For years, starting in 1973 at Panisse, I had tried to convince Vella Cheese company and others in Sonoma to give me some unpasteurized cream to make sauces like the French. For years they all stubbornly refused. Then I tried to get the cream from the Reading Terminal Market in Philadelphia, knowing full well that the Amish and Mennonites would not fool around ruining cream and butter by boiling the milk. But no dice. They would not ship unpasteurized cream across state lines.

So thirty years later, in a parking lot in Scottsdale, dipping fingers into a gallon of real cream and canary yellow butter that had come from Mennonites neighboring this farmer's property, I was moved almost to tears at what had finally come to pass.

While waiting to film the legendary happy hour at the Roaring Fork, we chilled some Gosset champagne. I took my first sip of this fabulous hand-made wine, spread some hand-churned butter on my hand-forged tortillas warmed over the fire, and sat back to watch the sun go down. Looking up at Camelback turning magenta in the moments before night fell, and knowing that we would soon be facing a 4 A.M. call for more filming the next day of another perfect sunrise over the Arizona desert, I poured another glass of rosy champagne, remembering that, in the immortal words of the Pink Panther, "champagne has the minimum of alcohol and the maximum of companionship."

THE THEORY OF EVOLUTION

Any winning restaurateur these days realizes that outstanding cooking starts with superb ingredients, and that a menu should be conceived from the marketplace rather than intellectual abstraction. The cornucopia of January in Santa Monica the day before Arizona was as plentiful as that of New York in August or September: sweet-tooth wild mushrooms looking like giant hedgehog mushrooms; cabbage in all its glory—cauliflower, cavallo nero, and several broccolis; purple, pink, and fire engine red mustard leaves; radicchio that was not magenta with white stripes but the other way around and with lime-green stripes running though the leaves as well; the onion family in all its glory—still-sweet cipollini picked that morning, fresh green garlic, every variety of chives with some of them flowering; Throgmorton Farm's vast array of fruits dried in the sun—white peaches, nectarines ugly when dried but with a perfume that made me swoon, six varieties of pears, hideous-looking but delicious persimmons, and an encyclopedic selection of dates, fresh and dried; ripe pomegranates and fresh-crop walnuts; and best of all, the citrus of Southern California at the peak of its season—Meyer lemons, kumquats, clementines, tangerines, "sweet lemons," five different kinds of grapefruit, crosses of grapefruit and oranges like pomelos, and a few others of mysterious parentage, like "manellos."

At the end of my walk in the market I ate a little box of wild strawberries from miniature rose grower Lore Caulfield, who that day had just a few handfuls of precious *fraises de bois,* or wild strawberries.

THE FOURTH INGREDIENT REVOLUTION

Inspired by my trip I set out again in 2002 to explore how non-restaurant America ate. I wanted to see what was going on in the towns of America, if what had been reported, that now home cooks could find ingredients in supermarkets that once were available only to top restaurants, was true.

The new supermarkets all seemed to have the word *fresh* somewhere in their names. All over America, even in unlikely places like Marathon Cay in Florida, I saw radicchio Treviso, mascarpone, American goat cheese, and perfect little green beans. Given this new shopping, the only thing good American home cooks needed was a television show to push them back to the stove. Why wouldn't anyone try Mario Batali's latest easy ravioli of fresh wonton wrappers? Or Lydia Shire's fresh tomato sauce, or make a sauce for steaks out of salted anchovies on the imported foods shelf, fresh basil, spring garlic, and new crop, not rancid organic hazelnuts from Oregon; give Martin Yan's Peking duck a try once having seen it on his *Chinatown;* or use the barbecued pork or roast duck in America's Chinatowns as the ultimate fast food at home, just chopped up with fresh herbs and cilantro on top of pasta or a cabbage salad? Or cook some white corn posole from Los Chileros de Nuevo Mexico, which specializes in "gourmet" New Mexico foods?

In late 2001, John Mariani in *Esquire* magazine had summed up the new chefs' cooking: "Simplifying, removing extraneous ingredients from their plates, and focusing more on essential flavors of the main ingredients."

The first revolution in American fresh ingredients occurred at Chez Panisse with freshness and local California ingredients.

The second started to occur in the last two years of the seventies, when *local* started to mean international because of the revolution in air-shipping of fresh ingredients like the ones I introduced to the California dining public at the California Culinary Academy.

The third was when American chefs picked up the mantra from the first revolution and helped spread farmers' markets and new supplies of organic, local, sustainable ingredients across the land.

The fourth was the current extension of the second, or the instant international Internet marketplace. *Local* and *fresh* and *seasonal* now mean wherever there is a field of superb ingredients, refrigeration, and an airfield nearby: South African wild mushrooms in New York in June; haricots verts from West Africa in California markets; fish from ten thousand miles away fresher than from a coastal United States locked in by storms.

USA, NOT CALIFORNIA

The public no longer sees these changes as a California phenomenon. Jeffrey Steingarten's end-of-the-millennium prediction in *Vogue* that there was a restaurant crash in the air, or that the next trend would be a gay cuisine, did not come true. Certainly his horror of famous chefs expanding their empires and leaving the new restaurants in the hands of inexperienced, lower-paid staff was often played out. But the choice of where to go in America to find the ingredients heretofore the realm of famous chefs was no longer a mystery. Culinary magazines like *Bon Appétit* celebrated these sources and started publishing the addresses and websites of where to find them.

A supplier like Portland, Oregon's Nicky USA, for example, published its quality guidelines, which were no longer about fresh versus frozen. Their rules went right to the heart of it all, to the kind of farming that is sustainable over a long period of time. By the end of the decade, these standards became the norm rather than the exception for small producers supplying restaurants of conscience: "raising animals humanely, on feeds without medication, animal by-products, or hormones."

By 2002 Chez Panisse used beef from Western Grasslands Inc. (since renamed Panorama Grass-Fed Meats). In May of that year, ranchers showed up at San Francisco's "Open Market Day" to talk about how their healthful, sustainably reared local beef was raised. That moment was a long way from thirty-four years earlier, when western ranchers would have shot at anyone with long hair from the radical streets of Berkeley preaching organic farming.

AN EXALTATION

In 1974 Richard Olney introduced me to fresh green almonds in the South of France. We ate them with cherries, over which I pined because they were so superior to the two varieties that I could buy back in the United States. Had anyone except an old-variety cherry farmer ever eaten one in the United States? I begged local suppliers for them for years to no avail. The May 2002 newsletter from GreenLeaf, San Francisco's revolutionary new produce supplier, was a manifesto of the revolution that had taken place. I could have bought Brooks, Burlat, and King Bing cherries, as well as unirrigated fruit from the foothills of the Sierras. My dishwashers at Panisse used to have to spend hours carving rosemary skewers, the rosemary and rose geranium flowers I had to steal on my way to work. Now here they were in a list that also included rue, fresh hearts of palm, popcorn shoots, cardoon, wild arugula, lovage for perfuming lobsters, nepitella mint, peppercress, and lemon balm. Stars' lettuce mix, which in the eighties took eight hours a day to make, was now just a phone call away. The tender lettuces mix was sucrine, majestic red, black jack, red perella, brunia, little gem, spreckles, freckles, roger, dark lolla rosa, four seasons, and green tango. It was enough to make one break into dance.

On rereading James Lipton's *An Exaltation of Larks,* which celebrates bounty and calls a collection of songbirds in the high months of summer an "exaltation," I wondered what the collective name for all this bounty should be. Strolling though Manhattan's Union Square farmers' market in 2002, seeing what New York, Long Island, and New Jersey alone can produce in August, I thought that the word was still *revolution.*

The first stand had bambino eggplant as well as white, purple, and purple-and-white-striped ones looking like a Karl Lagerfeld coat; there was Texas tarragon; Caribbean oregano; basil green, purple, and Thai; rosemary, thyme (lemon and flowering), black peppermint, lemon verbena, and seven kinds of mint, including apple. At stand number two I saw an entire regatta of radishes—watermelon, black, French breakfast with their white tips and white icicle (all white), as well as a whole section of tiny and giant red round ones; parsley root; tatsoi; long squash runners and their blossoms; mounds of tomatillos; small round carrots as well as long ones; bushels of limas; baby turnips; five kinds of beets; red, yellow, orange, and gold-and-green-striped cherry tomatoes; cranberry beans; microgreens; and pinterelle dandelions. At New York's Fox Hill Farm potato stand there were Yukon gold, whites, reds, russets, small red, carola, Norland red, brintje, Desiree, Augusta, Russian banana, agria, and French fingerling. But it was the onion stand that trapped me, as it always does.

It was next to a stand selling old-fashioned roses; the heady perfumes of the Duchesse de Brabants mingling with the smell of the glisteningly fresh onions made my mouth water. I saw a bread stand nearby, as well as some Vermont "European style" butter, and was tempted to make an onion–rose petal sandwich on the spot. After all, in Sydney as kids we used to make nasturtium ones. All I needed was some sea salt and Lampong pepper. And the onions in all their glory: salad whites, cooking yellows, rocambole, shallots on the stem, garlic tops about to flower, scallions large and small and white and red, purple and snow baby pearls, gold coin, luscious leeks, red cipolle, small red Italian, Kelshe (sweet and mild), and the Walla Walla sweets. I took home the Walla Walla, sliced them thinly, marinated them in *fleur de sel* and freshly squeezed blackberry juice for twenty minutes, and served them with a sauce of the rose petals ground up in a mortar with egg yolks and lemon juice, adding light French yellow extra-virgin olive oil to perfume and color the mayonnaise.

In January 2003 I received a letter explaining what ingredients I could expect to find in Minneapolis in February for my cooking demonstration promoting my new book, *Jeremiah Tower Cooks*. "We have a great game supplier with Peking duck, pheasant, and rabbit; any meat, including whey-fed lamb; fish and seafood no problem either. Of course, the White Earth Land Recovery Project's wild rice comes from here. Also fresh hothouse herbs, and a large Asian community with great markets. We have a Farmers' Market on full alert for whatever fresh ingredients you need: you can have the best, freshest organic eggs, farmstead butter, purest cream, goat cheese, and an extraordinary aged sheepsmilk cheese—all from pasture pampered animals."

Obviously the ingredient revolution has worked. What about the ingredient-driven food?

GIVING IT A GO: THE NEWER FOOD

American restaurant food had come a long way since the "sentimental" menu that, as Marian Burros reported in the new millennium, Alice Waters had just created for Marion Cunningham at Chez Panisse. Some of the diners' comments included:

"Marion would never put truffles in her chicken."

"Marion would want iceberg lettuce."

"Marion doesn't eat oysters."

Marion's mind was more on cookies.

Consider the difference of England's Jamie Oliver, who said in an article at that time on new English food that he was willing "to give it a go" with whatever he has seen that intrigues him. Like Peruvian food: "It has a really good social vibe, like tapas with lots of little bowls of this and that, a really refreshing way to eat." Or at England's Fat Duck, where the chef took whatever he fancied from the past fifty years of techniques and fresh ingredients to make his own, like sweetbreads cooked in hay and salt crust, crusted with pollen, and served with cockles à la plancha and parsnip puree. When he served red mullet with a velouté of coco beans, licorice, and vanilla, a reporter thought the mullet dish might be at odds with traditional tastes.

Which traditions? I wondered.

How old does a dish have to be before it becomes a tradition? Was El Bulli in Spain too new? I guess not, since the cooking world was soon covered in foam and the fire didn't go out.

The new American food had the same lineup as Jeffrey Steingarten used in *Vogue* to describe the newness of the "nouvelle cuisine" movement in France and its impact on America: "Hand-raised ingredients [nothing new in France], bought that morning [as it always had been], cooked at the last minute [new], and eaten only in season [as always], the return to cooking's regional roots [had been going on for decades in France and Panisse], and the banishing of formulaic sauces [new]."

A look at restaurant menus in nineties America shows that the earlier, wilder throwing of ingredients into the air like cards to see how they fell had, by 2010, settled down into more personal visions. Ingredients are chosen for their harmony on the plate rather than for pure novelty, as in "look what I've found." The Square in London showed a perfect example of the new sure-footed cooking, its menu listing dishes like pea soup with morel Chantilly, or steamed zucchini flowers with scallops and buttered crab, and a soup of peaches and strawberries with champagne.

Some visions remained true to the original: In August 1996 I went to the Chez Panisse twenty-fifth anniversary party.

For fifty-five dollars and 15 percent service charge we had:

Hors d'oeuvre
La Bouillabaisse de Lulu
Salade du Jardin
Compote Anniversaire
Sorbet de Cassis

The menu took me back to twenty-three years earlier, when I had to spend many hours trying to find fresh ingredients for my bouillabaisse at Panisse, shopping in Oakland, Berkeley, both Chinatowns, and from any foragers who had been out fishing and gathering. At this anniversary dinner, I wondered where all the famous ingredients had gone.

I could not believe my eyes when I read why Chez Panisse was voted the single best restaurant in the United States in 2001 by *Gourmet*, nor could I stop laughing at the irony. Green beans again. Could I ever escape them! "Sharply vinegared" and served as a first course with "an artfully rumpled heap of beyond-organic herbs," a drop of jelly, and "a swath of mayonnaise," the beans "vibrated" on the plate. Along with half a soft-boiled egg, this dish was reviewed as "the loveliest conceivable expression of a great cultural region." Really? The magazine drew the battle lines between what it said were the two schools of American cuisine: Chez Panisse was devoted to displaying nature at its best, Jean-Georges Vongerichten to bending nature to his will.

THE LIGHTNING BEHIND THE THUNDER

When I wrote the last menus at Stars in 1998, they celebrated a marriage of the old and the newest ingredients: foie gras sandwiches, boned rabbit saddles, wood-oven baked oysters and spiny lobsters, roast chicken broth soup served with ginger, foie gras, and Chinese black bean custard, and red and white Belgian endive leaves stuffed with quail egg and lobster rémoulade.

Or desserts with fresh lychee, rambutan, mangosteen, or ginger and jasmine flower sorbets.

By 2001, an event in New York organized by Charlie Trotter, David Bouley, and Australia's great Tetsuya "Tet" Wakuda used mostly new ingredients.

Dinner at the James Beard House
May 2001

WAKUDA
Scallop with foie gras, citrus and soy jelly

BOULEY
Striped bass, fennel-braised with saffron rose olive sauce

WAKUDA
Confit of Tasmanian soft-smoked ocean trout with kombu

TROTTER
Organic veal shank with soy beans and hijiki seaweed sauce

BOULEY
Braised beef cheeks with Catskill Mountain ramp spaetzle

TROTTER
Three custards: green tea panna cotta, chamomile crème caramel, Assam tea brûlée with melon sauce

BOULEY
Chocolate tart with pistachio ice cream

The dinner was a paean to flavor and textures. Tet's dish was a two-inch round of perfectly fresh sea scallop sliced an eighth of an inch thick. On top of it was a round of foie gras cut in exactly the same proportions. Nothing else was on the plate except for a little citrus juice, soy jelly, and olive oil. As the *Chicago Tribune's* Bill Rice said at the end of the meal, when we were all almost speechless: "Sometimes simplicity is just downright that simple," reminding me how far we had come in twenty years.

Sometimes too far.

At a dinner benefit for Share Our Strength at New York's Gramercy Tavern restaurant in 2001, the first course from Sydney's Rockpool restaurant seemed quite normal: salad of squid ink noodles. The chef from Seattle's Rover then served rabbit hearts with halibut. That seemed a bit off center. But when Paris's Petrossian caviar emporium offered a dessert of "Coca-Cola

Cajou of Coca-Cola emulsion, fruit and spice cookie, coconut sorbet and cashew sables," it seemed like outer space. I wondered what was going on with top chefs as the century passed into a new one.

GOURMET MAGAZINE'S NEW CHEF

I found it odd that Chez Panisse was the only restaurant on *Gourmet* magazine's list of the nation's top fifty restaurants whose website didn't feature, let alone mention, the name of the chef. Just the service charge. That brought up the question of what made a famous chef as the new millennium began. Perhaps there was a clue in *Gourmet's* saying that Alice Waters "is not so much a chef as an impresario." A concert master. Certainly by 2000 the best American chefs did seem to be marching to their individual music.

According to *Gourmet*:

Thomas Keller's the French Laundry aspired not so much to cook good food as to pursue fundamental truths revealed through food.

Wolfgang at Spago Beverly Hills served up passion and seriously glamorous dining.

Alan Wong in Honolulu was a true fusion of an organic, street-level blend of Chinese, Polynesian, and mainland American, lightly seasoned with imports from Japan, Mexico, and Korea—proving that Trader Vic's was the original fusion food forty years earlier.

Charlie Trotter was likened to "the Aleph," or that point from which every single thing in the world can be seen and from which Charlie cooked.

Ken Oringer in Boston was all about intensity of flavors, drawing on those of Maine, Japan, and Spain.

Nobu Matsuhisa was "the Escoffier of all things great and raw."

Clark Frasier and Mark Gaier at Arrows in Maine, who learned salad aesthetic at Stars, grew the greens in their kitchen garden so that the leaves' "immediacy is breathtaking."

Tom Douglas at the Palace Kitchen in Seattle created "campfire cooking fit for kings."

In New Orleans, Galatoire's, where on college trips from Harvard days I consumed more fried oysters and shrimp rémoulade than any human should, was still a restaurant that made one "giddy with pleasure."

Marcus Samuelsson at Aquavit made herring first acceptable and then chic.

Le Bernardin, always superb with the always impeccable Maguy Le Coze and Eric Ripert, was as if the Romans had built a temple to fish and shellfish cooking.

Jean-Georges Vongerichten, who gave us the absolutely brilliant early Vong with a recently departed Stars chef, was now giving a lot more.

Daniel Boulud's "piercing intelligence" and approach to classical French cooking got more flavor out of a single bell pepper than most restaurants did out of a whole truckload of foie gras.

Adornment in America was left to the David Rockwell dining rooms.

SIMPLE INGREDIENTS RULE

San Francisco food and wine critic Robert Finigan wrote to me in 2001 about the *San Francisco Chronicle*'s restaurant critic Michael Bauer, namely his latest off-the-tracks voluptuous excitement over the food at the redone Clift and its Asia de Cuba dining room. Bob was horrified at the bananas with fried calamari, and floored by Chinese-style fried rice with guacamole. Bauer's take, by contrast, was "marvelous" food. Bob wondered if "marvelous" meant the sheer marvel of being able to think it up, cook, and plate it, or whether the food was wonderful to eat. "When you conceived Stars," he said, "you brilliantly had the idea of an upscale bistro just right for its place and time, perfectly prepared dishes of historical and regional significance with excitements around the edges perhaps not previously experienced by most Stars' patrons." I replied that what turned me on then and what turns me on now are clean, pure, rich, and totally inspiring simple and complex flavors. The movie *Woman on Top*. Déjà vu all over again.

FLAVOR RULES

Now in danger from a runaway horse eclectic, we-can-do-anything cycle, the quality instead of quantity of ingredients was the only thing that could provide stability, besides knowing how to treat and present them. As a guideline in this culinary wooing of different cultures, ingredients, and flavors, I told my chefs to always remember their first paint box. First you discover primary colors. They are so wonderful, you feel they must be even more wonderful mixed together. Adding three more colors all you get is brown. Mud. It's the same with ingredients and flavors. A muddy result means that all the flavors stay on the same note, or slightly different ones all at once, without any structure. Just noise. A clear flavor has incredible clarity and purity, the culmination of perfect ingredients and masterly cooking, or sometimes just the ingredient. The clarity of a kilo tin of beluga caviar is in its "Here I am."

CHAPTER 37

WHAT NOW AND WHY

Eater restaurant editor Bill Addison summed up the state of Berkeley's Chez Panisse in 2014 in an article called "The Road to the 38" essential restaurants in America.

He introduced Panisse as the restaurant that "implanted the words 'local,' 'seasonal,' and 'sustainable' in our brains," as well as advancing a philosophy that "rerouted America's culinary trajectory" and still insists on a simplicity that "also generates its share of backlash." By 2016 everyone was back in line about simplicity, but where now is the inspiration coming from? I wonder. Is it still anything in California, or is it whatever is found to be great in not just the American cornucopia but the world's?

Bill's dining companion answered the California question. "This looks like something you'd serve at home," he said of the meal at Chez Panisse. Is "a little tuft of salad greens" with the salmon what we should be doing or an original Alice made cliched by time? It's "graceful," says Bill, but "nothing sets off fireworks." He added, "Lovely, and more transformative in doctrine than in experience. Am I dazzled by the meal? No . . . Just like eating at an old friend's house."

Do we even need a fiery spectacle to define a memorable meal?

The best American cooking in 2016 is inspired by the intent of the perfect salad green, but no longer a slave to the actual leaves, an intent whose culinary zeitgeist started at New York's Delmonico and the Four Seasons restaurants in 1900 and 1959, respectively. Both closed, but live on in their approach to making a restaurant and how to serve the food.

If much of what we know now as American food sprang from the James Beard consultancy at the "iconic" Manhattan restaurant, the Four Seasons, what has it really meant to all of us now that it has closed after fifty-seven years? An article in the December 14, 2015, issue of *New York* magazine tells us what regulars think. Mimi Sheraton, food writer and former *New York Times* restaurant critic: "It stressed seasonal, natural, and local foods long before that was thought of very much by anyplace else." Daniel Boulud, chef and restaurateur: "When I arrived in New York in 1982, I still remember where I was seated and the meal I had: the crab cakes, the rack of lamb, and a soufflé. It is the quintessential, classic American restaurant."

Are we back to that powerful and sustaining everyday simplicity in 2017?

THANK GOD FOR DÉJÀ VU

A back-to-the-future trend was identified by food writer John Mariani on Facebook in January 2016. "Good to hear that NYC's Eleven Madison Park is going '180 degrees' in the direction of simpler food, fewer dishes, no card tricks, no smoke and mirrors, no long recitations. This always happens—except perhaps in Chicago, where among some chefs more and more and more is better. As chefs get older they realize they need not do somersaults to impress guests who just want a fine meal."

Eleven Madison Park started in 2012 with an elaborate four-hour tasting menu celebrating New York City history. What domes of smoke covering sturgeon for a blini, or a picnic basket, or the waiters performing card tricks had to do with it was every customer's guess, if one they paid highly for. By 2015 chef Daniel Humm figured out that nothing exceeds like success, and went back to simplicity to keep the restaurant full. A Facebook announcement declared, "Patter from servers will be stripped down to what feels natural and pragmatic. Diners will be invited to steer the kitchen toward courses that sound right." Democracy in the halls of the Robespierres turning revolution into evolution! A ride back to the future, the clue being the customers now want to choose what they eat. No more showing off how many ingredients can fit on a plate and all the ways they can be cooked. Tout that more is less now, that less blabber from the waiters means more conversation among the guests. "Away with gimmicky," they might cry—and did. Eric Ripert, chef and co-owner of one of Manhattan's most perfect restaurants, Le Bernardin: "I don't want to be eating too much," as in five-hour tasting menus. As for waiter gimmicks, "Those experiences are not really New York because in New York we have so many other things to do." He points out that many diners just want to eat and don't want to talk to the waiters, or know "where the scallops are from."

That's the customers, but what about the chefs? In the *Observer Monthly* of December 13, 2015, they confessed the best things they had eaten all year.

René Redzepi, chef-owner of the world's sometimes most famous Noma restaurant in Copenhagen, hops on a plane any day to the Kadiköy market in Istanbul on his way to restaurant Çiya Sofrasi. He's "full of tradition but not afraid of innovating," like lamb stewed with dried cherries.

For London's chef Yotam Ottolenghi, the perfect meal was a platter of pickled herring from Russ & Daughters in New York: "These are the flavors which define New York for me."

For the chef and owner of the famous Arzak restaurant in Spain's San Sebastian, it was "Idiazábal cheese with a shepherd in the Urbia Mountains in the Basque country . . . with all the rich true flavor of the milk and the sense of the environment in which the mother had grazed."

It reminded me of Richard Olney teaching me in 1977 in the South of France the difference in flavors of the "same" goat cheese depending on what time of year the goats had been milked and whether they grazed in spring or winter pastures. Are we really going back to a real simplicity and not in the emperor's clothes now defrocked of frills and more-the-merrier ornaments?

Other chefs interviewed made it seem as if we are, at least in London. Sea urchins fresh out of the Irish Channel made one chef "realize how amazing nature is, and how little we should mess with our food." The development chef of the Gordon Ramsay Group adored sea salt ice cream from Ireland's County Kerry. Another chef was also in Istanbul at the Sultanahmet Köftecisi worshipping "lamb köftes grilled very simply over charcoal." England's food writer Fuchsia Dunlop was on her knees in front of the *khao chae* at Lai Rod restaurant in Bangkok: "grains of rice in iced water with flower petals, perfumed with candle smoke served with a platter of deep-fried relishes." Others mentioned shrimp in Mallorca cooked very simply over a grill with wood from the trees around the restaurant; or unpasteurized cream; a perfect baked pasta ("I've had millions of lasagnas over the years, but this blew my head off"); porcini in Tuscany, roasted whole with a bit of garlic and thyme, two hours after they were picked; lobster pasta; Tarte Tatin in Lamotte-Beuvron, France; my friend and great cook Anissa Helou, goat's curd mousse; and that giant of a chef from one of my favorite restaurants in the world, Fergus Henderson of London's St. John, the burger at the Four Seasons in New York.

Indeed, sometimes perfect food is just that simple.

There was nothing simple about "American cars so cool in the '50s, '60s, and '70s," but that's the analogy Mario Batali uses to point out the craft we need "to make sure that the twenty-first century isn't a footnote of the twentieth century—the American century." To not forget the hand craftsmanship that made those fabulous cars and their time. "And now the hand is coming back. And I think that has a lot to do with food. Farming is hip again and people are going to think about the things that they're contributing to society. I mean, if Americans have to produce things with their hands, and that's what food is all about. Hand-making this stuff is going to be the key to our success, to making us better. So cooks knowing the craft—even if they're not famous—trickles down to have a much larger effect on our society."

Revolutionary change from the rise of fast food (fast death) to its demise.

A FINAL WORD

A final word as to the veracity of all this. Having known M. F. K. Fisher fairly well, I know she wouldn't mind my including a thought from the beginning of her *To Begin Again,* talking about how her family accused her of never spoiling a story by sticking to the truth: It was a "plain lie," she said, "because I do not lie." Since she was a storyteller, I can think only of the Russian saying, "He lies like an eyewitness."

CHAPTER 38

WHERE IT ALL CAME FROM

A BIBLIOGRAPHY

"You are quite right," the count was saying. "The ideal cuisine should display an individual character, it should offer a menu judiciously chosen from the kitchen workshops of the most diverse lands and people—a menu reflecting the chef's alert and fastidious taste."
—Norman Douglas, *South Wind* (1917), quoted
in my journals, July 26, 1970

Inasmuch as what has happened to American cuisine since 2005 has been influenced by Spain's El Bulli and its continuation in Europe, like Noma, and a handful of well-known books from them, see Pau Arenos, and Arzak and Adria. Also Irving Davis's 1969 Catalan cookbook, which inspired many eye-opening combinations of ingredients for me. I have left this "classic" list as it was in 2003. Then every book listed was in my library (except for one), and I had read them all. All the quotations that are not from books are from magazines, press clippings, and my daily culinary and personal journals that I kept over the years. Any omissions tell a story, though not always.

A.W. *A Book of Cookrye*. London: Edward, 1591.
This book is as far back as you need to go in English. It is small, easy to read, and, apart from how to cook a crane, a curlew, a bustard, and a bittern, it shows the first faint stirrings of a modern organization table service for later centuries.

Acton, Eliza. *Modern Cookery for Private Families.* **London, 1845 and 1855.**
Because she has "truffles potted in butter" prepared "for the breakfast table," and that will always get my vote, and because she was a favorite of Elizabeth David (who gave me the book in 1974). My standby carrot soup of Chez Panisse in the early days was from Acton, using water instead of stock for pure vegetable flavors, as did Richard Olney and Marcel Boulestin before him. This is a book that comes from "instinct and sheer intelligence rather than experience," and it is more interesting than that of the later Mrs. Beeton, who copied her.

Adams, Charlotte. *The Four Seasons Cookbook.* **New York: Crescent Books, 1971.**
Read the foreword by James Beard for an introduction to perhaps America's most influential restaurant of the twentieth century. And notice the fiddlehead ferns, fried parsley, wild asparagus, and a large American wine list as early as 1959.

Alexander, Victoria, and Genevieve Harris. *A Taste of Australia: The Bathers' Pavilion Cookbook.* **Berkeley, CA: Ten Speed Press, 1995.**
Because the Bathers' Pavilion restaurant on the beach at Balmoral (near Sydney) was the West Beach Cafe, Trumps, and Michael's (Los Angeles) of Australia all rolled into one. What was New California decor and cooking became the New Australian, with Tony and Gay Bilson's Berowra Waters Inn, Neil Perry's Blue Water Grill at Bondi, Phillip Searle, Damien Pignolet, Tetsuya Wakuda, and a few others.

Alford, Jeffrey, and Naomi Duguid. *Hot Sour Salty Sweet.* **New York: Artisan, 2000.**
"A culinary journey though Southeast Asia," and no journey in the area of the Mekong Delta (southern China, Laos, Thailand, Cambodia, and Vietnam) has ever been more mouthwateringly photographed or written about—ever.

Ali-Bab. *Gastronomic Pratique.* **Paris: Flammarion, 1928.**
A book that includes a regime for how to eat very well without getting fat, showing that we did not invent concerns over eating healthfully. A very fashionable book for chefs to have read in the eighties. It grasps all your senses and elates the historian in you without a hint of cobwebs; rather it blows them away. It certainly did for me in 1974, when I used it at Chez Panisse, and then later at Stars.

Allen, Ida C. Bailey. *Mrs. Allen's Cook Book.* **Boston: Small, Maynard, 1917.**
Quite before her time with health concerns, her answer being to banish all bad cooking, even though she overcooks the vegetables by ten minutes.

America's Cook Book. **Compiled by the Home Institute of the** *New York Herald Tribune.* **New York: Charles Scribner's Sons, 1937, 1940; rev. ed., 1942.**
Included because my mother bought it the year I was born, and cooked with it for forty years. My copy is covered in food, stained, and dog-eared. And because it is very Rector's (restaurant) and a prequel to Beard. He must have known this book, or Josie Wilson did, when writing his monumental *American Cookery.*

Anger, Kenneth. *Hollywood Babylon II.* American ed. New York: E. P. Dutton, 1984.
I lived with Kenneth while he wrote the first *Hollywood Babylon,* almost ten years before this book was published. And because it shows Nick Ray and others in the film industry who, because of Alice Waters's boyfriend at the Pacific Film Archive at the time, were very much part of the scene of Chez Panisse. And because the cover shows what too many hamburgers, if they are not truffled, can do for you. Poor Liz.

Arenos, Pau. *Los Genios del Fuego.* Barcelona: Peninsula, 1999.
If you want to know what is going on in the most recent frontier of cooking, this is the book. It is visually in the style of *White Heat* and then Charlie Trotter's books, complete with the drawings done by the chefs to show how to present the dishes. All about ten geniuses of Spain in the vanguard: Ferran Adria, Jean Luc Figueras, Santi Santa Maria, and so on.

Aresty, Esther B. *The Delectable Past.* New York: Simon & Schuster, 1964.
The best contemporary of the fast passes at two thousand years of cooking, and still one of the easiest, most amusing, and educational to read. See also Jean-Louis Flandrin.

Aron, Jean-Paul. *The Art of Eating in France: Manners and Menus in Nineteenth Century France.* New York: Harper & Row, 1975.
An absolutely fascinating book! Its accounts of the magnificent Very's restaurant in Paris inspired me in 1976 to start thinking of the Stars concept: Could I have the likes of my hero Grimod de la Reynière eat there or in a café next door every week as he did at Very's?

Arzak, Juan Mari, and Ferran Adria. *Arzuk & Adria 2000–2001.* Spain, 1999.
This book was written to show the food that turned one century into another. These men should know. And the photograph of one of the world's great foods, *el jamón ibérico* (that most perfect of hams), makes my mouth water.

Audot, Louis Eustache. *La Cuisimère de La Campagne et de La Ville.* Paris: Audot, 1818.
This is the only book on this list that I do not have and have not read, but I mention it because I have been told it was the French home cookbook for a century after its publication and because again, that early on, it is about women's cooking.

Baldick, Robert. *Dinner at Magny's.* New York: Coward, McCann & Geoghegan, 1971.
One of the three books that really made me want to come up with the Stars concept and success. Just a brilliant book, and not only because the author is a fan of Huysmans! Magny's was the watering hole "of the leading novelists, critics, historians, and scientists of nineteenth century-France."

Barry, Naomi. "Escoffier." *Gourmet,* October 1989.
Because Naomi is a wonderful writer, and she really gets her man in this article.

Batterberry, Michael, and Ariane Batterberry. *On the Town in New York from 1776 to the Present.* New York: Charles Scribner's Sons, 1973.
Because these authors were in love with New York when it was not fashionable to be, and visionaries to see that the town would become the world's best culinary scene again, especially if anyone knew about its very colorful and creative past. Think truck farms run by a single restaurant (Delmonico's) on Long Island in the late nineteenth century.

Beard, James. *American Cookery.* Boston: Little, Brown, 1972.
This book shows that Jim knew how to take his place in history. Still, it ain't no Ali-Bab.

————. *Delights and Prejudices.* New York: Atheneum, 1964.
The best of his books, and maybe the only one he actually wrote. The true James Beard—or at least one of them.

————. *Fish Cookery.* Boston: Little, Brown, 1954; new ed., 1976.
Not the greatest book, even though it does have recipes for fresh sardines. But in 1976 James was already pointing out the severe marine "ecological changes" since the first edition. And because the inscription to me in 1976 says: "For Jeremiah— who knows so much! Love, James Beard."

————. The *James Beard Cookbook.* With Isabel E. Calvert. New York: E. P. Dutton, 1961; rev. ed., 1970.
Note that the copyright is 1959; you'll know how he was thinking that early on. In 1970 the publishers hailed this as a classic, "as essential to the modern American kitchen as the stove itself." James calls it "a basic cookbook." Not as good as the Rector's 1928 book, and it is already diluted by the home economics virus of the period after the world wars. But a Beard classic nonetheless.

Beaton, Cecil. "The Art of Table Decoration." *Gourmet,* December 1969.
Beaton is impeccable, and this advice is still amusing for the twenty-first century. In 1969 I read and recorded in my culinary notebooks: "A treat need not be a luxury; a banquet need not include caviar. Imagination is the most important ingredient."

Beck, Simone, with Louisette Bertholle and Julia Child. *Mastering the Art of French Cooking.* Vol. 1. New York: Knopf, 1961.
The book (especially the first volume) that launched a thousand young cooks into vats of butter, cream, and wonderful cooking.

Beebe, Lucius. The *Stork Club Bar Book.* New York: Rinehart, 1946.
One cannot visit the twentieth century without saying hello to Lucius Beebe. And this book, from one of New York's "various plush and chromium cocktail zoos," is all about the last time the city was at its height.

La Belle France: A Gourmet's Guide to the French Provinces. Preface by André Maurois. New York: Golden Press; London: Paul Hamly, 1964.
A stunning book that was countless years of inspiration for Chez Panisse and, early on, for my regional festivals. Perhaps no book more than this one inspired Alice Waters. See the newer and equally magnificent version of Robert Freson, *A Taste of France.*

Bemelmans, Ludwig. *La Bonne Table.* New York: Simon & Schuster, 1964.
A true New York boulevardier in the old style. Incredibly civilized stories of his "lifetime love affair with the art of dining" in the now-mythic places like L'Ousteau de Beaumanière in Provence, Le Pavilion in New York, and La Tour d'Argent in Paris. Everything from sausages and beer to caviar and champagne. Material originally from *Playboy* in 1960 ("Caviar"), *Holiday, Town & Country, Vogue,* and *The New Yorker.*

Bey, Pilaf [Norman Douglas]. *Venus in the Kitchen, or Love's Cookery Book.* New York: Viking Press, 1952.
Did the great Harry Cipriani know of this book when he wrote *Heloise and Bellinis?* This book is even more wonderful.

Bianchini, Francesco, and Francisco Corbetta. *The Complete Book of Fruits and Vegetables.* Illustrations by Marilena Pistoia. New York: Crown, 1975.
The colored illustrations tell more than a photo ever could. When this book came out, I bought it immediately and showed it to my partners at Chez Panisse with glee: Here were the things that I wanted to grow, the wild radish, the purslane, Treviso, New Zealand spinach, and the sea rocket and borage I had cooked with in Maine. I was given a copy by Linda Guenzel, who wrote *The Chez Panisse Menu Cookbook;* she inscribed it by quoting Larousse on what is a vegetable, and then said: "You, the high priest of all culinary, have given us vegetables as Larousse may never have known."

Bittman, Mark. *How to Cook Everything.* New York: John Wiley, 1998.
The new *Joy of Cooking.*

Blanc, Georges. *The French Vineyard Table.* New York: Clarkson Potter, 1997.
The most visually evocative and beautifully done of the French chef books of the nineties, by my favorite French country chef, who carried on the cooking of the amazing women of Vonnas and Lyons.

Bober, Phyllis Pray. *Art, Culture, and Cuisine.* Chicago: University of Chicago Press, 1999.
A very impressive and illustrated culinary history that "examines cooking through the dual lens of archaeology and art history." Finally someone who can explain what that classic period of reclining while dining was all about.

Boeckmann, Susie, and Natalie Rebeiz-Nielsen. *Caviar.* London: Mitchell Beazley, 1999.
Called the definitive book, it probably is, if you read it with the Inga Saffron book. The book inspires one to go out and eat caviar—while one still can.

Borrel, Anne, with Alain Senderens and Jean-Bernard Naudin. *Dining with Proust.* New York: Random House, 1992.
This could have been a very silly book. But the food is real, thanks to the great Parisian chef Alain Senderens, who understands the grand presentations of the era. The food in the very good photographs is historically correct and delicious looking. What a way to learn history, with Nesselrode pudding, spiced beef in jelly, and the "Lunch at Reveillon: scrambled eggs with bacon, lobster American style, hare à l'allemande, rose, and macaroon preserve." Divine.

Bourdain, Anthony. *Kitchen Confidential.* New York: Bloomsbury, 2000.
In Bourdain's own words, "Twenty-five years of sex, drugs, bad behavior, and haute cuisine." Adored this book, laughed and cried (in terror of recognition) all through it. And made me want to do it all over again. The restaurant business, not cry. Though some would say they are the same thing.

Boulestin, X. Marcel. *Ease and Endurance.* London: Home & Van Thal, 1948.
Elizabeth David gave me this book on "the first day of summer, 1978," after a seven-hour lunch. It shows how Boulestin covered the twenties, thirties, and forties, mixing artists, socialites, and food. See page 90 for the description of his new restaurant in Covent Garden. He used the artists of the day, creating a decor that should make decorators today gasp in admiration. And because thirty-five years later I tried to buy the place.

———. "Finer Cooking." *Vogue,* London, 1923–.
Read anything by Marcel, and this is a very good introduction.

———. *What Shall We Have Today?* London: William Heinemann, 1931.
If you want to see Elizabeth David before Elizabeth herself, this is her hero and mentor with his relentlessly modern mind. As a young man he was secretary to the Colette-Willy ménage, then escaped the drama of that household and, already an Anglophile (taking Colette to tea at the English Dairy in Paris), fled to England, taking with him a few Modiglianis that he had bought for twelve pounds. *Simple French Cooking for English Homes* came out in 1923, written for single people and working

women who have to cook without much money or time. Sound familiar? Think Richard Olney, only fifty years earlier: "All these soups . . . must be made with plain water. When made with the addition of stock they lose all character and cease to be what they were intended to be." No statement could be more "modern" in every way, or more cutting-edge. Also because he says that on charcoal is the only way to grill.

Boulud, Daniel, and Peter Kaminsky. *Chef Daniel Boulud.* **New York: Assouline, 2002.**
A day in the life of Daniel, and a wonderful book if you can get past the crazy graphics. I can.

Bradley, Richard. *The Country Housewife and Lady's Director.* **London, 1727, 1732, 1736; repr. 1736 ed. London: Prospect Books, 1980.**
A vastly entertaining and intelligent book with recipes inspiring for now—look at the Sorrel Tart and the Small Suckers of Artichokes. Not at all esoteric, until we get to the Viper Soup.

Brillat-Savarin. *Physiologie du Gout.* **Paris: Michel Levy Frères, 1873.**
Is any comment necessary? Well, perhaps. See Lucien Tendret.

Brown, Eleanor, and Bob Brown. *Culinary Americana.* **New York: Roving Eye Press, 1961.**
One hundred years of cookbooks, published in the United States from 1860 to1960—so an invaluable bibliographical resource.

Brown, Helen. *Helen Brown's West Coast Cook Book.* **New York: Little, Brown, 1952.**
Helen was an absolute favorite of James Beard. This was stuff for the public, *McCall's, House & Garden,* and so on, and is so very American. It gave me the nerve in 1976 to start putting the origins of ingredients on the menu.

The Browns. *America Cooks.* **Garden City, NY: Halcyon House, 1940.**
"Favorite Recipes from Forty-eight States," including Scuppernong Pie and a traditional breakfast from the Shenandoah Valley. Packed with Americana before the canned and frozen foods.

Bullock, Mrs. Helen. *The Williamsburg Art of Cookery.* **Williamsburg, VA: Colonial Williamsburg, 1939.**
Very entertaining, but what rivets me is the account of the books consulted for this work: Hannah Glasse, Miss Leslie, John Farley, Mrs. Mary Randolph's *The Virginia Housewife.* Perfect taste!

Capon, Robert Farrar. *The Supper of the Lamb.* **New York: Doubleday, 1967.**
An inspiring book. Included here for the preface; for the dedication, which is to his wife, whom he calls "the lightning behind all this thunder," because he believes that

an onion can save you from hell, and because he says, "The world exists, not for what it means but for what it is. The purpose of mushrooms is to be mushrooms; wine is in order to be wine: things are precious before they are contributory." That is the cook's true guide.

Carson, Rachel. *The Silent Spring.* Boston: Houghton Mifflin, 1962.
A huge influence on me in the early sixties, which after my early foraging efforts in the 1960s, and later, in the early seventies, made me want to start growing our own produce and recycling for the restaurants.

Chamberlain, Samuel, and Narcissa Chamberlain. *Bouquet de France.* New York: Gourmet Books, 1952.
Defining the art of a culinary tour, in the days when you could just drop by almost anywhere in France and get a good meal. A sensibility we should recover.

Cherikoff, Vic, and Jennifer Isaacs. *The Bush Food Handbook: How to Gather, Grow, Process and Cook Australian Wild Foods.* Balmain, Australia: Ti Tree Press, n.d [1990s].
This is serious book. Not a Birkenstock in sight. It shows how seriously the Australians took over from California in reworking regional aesthetics to make a new culture and cuisine. Fascinating book and beautifully presented.

Child, Mrs. *The American Frugal Housewife.* Boston: Carter, Hendee, 1832.
One can tire of the thousands of household management books, but this one is small and powerful. And this woman, at a time when a woman could not go into the supper room at a party unless escorted by a man, was a newspaperwoman, magazine editor, gardener, novelist, poet, reformer, and a friend of Whitman, Lowell, and Bryant. She also hid runaway slaves, and her first important antislavery writing in America nearly ruined her.

Cipriani, Harry. *The Harry's Bar Cookbook.* New York: Bantam Books, 1991.
My hero.

———. *Heloise and Bellinis.* New York: Little, Brown, 1986.
When I read this book I knew that Harry at Harry's in Venice and Tom Margittai at the Four Seaons in New York were having as much fun as restaurateurs as I was!

Cocteau, Jean. *Past Tense (Diaries).* New York: Harcourt Brace, 1987.
Because the highly intelligent Ezra Pound thought Cocteau was the most intelligent Frenchman he had met, along with Francis Picabia. For "Eggs Picabia" see Alice B. Toklas's cookbook.

Colette. *Prisons et Paradis.* Paris: Librairie Arthème Fayard, 1986.
For the truffles and her sensibility about everything, including food.

————. *The Pure and the Impure*. New York: Farrar, Straus & Giroux, 1967.
"To receive from someone happiness—is it not to choose the sauce in which we want
to be served up?"

Conrad, Barnaby. *Absinthe*. San Francisco: Chronicle Books, 1988.
Now that absinthe is legal again in Europe, and being manufactured in Thailand as
well as in Spain and France, one should read about this most subtle green elixir to
be sipped at "the green hour" because, as someone said, "Absinthe makes the heart
grow fonder."

Cooking. Edited by Barbara Kafka. Stamford, CT: Cuisinart Publications, 1978–.
Great little magazine edited by the phenomenally brilliant Barbara Kafka. Writers are
Naomi Barry, James Beard, Gault and Millau, Abby Mandel, Elizabeth David, and
so on. Read also all the books by Barbara, including the wonderful book *Roasting*.

Core, Philip. *Camp: The Lie That Tells the Truth*. Foreword by George Melly.
London: Plexus, 1984.
Not just because the book is dedicated to me, "champagne en campagne," but be-
cause it covers a lot of my early imprints and aesthetic lessons: Aubrey Beardsley,
Cecil Beaton, Prince Yusupov, the Sitwells, the sixties, Robert de Montesquiou and
Boni de Castellane (the Belle Époque's most elegant men), Jean Cocteau, Edward
James, Ronald Firbank, Diaghilev, D'Annunzio (the perfect peaches, in the perfect
bowl, all wrapped in the perfect silk scarf—all made at his villa), Noël Coward,
Colette, Carême (who made the campiest remark of all of them about the fine arts
being five in number, including pastry making, of which architecture is a branch),
Capri, Jean-Michel Frank, Christian Bérard, and Lou Reed. These are all the people
who made the most of their faults, because after all, "Camp is a disguise that fails."

Courtine, Robert. *The Hundred Glories of French Cooking*. New York: Farrar,
Straus & Giroux, 1973.
A book wonderful for its unparalleled illustrations—the beautiful chefs in boots, the
photo of Curnonsky at lunch, the fish market section at Les Halles. Treat yourself.

Cox, Mrs. Samuel R. *The Parker Cook Book*. Abilene, TX, 1932.
Not the Parker House hotel cookbook, but in this one, for the Presbyterian Church,
they still ate caviar, and the nonalcoholic drinks are state of the art.

Craddock, Harry. *The Savoy Cocktail Book*. London: Constable, 1930.
If you haven't seen the design of this perfect Art Deco book, you are really missing out.
The ultimate recipes, and then there is the foreword to the wine section, by Colette.

Crowninshield, Frank. *The Unofficial Palace of New York: A Tribute to the
Waldorf-Astoria*. New York: Waldorf-Astoria, 1939.
For the Sert murals, the chapter by Elsa Maxwell, and the American menus with

Diamond Back Terrapin, Chicken California Style, Roast Mountain Sheep, and Basket of Lobster, all at one dinner in 1899. See the 1937 menu for an "Idaho Dinner," which then called out the origins of the ingredients: Snake River, Twin Falls, Sawtooth Range, Jerome County, Boise Valley, and Lone Pine, Idaho.

Culinaria. Cologne: Konemann, 1998.
Huge, glossy books that entice you to pick them up and then make you think nothing this obvious-looking could be good. They are, and full of gripping information and illustrations. The United States, France, and Italy are the ones I have.

Curnonsky. *Traditional Recipes of the Provinces of France.* Translated by Edwin Lavin. London: W. H. Allen, 1961.
The book from which I did the famous Curnonsky festival at Chez Panisse, and the book I used to give as Christmas presents. A beautiful book—if a bit recherché.

David, Elizabeth. "Edouard de Pomiane." *Gourmet,* March 1970.
Because it opens with "Art demands an impeccable technique; science a little understanding."

———. *French Provincial Cooking.* New York: Harper & Row, 1960.
I was handed this book on my first day of work as executive chef at Chez Panisse by Gene Opton, the woman running it at the time, and was told it was the bible to cook from. Very great book, and Elizabeth's main work as far as most people are concerned.

———. "Marcel Boulestin." *Gourmet,* August 1969.
The article that turned me on to Boulestin, and again on to Elizabeth.

———. "Norman Douglas." *Gourmet,* February 1969.
Because on the back page of Elizabeth's copy of *Old Calabria,* Norman wrote: "Always do as you please, send everybody to Hell, and take the consequences. Damned good rule of life."

Dalí, Salvador. *Les Diners de Gala.* New York: Felicie, 1973.
Pure Dalí, and how to sodomize a leg of lamb. As I did at Chez Panisse right after reading it. Full-color food from Paris's Lassere, Maxim's, and La Tour d'Argent.

Davidson, Alan. *The Oxford Companion to Food.* Oxford: Oxford University Press, 1999.
In the tradition of the great dictionaries of food (see Dumas), this is Alan at his best—erudite, and not afraid of his always-riveting opinions. A must for food reference today.

Davis, Irving. *A Catalan Cookery Book: A Collection of Impossible Recipes.* **Edited by Patience Gray. Paris: Lucien Scheler, 1969.**
Inasmuch as some knowledgeable people say that right now the best and most daring food in the West is in Spain, and because I have loved this book and the food in it since it was published. Inspiring the food at Stars. Rabbit with snails indeed! Pretty good with monkfish, too—the snails, I mean. In the early seventies people thought I was mad for pushing this food and this book. See Arzak and Adria, and Pau Arenos.

De Croze, Austin. *What to Eat and Drink in France.* **London: Frederick Warne, 1931.**
Written "for tourists so they can choose from any province [of France] the typical local dishes." Important early Chez Panisse source.

De Gouy, Jean. *La Cuisine et La Patisserie Bourgeoises.* **Paris: Lebegue et Cie, 1896.**
Because this book is understandable to all, "à la portée de tous," and because you will need this one to explain all the other ones. French cookbooks, that is.

De Groot, Roy Andries. *The Auberge of the Flowering Hearth.* **New York: Bobbs-Merrill, 1973.**
This book blew me away, made me fall in love with France again, love De Groot again, and after I made everyone read it, and saw they loved it, set me off on a cooking frenzy of renewed enthusiasm at Chez Panisse in 1973. One of the books you would take in an overnight bag—your only luggage—when banished to a desert island. Also a huge favorite of Alice Waters.

Douglas, Norman. *South Wind.* **London: Martin Secker, 1917. (Reprinted many times since first publication.)**
"'You are quite right,' the count was saying. 'The ideal cuisine should display an individual character, it should offer a menu judiciously chosen from the kitchen workshops of the most diverse lands and people—a menu reflecting the master's alert and fastidious taste.' *South Wind.*" Quoted in my journals, July 26, 1970.

Dubois, Urbain, and Emile Bernard. *La Cuisine Classique.* **Paris: Chez les Auteurs, 1856.**
Not just for the illustrations of those divine garnishes stuck on skewers (like whole truffles pierced with cockscombs and crayfish), or for the uniquely understandable descriptions of pieces montées, but because this book tells exactly what the difference is between the two services, French and Russian. From what I still hear of these terms bandied around in culinary academies, this book should be reread. Also, the style of the recipes is beautifully direct, straightforward, and definitive, and just before the similarly inspired Escoffier.

Ducasse, Alain. *Flavors of France.* **New York: Artisan, 1998.**
Finally a book by a chef (one of the most famous in the world) that is the food you can cook from, and the photographs show you can. Alain knows that more than four main ingredients on a plate is too many.

Ducasse, Alain, and Jean-François Piège. *Grand Livre de Cuisine d'Alain Ducasse.* **Paris: ADP, 2001.**
Not since Prosper Montagné's *Larousse Gastronomique* (1938), Escoffier's *Le Guide Culinaire,* and Henri-Paul Pellaprat's *L'Art Culinaire Moderne* (1935) has a chef accomplished a work that codifies the cooking of a nation and the time. This one does.

Dumas, Alexandre. *Dictionary of Cuisine.* **Translated by Louis Colman. New York: Simon & Schuster, 1958.**
My bedside reading in college, and I could not wait to buy the unedited version. I never tire of this book. See Alan Davidson and Waverley Root. This edition was severely cut. The new, less edited one is Alexandre Dumas, *Le Grand Dicuonnaire de Cuisine* (Turin: Henry Veyrier, 1978).

Dumaine, Alexandre. *Ma Cuisine.* **Paris: Pensée Moderne, 1972.**
Richard Olney, in our correspondence in 1973, told me to read this. Dumaine became my model. I wanted a restaurant that people would think "worth the journey."

Dupleix, Jill. *New Food: From the New Basics to the New Classics.* **Port Melbourne, Australia: William Heinemann, 1994.**
Tells the story of why the nineties were not going to be the eighties. This woman loves to think, eat, write, and tell you all about it. Very clever indeed.

Durack, Terry. *Yum.* **Port Melbourne, Australia: William Heinemann, 1996.**
Yum indeed. By the husband of Jill Dupleix, this book is very nineties, or the new Australian intelligence, the worldwide view. There is a list of who he thinks are the best chefs and restaurateurs in the world at the time of his writing, including my favorites Bruno Loubet of London's L'Odéon, Georges Blanc, of course, Arrigo Cipriani, and Pierre Koffrnan.

Durrell, Lawrence. *The Black Book.* **Paris: Obelisk Press, 1938; New York and Paris: Olympia Press, 1959.**
Because the book opens with "Today there is a gale blowing up from the Levant," the wind withering the soft gold shavings of hair along the thighs. "The very nipples turn hard and black on the breasts of women, while the figs roast." Who needs a cooking lesson? And if it isn't about food it is all the senses that cooking conjures up. The hero tastefully identifies the scent on the air: "It's the girls' bogs again!" Such an amateur of odors must be admired. How did he know it was girls? This is the book to read if dining alone.

Ebert-Schifferer, Sybille. *Still Life.* New York: Harry N. Abrams, 1999.
A thousand words to describe what food was on artists' and other people's minds—
and then there are the paintings.

Escoffier, Auguste. *Le Guide Culinaire.* Paris: Flammarion, 1903; 3d ed., Paris:
E. Grevin, 1912.
There was an edition in 1907 as well, but the 1912 has the introductions of both
the second and the first, and these are the beginning of modern cooking. Do not
overlook the mention of his "maître" Urban Dubois. And the pieces on stocks and
"fonds" are the bible to this day. Also the book I used for the Escoffier festival at
Chez Panisse in 1974, which put the restaurant on the local and national map.

———. *Ma Cuisine.* Translated by Vyvyan Holland. London: Paul Hamlyn,
1965.
My first cookbook as a teenager and the first that I read constantly from cover to
cover. The mainstay reference for my recreational graduate school cooking binges
and early lessons.

Escoffier, Auguste, ed. *Le Carnet d'Epicure.* Paris, 1908–12[?].
A lesson in culinary history that cannot be missed. Check out the Salad Folle—with
haricots verts, foie gras, lobster, hazelnut oil, and so on—in 1908, sixty years before
everyone thought they had invented it.

Evelyn, John. *Acetaria, A Discourse of Sallets.* London: B. Tooke, 1699.
Because three hundred years later everyone agrees this is one of the truly delightful early cookbooks: the dedication is totally mad, the preface about the "universal
plantation" is deranged, 90 percent of this "cookbook" is about gardening and life,
only 10 percent is about recipes (a delicious one for artichokes). Not a cookbook at
all, but read it and see how serious and how much fun the seventeenth century was
for cooks.

Farley, John. *The London Art of Cookery.* 7th ed. London, 1792.
Farley was the "principal cook at the London Tavern." If you do nothing else with
this democratically approached and concisely worded book, look at the plates showing the arrangement on the table of the various dishes per course—many books talk
about this "French" service, but few show how it was done. This is "Simple Food,"
and the recipes are beautifully written.

Farmer, Fannie Merritt. *The Boston Cooking-School Cook Book.* Boston: Little,
Brown, 1937.
A bit overrated but historically interesting, and do not bother with any editions after
this one. Read "a few rules for successful dining": as in use foods only at the height
of the season, use generous-size plates so the food is not crowded, think always of the
wine and how the food will affect it, and so on. All this in 1937!

Fashions in Foods in Beverly Hills. Beverly Hills, CA: Beverly Hills Woman's Club, 1931.

If there was any doubt what America ate after the fall of American food (post–World War I) and before the revolution, here it is. Carrot Ring, Tamale Pie, Goulash, Cottage Cheese Salad, Wakimoli Salad, and Divinity. Most of it pretty good, which is why most of the country is still eating it!

Fernandez-Armesto, Dr. Felipe. *Food: A History.* London: Macmillan, 2001.

From the invention of cooking to feeding the giant maw of the contemporary world.

Fielding, Daphne. *The Duchess of Jermyn Street: The Life and Good Times of Rosa Lewis of the Cavendish Hotel.* Boston: Little, Brown, 1964.

Because if you did not see the show from the BBC more than three times you are deprived. The way I always wanted to treat my customers, and did. An absolute inspiration for any truly inspired restaurateur! From kitchen maid to culinary genius, mistress of the king, and prankster extraordinaire, one of the great individualistic women of the century. And discreet to boot.

Firbank, Ronald. *Concerning the Eccentricities of Cardinal Pirelli.* London: Duckworth, 1926.

Thank God there is one mention of food, "white menthe" (and then only because the dog was covered in it); otherwise I could not include this inspiration of my college years.

Flandrin, Jean-Louis, and Massimo Montanari. *Food: A Culinary History from Antiquity to the Present.* New York: Columbia University Press, 1999.

Jacques Pépin said this book is "essential reading for the historian and the lover of social studies as well as the modern cook and gourmet." The title says it all: if you are interested in food, this is the book for you.

Foods of the World. Edited by Time-Life Books, James Beard and Michael Field, consultants. New York: Time-Life Books, 1970.

I have to mention Michael Field. Cathy Simon, Michael Palmer, and I cooked a lot from his *Michael Field's Cooking School* when we were in college. I could never get a straight answer out of anyone, let alone Beard, about what he was like. When asked, Beard would get quiet, as when he knew someone was talented, admired the talent, but for some private reason didn't want to praise it. Anyway, these books were of enormous excitement and inspiration to me and my friends. I could not wait for the mail to bring the new issue. *Vienna* was good, *Classic French* wonderful, and *American Cooking: Southern Style* was the one most of my friends cooked from and the one that got us all on to Thomas Jefferson and hams. Still a great read.

La France à Table. Rue de Castellane, Paris, early 1930s.

A magazine with writers like Colette, Gaston Derys, Austin de Croze, Curnónsky talking about cooking. When they talk about cooking in the ashes of the fire, for example, it is the true flavor of the regions and countryside of France.

Franz, Mark. *Farallon.* San Francisco: Chronicle Books, 2001.
Definitely a chef's and a beautiful book. For those who love to cook fish and want to know all about it, Mark tells you how.

Freson, Robert. *The Taste of France.* New York: Stewart, Tabori & Chang, 1983.
One of the most stunningly beautiful photography cookbooks ever, and one that created a style. The writers include Richard Olney, Ann Willan (La Varenne), Jill Norman (Elizabeth David's literary executor), Alan Davidson, and Caroline Conran.

Fussell, Betty. *I Hear America Cooking.* New York: Viking Press, 1986.
Because she educates us away from the traps of slavishly believing in "authentic" and "regional" without knowing where the worth of the concepts lie.

Gattey, Charles Neilson. *Foie Gras and Trumpets.* London: Constable, 1984.
For those who love to give grand and expensive parties, or who love to read about them. You have not lived until you have read about Kessler's "gondola party" for the English king, or "the Awful Seeley Dinner" when Little Egypt was served naked from a pie and the police had to raid Sherry's (again). The Savoy, Boulestin's, the Waldorf, Delmonico's, Rector's. All these great restaurants and the dish about them is all here.

Gibbons, Euell. *Stalking the Wild Asparagus.* Philadelphia: McKay, 1962.
The father of foraging, and the book that inspired me in the sixties, on the beaches of Maine and at my Massachusetts farm, before I got into the restaurant business, to grow my own and to forage.

Ginor, Michael. *Foie Gras: A Passion.* New York: John Wiley & Sons, 1999.
A book about this delicious fat that really works. The best I know in English on the subject.

Glasse, Hannah. *The Art of Cookery, Made Plain and Easy.* Alexandria, VA: Printed for the author, 1805.
Because, according to John and Karen Hess, it was "the most popular cookbook in the colonies." And for the section on American cooking.

Gopnik, Adam. "Is There a Crisis in French Cooking?" *New Yorker,* April 28 and May 5, 1997.
A piece of extraordinary intelligence. The fickle muse of French cooking, and where does she sit?

Gordon, Peter. *The Sugar Club Cookbook.* London: Hodder & Stoughton, 1997.
The jacket says that Gordon is the Alastair Little (eighties) of the nineties. He's cool.

A book of the "de rigueur" (though I hope not "rigor mortis") Marco Pierre White design school. He's really searching the world for great flavors, but see the Australians ten years earlier.

Goloub, Hélène. *100 Recettes de Cuisine Russe.* **Paris: Self-published, 1924.**
Perfect recipes for a cuisine that, for a dinner party, is still the most impactful.

The Good Cook. **Richard Olney, consultant; editors of Time-Life. London and Alexandria, VA: Time-Life Books, 1979-**
The best how-to teaching books there are, especially the English edition, and a series that I worked on with Richard, as well as doing a few of my own in Virginia. This series changed "how to" food photography for good.

Griffini, Orso Cesare, and Frances E. Vieta. *I Tartúffi.* **Rome: Trevi Editore, 1973.**
The book that, when I bought it in 1974, made me want to be the first to bring fresh truffles to California—and I was.

Grigson, Jane. *The Art of Charcuterie.* **New York: Knopf, 1968.**
It is not generally known how influential this book has been, but every time you taste a succulent double pork chop in America, it is because the chef read this book. All the brining done now in American restaurants is because of Jane. Cook pork or poultry without this book? Not well.

———. *British Cookery.* **New York: Atheneum, 1985.**
A celebration of regionality by this most wonderful of women. Superb.

Guenzel, Linda R. *Beyond Tears: The First Eight Years.* **Illustrations by David Lance Goines and Wesley B. Tanner. Berkeley, CA: Chez Panisse, 1979.**
The collection of menus from August 28, 1971, to December 30, 1978, the day before my last day at the restaurant. The first chef was Victoria Kroyer, who later opened Pig by the Tail charcuterie across the street. I was the second. Linda knew this was the important period, as did Darrell Corti when he sent a funeral wreath in 1974 after my week of Escoffier dinners: "Chez Panisse can never be this great again."

———. *The Chez Panisse Menu Cookbook.* **New York: Random House, 1982.**
The inscription in the copy given to me by Linda is "To Jeremiah—The inspiration, the raison d'etre, the *creator* of so much on these pages—without you, there would be no Chez Panisse, no cookbook. Truth shall triumph."

Guérard, Michel. *La Cuisine Gourmande.* **Paris: Robert Laffont, 1978.**
This and the Troisgros book, with its revolutionary food and plate presentations,

changed it all for young chefs in the United States. Nora Ephron said that this food did not have any impact on the way Americans eat at home, but to the extent that food magazines or TV shows have any effect on that eating, she's wrong. But she's right inasmuch as, in the hands of untalented cooks, the food became "non-nouvelle cuisine," prompting Paul Bocuse (the self-proclaimed leader of the Young Turks) to say that "so-called" nouvelle cuisine "usually means not enough on your plate and too much on your bill."

Guillot, André. *La Grande Cuisine Bourgeoise.* **Paris: Flammarion, 1976.**
This is the "cuisine bourgeoise," as opposed to the "cuisine de la noblesse" that existed before the French Revolution. The three principles of this cooking are the best products (not the rarest), diversity of the dishes that can make up menus, and the rule of economy (nothing wasted). This book explains also how the change in politics and constitutions set the culture of how we eat today. Read the brief historical analysis of the rise of bourgeois cooking.

Hartley, Dorothy. *Food in England.* **London: MacDonald & Jane's, 1954–75.**
I can't remember if Elizabeth David admired Hartley's scholarship or not (God help anyone whose work she didn't), but I find the book great reading. Look at the unique and amazing sketches of ranges and roasting equipment. The food, she says, is "old fashioned, the way we [English] like it." And when it's "open apple tart after the pig," with clotted cream, so do we all.

Hay, Donna. *The New Cook.* **Sydney: Murdoch Books, 1997.**
There are several books in this series of material from Australian *Marie Claire,* and I find them all visually inspiring. The photographs and the contents never fail to make me want to cook, and to conjure up new dishes. The price of the books is very right.

Hazan, Marcella. *Essentials of Classic Italian Cooking.* **New York: Knopf, 2001.**
The way to get the best of the genius of Marcella in one book, this one comprising both *Classic Italian Cookbook* and *More Classic Italian Cooking.*

————. **Marcella's** *Italian Kitchen.* **New York: Knopf, 1986.**
Because, as I said on the back cover for her: "A perfect book . . ."

Herbst, Sharon Tyler. *Never Eat More Than You Can Lift.* **New York: Broadway Books, 1997.**
If you like books with "sayings" on food and wine, this is it. My favorite has always been what Lily Bollinger said about champagne, and she would have known: "I drink it when I'm happy and when I'm sad. Sometimes I drink it when I'm alone. When I have company I consider it obligatory. I trifle with it if I'm not hungry and drink it when I am. Otherwise I never touch it—unless I'm thirsty." On my tombstone I hope.

Hess, John L., and Karen Hess. *The Taste of America.* New York: Grossman, 1977.

Read this if for no other reason than it made most of the famous names in the United States purple with rage, spluttering with outraged pride. I adored it. Seemed to me to hit what was going on with the commercial food industry in America at the time fairly squarely on the mark.

Hess, Karen. *Martha Washington's Booke of Cookery.* New York: Columbia University Press,1981.

When I recommend centuries-old cookbooks here, I do cringe slightly with fear at how difficult the print and the language may be to decipher, let alone some of the terminology. This book is completely noted and annotated ("*Layes* is an old word for layers; *porringers* are individual bowls") and therefore makes easy and fascinating reading of this family manuscript and treasure trove of "culinary secrets of some of our earliest colonists, part of our American heritage from England."

Hierneis, Theodor. *The Monarch Dines.* London: Werner Laurie, 1954.

Memories of a cook at the court of Ludwig of Bavaria. I am still trying to figure out why I was given this book on my twenty-first birthday! I do know that I took one look at the photo of the kitchen at Neuschwanstein, and at the one of the dining room at Schloss Linderhof, and knew I had to live in that kitchen or make a house like it. Pure Minoan arches and vaulted ceilings. Every anniversary of Ludwig's last meal (before strolling out of the embrace of his valet into that of the lake) was celebrated in my restaurants.

Hirtzler, Victor. *The Hotel St. Francis Cook Book.* Chicago: Hotel Monthly Press, 1919.

Quite a modern book still. The "art of cooking developed in the hotel business, which, in America, now leads the world." The book is organized with a breakfast, lunch, and dinner menu for each calendar day of the year with some recipes selected from each. The food is caught halfway between Europe and the United States, and is very schizophrenic about the choice of English or European languages to name the dishes. But nothing American is left out. There is no grip on the book's own region of California yet, except for the oysters.

Holyfield, Dana. *Swamp Cookin' with the River People.* Berkeley, CA: Ten Speed Press, 1999.

Like *White Trash Cooking,* this little book has a ring of truth, is hilarious, and I love the photographs of Louisiana swamp critters and how they are cooked outdoors.

Hom, Ken, and Pierre-Jean Pebeyre. *Truffles.* Paris: Hachette, 2001.

If anyone knows more about black truffles than the Pebeyre family of Périgord, I don't know who it could be. And until you have cooked Ken's tastou (truffle sandwiches) or the oeufs â la cocque, sauce truffe (soft-boiled eggs with black truffle sauce), you have not lived to the fullest. The photograph of Pierre-Jean's grandfather Alain sniffing truffles through his long, white beard has been constantly on my kitchen or restaurant wall since my first days at Chez Panisse.

Hopkinson, Simon. *Roast Chicken and Other Stories: Second Helpings.* London: Macmillan, 2001.
Wonderful unpretentious essays by the chef who started Bibendum restaurant in London.

Huysmans, Joris-Karl. *À Rebours.* Paris: Fasquelle Éditeur, 1955.
An important book to understand the sensibility of the nineteenth-century fin de siècle and the world of Ritz and Escoffier. It is the book that, along with Rechy's *City of Night,* ruined my twenties, as Gide's *Faux-Monnayeurs* did my teens.

Jackson, Stanley. *The Savoy.* New York: E. P. Dutton, 1964.
You don't have to have stayed in one of the Thames suites to appreciate the wonderfully English understated outrageousness of this book, and its social history of several eras.

Janson, Charles William. *The Stranger in America.* London: Albion Press, 1807.
All about the "genius, manners, and customs of the people of the United States," written by a European. You get an idea of the view from the following excerpt (about an American woman in an English household) that "is truly characteristic of American politeness." When asked to drink tea she replied: "Tea, indeed! No—I have drank [*sic*] none of that cursed stuff since the affair at Boston. I swallow a beef steak or a piece of fat pork for breakfast and supper, and wash it down with a quart of cider—that's my way!" No Thomas Jefferson in that woman's family!

The Joy of Truffles. Cologne: Evergreen Benedikt Taschen, 1998.
One of the most beautiful food books ever published. The photographs of food set the standard. The photo of the braised black truffle with sherry butter makes me want to dive into it.

Kaytor, Marilyn. *"21": The Life and Times of New York's Favorite Club.* New York: Viking Press, 1975.
The other book that made me think of creating the Stars concept. This is the book if you want to know the history of the first fifty years of the twentieth century in New York, and was there ever a more debonair restaurateur than Pete Kriendler?

Keenan, Brigid. *Dior in Vogue.* Foreword by Margot Fonteyn. New York: Harmony Books,1981.
Look at Le Coudret, Christian Dior's Mill House near Fontainebleau. The dining room and the photo of Dior, chicest of men, making raspberry liqueur in the kitchen of the same old mill house with his very un-chic dog Bobby. As for the mill: "There

were white walls and dark beams, stone-flagged floors, simple furniture gleaming with the patina of age and care, big country cupboards smelling of lavender." The unpretentious style of a gentle genius.

Keller, Thomas. *The French Laundry Cookbook*. New York: Artisan, 1999.
The book that raised the bar for chefs' cookbooks to infinity. Stunningly beautiful, inspirational, and challenging for most.

Kennedy, Diana. *The Cuisines of Mexico*. New York: Harper & Row, 1972.
I bought this in 1974, and it still inspires me. The front flap says Kennedy is in the "tradition of Elizabeth David and Jane Grigson." Personal, opinionated, and true. As a cookbook should be. See also the new books, including *My Mexico*.

Kettner's Book of the Table. London: Dulan, 1877.
Because it is an inspirational book that believes that "[i]f the nature of the ingredients be well known, much fewer will do." After many readings, never tired.

Knapik, Harold. *Haute Cuisine Without Help*. New York: Liveright, 1971.
A charming book by a friend of Alice B. Toklas, for whom he cooked. He wrote it to show that you don't have to be French to cook superb food. Even in 1971 he wanted to tell the public about the horrors of canned anchovy filets, and the glories of salted whole ones. This is all about the origin and the quality of the ingredients. Read the bit about poached eggs.

Kuh, Patric. *The Last Days of Haute Cuisine: America's Culinary Revolution*. New York: Viking Press, 2001.
Another look (and a very intelligent one) at the story of *California Dish*.

Lang, George. *Nobody Knows the Truffles I Have Seen*. New York: Knopf, 1999.
And I wonder how many know the huge achievements of George Lang and the contributions (see the Four Seasons, Restaurant Associates, and how we view catering in America today) of the amazing George. Read about it all here. As well as in other books.

Lanta, Anna Tasca. *The Heart of Sicily*. New York: Clarkson Potter, 1993.
Because surely in any cook's heart there is a little or a lot of Sicily? I adore this book (see the photos of tomatoes drying in the sun and how it is *really* done), this family, and their Regaleali wines grown in the heart of Sicily.

La Varenne, Sieur de. *Le Vray Cuisinier François*. Amsterdam: Chez Pierre Mortier, 1651 (Larousse).
This father of French cuisine started his career as chef by pimping for Henri IV, the king who wanted a chicken in every subject's pot. My bible when I was a lad,

Larousse Gastronomique, told me that La Varenne's "recipes can be used today," so I did. I used the raspberry vinegar recipe and later, at Stars, the squab cooked in it. (See *Jeremiah Tower's New American Classics*).

Lawrence, R. de Treville, Sr. *Jefferson and Wine.* The Plains, VA: Vinifera Wine Growers Association, 1976.
Not just for Jefferson's letter in 1787 to Chateau d'Yquem asking to buy some wine, or his wine-loving correspondence with my ancestor John Rutledge, but the one of two books that in 1976 made me think of American food, and of calling it "California," in particular.

Le Duc. *Crustacés, Poissons et Coquillages.* Paris: Jean-Claude Lattes, 1977.
The book from the restaurant in Paris that changed the way we all looked at cooking fish. A big influence on me in 1977.

Leslie, Miss. *Directions for Cookery in Its Various Branches*. Philadelphia: Henry Carey Baird, 1853.
What this woman, writing with huge success (in sales) for other women who have to cook for their husbands, hates: "washy soup, poultry half raw, gravy unskimmed, and vegetables undrained; to say nothing of ponderous puddings, curdled custards tasting of nothing, and tough pastry." Many of the professional cooks on line in the United States today don't know about skimming sauces. And she knew then that bad food makes bad moods, and that only food cooked according to proper procedures is good for one's health.

Lewis, Edna. *The Taste of Country Cooking.* New York: Knopf, 1976.
My copy is marked "From James Beard, August 1976." After I read it, and after my California Dinner at Chez Panisse, I knew we were onto something emphasizing American food, as Jim had told me all along.

Machen, Arthur. *Dog and Duck.* New York: Knopf, 1924.
Because: "If a man talks to me of the sacred cause of Humanity, I lock up my few silver spoons." And "But he who speaks well of port is, as the Greeks said of their best men, beautiful and good."

McClure, Michael. *Meat Science Essays.* San Francisco: City Lights Books, 1963.
This was a bible for me as a college freshman, thanks to my roommate, the poet Michael Palmer. A book "that may turn out to be a significant one for his generation. Its themes are suicide, death, revolt, sexuality & drugs, Artaud, Camus, and liberty"— all the things that obsessed me in the sixties, other than Escoffier's *Ma Cuisine* and John Rechy's *City of Night.* And for the essay on cocaine (so that the night it was introduced to Berkeley, on top of the low freezer in the kitchen of Chez Panisse, I was ready). And for the culinary chapter: "The Mushroom."

Margittai, Tom, and Paul Kovi. *The Four Seasons.* New York: Simon & Schuster, 1980.
"The ultimate book of food, wine, and elegant dining" is what the cover says, and certainly the restaurant is "one of the world's great restaurants." Read also the foreword by James Beard, who calls the restaurant "a gastronomic legend." How true.

Marinetti, Filippo Tommaso. *The Futurist Cookbook.* Italy, 1932; London: Trefoil, 1989. Translation: Bedford Arts, San Francisco, 1989.
Because the New York chef David Burke proved Marinetti correct, probably without even knowing it: Tyrrhenian Seaweed Foam with Coral Garnish, for example. And Excitant Gastrique. And because the book is hilarious and vastly intelligent.

Matron, Fred J. *Jean-Louis: Cooking with the Seasons.* Charlottesville, VA: Thomasson-Grant, 1989.
The ultimate chefs' photograph cookbook of its time, and one of the best and most influential of the last part of the American twentieth century. Having nothing to do with the seasons, but all about presentation, and style-setting presentation it is, a style that capped the eighties and sent the young nineties into a swoon. Thousands of up-and-coming chefs aspired to this cooking, with mixed results.

Marshall, A. B. *The Book of Ice.* London: Simpkin, Marshall, Hamilton, Kent, n.d. Another publication of his, *The Table,* was published in 1886.
Given to me by Elizabeth David, "a reminder of your summer with me in London 1978. With Love." Because we both wondered whether the first household ice cream makers were in the United States or England. Read about cucumber ice cream, white coffee ice cream, and Spanish nut and cookies ice cream. All a hundred years before Ben & Jerry's went public.

Médecin, Jacques. *La Cuisine du Comte de Nice.* Paris: Juillard, 1972.
Given to me by Alice in early 1974, this, Elizabeth David, and (for me) Richard Olney were the books that formed Chez Panisse until I decided to take it truly regional in 1976. A book that influenced a lot of people, many of whom went "Mediterranean."

Menon. *La Cuisinière Bourgeoise.* Paris: Guillyn, 1746.
One of the great cookbooks of all time, as both Richard Olney and Elizabeth David told me over and over again until I read it: "Simple dishes, good ones, and new ones, for which I have given easily understandable instructions." And a book that was one of the first to write about women's cooking in the home.

Montagné, Prosper. *La Grand Livre de La Cuisine.* Paris: Flammarion, 1929.
A beautiful monster of a book, with Philéas Gilbert (partner with Escoffier in *Le Guide Culinaire)* doing a preface, and Henri Béraud's look at the future that would suggest the pot-au-feu had hyperbolic magic mushrooms in it. Read it for the lunch

menu of February 2, 1926, the centenary of Brillat-Savarin. It is the menu that Béraud regretted "all his life that he had not assisted at its preparation." I now regret not having been there. And what an extraordinary modern menu it is, considering how mad they could have gone, being that close to the previous century: "Rissoles of foie gras and sausages cooked in Chablis for hors d'oeuvre, Beaujolais for aperitif; an 'omelet du Cure' with La Mission Haut-Brion; stewed eels in a coulis of crayfish, Cheval Blanc; a truffled turkey, Côte de Nuits of Bouchard; Salade de l'émigré; Cheeses, another Bouchard Reserve; pyramids of meringue with vanilla ice cream flavoured with rose petals, Heidsieck and Pol Roger; Fruit, coffee, cognac, liqueurs." Now that's a lunch!

————. *Larousse Gastronomique: The Encyclopedia of Food, Wine, and Cookery.* Introduction by Auguste Escoffier and Philéas Gilbert. Edited by Charlotte Turgeon and Nina Froud. New York: Crown, 1961.
Get started on this translation, then buy the earlier French editions for all the edited-out details in the English-language editions. The book other than Escoffier's *Ma Cuisine* that I read ceaselessly in college.

Morris, Helen. *Portrait of a Chef: The Life of Alexis Soyer.* Cambridge: Cambridge University Press, 1938.
As a model chef "Soyer was vain, a poseur, a fop, an eccentric, a brilliant inventor, and a magnificent organizer." He was the "lie that tells the truth." And he designed the vast kitchens of the Reform Club. And he once fed twenty-two thousand poor people Christmas dinner for free. Anyone who thinks he or she is a grand chef should read this book first.

Nignon, Édouard. *Eloges de la Cuisine Française.* Paris: Édition d'Art H. Piazza, 1933.
A true Scorpio, and slightly mad. And a brilliant foreword by Sacha Guitry that I have quoted often. Read also Nignon's *Les Plaisirs de La Table* (Paris: Jacoub & Aulard, 1930), which is truly a pleasure. No one has more fun than Nignon. Also because if you look under the bed of any of the most famous chefs since 1960 (at least literate ones), you will find one of Nignon's books. Nignon was chef at Paillard in Paris, then at Claridge's in London.

O'Donnell, Mietta, and Tony Knox. *Great Australian Chefs.* Sydney: Bookman Press, 1999.
If you had any doubt that the culinary revolution moved to Australia after California, before moving on to England, this book will convince you.

Olney, Richard. *The French Menu Cookbook.* New York: Simon & Schuster, 1970.
Because it was dedicated to Georges Garin, the inspiration, if an irascible one, for the Young Turks of the seventies in France. As in vegetable purees. And because when I

read this book when it came out in 1970, I began a correspondence with Richard, and it was my personal (not the official) bible when I started at Chez Panisse.

————. *Simple French Food.* New York: Atheneum, 1975.
Not just because my book is inscribed "For adorable Jeremiah," but because when Richard told me he was going to write it, I said we would have to do a two-week festival of the dishes at Chez Panisse to introduce him and his food to California.

————. *Yquem.* Paris: Flammarion, 1985.
Because it is fascinating to see the menus from 1867 to 1985 that have served this famous wine, including the one I did at Chez Panisse in 1975, "An American Menu," with only Sauternes served with the food. The pairing of rich roast beef with d'Yquem came from Prince Yusupov (the one who assassinated Rasputin) as told to me by the mentors of my teens, Count Cheremetev and my Russian uncle.

Orwell, George. *Down and Out in London and Paris.* New York: Harper & Brothers, 1933.
For anyone interested in working in the restaurant business, this book is a must, before reading its pupil, *Kitchen Confidential* by Anthony Bourdain.

Pellaprat, Jean-Henri. *L'Art Culinaire Moderne.* Castagnola, Switzerland: Jacques Kramer, 1956. English translation as *The Great Book of French Cuisine.* New York: Thomas Y. Crowell, 1966.
That is exactly it: a great book. What it was like to eat at Maxim's, if you don't have their book.

————. *The Great Book of French Cuisine.* Jeremiah Tower translation. New York: Vendome Press, 2003.
The iTunes preview says; "Henri-Paul Pellaprat and Jeremiah Tower, master chefs of the nineteenth and twentieth centuries, have created a reference cookbook that will shape great chefs and great cooking in the twenty-first century." An exaggeration of me, but not of Henri-Paul. But I did go through two thousand recipes and rewrite them. As well as removed all the 1960s American home economics rubbish from the book.

Pépin, Jacques. *Complete Techniques.* New York: Black Dog & Levanthal, 2001.
A compilation of the brilliant how-to photographs of *La Technique* (1976) and *La Méthode* (1979) that helped me through so much in the kitchen, since I was never taught professionally, and when I started at Chez Panisse, there wasn't anyone else who was either. Thank you, Jacques.

Peterson, James. *Sauces.* New York: Van Nostrand Reinhold, 1991.
The first person after Escoffier's introduction to stocks and sauces to get it right—perfectly. A book that I wish I had written.

Petits Propos Culinaires. **Edited by the Davidsons. London: Prospect Books, 1979–.**
A wonderfully mad and fascinating little collection of books, and in this first edition Nathan d'Aulnay (Richard Olney) and I printed recipes for use in the Time-Life *Good Cook* series. Elizabeth David was intrigued and did "Hunt the Ice Cream," the wonderful Elizabeth Lambert Ortiz did "Coriander," and in later editions, like No. 26 in 1987, the booklets were already looking at Australia, with the visionary "Symposium of Australian Gastronomy."

Picture Cook Book. **New York: Time, 1958.**
Full-on 1950s. Look at page 119: The shoes are more beautiful than the food, not to happen again until the nineties and Manolo Blahnik! And page 154, the clothes at the barbecue! Then look at the restaurant section and see the food of Fernand Point (see below), the photograph and food of the great Alexandre Dumaine at the Hôtel de la Côte-d'Or in Saulieu (see above), and Ernie's in San Francisco, just to see the very spooky photo of the chef Ermete Lavino, who is the identical twin to the Ernie's chef of thirty years later, Jackie Robert. Yes, this book is a treasure of the mouth-hanging-open-in-wonderment variety.

Point, Fernand. *Ma Gastronomie.* **Wilton, CT: Lyceum Books, 1974.**
You have to love a man who drank a magnum of champagne while being shaved, and who was the culinary father to Paul Bocuse and a host of other Young Turks, like Thomas Keller in Napa, and Tony Bilson in Sydney. And was other book I was supposed to look at when I was hired at Chez Panisse. See in this book.

Pollan, Michael. *The Botany of Desire.* **New York: Random House, 2001.**
A book on apples, potatoes, marijuana, and tulips that reads like a thriller. A perfect book.

Pomiane, Édouard de. *Cooking with Pomiane.* **Oxford: Bruno Cassirer, 1976.**
One of Elizabeth David's favorites, and one she told me to read for writing the Chez Panisse menus. And because he had a radio show on food in the 1930s, as well as tried to teach the French to eat the way we do now: with health in mind, but without sacrificing great flavors and meals.

———. *French Cooking in Ten Minutes.* **New York: Farrar, Straus & Giroux, 1977.**
No wonder Elizabeth David adored him, and here for the simplicity and ease of recipes. Who says you can't put together a meal in your little apartment!

Practical Housekeeping: A Careful Compilation of Tried and Approved Recipes. **Wilton, Ohio, 1876.**
This is the mother of all housewives' companions, dedicated to the "Plucky House-wives of 1876, who master their work instead of allowing it to master them." The material later (1883) became *Buckeye Cookery,* which was reprinted by Dover.

Ramsay, Gordon. *Passion for Flavor*. London: Conran Octopus, 1996.
The foreword is by Guy Savoy, the French chef we Americans trounced in 1983 in Newport in front of one hundred U.S. food journalists. Another book after the school of Marco Pierre White, a very nice book to cook from, and a new "cuisine Légère" all over again. Richard Olney liked Gordon's restaurant Aubergine, though perhaps not for the cappuccino soup presentation. Or before he became a clown instead of an inspirational chef.

Ranhofer, Charles. *The Epicurean*. New York: Dover, 1971.
By the chef at the great Delmonico's in New York (this material is from 1862 to 1894). A book I bought in February 1974, but the bell did not go off in my head until two years later; when reading it again, I saw that all the menus used English words and terms, and I saw the dishes inspired by California (the corn soup from Mendocino) and immediately wrote the California Regional Dinner, which started a revolution.

Rann, Evelyn. *After the Theatre Lunch*. [Minneapolis]: Buzza Company, [1930s].
This little pamphlet book has a beautiful and charming late Deco design that could easily be the inspiration for David Lance Goines, of Chez Panisse poster fame. The written material is straightforward with a lot of American class.

Rawlings, Majorie Kinnan. *Cross Creek Cookery*. New York: Charles Scribner's Sons, 1942.
One of the ultimately American cookbooks, and it inspired me to do a Florida Regional Dinner at the Santa Fe Bar & Grill in 1982. When I was asked, "Is this Floridian cuisine?" I answered, "It should be." Rawlings gives the recipe for the divine Black Bottom Pie.

Ray, Cyril, ed. *The Gourmet's Companion*. London: Eyre & Spottiswoode, 1963.
About all the greats in the very intelligent prose of the first part of the twentieth century. From Virginia Woolf, André Simon, Elizabeth David, Pilaff Bey (Norman Douglas), E. M. Forster, Hilaire Beloc ("His sins were scarlet, but his books were read"), and the like.

Rector, George. *The Rector Cookbook*. Chicago: Rector, 1928.
The only nonliving restaurant other than Delmonico's that was a model for Stars of San Francisco: "Rector's was the supreme court of triviality, where who's who *went* to *learn* what's what." The customers were "champions, challengers, opera stars, explorers, captains of industry, and lieutenants of sloth; gamblers, authors, and adventurers, [and] all celebrated their temporary successes with a night at Rector's." The book has very American food at its best. The European heritage was there, but it was worked over into a new image and taste. My grandmother's favorite book—for her cook.

Reynière, Grìmod de la. *Almanach des Gourmands.* 8 vols. Paris: Chez Maradan, 1803–12.
The first book that Richard Olney told me in 1973 to buy and, with my first spare money from Chez Panisse, I did. Four of them. Wonderful, brilliant, and an inspiration to many great chefs and writers (see Lucien Tendret).

Ripert, Eric, and Michael Ruhlman. *A Return to Cooking.* New York: Artisan, 2002.
The first chefs' cookbook that measures up visually after Thomas Keller's book, *The French Laundry Cookbook,* and surpasses it in usability by the home cook. One is swept along by the personal passion of Eric and his rediscoveries.

Ritz, Marie Louise. *César Ritz.* Philadelphia: J. B. Lippincott, 1938.
Because whatever ideas you have about perfectionism will forever change after you have read about this genius's work habits. Mine did.

Rodriguez-Hunter, Suzane. *Found Meeds of the Lost Generation: Recipes and Anecdotes from 1920's Paris.* Winchester, MA: Faber & Faber, 1994.
Hilarious, adorable. and a must for anyone who wonders how greats gave great parties to without a lot of money. Or with.

Roman, Philippe. *Cochon: Rimailles et Ripailles.* Paris: Jean-Paul Rocher, 2003
As elegant a little book as you will ever find if you like poetry on how to feast on pig.

Rombauer, Irma S., and Marion Rombauer Becker. *Joy of Cooking.* Indianapolis and New York: Bobbs-Merrill, 1975.
One of the greatest cookbooks ever. Originally published in 1931, it now makes later editions of Fannie Farmer look like Mobil guides. If you had to have one cookbook, this could be it. See Bittman.

Root, Waverley. *Food: An Authoritative and Visual History and Dictionary of the Foods of the World.* New York: Simon & Schuster, 1980.
My favorite dictionary of food, along with Alexandre Dumas's and Alan Davidson's two hundred years later. See also *The Food of France* and *The Food of Italy.*

Sackville-West, Vita. *V. Sackville-West's Garden Book.* London: Michael Joseph, 1968.
Because Alice Waters gave it to me on May 7,1974, thinking that this was what I was talking about as I was pushing starting a farm of our own. Obviously she had never seen Sissinghurst, where my mother used to take me to teach me gardening, or known about the inherited fortune that maintained it. In California we ended up with lettuce and a few geese.

Saffron, Inga. *Caviar.* New York: Broadway Books, 2002.
Subtitled "The Strange History and Uncertain Future of the World's Most Coveted Delicacy." So read it and eat it while you can.

Saint-Ange, Madame E. *La Bonne Cuisine*. Paris: Larousse, 1927.
Because she is a cult. Decide for yourself if it is by 1927 "the most practical cookery book in the French language" (Elizabeth David) or not. It is certainly more practical for the home cook than Escoffier's *Guide Culinaire,* and it's one of the first cookbooks truly in love with precision. It is interesting that Elizabeth adored this book, since her books are anything but precise from the point of view of anyone but a natural cook.

Sanger, Marjory Bartlett. *Escoffier.* New York: Farrar, Straus & Giroux, 1976.
One of the best books about the Man.

Sarris, Stan, and Rodney Adler. *Banc.* Sydney: New Holland, 1999.
An Australian version of the "day in the life" of a restaurant, beautifully photographed, and with good recipes of food and drink.

Schlosser, Eric. *Fast Food Nation*. Boston and New York: Houghton Mifflin, 2001.
"The dark side of the American meal." A view of what is wrong with modern America through what it eats. Brillat-Savarin's "you are what you eat" comes horrifyingly true.

Schofield, Leo. "California Cuisine." Australian *Gourmet,* April 1986.
Sometimes it takes an outsider to see what's going on. What is truth and what is myth. Leo is a giant in this. An elegant man.

Schuman, Charles. *American Bar.* New York: Abbeville Press, 1995.
After the *Savoy Cocktail Book,* and on a par. One of the best books on bartending and drinks.

Serventi, Silvano. *La Grande Histoire du Foie Gras.* Paris: Flammarion, 1993.
An exceptionally beautiful book, superbly done, and with it and Michael Ginor's book, you have the whole foie, as it were.

Simon, André. *A Concise Encyclopaedia of Gastronomy.* London: Wine and Food Society, 1940–48.
Brilliantly told and organized by category, like "Fish" and "Meat." On buying fish: "Look at the fish, it tells its own tale." The section on "Ham" is the best on the subject I have ever seen.

———. *A Flummery of Food: Feasts for Epicures.* London: Little Books, 2004.
A color-illustrated pocket book with Simon's choice of writers and their articles that are as charming as his own.

Sitwell, Edith. *English Eccentrics.* London: Penguin Books, 1971.
How could you have an informed sense of humor about the twentieth century if you

have not read this? Or feel so well about how much you drink? Not as much, one would hope, or as colorfully, as Squire Mad Jack Mytton, who drank eight bottles of port a day, and his horse, Baronet, not much less. He spent half a million (tens of millions today) doing it, and set fire to his nightshirt to cure the hiccups. A barrel of fun, as it were.

Slater, Nigel. *Appetite*. New York: Clarkson Potter, 2000.
Subtitled "So What Do You Want to Eat Today." This book will always answer that question that never ends. Nigel is a genius.

Smith, Delia. *Delia's How to Cook*. London: BBC, 1998.
A friend of mine in London said of Delia that all her recipes always work. If you are interested in basics, Delia's television shows and books are the ones to watch and cook from. She is the doyenne of British cooking.

Solomon, Charmaine. *Encyclopaedia of Asian Food*. Boston: Periplus Editions, 1998.
Exhaustive and fascinating. Charmaine has always known the most from a Western perspective, and she was one of the first to know.

Spoeri, Daniel. *The Mythological Travels*. New York: Something Else Press, 1970.
Magic mushroom surrealism unsurpassed.

Steingarten, Jeffrey. "Meals of the Millennium." *Vogue,* November 1999.
Because this, and anything Jeffrey writes, is worth reading.

Stout, Rex. *The Nero Wolfe Cookbook*. New York: Viking Press, 1973.
The Nero Wolfe mysteries were some of the first books I read that made me want to cook, and here are the recipes.

———. *Too Many Cooks*. New York: Farrar & Rinehart, 1938. Reprinted New York: Bantam, 1983.
Because in 1970 I read it again and listed the wonderful food in praise of America: Creole Tripe from New Orleans; Missouri Boone County Ham—cooked with vinegar, molasses, Worcestershire sauce, cider, and herbs; Chicken in Curdled Egg Sauce—almonds, sherry, Mexican sausage; Tennessee Opossum; and Philadelphia Snapper Soup. See previous entry.

Szathmary, Louis, advisory ed. *Cookery Americana*. New York: Arno Press, 1973.
A series of twenty-seven cookbooks, including *Fifty Years of Prairie Cooking*, that "chronicles a fascinating aspect of American social life over the past 150 years." Truly an insight into what we have lost in the menu since the First and Second World Wars. Most of the household management and church societies material that fills these books is not "cottage cheese omelet" and "rinkum tiddy."

Talleyrand, Charles-Maurice.
Anything on the lifestyle of this great diner is worth reading. A man who continued, because of a complete lack of scruples, to eat famously well throughout the people's revolution against excess, and lived through all the next royalist, imperial, and populist regimes. After all, his chef was Antonin Carême, one of the greatest chefs of all time, and mentor to Escoffier as well as Dubois and so on. And because Talleyrand was the first to figure out that entertaining should be tax deductible.

Tendret, Lucien. *La Table au Pays de Brillat-Savarin.* **Mâcon: Protat Frères, 1892.**
"A small masterpiece," Richard Olney calls it. This book inspired many, like the legendary Alexandre Dumaine, the greatest chef in France in the mid-twentieth century. The famous Poularde au Vapeur is from Tendret, going from Dumaine on to Fernand Point and his pupil Bocuse. The Aga Khan would go to France just to dine on this sublime chicken at Dumaine's.

Tirel, Guillaume (Taillevent). *Le Viandier.* **Paris, 1373–80; Paris: Pichon and Vicaire, 1892. .**
Tirel was the head cook to French dukes and to Charles VI. Read this if for no other reason than that this collection of manuscripts is the first French cookbook, and to learn to cook with almonds, and for the miracles of verjus in cold soups thickened with almonds. Oeufs de Truite (trout eggs) not bad either.

Toklas, Alice B. *The Alice B. Toklas Cook Book.* **1954; New York: Anchor Books, 1960.**
A book "of character, fine food, and tasty human observation," according to Janet Flanner (American journalist in Paris). The book that I cooked from endlessly in college, and then afterward cooked from for the Gertrude Stein dinner at Chez Panisse. Try the Eggs Francis Picabia, but the most food-splashed page is for "A Tender Tart," everyone's favorite kind.

Toulouse-Lautrec. *Chez Maxim's.* **New York: McGraw-Hill, 1962.**
Alice Waters's favorite book, and looking at the photo of the countess in her fifties mink entering Maxim's to greet the owner, Louis Vaudable, you will know why. For the lovers of chicken "in half mourning," this is it. And because, with the Baron de Ladoucette, I had one of the best meals ever at Maxim's.

Tower, Jeremiah. *America's Best Chefs Cook with Jeremiah Tower.* **Companion to the PBS Series. New York: John Wiley & Sons, 2003.**

———. "Crowned with Roses—A Four Second Perfume." Unpublished, 1972.
"Memoirs of a Harvard Graduate, 1961 to 1972." In the introduction I wrote, "I will speak, like Arthur Machen, of certain tastes. But unlike he, who dared retribution by admitting a Germanic liking for apple sauce with his roast goose when

nationalism made such an admission risky, I will dwell on a revival, and so avoid the ire of all but the most dull."

———. *A Dash of Genius.* Amazon Kindle Single, 2014.
My book on Auguste Escoffier.

———. *Jeremiah Tower's New American Classics.* New York: Harper & Row, 1986.
My first cookbook. James Beard Foundation winner.

———. *Jeremiah Tower Cooks: 250 Recipes from an American Master.* New York: Stewart, Tabori & Chang, 2003

Troisgros, Jean, and Pierre Troisgros. *Cuisiniers à Roane.* Paris: Robert Laffont, 1977.
The other book that changed my and other American chefs' views of cooking and presentation of their food. See Michel Guérard.

Trotter, Charlie. *Meat and Game.* Berkeley, CA: Ten Speed Press, 2001.
I mention this one to remind you to look at the whole series of Charlie's restaurant cookbooks.

Tsuji, Shizuo. *Japanese Cooking: A Simple Art.* New York: Kodansha International, 1980.
The first book that we saw in America to set down the art of this cooking and still influential.

Villas, James. *American Taste: A Celebration of Gastronomy Coast to Coast.* Foreword by James Beard. New York: Arbor House, 1982.
Because when I was planning the Celebration of American Chefs for 1983 as the first big function of the AIWF, this book was the inspiration to make me insist, against the pressure of New York and Los Angeles chefs, that we find chefs from all over the land. And because James Villas is the writer who champions simple American food, and knows more about it than anyone. See below.

———. "From Our Abundant Land: At Last, a Table of Our Own." *Town & Country,* June 1976.
Read also Villas's *At Table: A Passion for Food and Drink* (New York: Harper & Row, 1988), and *Between Bites* (New York: John Wiley & Sons, 2002). All Villas's books are fascinating, impeccably written, and historically important.

Visser, Margaret. *The Rituals of Dinner.* New York: Grove Weidenfeld, 1991.
A book on the "origins, evolution, eccentricities, and meaning of table manners." Fascinating. How and why we eat together.

Warne, Frederick, & Co. *Every-Day Cookery: For Families of Moderate Income.* Covent Garden, London, c. 1900.

This extraordinary little book, of only 150 pages, by a publisher who did "useful books," "model manuals," and so on, sold this for one shilling and actually thought that roast partridge on a platter with its garnish of vegetables, or a whole turbot, was for moderate income (in those days, chicken was the luxury poultry). Read this delightful book and see why Elizabeth David adored it so, how it formed her style, and why she gave it to me.

Warner, Richard. *Antiquitates Culinariae; Or Curious Tracts Relating to the Culinary Affairs of the Old English.* London: R. Blamire, 1791; reprint, London: Prospect Books, 1981.

Because it includes *The Forme of Cury,* thought by most to be the finest of the old English cookbooks: "a roll of ancient English cookery, compiled about 1390, by the master cooks of Richard II." Read it now, eat the latest and best food in London now in places like St. John's, and remember this fourteenth century.

Wechsberg, Joseph. "Brillat-Savarin." *Gourmet,* March 1970.

Thank God someone has some objectivity about this god of gourmets. And because anything by Wechsberg is worth reading. See also his charming *Blue Trout and Black Truffles* (New York: Knopf, 1966).

White, Marco Pierre. *White Heat.* London: Pyramid Books, 1990.

A visionary book (as you can tell by the countless imitations after it was published) that set the style for a "day in the life of a restaurant" and the handheld camera that is part of the action of the restaurant.

Wolfe, Linda. *The Literary Gourmet.* New York: Random House, 1962.

Because this book is beautiful and really fun to read, and because The Four Seasons restaurant tested the recipes. Appropriately, since its "imaginative modern cuisine is based on the best achievements of the past" and "brings these historic recipes once again to life." Tripe from Shakespeare, crayfish soufflé from Gogol, crème au chocolate ice cream from Dumas, suckling pig and kasha from Chekhov, velvet cakes—naturally—from Wilde, and for the dinner at the chateau of the Marquis de Vaubyessard. The one to which Emma Bovary goes. "One of the most seductive dinner parties in literature," the perfumes of the flowers and of the fine linen, the fumes of the viands, and the odor of truffles all enveloping Emma as she enters the dining room.

Woolf, Virginia. *Orlando.* London: Hogarth Press, 1928.

The dinner Orlando did at the embassy in Constantinople at the end of the great fast of Ramadan: "gold plate . . . candelabras . . . negroes in plush breeches . . . pyramids of ice . . . fountains of negus . . . jellies made to represent His Majesty's ships . . . birds in golden cages . . . gentlemen in slashed crimson velvet . . . oceans to drink," and so on. The 1978 Orlando dinner was the last that I ever cooked at Chez Panisse.

Zachs, Richard. *History Laid Bare: Love, Sex, and Perversity from the Ancient Etruscans to Warren G. Harding.* New York: Harper Perennial, 1995.
If you want to know what other things other people have also and always eaten, read this and wonder. And laugh.

INDEX

ABOUT THE AUTHOR

JEREMIAH TOWER began his career as chef and co-owner of Chez Panisse in Berkeley, California, and later ran several other successful restaurants, including Stars in San Francisco and the wildly successful Peak Café in Hong Kong. He is the author of *Jeremiah Tower's New American Classics* and *Jeremiah Tower Cooks,* as well as the host of PBS's *America's Best Chefs* and the author of the companion book, *America's Best Chefs with Jeremiah Tower.* In 1996 the James Beard Foundation named him the Outstanding Chef in America. Tower lives in New York City. His culinary memoir, *California Dish,* was published in 2003, his new book, *Table Manners: How to Behave in the Modern World and Why Bother,* is forthcoming in the fall of 2016. *The Last Magnificent* is showing at film festivals around the United States and in major theater markets starting in March 2017 and soon thereafter on CNN and Netflix.